A Guide Book of
BARBER SILVER COINS

A Complete History and Price Guide

Q. David Bowers

Foreword by
Kenneth Bressett

Whitman Publishing, LLC
PUBLISHING SINCE 1934
www.whitman.com

A Guide Book of
BARBER SILVER COINS

Whitman Publishing, LLC
PUBLISHING SINCE 1934
www.whitman.com

3101 Clairmont Road, Suite C, Atlanta, GA 30329

Correspondence concerning this book may be directed to the publisher, attn: Barber Silver Coins, at the address above.

ISBN: 0794843158
Printed in China

Disclaimer: Expert opinion should be sought in any significant numismatic purchase. This book is presented as a guide only. No warranty or representation of any kind is made concerning the completeness of the information presented. The author, a professional numismatist, regularly buys, sells, and sometimes holds certain of the items discussed in this book.

Caveat: The value estimates given are subject to variation and differences of opinion. Before making decisions to buy or sell, consult the latest information. Past performance of the rare coin market or any coin or series within that market is not necessarily an indication of future performance, as the future is unknown. Such factors as changing demand, popularity, grading interpretations, strength of the overall coin market, and economic conditions will continue to be influences.

Other books in Bowers Series include: *A Guide Book of Morgan Silver Dollars; A Guide Book of Double Eagle Gold Coins; A Guide Book of United States Type Coins; A Guide Book of Modern United States Proof Coin Sets; A Guide Book of Shield and Liberty Head Nickels; A Guide Book of Flying Eagle and Indian Head Cents; A Guide Book of Washington and State Quarters; A Guide Book of Buffalo and Jefferson Nickels; A Guide Book of Lincoln Cents; A Guide Book of United States Commemorative Coins; A Guide Book of United States Tokens and Medals; A Guide Book of Gold Dollars; A Guide Book of Peace Dollars; A Guide Book of the Official Red Book of United States Coins; A Guide Book of Franklin and Kennedy Half Dollars; A Guide Book of Civil War Tokens; A Guide Book of Hard Times Tokens;* and *A Guide Book of Mercury Dimes, Standing Liberty Quarters, and Liberty Walking Half Dollars.*

Contents

FOREWORD

I have never ceased to appreciate the imprint left on our coins by the artistry of Charles E. Barber. Whenever I see a Barber coin of any denomination, my thoughts go back to a time when coins with his designs were still relatively common in everyday commerce. It is perhaps unknown to some collectors today that many of those workhorse coins actually remained in active circulation well into the 1940s, and even a few remained to the 1950s. Back then it was not uncommon to find many of the older dates in change, and some of those even had mintmarks that told us where they had been made. Having such a ready supply of collectible items easily at hand was incentive enough to inspire any budding numismatist to attempt assembling complete sets.

I think the reason Barber coins stayed in use for such a long time was because of their imposing design, their apolitical theme, and their endurance—that is, even after decades in circulation the dates and mintmarks were still clear. Their basic identity remained intact.

These were *real* coins in every sense of the word. They felt worth their value in silver, and were symbolic of everyman's pride in America. The simplicity of their design and boldness of expression eventually made them a popular favorite of everyone who used them. They were also a product of a time when Americans knew how to make do with things that were more practical than new or ideal. The idea of changing to a more modern mode did not occur in earnest until 1916, sparked by a public desire for something more symbolic of a nation recently thrust into war.

In this book you will find that Q. David Bowers presents a fresh landmark account of Barber coinage touching on every aspect of availability, condition, varieties, history, and collectibility of these fascinating coins. When they were actually in daily use there were few thoughts about such things. They were simply the coins of the day and were only of nominal interest—except to those who sought to collect them from circulation. The more advanced collectors, much fewer in number, could purchase pieces in Uncirculated condition at prices under $5 for common Philadelphia issues; about the same price as for a common silver dollar at that time, although the equivalent of about $50 in today's inflation adjusted dollars.

The Barber quarter was the coin of our fathers. It was the coin that gave rise to the now outdated saying "Shave and a haircut, two bits." For a quarter was actually the going price in a tonsorial visit of that day, though *two bits* was a reference to the quarter's precursor, the Spanish-American two-*reales* coin. (At the time, this was a familiar expression.) In other words this quarter was the original *barber* quarter in every sense of the word.

It was only after 1893 that collectors became interested in the mintmarks found on these and other United States coins. Prior to that, mintmarked coins were just considered to be varieties, and collectors were quite content to save only one coin of each date regardless of whether or not it had a mintmark. The big change in collector consideration came about with the publication of *Coinage of the United States Branch Mints* by A.G. Heaton in May of 1893. However, even in later years of the Barber coinage, few people other than avid collectors paid much attention to the mintmarks. Serious collectors usually preferred a single Proof example of each date rather than concentrating on Uncirculated specimens or those with mintmarks.

When I began collecting in the early 1940s, I sought to find one Barber coin of each date and mintmark in circulation. I soon learned that there were some key pieces that simply did not show up in the New England area. Those made in San Francisco were the toughest because coins did not move about extensively in those days. Yet, it was fun looking for them, and it was often rewarding even when the condition of some pieces was less than desirable. My perseverance was spurred on by an older friend who had once been a toll booth fare collector in a New York subway. Over the years, from about 1930 to 1950, he had collected one of each date and mintmark of every regular-issue circulating United States copper and silver coin, most of them at face value from change! Only a couple of the rarer pieces were purchased from dealers, and those with the profit from duplicate scarce coins that he had found.

One of my ambitions at that time was to save a set of 1892 coins in anticipation of what I was sure would almost certainly become a huge celebration of the discovery of America. Purchasing nice specimens of that date was no problem. Many people saved them in unused condition because they were the first year of issue. Yes, I proudly exhibited them in 1992, along with some gold and silver coins of Ferdinand and Isabella, only to find that by then the exploits of Columbus were largely ignored or disrespected with the new-day recognition that he was not the first to discover America. Still, the thrill of owning those pieces, now nearly 125 years old, is inspirational for me.

There is no going back to those halcyon days of finding Barber coins in circulation. Today there is a new era of interest in these classic items, and one with new attitudes about the value and desirability of mintmarks, condition, and varieties. It is also a time when these coins can be more fully appreciated for their place in our nation's numismatic history.

Such are my memories of Barber coinage. I am sure you will have equally memorable experiences with your interest in them, and positive that your enjoyment of collecting them will be greatly enhanced by all you will find in Dave Bowers's comprehensive book on this subject. Collector interest in these coins is sure to be brought to a new height through the information presented here.

Kenneth Bressett
Senior editor, *A Guide Book of United States Coins*

Introduction

Starting in the early 1950s, when I discovered the world's greatest hobby, numismatics, reading about the history and tradition of coin collecting became a prime interest of mine. It still continues to this day.

In 1953 I began dealing in coins on a part-time basis. Barber coins were among my favorites. Not long afterward I started a collection of Proof Barber half dollars with one of each date from 1892 to 1915. The dates through 1912 were priced at about $7 to $9 each. The 1913 was more expensive, and the 1914 and 1915 cost into three figures, as a Virginia collector was hoarding those two years. Some coins offered were hairlined, others were gems. There was no difference in price. This may seem unusual to read today, but if you look through issues of *The Numismatist* and *The Numismatic Scrapbook Magazine* of that era you will see that Proofs were often called "brilliant," but without other modifiers. Similarly, the *Guide Book of United States Coins* simply listed "Uncirculated" and "Proof."

B. Max Mehl, the famous Fort Worth, Texas, dealer, became a friend, and we had a number of conversations prior to his passing in 1957. On one memorable evening he, Abe Kosoff, Abe's wife Molly, and I all had dinner at an ANA convention. By that time we had become acquainted through letters and telephone calls. When I published my first catalog in September 1955 he sent me a letter of congratulations.

During one conversation we discussed Barber silver coins. I mentioned that I had recently purchased a group of Barber dimes that Mehl had sold around 1908 or 1909. The paper envelopes were marked just with dates such as 1901, 1902, and so on. Upon inspection some coins had mintmarks. I asked why the mintmarks weren't reflected in his labels, and he replied to the effect, "Most collectors just wanted dates, and modern mintmarks were not very important then." He also mentioned that around that time he was on a train trip, and in going to the dining car he forgot to take money with him. He did have a briefcase of rare coins. When he received his bill he extracted a Proof Barber half dollar and used it to buy lunch! Of course, back then such a coin was not worth much over face value.

In an early visit to Stack's in New York City I was shown a Proof 1913 half dollar (considered to be much more desirable due to the comparatively small mintage for circulation strikes) and bought it for $25. To give a reality check: the American dollar had a greater buying power back then. A hotel room in the Park Sheraton Hotel near Stack's cost $16 per night. Coca-Cola was a nickel a bottle, the same price charged for a pay phone call. A nice restaurant lunch was about a dollar, including tip. When McDonald's first went into business in the 1950s hamburgers were 15 cents each. Some new cars were less than $2,000 each.

In circulation I could find well-circulated Barber half dollars from time to time, but hardly any dimes or quarters. In 1957 I paid the record price of $4,750 for a beautiful Uncirculated 1894-S dime rarity—a coin for which 24 were minted and just eight are known today. I was a student at Penn State at the time. This stirred up a lot of newspaper stories, a feature in *Seventeen* magazine, and other publicity. I was invited to appear on NBC's *Today Show*, with my transportation paid and a three-day complimentary stay at the Waldorf-Astoria. I received over 6,000 letters, typically saying something like, "I have an even older dime, an 1892."

Ambassador R. Henry Norweb contacted me about the dime. After owning it for a while and visiting it occasionally in a safe deposit vault, I sold it to him for $6,000. He gave it to his wife, Emery May Holden Norweb, as a gift. Both of the Norwebs, famous in American numismatics, became fine friends. I have many nice memories of visits with them, including in Cleveland, their main home, at their premises on the top floor of the River House in New York City (Henry Luce, founder of *Time* magazine, had a lower floor), and at their summer seaside home in Boothbay Harbor, Maine. In the 1990s I auctioned their estate collection, including the 1894-S dime. In the same decade, my company sold the Louis E. Eliasberg Collection, which contained a complete run of Barber coins, most in superb gem preservation. During this decade, David Lawrence, the preeminent scholar in the Barber field, corresponded regularly with me, reviewed coins to be auctioned by me, and helped me in many other ways. In 1994 when he published the second edition of *The Complete Guide to Barber Quarters* he invited me to write the foreword, which I did.

There is a peculiar, perhaps even unique aspect to Barber coins. Probably more than 95 percent of the pieces in existence are in grades of About Good and Good! This is because the design—of the obverse in particular—caused the coins to lose detail quickly. By 1935 a Barber coin that was minted just 20 years earlier, say in 1916, was likely worn down to virtual smoothness. I say more about this in chapter 2. For many varieties with mintages in the high hundreds of thousands or the millions, Extremely Fine and About Uncirculated coins are very scarce, and Mint State coins are *rarities*. Curiously, there are some exceptions. The 1913-S quarter comes to mind. In Extremely Fine and About Uncirculated grades the 1913-S is rarer than Mint State coins of the same variety.

The Treasury Department made no particular effort to call them in, and by the 1930s untold millions of Barber coins were still in circulation. In that decade the collecting of coins by dates and mintmarks became popular. With albums and, later, folders many people began searching for Barber coins, especially dimes due to their low face value.

In contrast, the design of Liberty Seated silver coins, the predecessors to the Barber issues, held up well in circulation, and a coin in use for 20 years might still be in the grade Very Fine. Today the Liberty Seated coins in collectors' hands are mostly worn, but grades such as Fine, Very Fine, and Extremely Fine are common.

As time went on, I bought and sold many Barber coins. The vast majority of my sales were by filling "want lists" for customers. Price was much more important than quality to most buyers, and I lost much business as I graded strictly and paid fair market prices for choice examples. Bargain seekers would rather have a rubbed Proof for, say, $20 than a gem for $30, and wouldn't know the difference.

Uncirculated Barber quarters and half dollars were especially hard to find if choice. The term *Mint State* was known then and, in fact, had been used in the 19th century, but *Uncirculated* was the description everyone used. I recall that Ray Byrne, a client from Pittsburgh, told me he was going to build a collection of Barber quarters in that grade. Within a year he told me he gave up, as even less valuable examples could not be found, and he had made very little headway.

As you read through the chapters to follow you will learn all about Barber dimes, quarters, and half dollars. Quite unlike many later series, the grades of About Good and Good are widely sought and actively collected in the Barber series. Of course, Fine, Very Fine, and higher grades are more desirable, but the cost of some, especially in Mint State, can be a deterrent to all but the most financially fortified enthusiasts. Gem examples of such varieties as 1896-S, 1901-S, and 1913-S quarters and 1904-S half dollars cost more than a fine, top-of-the-line sports car. In actuality, very few Barber specialists seek to build Mint State sets. Lesser grades satisfy.

In lower grades, completing a full set of dimes, quarters, and half dollars is a reality for most collectors—the rare 1894-S dime being the only exception. The era in which Barber coins were minted and first circulated is one of the most interesting and evolutionary in American history and is the subject of chapter 3.

I hope you will gain new appreciation for Barber coins and enjoy this book about them.

Q. David Bowers

How to Use This Book

Barber coins were struck during the Gilded Age and the Progressive Era. Both were ages of unprecedented technological progress, which was showcased in almost yearly expositions around the United States. One such, the World's Columbian Exposition, held in Chicago in 1893, showcased the new Barber designs along with incredible advancements in electric lighting. The Panama-Pacific International Exposition was another landmark exposition held in San Francisco in 1915 to celebrate the opening of the Panama Canal. Each chapter in this book opens with a picture of one of the many expositions held during the period of Barber coinage. These pictures are taken from souvenir prints and postcards such as the postcard displayed at the bottom of page ix.

The typical entry for a coin by date, and mintmark where applicable, contains the following information:

Circulation-strike mintage: Figures are from *The Annual Report of the Director of the Mint.* The mintage figure is often unrelated to the numismatic rarity of coins today, due to exportation (such as to the Philippines beginning in 1898), melting, and unusual distribution. Many such circumstances are explained in the text.

Proof mintage: Treasury Department records are the source for Proof mintage figures.

Availability in Mint State: Estimates are given by the author in consultation based on long-time personal experience plus other sources including specialists, specialized texts, information published in the *Journal of the Barber Coin Collectors' Society*, and elsewhere. Population reports issued by the Professional Coin Grading Service (PCGS) and the Numismatic Guaranty Corporation (NGC) have been reviewed by the author, but their information has been taken into consideration with a large grain of salt. Countless coins graded, for example, MS-63 in the 1990s have "graduated" to be MS-65 today, the result of "gradeflation." A glance at population reports from the early 1990s shows very few MS-66 coins in proportion to MS–64 and 65. Today MS-66 coins abound. Mentioning this is an important caution for sophisticated readers, as many offerings of coins quote such reports as the ultimate definition of rarity. Further, as explained in chapter 2, the certified grade of a coin sometimes has little to do with its overall numismatic desirability. Most connoisseurs would prefer a sharply struck MS-63 coin with beautiful eye appeal to a much more expensive MS-65 that is dark and unattractive.

Availability in circulated grades: These figures are educated guesses based on the relative quantities and grade levels seen by the author and the many consultants and sources, often including extensive information from the *Journal of the Barber Coin Collectors' Society.*

Characteristics of striking: Often within a given date and mintmark many different die pairs were used. One rule does not fit all. There are, however, some general observations for many varieties, and these are given. New Orleans coins are often weakly struck in areas. In contrast, San Francisco coins are usually sharp. For many coins, cherrypicking will result in buying sharp coins at no extra cost, for the certification services do not mention sharpness of strike.

Availability in Proof format: Comments are given concerning rarity and grade ranges. Selected Proofs are pictured in galleries at the end of each denomination's chapter.

Notes: Under this heading are comments on unconfirmed varieties, comments on distribution, historical notes, and other information that may be interesting or relevant.

Market values: These values represent estimated market averages for typical coins in given grade categories. Especially attractive examples of rarities may sell for more at auction. In all instances these are given as a general market guide. As this book is expected to be in print for a number of years, consult current sources before buying or selling.

Certified populations: These populations were compiled from the population reports of the Numismatic Guaranty Corporation (NGC). Proofs which are graded below PF-60 are impaired Proofs: impaired Proofs are not discussed in the prose of the catalog, but impaired proofs certified between PF-50 and PF-59 are shown in the certified population chart under the head PF-50.

Varieties: Widely recognized varieties are discussed under this head.

A souvenir postcard from the Pan-American Exposition of 1901, a vignette from which is featured on the following page. Above are two vignettes taken from other exposition postcards from the period of Barber coinage.

Chapter One

New Coinage of 1892

1892, Barber, half dollar.

The Legacy of Silver Coinage

In 1892 a change was made to the dime, quarter, and half dollar to replace the Liberty Seated design, which had been in continuing use since its inception across various denominations from 1836 to 1839 and had been the subject of much criticism in recent years. The Liberty Head design by Charles E. Barber was adopted amid some discussion and controversy. This was simply the latest chapter in silver coinage motifs.

The first federal dimes were made at the Philadelphia Mint in 1796 and featured the Draped Bust obverse combined with the Small Eagle reverse. In 1798 the Draped Bust obverse was retained in combination with the new Heraldic Eagle reverse. The Capped Bust type was introduced in 1808 and continued till 1837, when it was replaced by the Liberty Seated design. With some alterations, this last style was continued till 1891. The "cereal wreath" reverse of the Liberty Seated design was the only motif continued into the succeeding Barber series.

Dimes were first struck in 1796. This motif was also used in 1797.

In 1798 the Heraldic Eagle reverse was introduced. This was continued in use through 1807.

Capped Bust dimes were made from 1809 to 1837.

Liberty Seated dimes without obverse stars were struck at the Philadelphia Mint in 1837 and the New Orleans Mint in 1838.

Liberty Seated dimes with obverse stars were made in several variations from 1837 to 1860. The "cereal wreath" reverse was introduced in 1860, when the legend replaced the stars. This reverse was continued after 1891 in the Barber dime series and used until 1916.

The designs of quarters followed the same general line, but with some differences in starting dates. In 1796 the Draped Bust obverse was used with the Small Eagle reverse, after which no coins of this denomination were made until 1804, when the reverse was changed to the Heraldic Eagle type, which was continued through 1807, after which there was no coinage of this denomination until 1815, when the Capped Bust type was used for the first time. In 1838 the Liberty Seated motif was introduced. This was continued with some changes through 1891, after which year the obverse and reverse were redesigned by Charles E. Barber.

Half dollars were first coined in 1794, and these were of the Flowing Hair type also used in 1795. In 1796 and 1797 the Draped Bust obverse and Small Eagle reverse were used, followed by a gap in coinage until 1801, when the reverse was changed to the Heraldic Eagle style. The Capped Bust type with lettered edge was made from 1807 to 1836, followed by Capped Bust styles with reeded edge and two different reverses from 1836 to 1839. In 1839 the Liberty Seated type was introduced, and it continued with variations through 1891, after which year the obverse and reverse were redesigned by Charles E. Barber.

CHANGES PROPOSED

As much as the Liberty Seated coins of the late 1830s through 1891 are admired by numismatists today, by the mid-1800s, at which time they had been in use for more than a decade, the design was subject to criticism. They did not appeal to everyone. Many proposals were made for making changes to the denominations featuring Liberty Seated. From the 1850s onward quite a few different pattern coins were made with different motifs, some being food for thought for design changes, but many, if not most, had been made as special pieces for sale to numismatists. The making of such patterns ended in 1885, mostly in response to a hue and cry from collectors that the secret distribution of such pieces was unfair. Still, calls for new motifs persisted.

Quarters were first struck in 1796, as shown here, after which no coins of this denomination were made until 1804.

In 1804 the Heraldic Eagle reverse was introduced. This was continued in use through 1807.

Capped Bust quarters were made from 1815 to 1828, with a large diameter. The design was continued from 1831 to 1838 with a reduced diameter.

Liberty Seated quarters were made in several variations from 1838 to 1891.

The first half dollars of 1794 were of the Flowing Hair style, a design continued in 1795. The lines on the portrait are Mint-caused adjustment marks.

The Draped Bust obverse, Small Eagle reverse half dollars were struck in 1796 and 1797, after which the next coinage of the denomination was in 1801.

In 1801 the Heraldic Eagle reverse was introduced on the half dollar. This was continued in use through 1807.

Capped Bust half dollars with lettered edge were made from 1807 to 1836. The motif was continued through 1839 in two versions with a smaller diameter and reeded edge.

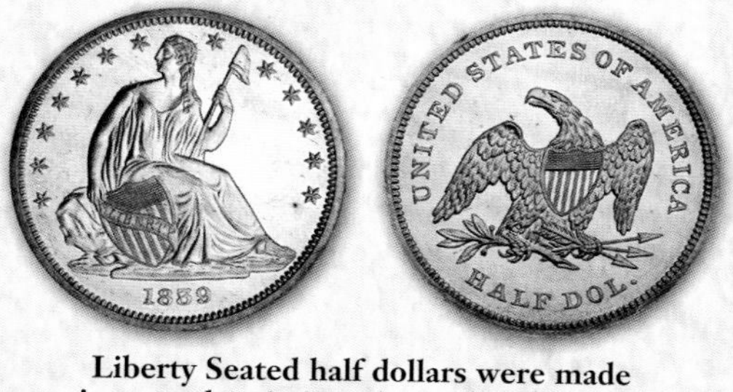

Liberty Seated half dollars were made in several variations from 1839 to 1891.

In *The Annual Report of the Director of the Mint* for 1887, James P. Kimball, the director of the Mint, endorsed the making of new designs. In October 1889, Edward O. Leech became Mint director, succeeding Kimball. Leech invited 10 leading artists to redesign the silver dime, quarter, and half dollar.[1] The dollar motif designed by assistant engraver George T. Morgan was relatively new, having been introduced in 1878, and was not a candidate for change (although at the time various outside critics suggested that a new design would be desirable). Leech did not consult the Engraving Department at the Philadelphia Mint about the contest. Traditionally, new coinage motifs had originated with the artists and engravers in Philadelphia, not from artists in the private sector.

Edward O. Leech, the Mint director who took office on October 16, 1889, soon called for a change in the design of the dime, quarter, and half dollar.

The artists who received the invitation discussed the matter among themselves and then wrote to Leech to state that they would only do this if $100 would be paid for each sketch submitted and $500 for each accepted design. Otherwise a lot of time and effort would be wasted, as only a few designs were to be chosen from the many desired to be submitted.

This response was not satisfactory to Director Leech. On April 4, 1891, he sent a "Circular Letter to Artists" inviting nearly 300 recipients to submit ideas:

> 1. They must be presented in the form of models or medallions in plaster, the models to be from 4 to 8 inches in diameter; a separate design to be submitted for the obverse and reverse of the silver dollar, and separate designs for the obverse of the half dollar, quarter dollar, and dime.
> 2. The models must be in what is known as "low relief," suitable for coins.
> 3. Each model submitted must be complete, with the denomination of the coin, and only such inscriptions as are required by law, together with the date (year).
> 4. The models must be submitted under seal to the Director of the Mint on or before June 1, 1891.
> 5. An award not to exceed $500 will be made for each design accepted.
>
> Full facilities will be afforded at the Mint at Philadelphia to artists who may desire to examine coins belonging to the cabinet of that institution.
>
> The following is a list of the coins for which new designs are proposed, with the diameter and thickness of each . . .

The project was publicized. *Banker's Magazine*, June 1891, included this:

> **New Designs for the Silver Coins**
>
> Among the wise acts of the last Congress was a law authorizing the director of the Mint to have new designs prepared for the silver coins. The designs that have so long been in use have often been criticized. It has been asserted that to cover the entire surface of the coin an inch and a half in diameter with a single figure indicates a poverty of design. Again, it has been asserted that the wings of the eagle on the reverse

side resemble pancakes more than wings, and that the liberty on the half dollar and quarter represents a homely woman with a scrawny neck sitting in a very trying way on the sharp corner of a shield, and that the eagles of these coins have a distinctly drunken appearance, with a beak like the nose of a rhinoceros.

While these criticisms may be too severe, it has long been acknowledged that the artistic conception is as poor as their mechanical execution is excellent. The Director of the Mint, Mr. Leech, has decided to avail himself of the opportunity made by a law of the last Congress authorizing him to adopt new models of the national emblems for use upon the coins. He has already communicated with such American artists and sculptors as he could conveniently get at, inviting the submission of five designs, and offering a payment of $500 for each design selected.

The obverse and reverse of the silver dollar, and the obverse only of the half dollar, quarter dollar and dime, are to be the coins and sides affected by his proposals. The models must be presented in the form of medallions in plaster, in low relief, and with no other inscriptions than are authorized by law. These for the silver dollar are the words "Liberty" and "United States of America," and it is also required that upon the reverse of this coin shall be the figure of an eagle. Upon the obverse of the other three coins there must be an impression emblematic of liberty and an inscription of the word "Liberty."

These conditions met, the opportunity of invention is unlimited. Mr. Leech will supply to anyone desiring them copies of his circular offer and the law. It is to be hoped that the sums offered for the designs are sufficiently large to tempt artists to display their utmost skill. For many years the mechanical execution of our coins has been of the highest order, and there is no reason for remaining so far below other enlightened nations in their artistic appearance.

Three judges were invited to review the new round of submissions: Chief Engraver Charles E. Barber of the Mint, Boston engraver Henry Mitchell, and sculptor Augustus Saint-Gaudens. On June 3 they submitted this report to Director Leech:

Charles E. Barber.

Augustus Saint-Gaudens.

Dear Sir:

We would respectfully report that in conformity with your written request we have opened in the presence of the director of the Mint the new designs or models submitted for the silver coins of the United States, under Department circular of April 4, 1891, and have carefully examined the same.

We are of the opinion that none of the designs or models submitted are such a decided improvement upon the present designs of the silver coins of the United States as to be worthy of adoption by the government.

We would respectfully recommend that the services of one or more artists distinguished for work in designing for relief be engaged at a suitable compensation to prepare for the consideration of the Department new designs for the coins of the United States.

Very respectfully,
Henry Mitchell
Augustus St. Gaudens
Chas. E. Barber[2]

Subsequently the *American Journal of Numismatics*, July 1891, included an article on the project under the title "The New Designs for Our Coinage." Excerpts:

. . . It was publicly stated, when these proposals appeared, that the inducements offered by the government were not sufficient to elicit suggestions of value, much less complete designs for the purpose. Artists who might have given thought to the matter, complained that their time would be wasted, as they would receive nothing for their labor unless their models were accepted; and the result seems to have been, as was anticipated, a complete failure to produce anything that would unite beauty with utility and the practical necessities involved.

When the director of the Mint suggested to the engraver at Philadelphia that he get someone to assist him in some special work that was under way, he replied that he did not know of anyone in the United States who was competent even to assist in this work. During the recent competition the celebrated sculptor, Augustus Saint-Gaudens, who was one of the judges in the contest, told Mr. Leech that he knew of only four artists who were competent to do this class of designing, and that three of them were in France and he was the fourth. He could say this without egotism, for he made a special study of this subject before he attained celebrity as a sculptor. Admitting most willingly the pre-eminent genius of Mr. Saint-Gaudens as a sculptor, we fear that he can hardly be said to have shown equal talent for producing designs adapted to coinage.

We understand that the design favored by the latter gentleman was something after the rude but beautiful coinage of the Greeks. But these designs it would be impossible to follow, and Mr. Barber said in a recent interview, that there was no machinery in existence to coin such pieces as cheaply and as quickly as was necessary. Doubtless American ingenuity could overcome this difficulty, but there are others which cannot be overcome. No three coins could be piled with stability; the third would inevitably fall; their high relief would not sustain the constant wear of circulation without soon being defaced, the protecting rim on our present coins not being compatible with such devices; their irregularity, and that is one of the chief features advocated by those whose suggestions seem to have been sought, would prevent their use, and at the same time make an easy field for counterfeiters.[3]

The *Boston Transcript*, July 31, included this:

> "It is not likely that another competition will ever be tried for the production of designs for United States coins." said Mr. Leech, the director of the Mint, yesterday. "The one just ended was too wretched a failure. Doubtless it was the first contest of the sort ever opened by any government to the public at large. The result is not very flattering to the boasted artistic development of this country, inasmuch as only two of the three hundred suggestions submitted were good enough to receive honorable mention . . ."

As the contest did not yield any satisfactory results, later in July Director Leech traveled to Philadelphia to discuss the matter with the artists at the Mint, including Chief Engraver Charles E. Barber and his two associates, George T. Morgan and William Key. Still seeking to make design changes, he asked each to make some sketches for the dime, quarter, and half dollar—one uniform obverse for each of the denomination, featuring a head similar to that found on certain French coinage.

The reverses of the quarter and half dollar were to be adapted from the Great Seal of the United Sates—what had been called the Heraldic Eagle design when used on coinage generations earlier. At a quick glance the dime's reverse was to remain unchanged from the "cereal wreath" motif created in 1860, but slight differences were made. In due course Leech returned to the Mint, viewed the sketches presented, and took them back to the Treasury Department in Washington for review by senior officials.

Chief Engraver Barber Chosen

In July 1891, Director Leech, having accomplished nothing with artists in the private sector, tapped Chief Engraver Charles E. Barber to prepare coinage designs. Barber set about the task, sometimes allowing his designs to depart from his instructions—in one case creating a reverse inspired by the Una and the Lion reverse on the 1839 British £5 gold coin, it was said. Barber had a mind of his own and had a higher opinion of his talent than did others in the community of artists. The New York City contingent in particular thought his work on medals was sub-par, and it is said that Saint-Gaudens called his art "wretched." However, Barber was in charge of finalizing coin designs that had been accepted by the Treasury, and he resented the input of sculptors from the private sector.

By early August, Barber had created a head of Liberty that was acceptable to Director Leech. The Great Seal motif caused problems when the design shown to Leech was found unacceptable. Barber wanted stars with five points while Leech wanted six, and the director did not like the way E PLURIBUS UNUM was placed on a ribbon crossing the neck of the eagle. On October 2, Barber wrote to Leech:

> I am quite willing to make any change in design, provided the suggestion in my mind is a good one, but I must ask that criticism come to an end before I am too far advanced with the die . . .[4]

This did not sit well with Leech, who informed Barber that he was to do as he was told. Period. Patterns were created, some adjustments were made to the Great Seal, and these were shown to others in the Treasury Department. Examples were given to President Benjamin Harrison, who took them to a Cabinet meeting where they were discussed. Leech was on hand and assisted the Cabinet with the evaluation. The president made the suggestion that the word LIBERTY be strengthened on the obverse. Clouds at the top of the reverse were to be eliminated. The matter was finalized soon thereafter.[5]

Shortly afterward the Treasury Department issued this description of the new design:

> On the obverse, Head of Liberty looking to the right; olive wreath around the head and Phrygian cap on the back; on the band or fillet on the front is inscribed "Liberty"; and surrounding the medallion are 13 stars to represent the 13 original states. Directly over the head at the top of the coin is the legend "In God We Trust," and beneath the bust the date.
>
> On the reverse appears the seal of the United States, as adopted in 1782, represented by an eagle with open wings, on the breast a shield, in the dexter claw an olive branch and in the sinister claw a sheaf of arrows, representative of peace and war. In its beak the eagle holds a scroll with the motto "E Pluribus Unum" ensigned above, and about the head with 13 stars environed by clouds.[6]

COIN NEWS IN THE POPULAR PRESS

This information was sent out to newspapers and magazines, and many articles appeared in print. The *Boston Herald*, November 6, 1891, ran this headline, "Ugly Models of the Present to Be Superseded, Artistic Half and Quarter Dollar and Dimes Coming in January." The text included these comments:

> The new designs for the fractional silver coins which have been completed at the Treasury Department are a great improvement over those now in use.
>
> Mr. Leech, the director of the Mint, has taken much interest in improving the artistic standard of the coins, and has finally obtained devices which approach his idea of what model devices should be . . . He opened the competition at first to prominent American artists, but failing to obtain any designs which precisely suited him, he took up the subject himself in consultation with the engraver at the Philadelphia Mint and obtained, after considerable study, the devices which have been adopted. Mr. Charles E. Barber is the engraver of the Mint who has made the models, and several experimental pieces were struck in silver before the new designs were adopted.
>
> The question what constituted a design "emblematic of liberty," was somewhat mooted, and some of the designs proposed figures of Washington on horseback or historical scenes. Director Leech . . . finally decided that the best device was the head of the goddess similar to that which figures on the silver pieces of the French Republic. The head which he has adopted, however, is different in its lines from any other which has appeared on coins, and is considered in its well-rounded classic outlines more beautiful than any which has been used. The head will take the place on the silver half and quarters of the present complicated seated figure, whose lines are so indistinct. . . .
>
> The engraving department of the Mint at Philadelphia is working energetically to have the dies with the new designs ready for use at the beginning of the new year. Soon after New Year's, therefore, people may expect to get the artistic new coins in place of the present ugly models.

Thus the "ugly" Liberty Seated motif was scheduled to be replaced. Would there be a dawning of public enthusiasm for the new motifs? It was hoped so. However, this was not to be.

Harper's Weekly, November 21, 1891, included this scathing article by Jno. Gilmore Speed illustrated by a *rather crude* image of an 1891 pattern supplied by the Treasury Department:

The Design for the New Silver Coins

The mountain has labored and brought forth a mouse.[7] There was much ado last spring about selecting a design for the new silver coins to be made by the mints of the United States. The director of the Mint, Mr. Leech, took a great deal of advice from artists and invited suggestions as to the design to be adopted, and then chose to have the new coins modeled in the department by the engraver of the Mint.

The result is now before us and is another illustration of the truth, which Buckle carefully formulates, that as a rule the good legislative enactments are only those which repeal standing laws made by previous legislatures, and that nearly all laws are bad.[8] The law of Congress in regard to the new coins contained clauses which did not give a very wide discretion to the Director of the Mint in the selection of a designer for the new coins, and it also restricted the artist in any work he chose to attempt. The law said, "There shall be upon one side an impression emblematic of Liberty, with an inscription of the word 'Liberty' and the year of coinage, and upon the reverse the figure of an eagle with the inscriptions 'United States of America' and 'E Pluribus Unum,' and a designation of the value of the coin." The director of the Mint was further empowered to give $500 for each accepted model.

He invited a number of sculptors and artists to submit designs, but last spring many of the best men joined in a communication declining to participate in a competition in which even those who were successful would be but poorly paid for the work done. However, this was not the only reason which influenced them in declining. If an American artist had felt that he was doing something to prevent his government from making an artistic blunder he would have been willing to waive the question of compensation; but the other conditions were too hard. The time given in which to make the designs was only six weeks, and this was considered too short a period during which first-class work could be done. In addition, again, these artists were not asked to make designs for the whole coin, but for only one side.

Knowing that the department would probably employ some incompetent artisan to make the other side, artists of standing were indisposed to have their work thus spoiled by part of the coin being good, and the rest atrociously bad. The design adopted shows that this is precisely what would have happened, and the artists who foresaw such a probability were wise in their judgment. A painter making a design would have needed to ask the assistance of a sculptor or other designer as to the

Illustrations from the article above.

modeling, and it will readily be seen how very inadequate was the compensation proposed. But this was not, as has been said, the cause which impelled all of them to decline to compete, though, to be sure, some of them could have but poorly afforded to do work for nothing, even when that work was for the United States government. However, many designs were sent in, and all of them were rejected as unsuitable, though it is scarcely possible that there was not among them one or more much better than that which has been adopted, and the pictures of which are printed herewith. This is the work of Mr. Barber, who has held a position in the Mint for some seventeen years, and who is responsible for some of the other coins now in circulation.

There can be no doubt whatever that the mechanical conditions under which coinage is carried on by modern nations are somewhat adverse to the sculptor's art. That the loss in metal by abrasion shall be reduced to a minimum, the relief must be very low, and not much more than a mere film. This was not required in ancient coins, many of which were in high relief, and admitted of many artistic effects not possible today. Indeed, the difficulties in the way of making a good modern coin are so great that Mr. Augustus Saint-Gaudens did not hesitate to say that in his opinion there were only three or four men in America capable of designing a really admirable coin.

"But," said he, looking at a photograph of the new design made by Mr. Barber, "there are a hundred men who could have done very much better than this. This is inept; this looks like it had been designed by a young lady of sixteen, a miss who had taken only a few lessons in modeling. It is beneath criticism, beneath contempt. I told Mr. Leech," he said, continuing, "that if he invited several Frenchmen, whose names I would furnish, to give designs, he would be able to turn out a really 'swell' coin. But it appears that this was not possible under the law. But under the law he could certainly have obtained something better than this. I then offered to give him the names of several Americans, either of whom if given a commission could have made a good design; but this suggestion of mine was not acted upon. I am opposed to going to shops for artistic designs, but he could have done infinitely better by going to either of the great silversmith establishments for his designs. There are hundreds of artists in this country, any of whom, with the aid of a designer, could have made a very respectable coin, which this is not. Indeed, I cannot see that it is any improvement in any regard upon the old coins."

Mr. Kenyon Cox, when shown the photographs of the new design, sniffed the air as though it were foul, and said, impatiently, "Every time the government has anything to do in art matters it shows its utter incapacity to deal with such things." When he was asked to express an opinion of the design, he looked at it a moment and said, "It is beneath criticism," and then added, "I think it disgraceful that this great country should have such a coin as this." Mr. Cox was disinclined to say more, for he evidently felt very strongly on the subject, and was too full of disgust at the artistic inferiority of the new design to express himself freely and still preserve his amiable politeness.

Mr. J.S. Hartley, the sculptor, who, when I called at his studio, had just put the finishing touches on his model for the heroic statue of Ericsson to be placed in the Central Park, examined the photographs carefully. Of the reverse side of the coin, which shows a heraldic eagle carrying a shield on its breast, and in its claws an olive branch and a bunch of arrows, Mr. Hartley did not think very badly, though he found nothing particular in it to praise. Of the obverse side, however, with a head of Liberty wearing a Phrygian cap and a laurel wreath, he said that it was evidently the work of an amateur who had mastered very few of the rudiments of modeling. The head he thought unintellectual, and the face even worse, as it suggested that of a disreputable woman just recovering from a prolonged debauch.

Such were the opinions of three distinguished American artists. The photographs were then shown to a dealer in coins, who is a learned numismatist, but whose relations with the Mint in his business made it inexpedient for him to criticize the work of that department in his own name. He said that, compared with really good modern coins, there was little if anything to commend in this, but he thought that after the coins had been seen, and we got accustomed to them, we would probably like them better. He confessed that he rather liked the reverse of the coin, and, as an American, he was glad that Congress had stipulated that the eagle should be preserved on the new coins. The head of Liberty he thought was very poor and unsatisfactory, and much inferior to many of the designs which in time past the government had declined to use. And he saw no reason or propriety in placing the words "In God we trust" on the coin.

Several designers were also visited, and to them were the photographs shown. Without exception they pronounced the work to be devoid of merit, and no improvement whatever on the old coins. Such seems to be the universal opinion of the new design of those qualified to judge in such matters. But it has been adopted, and on the 1st of next January the mints will begin stamping the coins with dies made from Mr. Barber's design. And so it will continue until Congress does a good act by repealing a bad law, and enable the government officials to secure the services of men competent to make designs more worthy of the country.

The *American Journal of Numismatics* reviewed the designs in its issue of January 1892:

The New Silver Coins

The new silver coinage of half and quarter dollars, and dimes was put in circulation early in January. The dollars have not yet made their appearance. It is not certain that they will, at present. These coins differ in their devices from previous issues, in bearing a bust of Liberty instead of the seated figure used for so many years, which is a return to the type used early in the present century, and the eagle has its wings raised, somewhat as on the gold coins. . . .

The general effect is pleasing. Of the three the dime is to many the most attractive piece. The head of Liberty is dignified, but although the silly story has been started that the profile is that of a "reigning belle" of New York, she can hardly be called a beauty; there is a suggestion, difficult to define, yet perceptible, of the classic heads on some of the Roman coins, and a much stronger suggestion of the head on the French francs of 1871 and onward; but there is a fullness in the upper lip which detracts from the expression, and a slight swelling on the back of the neck, that led one irreverent critic to remark "she is going to have a boil," and another to say "the throat is that of a gladiator!"

The eagle is a compromise between the buzzard on the dollar,[9] and the heraldic eagle on the gold coinage: the wings are not so erect, and are more widely expanded, and their tips extend nearly to the rim: it has not the slender neck and body of the conventional eagles on the German coins, nor their serrated pinions, but the legs and talons are wide-spread, and decidedly heraldic in their treatment; the head is spirited and well-drawn.

The relief on these pieces is about the same as on previous issues; the limitations of the modern method of striking, and the impossibility of piling coins where the device is in high relief, as noted in a former number of the *Journal*, have prevented the carrying out of the frequent suggestions to make the devices stand out more boldly than heretofore.

From this description it may be fairly inferred that in many respects these coins are an advance on what has hitherto been accomplished, but there is yet a long distance between them and the ideal National coin. Perhaps that will never be reached. The mechanical difficulties are numerous, and there has as yet been no way discovered by which these can be overcome and the proper thickness, weight, and size required for coins of such general circulation be preserved.

It must be admitted that if coins should approach more nearly to medals in the matter of "relief" they would rapidly lose their beauty and suffer serious loss by attrition. The American genius for invention has not yet turned itself in this direction to any extent, but those who have studied the problem most carefully, seem to have come to the conclusion that coins of the highest type of art will be struck for popular use about the same day that the quadrature of the circle shall be exactly accomplished.[10]

Mintage of the Barber Coins Begins

Minting of the Barber coins commenced on January 2, 1892. The first delivery to the cashier consisted of $2,000 in dimes, $1,000 worth of quarters, and $5,000 in half dollars. A shipment of $50 face value was sent that day to Mint Director Edward O. Leech in Washington. These were received on the 4th, at which time a set of the three denominations was given to President Grover Cleveland, and other sets were given to Leech's friends.[11]

Coining press on view for visitors to the Philadelphia Mint in the early 1890s. The attendant takes blank planchets from a bin to her left and drops them into a vertical brass tube that feeds them one by one into the press. (*Harper's Weekly*, September 3, 1893)

There was a problem with the relief being too high on the quarters and the half dollars, this newspaper account being typical commentary on the matter:

> Bank cashiers complain that the Goddess of Liberty on the newly minted quarters and half dollars is too plum. The coin cannot be stacked in piles of $5 and $10 as has been the custom on bank counters from time immemorial, for this reason. The figure of the Goddess is an artistic success, but the men who handle money in the banks do not admire it.[12]

Half dollars in particular were criticized as not being satisfactory for poker chips. Chief Engraver Barber adjusted the quarter design, but if there was a problem with the half dollar, no record has been found of any correction.

As might be expected and had been generally true of nearly all new designs, citizens hastened to criticize the new coinage, adding to the criticisms already in print from those who had reviewed the motifs prior to their being coined. From an early account:

Art in Silver Coins

> During the week which closed last Saturday some of the new coins issued by the United States government crept into circulation and were commented on by beholders from different points of view. The coinage is limited to three pieces, the dime, quarter and half-dollar, and all three present in differing sizes the same designs for obverse and reverse.
>
> On one side there appears a spread-eagle and on the other the profile of a head surmounted by the legend: "In God We Trust." The eagle is a meager and ill-fed specimen of our noble bird and the profile is that of a goddess of liberty, though it looks like the head of the ignoble Emperor Vitellius with a goiter. To be extremely frank, these new coins are not artistic. Even this mild statement is unduly flattering to the designers.
>
> Some time ago Mr. Wanamaker introduced an acceptable reform by abolishing the bottle-green postage stamp and putting a cherry-red one in its place—a stamp that is in place on a wedding invitation as well as on a letter of condolence. But it seems that

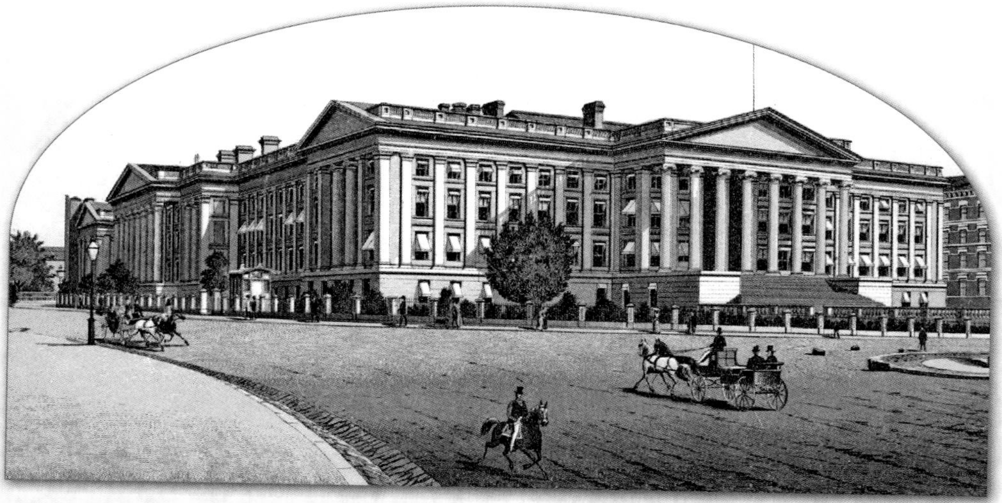

The Treasury Building in Washington, D.C., as it appeared in the early 1890s. (J.F. Jarvis, *Views*)

a similar effort at reforming the coinage is sure to result a great deal less fortunately. The nation has poor luck in getting up designs for coins. The reason is not apparent unless it be that sufficient inducements are not offered to bring our really good designers into competition. However, money has another end than that of satisfying aesthetic people. Presumably no one will object to having a quantity of the new coins in his possession, even if he does not admire them.[13]

The *Washington Star* printed this concerning the distribution of the new coins from the Treasury Building in Washington, D.C.:

Rich Uncle Sam

How He Gives Out Change to the People.

He Is Passing Thousands of Dollars' Worth of the New Coins Over His Counter Every Day. How It Is Done:

Silver change of the new patterns is being dispensed at the rate of thousands of dollars daily over what may be called the change counter of the nation at the Treasury. It is done up prettily in little paper *rouleaux* [rolls] each contain $5 in dimes, quarters and halves. It is put up in coarse muslin bags, holding $50 each, with paper tags attached. On every such bag is marked the weight, which could be two pounds twelve and a half ounces for new and unabraded coins, together with the date of the weighing and the signature "J.," which stands for Jerry Jones, the official weigher. Ordinarily such subsidiary pieces are not given out over the counter in sums of less than $5, but to satisfy public curiosity and also for the sake of getting it in circulation, everyone is permitted for the present to procure the freshly designed silver money in as small quantities as may be desired.

The new coins are brought from the Philadelphia Mint, where they are made, in wooden kegs. In each keg are five sacks, holding $1,000 each. They are delivered by the United States Express at the basement on the east side of the Treasury, and are wheeled on small trucks to the counting-room. In the apartment deft fingered young ladies sit at tables with stacks of glittering silver in front of them. They take a double handful at a time, quickly spread out the bright pieces in a layer over the board, and pick them off the edge by the numbers necessary to fill the rouleaux. For making these rouleaux small paper tubes are prepared by the messengers of the division in their leisure moments. The rapidity with which they are filled and closed at the end is astonishing. Finally they are placed in drawer-like boxes, each of which contains exactly $200. So accurately are they made to hold just that amount that the absence of a single coin would be likely to make the shortage visible. Every such paper roll of silver is weighted after being filled in the same way as the bags are.

It is interesting to stand behind the change counter upstairs in the cash rooms and see how the business is carried on. The official in charge is enclosed within a wire cage, surrounded on every side by sacks of money in every shape. Piled on the floor are bags of silver and the boxes filled with rouleaux, just as they have been brought up by the elevator from the counting floor beneath. Besides the smaller coins there are bags of silver dollars, each containing $50 or $100, rouleaux holding ten silver dollars each, nickels in muslin bags of $25, and paper bags of $1 and $5, and pennies in muslin bags of $5 and paper bags of $1. At the left of the paying teller is a drawer divided into compartments exactly the size of greenbacks, and filled with bank and treasury notes and silver certificates of every denomination. The aggregate sum at hand seems enormous, but people come in such rapid succession to the window that presently the supply of small bills runs low. In response to an order conveyed by a messenger two packages are brought, each a foot cube, and neatly done up in brown paper with a label. The official in charge of the change cuts them open with his pen-knife. In one of them is found 4,000 one dollar notes, and in the other as many two dollar notes. Whenever the teller needs more cash of any kind he simply fills out a blank and signs his initials. The vault clerk delivers to him the money and charges it against him.

Packing cloth bags of coins into barrels for shipment at the Philadelphia Mint. (Underwood & Underwood U-191237)

A photographic view of the Cash Room. (Panel from Underwood & Underwood stereograph U-105983)

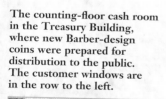

The counting-floor cash room in the Treasury Building, where new Barber-design coins were prepared for distribution to the public. The customer windows are in the row to the left.

All the fractional paper currency that comes in for redemption is handed directly over the change counter, new money being given for it. One day last week, a package of it, containing $71.72 was received in this way—the biggest single consignment that has reached the Treasury for a year. The little notes, neatly done up in a bundle, were so old and worn that the engraving on them was hardly distinguishable. Some curious stories might have been told about them doubtless. Perchance they formed a portion of some miser's hoard, hidden away ever since the war [The Civil War]. Anyone who has a portion of a bill and has lost the rest can get a fresh one for it by applying at the same counter. Three-fifths of a ten dollar note is worth $10, two-fifths is worth $5, but a lesser fragment must be accompanied by an affidavit, telling how the balance was destroyed. Among the coins sent in from banks are a great many mutilated and foreign ones. They are thrown out in the counting room. All old copper cents [Large Cents] are kept and sent to the mint for re-coining. Likewise it is with the nickel three-cent and two-cent pieces.—[*Washington Star*][14]

Coverage of the new Barber coins was soon trumped by announcements of the new souvenir (as they were called) half dollars being prepared for the World's Columbian Exposition. This inspired a flood of comments about the commemorative design, though most were humorous or negative.[15] The regular-issue dimes, quarters, and half dollars were no longer newsworthy.

A Modern Review

In contrast to comments of years earlier, Cornelius Vermeule, numismatist and a curator at the Museum of Fine Art, Boston, writing in 1971, praised the Barber design to the skies:

The designs of Barber's coins were more attuned to the times than even he perhaps realized. The plumpish, matronly *gravitas* of Liberty had come to America seven years earlier in the person of Frédéric Bartholdi's giant statue on Bedloe's Island in New York Harbor.[16]

Such sculptures, whether called Liberty or Columbia or The Republic or a personification of intellect, were dominant themes of the Chicago World's Fair, the Columbian Exposition of 1892, termed by Saint-Gaudens "the greatest meeting of artists since the fifteenth century." Chief among these statues was Daniel Chester French's colossal *Republic*, a Pheidian matron holding aloft an eagle on an orb in one hand and a Liberty cap on an emblem in the other. The heavy profile, solemn eyes, thick jaw, and massive neck of the statue are in harmony with what Charles Barber had created for the coinage in the year of the Fair's opening.[17]

Of all American coins long in circulation, no series has stood the wearing demands of modern coinage as well as the half dollar, quarter, dime developed by the chief engraver at Philadelphia. Liberty's cap, incised diadem, and wreath of laurel were designed to echo all the depth and volume of her Olympian countenance. These classical substances are offset, almost literally, by sharply rectangular dentils of the raised rims and by the strength of thirteen six-pointed stars.

On the reverse of two large coins, an equal constellation of stars has five points and is clustered above the eagle's shaggy, craggy profile. On both sides the simple dignity of motto, legend, and denomination binds the pictorialism into a cohesive tondo. The wealth of irregular surfaces and sharp angles is an almost electrifying aesthetic experience. The wreath of the dime's reverse carries the plasticity of the eagle's feathers into miniature dimensions and entwines the less complicated inscription in forthright fashion. This wreath also exhibits its own freshness and sculptural activity; leaves, berries, and stems are alive with a carefully controlled sense of nature. Even when these coins have been nearly smooth, their outlines suggest the harmony of interior detail in careful planes of relief that make Uncirculated specimens a pleasure to contemplate. The sculptor was unsurpassed in the mechanics of creating a durable design of monumental validity.[18]

Aspects of Minting

To produce the 1892 dies the artists at the Mint made the design in larger form in clay, from which an impression was taken in plaster, from which a metal cast was made. After retouching the details, a pantograph lathe, or reducing machine, was used to make hubs from which master dies were created.

Production of the dimes, quarters, and half dollars for circulation took place at the three mints then currently in operation—Philadelphia, New Orleans, and San Francisco (see appendix III). The new Denver Mint coined pieces starting in 1906. After 1909 the New Orleans Mint shut down forever. Coinage of all three denominations usually, but not always, took place at each of the mints in each year. Dimes and quarters of the Barber design were made through 1916, when they were replaced by the Mercury and Standing Liberty designs respectively. Barber half dollars were made through 1915, followed in 1916 by the Liberty Walking motif.

The Life of Coinage Dies

In *The Annual Report of the Director of the Mint* information was occasionally given concerning the production life of coinage dies. If one die in a coining press failed due to cracks, the other die would continue in use. Endeavoring to sort this out, Russell Easterbrooks estimated these figures:

> 1907: Dime: 92,345 coins per die, quarter 60,218, and half dollar 36,071.

The 1908 *Report* gave precise information as to the highest and lowest number of coins struck by a single die:

> Dime: 515,476 highest for an obverse die, lowest 2,589. Lowest for a reverse die (highest not given).
>
> Quarter: Obverse information not given. Records including both sides were for a reverse 660,352 highest and 6,700 lowest.
>
> Half dollar: 468,850 highest for an obverse die, lowest not given. Highest for a reverse not given, lowest 3,000.[19]

In calendar year 1913 the average number of coins struck per die at each mint was:

Denver Mint Die Life (1913)

Quarter: 86,507 obverse; 107,211 reverse.

Half dollar: 75,472 obverse; 68,931 reverse.

Philadelphia Mint Die Life (1913)

Dime: 166,152 obverse; 201,756 reverse.

Quarter: 100,308 obverse; 167,180 reverse.

Half dollar: 101,198 obverse; 101,198 reverse (indicating the die pairs were probably replaced at the same time).

San Francisco Mint Die Life (1913)

Dime: 177,319 obverse; 132,989 reverse.

Quarter: Two pairs of dies were used to strike just 40,000 coins.

Half dollar: 92,214 obverse, 215,166 reverse.[20]

In calendar year 1914 the average number of coins struck per die was much lower on average:

Denver Mint Die Life (1914)

Quarter: 45,568 obverse; 81,441 reverse.

Half dollar: 51,698 obverse; 68,931 reverse.

Philadelphia Mint Die Life (1914)

Dime: 124,852 obverse; 133,564 reverse.

Quarter: 63,736 obverse; 84,016 reverse.

Half dollar: 53,423 obverse; 53,423 reverse (indicating the dies were changed at the same time).

San Francisco Mint Die Life (1914)

Dime: 162,079 obverse; 138,925 reverse.

Quarter: 70,934 obverse; 70,934 reverse.

Half dollar: 63,468 obverse; 114,243 reverse.[21]

It might be an interesting exercise to carefully study Barber coins of 1913 and 1914 to see if die life can be correlated with the sharpness of strike.

For obverse dies, four-digit logotypes were used to punch the date into dies through 1908, after which the date was part of the master die. Because of this, coins from 1892 to 1908 vary slightly in date positions for a given year and mint. Under a strong magnifier differences can be seen for such characteristics as the position of the 1 in the date to Barber's initial B in the neck above, and the distance of the first and last date digits from the denticles in the border. On dimes the differences are often so subtle that they cannot be detected. On quarters and half dollars the differences are more noticeable. From 1909 onward the dates were in the hub dies and there were no longer differences within a given year and denomination.

For reverse dies of all dates, the mintmarks were punched in by hand. Within a given year they sometimes varied in size, the most famous of such being the "Micro o" 1905-O dime and the rare "Micro o" 1892-O half dollar. These variations resulted from mintmarks intended for use on one denomination being inadvertently used on dies of another value. D and S mintmarks also varied in size, but such differences have not attracted a wide audience. There are also many instances of mintmarks showing doubling from two

Mintmarked Coins Showcased in 1893

In 1892 there were four mints operating in the United States: Philadelphia, Carson City, New Orleans, and San Francisco. Carson City made only one silver denomination—the dollar. The other three mints produced silver coins from dimes to dollars, including the three Barber issues launched in 1892.

At the time there was hardly any numismatic interest in coins with mintmarks. Collectors sought dates only, and the presence or absence of a mint letter was not important. Not even the Mint Cabinet curators in Philadelphia were interested in adding pieces from each mint each year.

A small advertisement in *The Numismatist* in May 1893 would change the very foundations of American numismatics, although no one knew it at the time. Placed by Augustus G. Heaton, the notice offered for sale *Mint Marks*, noting:

Augustus G. Heaton.

> This treatise just published in handsome and substantial pamphlet form is based upon a close study of the subject during the accumulation of an almost complete collection of silver "mintmark" pieces.
>
> Every alert collector of United States coins from 1838 to the present day will require it. It has full descriptive lists of the branch mint dates of every denomination, and of many hitherto unknown varieties, indications of scarcity and value, comparisons with Philadelphia issues, historic suggestions and other material of great interest to numismatists.
>
> It is the only guide book to a new field now eagerly invaded. Several prominent collectors who have seen the manuscript commend it highly, and leading coin dealers have welcomed the treatise as a timely and much needed work.

Heaton, a facile writer, listed 17 reasons for collecting mintmarks, as delineated below:

Causes of Attractiveness

1st. Mint Marks in their progressive issue at New Orleans, Dahlonega, Charlotte, San Francisco, and Carson City show the direction of our country's growth and its development of mineral wealth.

2d. Mint Marks in their amount of issue in varied years at different points offer the monetary pulse of our country to the student of finance.

3rd. The denominations of any one Branch Mint, in their irregular coinage and their relation to each other at certain periods, indicate curiously the particular needs of the given section of the land.

4th. A knowledge of the Branch Mint coinage is indispensable to an understanding of the greater or less coinage of the Philadelphia Mint and its consequent numismatic value.

5th. A knowledge of the coinage of the different Branch Mints gives to many usually considered common dates great rarity if certain Mint Marks are upon them.

6th. Mint-Mark study gives nicety of taste and makes a mixed set of pieces unendurable.

7th. Several dies were used at Branch Mints which never served in the Philadelphia coinage, and their impressions should no longer be collected as mere varieties.

8th. The very irregularity of dates in some denominations of Branch Mint issues is a pleasant exercise of memory and numismatic knowledge.

9th. This irregularity in date, and in the distribution of coinage, gives a collection in most cases but two or three, and rarely three or more contemporaneous pieces, and thus occasions no great expense.

10th. As the Branch Mints are so far apart their issues have the character of those of different nations, and tend to promote correspondence and exchange, both to secure common dates in fine condition and the rarities of each.

11th. The United States coinage has a unique interest in this production at places far apart of pieces of the same value and design with distinguishing letters upon them.

12th. As Mint Marks only occur in silver and gold coins they can be found oftener than coins of the baser metals in fine condition, and neither augment or involve a collection of the minor pieces.

13th. As Mint Marks have not heretofore been sought, or studied as they deserve, many varieties yet await in circulation the good fortune of collectors who cannot buy freely of coins more in demand, and who, in having access to large sums of money, may draw therefrom prizes impossible to seekers after older dates.

14th. The various sizes of the mint marks O, S, D, C, and CC, ranging from the capital letters of average book type to infinitesimal spots on the coin, as well as the varied location of these letters, defy any accusation of monotony, and are far more distinguishable than the characteristics of many classified varieties of old cents and 'colonials.'

15th. Mint Marks include noble enough game for the most advanced coin hunter, as their rarities are among the highest in value of United States coinage, and their varieties permit the gathering in some issues of as many as six different modern pieces of the same date.

16th. The face value of all the silver Mint Marks to 1893, being less than one hundred and fifty dollars, they are within the means of any collector, as aside from the economy of those found in circulation, the premiums for rarities are yet below those on many coins of far inferior intrinsic worth.

17th. As the new Mint at Philadelphia will have a capacity equal to all existing United States Mints, it is probable that others will be greatly restricted or even abolished in no long time, and that Mint Marks will not only cease as an annual expense, but be a treasure in time to those who have the foresight to collect them now.

Heaton was a Renaissance man in his day. His primary occupation was that of an artist. His painting, *The Recall of Columbus*, hangs in the Capitol rotunda and is pictured on the 50-cent commemorative stamp made for the World's Columbian Exposition. He was a skilled poet as well, and he contributed many coin-related rhymes to *The Numismatist*. In 1894 he was elected president of the American Numismatic Association. The *Mint Marks* study sold well. Within a year, at least several dozen numismatists were in the pursuit of mintmarked coins, and some of these wrote to the various mints to seek current issues—mostly dimes, as they were the most popular denomination. Due to handling, many coins obtained directly from the mints were less than gem quality. Philadelphia coins without mintmarks were usually ordered in Proof format. There was little desire for current circulating issues. As a result, high-level, Mint State Philadelphia coins that survive today did so as a matter of chance, not intent.

It was not until well into the 20th century that interest in mintmarks became widespread. As a result, relatively few Barber coins were saved in Mint State during the 1890s and in the early years of the 20th century. Heaton's *Mint Marks* treatise seems to have been most influential for dimes. It is likely that by 1904, a decade later, no more than a dozen or so collectors specialized in half dollars. Generations later, many Barber issues with large mintages were found to be rare in high grades.

Numismatic Interest During the Barber Years

In their era the Barber design received a lot of bad press, as described in the preceding chapter. The coins were not at all popular with numismatists, and few set about building collections of them. The most interest was in Proofs, the mintage numbers for which were well below 1,000 coins in each year except for 1892. Even interest in these waned, and by the last year Proofs were made—1915—the mintage was only 450, a slight uptick from the record low of 380 the year before. There were a number of issues under similar circumstances in that era. Hardly anyone collected Morgan silver dollars other than the yearly Proofs until that denomination was discontinued in 1904. The 1908, Indian Head, quarter eagles and half eagles by Bela Lyon Pratt were severely panned in the pages of *The Numismatist*, and hardly anyone collected them either.

Today such apathy accounts for the remarkable situation that for many Barber dimes, quarters, and half dollars with mintages over a million, fewer than 100 Mint State–65 or finer coins exist today. A buyer with an unlimited budget who seeks to acquire one of each date and mintmark of Barber half dollar from 1892 to 1915 in MS-65 or better grade and with good eye appeal must expect to spend at least a decade in the effort, and even that might not be enough time. In contrast, anyone seeking to form a collection of gem Liberty Walking half dollars from 1916 through 1947 can probably get most of the various dates and mintmarks within a week and all of them within a month. This contrast is simply amazing.

The Barber Coin Collectors' Society

While old-time newspaper accounts panning the Barber design are interesting to read, as are contemporary complaints about Morgan dollar and Liberty Seated coin motifs, they do not have much relevance to modern numismatics. The Barber Coin Collectors' Society, formed in 1989, is dedicated to all of the coins created by Chief Engraver Charles E. Barber, including Liberty Head nickels (1883 to 1913) and, in passing, various commemoratives. The *Journal of the Barber Coin Collectors' Society* includes articles covering the rarity of various issues in different grades, illustrations of interesting die varieties and unusual pieces, advice on buying and selling, and more.

Today, Barber dimes, quarters, and half dollars are enthusiastically collected. However, Mint State and Proof coins are the *crème de la crème;* forming a complete or nearly complete collection of such is very expensive; and in the entire history of numismatics no one has ever done this at the gem MS-65 and Proof-65 levels. Not even the Eliasberg Collection auctioned in 1996 and 1997 achieved this goal, although it came very close. A reasonable goal for a well-financed connoisseur is to seek certified MS-63 coins, patiently searching for nice strike and eye appeal.

Happily, the completion of collections of each of these three denominations, excepting the 1894-S dime, is very doable in such grades as About Good and Good. These constitute the vast majority of Barber coins in numismatic hands and are also the focus for the members of the Barber Coin Collectors' Society, although most members seek higher circulated grades up to About Uncirculated. Today probably 95 percent of the remaining Barber coins from the 1890s are in grades such as About Good (AG-3) and Good (G-4), and for 20th-century issues the typical grade is G-4.

As noted in the introduction, the reason for this is that Barber coins were not widely collected until the 1930s and 1940s, by which time most had been in circulation for a long time. Even coins in Very Good grade, defined as having several letters in the word LIBERTY readable, form only a tiny percentage of existing coins.

JOURNAL
OF THE
BARBER COIN COLLECTORS SOCIETY

VOLUME I, #1

SPRING, 1989

UNITED STATES OF AMERICA 1894 — ONE DIME

1894-s Dime: The Classic Barber Rarity

In this Issue...

- Cover story...*The Mystery of the Classic Barber Rarity*
- *Why a Barber Coin Collectors Society?* Steve Epstein
- *Barbers - An Overlooked Series* David Lawrence
- *Question & Answer Column*
- *Barber Knowledge Barometer*
- *Barber Coinage Library*
- *Dealer Bourse*
- *Barber Barter*
- *Member Feedback Form*
- *Membership Information*

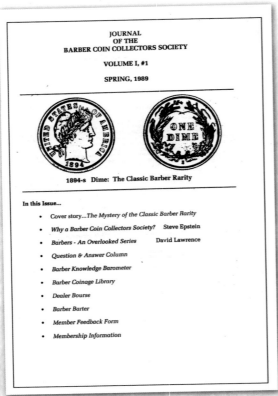

Cover of the first issue of the *Journal of the Barber Coin Collectors' Society*, spring 1989.

This rare 1901-S quarter, graded AG-3, shows decades of wear. Even so, it would be highly desirable to most specialists and has a market value well into four figures.

In the Barber series, and also the earlier Liberty Seated series, the collecting of coins in grades such as Good, Very Good, Fine, and other levels below Mint State is popular with serious numismatists. This is in contrast to many later series from the mid-1900s to date, in which Mint State and Proof coins form the center of most attention, but worn pieces are often overlooked, except for those acquired by casual collectors filling albums and boards.

Of course we all know that in certain early series—say state copper coins of the years 1785 to 1788—worn coins are the rule, and for many varieties the finest-known examples are from Good to Fine. For Vermont copper coins from 1785 to 1788 typical grades are Very Good to Very Fine, often poorly struck and on defective planchets. These have a special charm for their rusticity—like folk art. A longtime collector can enjoy examining such a coin under magnification, while a modern MS-70 commemorative, perfectly struck and without a blemish, would hold little interest. In contrast, many newcomers to the hobby are not tuned in to worn examples—which can appear to be coins that have been there and done that, serving their duty in commerce.

Coin Collecting Becomes Widely Popular

In the 1930s coin collecting became widely popular with the general public for the first time. This was caused by a confluence of several events.

In 1934 Wayte Raymond and the Scott Stamp & Coin Co. published the first large edition of the *Standard Catalogue of United States Coins*, the only reference to give mintage figures as well as prices of coins in various grades. It became wildly popular and was sold in various editions through 1958. Raymond also promoted his line of National holders. For the first time coins could be mounted in cardboard pages with clear cellulose acetate slides on both sides, permitting them to be nicely stored and displayed at the same time.

Whitman, starting with its "Penny Board," published a line of panels, later supplemented by inexpensive blue folders, in which to collect many series. Barber coins were labeled as "Morgan" coins—for example, Barber dimes were labeled as Morgan dimes. This inaccuracy appeared in many other products and publications as well, never mind that Barber's initial B was prominent on the obverse of each coin. Most often such coins were called Liberty Head issues. The Barber name did not become popular in conjunction with these issues until later.

Another contributing influence to this surge in numismatics was the popularity of hobbies in general during the Depression. Home crafts, jigsaw puzzles, stamp collecting, and

Whitman "Morgan Dime—Liberty Head" panel of 1938 filled with coins taken from circulation in that era. The average grade is G-4.

other pursuits attracted many devotees. Taking Barber dimes from circulation in the 1930s was affordable to many. In contrast, holding onto quarters and half dollars represented an investment that many people had to think about carefully.

According to the Bureau of Labor Statistics, in 1935 the average weekly wage for someone employed in manufacturing was $21.06 for 36 hours of work. In the making of cotton goods the figure was $13.07 for a week of 34.6 hours. In the same year a worker in the wholesale trade earned an average of $26.93 for a 41.3-hour work week, and in year-round hotels the typical worker earned $13.57 by working 47.8 hours. It took a hotel employee three and one-half hours to earn a dollar. A Barber half dollar taken from pocket change represented nearly two hours of work—that is, for those lucky enough to be employed. The Depression held sway, and many people were idle.

CIRCULATION FINDS

A number of inventories of Barber coins put away as general pocket change in the 1930s and 1940s survive today. These show pieces that were in general circulation at the time. Naturally, later issues with large mintages are found in such lists more often than early low-mintage coins, especially mintmarked coins of the 1890s. Any inventory would vary depending on the geographical location in which it was gathered.

In *The Numismatic Scrapbook Magazine*, November 1938, Dr. J. Robert Schneider of Rock Island, Illinois, listed the Barber dimes and quarters he had found in circulation from November 1937 to September 20, 1938.[1] The grades were not given, but it can be assumed that most if not all were AG-3 and G-4.

Barber dimes:

1892: 6	1900: 12	1905-O: 1	1908-O: 1	1912: 52
1892-O: 2	1900-O: 1	1905-S: 8	1908-S: 10	1912-D: 29
1893-S: 1	1900-S: 3	1906: 19	1909: 18	1912-S: 5
1894-O: 1	1901: 24	1906-D: 9	1909-D: 1	1913: 47
1896: 1	1901-O: 7	1906-O: 3	1909-O: 1	1914: 45
1897: 6	1901-S: 2	1906-S: 5	1909-S: 4	1914-D: 27
1897-S: 1	1902: 27	1907: 36	1910: 20	1914-S: 5
1898: 14	1902-O: 5	1907-D: 2	1910-D: 4	1915: 18
1898-O: 2	1903: 19	1907-O: 6	1910-S: 2	1915-S: 2
1898-S: 1	1903-O: 8	1907-S: 5	1911: 41	1916: 41
1899: 16	1904: 18	1908: 18	1911-D: 22	1916-S: 11
1899-O: 3	1905: 17	1908-D: 15	1911-S: 6	Dateless: 7

Barber quarters:

1892: 29	1895-S: 2	1900: 40	1904: 5	1907-S: 5
1892-O: 1	1896: 21	1900-O: 9	1904-O: 1	1908: 29
1892-S: 5	1896-O: 2	1900-S: 6	1905: 29	1908-D: 33
1893: 16	1897: 37	1901: 24	1905-O: 8	1908-O: 49
1893-O: 6	1897-O: 4	1901-O: 2	1905-S: 6	1908-S: 1
1893-S: 3	1897-S: 2	1902: 45	1906: 32	1909: 61
1894: 8	1898: 47	1902-O: 10	1906-D: 9	1909-D: 34
1894-O: 4	1898-O: 9	1902-S: 3	1906-O: 12	1909-O: 2
1894-S: 3	1898-S: 5	1903: 37	1907: 54	1909-S: 12
1895: 17	1899: 73	1903-O: 12	1907-D: 8	1910: 11
1895-O: 7	1899-O: 9	1903-S: 2	1907-O: 19	1910-D: 7

Barber quarters *(continued)*:

1911: 25
1911-D: 8
1911-S: 2
1912: 38
1912-S: 2
1913: 4
1913-D: 7
1914: 50
1914-D: 22
1914-S: 3
1915: 30
1915-D: 20
1915-S: 4
1916: 19
1916-D: 54
Dateless Philadelphia: 13
Dateless New Orleans: 9
Dateless San Francisco: 1
Unidentifiable: 19

In Ann Arbor, Michigan, a citizen set about hoarding silver coins in the early 1940s. In September 2004 Tim Glaue, a Barber coin enthusiast, received a call from a friend who was excavating the foundation of the Michigan home. The friend reported that two glass canning jars filled with coins had been found along with a newspaper dated May 26, 1940, put there when the foundation was built.[2] Tim visited the scene and counted 1,193 coins, including 502 quarters, 690 half dollars, and a single Peace silver dollar, the most recently coined issue. There were 36 Barber quarters and 30 Barber half dollars. These consisted of the following:

Barber quarters:

1893: 1 (AG-3)
1893-O: 1 (AG-3)
1897: 1 (AG-3)
1898: 1 (AG-3); 3 (G-4)
1899: 1 (AG-3); 4 (G-4)
1901: 2 (AG-3); 1 (G-4)
1902: 1 (AG-3); 2 (G-4)
1904: 1 (AG-3); 1 (G-4)
1905: 1 (AG-3)
1906: 1 (AG-3)
1908: 1 (AG-3); 1 (F-12)
1908-D: 1 (AG-3)
1909: 1 (AG-3)
1909-D: 2 (G-4)
1909-O: 1 (AG-3)
1911: 1 (AG-3); 1 (G-4)
1914: 1 (G-4)
1915: 1 (G-4)
1916: 1 (G-4)
1916-D: 1 (AG-3); 1 (G-4)

Barber half dollars:

1894: 1 (G-4)
1895-S: 1 (G-4)
1896: 1 (G-4)
1899: 1 (AG-3)
1900: 1 (G-4)
1901-O: 1 (G-4)
1902: 1 (AG-3)
1902-O: 1 (VG-8)
1905-O: 1 (G-4)
1906: 1 (G-4); 1 (VG-8)
1907: 1 (AG-3); 1 (G-4)
1907-D: 1 (AG-3); 1 (G-4)
1907-S: 1 (G-4)
1908-O: 1 (G-4)
1909-O: 1 (AG-3)
1910-S: 1 (F-12)
1911: 1 (G-4)
1911-D: 1 (G-4)
1912: 1 (G-4)
1912-D: 1 (G-4); 1 (VG-8)
1912-S: 2 (G-4)
1913-S: 1 (AG-3)
1914: 1 (VG-8)
1914-S: 1 (VG-8)
1915-D: 1 (AG-3)

In 1947 a customer of the Manchester, New Hampshire, Savings Bank was given a cardboard folder that had spaces for 30 dimes to be inserted—the Pocket Dime Saver—to encourage thrift. In ensuing months the Manchester resident inserted several Liberty Head (Barber) dimes from circulation into the savings board. The inventory is as follows, providing a view of what was possible to find at the time. It is seen that G-4 is the standard grade without a single coin in better condition:

Barber dimes:

1901: 1 (Fair-2); 1 (G-4)
1901-O: 1 (G-4)
1902: 3 (AG-3)
1905: 1 (G-4)
1906: 1 (AG-3); 1 (G-4)
1906-S: 1 (G-4)
1907: 1 (Fair-2); 1 (G-4)
1907-O: 1 (G-4)
1908: 1 (G-4)
1908-D: 1 (G-4)
1911: 1 (G-4)
1911-D: 1 (G-4)
1911-S: 1 (G-4)
1912: 1 (AG-3); 1 (G-4)
1912-D: 2 (G-4)
1912-S: 1 (G-4)
1913: 1 (G-4)
1914: 1 (G-4)
1914-D: 1 (AG-3); 1 (G-4)
1916: 1 (AG-3); 2 (G-4)

In the 1950s, when I first discovered numismatics, thousands of collectors had Whitman folders for Barber dimes, quarters, and half dollars. By that time most such coins had disappeared from circulation, except for half dollars. When seen these were usually well worn, AG-3 was the typical grade. There were, however, good supplies of Barber coins in dealers' inventories, these being coins that had been picked out from the 1930s onward.

In the 1940s three men who sold subway tokens in New York City—Herb Tobias, Max L. Kaplan, and Morris Moscow—fished tens of thousands of worn Barber coins from the change they received. These three men also found many 1942 Over 1 dimes and profited from them. I recall that Tobias, in the 1950s—by then a dealer in many other coins as well—had a huge stock of circulated Barber coins that he had accumulated in the 1940s when he was a cashier selling tokens for the New York City subway system. In the 1990s Littleton Coin Co. bought many of Morris Moscow's coins through his brother-in-law George Shaw, who handled the Moscow estate.[3]

A cardboard folder filled with Barber dimes, issued by the Manchester Savings Bank.

Liberty and Rarity

There is a curious aspect regarding the survival of Barber silver coins. The Official ANA Grading Standards and other published references define a coin in Fine-12 (F-12) grade as having all of the letters in LIBERTY visible on the obverse. The zinger is that the design is such that the word is on one of the areas of highest relief, and with only a minimum amount of circulation the letters started disappearing. A coin in circulation for only a few years likely would have just a few of the letters still visible, and in 20 years they would all be gone.

A correctly graded F-12 Barber coin usually has all of the other details as sharp as might be found on a Very Fine or even Extremely Fine coin in another series! By the 1930s, as demonstrated by the inventories given above, most Barber coins were worn down to AG-3 or G-4, including varieties that were scarcely 20 years old. In contrast, the predecessor series of Liberty Seated dimes, quarters, and half dollars could circulate for 20 or 30 years and still be in F-12 or better condition.

An explanation of this grading nicety contributes to understanding why Barber coins above G-4 represent only a tiny percentage of the pieces in numismatic hands today.

The Three Denominations

As a guide to each series, these three books written and published by David Lawrence in the early 1990s are essential: *The Complete Guide to Barber Dimes*, *The Complete Guide to Barber Quarters*, and *The Complete Guide to Barber Halves*. As a memorial to his father, David's son, John Feigenbaum, has made these available free of charge on the Web site davidlawrence.com (which is also tied into the Barber Coin Collectors' Society Web site).

Several books by Kevin Flynn take a somewhat different tack and emphasize repunched dates and mintmarks, misplaced dates, and reproduce original Mint and Treasury correspondence. These contain much useful information as well. The titles of these works are: *The Authoritative Reference on Barber Dimes*, *The Authoritative Reference on Barber Quarters*, *The 1894-S Dime: A Mystery Unraveled*, and *The Authoritative Reference on Barber Half Dollars*.

Of the three Barber denominations, dimes are the easiest set to complete, except for the 1894-S, of which only eight are known (see appendix II). In G-4 grade there are none that are difficult to find, although the 1895-O is rarer than the others and is most expensive. A set of mixed Extremely Fine and About Uncirculated coins is a challenge, with several varieties priced in the hundreds of dollars, and the 1895-O in the low thousands. Time was when such a set might take a year or more to complete—in pre-Internet days. Today, more coins can be bought and more quickly. This is good and bad. Instant gratification in any hobby usually leads to waning interest. The thrill of the hunt is always desirable and promotes numismatic longevity. A set in MS-63 grade will take time to complete and is, of course, more expensive. An MS-65 set might take several years to finish, especially if good strike and eye appeal are added to the equation.

Quarter dollars are very popular to collect. The key issue is the 1901-S, the rarest and most costly in the series. The 1913-S is the second most expensive, followed at a distance by the 1896-S. AG-3 and G-4 grades are the most available. Filling an album with these can be an enjoyable pursuit. At the EF and AU levels, such a set is a real challenge. For the connoisseur with a well-fortified bank account, MS-63 is an attractive possibility. This will take some time to do. As to MS-65, this will take years. Among the quarters, the issues of 1892 are particularly interesting for their reverse varieties.

Barber half dollars are the one series without any truly rare issues in circulated grades. In grades such as AG and G the 1892-O, 1892-S, 1893-S, 1896-S, 1897-O, 1897-S, 1914, and 1915 each cross the $100 line. Building a set in EF and AU grades is a challenge. Among higher grades, a set in MS-63 hand-selected for strike and eye appeal will likely take several years to complete. As to MS-65, you might as well forget it! The 1904-S seems to be the scarcest in gem Mint State closely followed by the 1896-O. Apart from dates and mintmarks there is one variety, the 1892-O Micro o, that is very popular and also quite rare. This can be an optional addition to any set.

Here is a *secret:* There are many Barber coins that are really scarce in high grades and more than a few are rarities in gem Mint State. Some of these are not well known, with the result that prices in *A Guide Book of United States Coins* and other references are bargains compared to the coins' availability.

For those who like history, contemplating the era in which these coins were struck adds a lot of interest and appreciation to collecting. The next chapter is devoted to this aspect.

ESTIMATING COIN POPULATIONS

It is useful to estimate how many of each Barber coin survives today. The process of doing so is a combination of art and science. Such estimates began large scale after the Professional Coin Grading Service (PCGS) was established in 1986 and Numismatic Guaranty Corporation (NGC) began business in 1987. After they got underway, each published population reports listing the coins they had certified in various grades. Today, such reports have matured and are one of several useful guides. Often they are cited as *the* source for rarity. This can be very misleading.

For enlightenment in regard to rarity take a look at population reports from the mid-1990s and you will see that relatively small percentages of Mint State coins are graded MS-66 or 67. Today, multiples more are. This is largely a result of "gradeflation."

Among Barber quarters the 1901-S is the key issue. Only 72,662 were minted, and this was in an era in which only a few collectors were interested in mintmarks. Most went into circulation. In the 1930s, when albums and folders made numismatics a dynamic hobby, the 1901-S was recognized as being rare, and many were captured by collectors. In contrast, 6,540,800 were minted of the 1916-D, Barber, quarter, and in the 1930s and 1940s collectors who desired a single example found one easily, but they did not save duplicates. In the 1970s when silver bullion rose to unprecedented highs, well-worn 1916-D quarters were worth more if melted than their *Guide Book*–listed values to collectors. Likely, many dealers and collectors who had duplicates sent them to the melting pot. Those held by the public were mostly preserved.

In this book I estimate that only 8 to 12 1901-S quarters survive in grades of MS-65 or higher, and in worn grades, mostly AG-3 and G-4, about 1,800 to 2,200 exist. For the 1916-D I estimate that 1,500 to 2,000 gem Mint State coins survive and for circulated grades 50,000 to 60,000. Using just the PCGS Population Report for January 2015 these figures are revealed:[4]

1901-S Barber quarter: 517 certified in grades from Fair-2 to AU-58. 31 Mint State, including 8 examples in MS-65 and above. The 31 Mint State coins no doubt include many resubmissions, possibly netting to less than half that number of *different* coins. Of the original mintage of 72,662 pieces 1 coin in 333 has been to PCGS.

1916-D Barber quarter: Only 62 certified in grades from Fair-2 to AU-58. 754 Mint State including 673 examples in MS-65 and above. Only 1 coin in 8,999 of the original mintage of 6,540,800 has been to PCGS.

The above seems to demonstrate that valuable coins such as the 1901-S in *any* grade have a much higher rate of submission than do less valuable ones. There is not much value to circulated 1916-D quarters, so not many have been submitted. The above figures can be expanded proportionately if NGC numbers are added, making the 1916-D seem even more rare in comparison to the 1901-S—which it is not!

Further regarding the understanding of population reports: in 1884 at the Carson City Mint, 1,136,000 Morgan dollars were struck. Most of these went into storage at the time. In 1964 the Treasury Department found that 962,638 coins, amounting to 84.7 percent of the original mintage, were still in vaults in the Treasury Building in Washington. These were turned over to the General Services Administration, which publicized them extensively and, starting in 1972, offered them in mail bid sales. Eventually all of these sold, and at nice premiums. As of a study I did on October 8, 2014, PCGS and NGC combined have only had 153,354 certification events. I say "events" as this number does not represent different coins. There have been many resubmissions. *Only 16% of these coins sold at a premium have been certified.*

Some published estimates have been based on eBay offerings. These too need to be taken with a grain of salt. A 1901-S quarter in G-4 grade worth thousands of dollars is a candidate for offering on eBay or elsewhere on the Internet. A 1916-D quarter in the same grade has a market value of less than $10 and escapes notice. In comparison to 1901-S listings it appears to be rare, which it isn't.

The matter of "gradeflation" is important. More than a few certified MS-65 coins were graded at lower levels earlier, and this is also true of VF, EF, and other categories in which a coin has significant value. Resubmissions are a part of gaming the system and are profitable to both the players and the grading services, but statistics are distorted in the process.

I suggest that very few Barber coins were deliberately saved as souvenirs or mementos by the public, except for some quickly-fading interest when they were introduced in 1892. By the 1930s, when collectors became interested, probably some small percentage of the original mintages survived—somewhat less than 1 percent estimated for pre-1900 dates, and 1 percent or more estimated for later issues. In search of reliable population information, I have reviewed information from many surveys published in the *Journal of the Barber Coin Collectors' Society*. Some issues, certain 1907-S coins for example, seem to exist in fewer numbers than expected. In particular David Lawrence's books have been valuable, for as a dealer he bought and sold countless thousands of coins and kept records of them.

Focus on Proof Coins

Some comments about Proof coins are appropriate. When struck and carefully removed from the coining press, each Proof was flawless—what would be called a high numerical grade today. However, the reality is that the vast majority of Proof Barber silver coins minted from 1892 to 1915 are less than Proof-65 grade. Why?

The explanation is that from the late 1800s until the late 1900s, "brilliant is best" was the common philosophy of collectors, dealers, and museums alike. In a visit to Philadelphia in the summer of 1903, Farran Zerbe examined the Mint Cabinet of coins on view there. The condition of certain United States coins was less than ideal:

> I found many of the silver Proof coins of late years partially covered with a white coating. On inquiry I learned that an overzealous attendant during the last vacation months when the numismatic room was closed took it on himself to clean the tarnished coins, purchase some metal polish at a department store, and proceeded with his cleaning operation. Later a coating of white appeared on the coins, which was now slowly disappearing. I expressed my displeasure at this improper treatment of Proof coins, and the custodian explained, "That is nothing. I have been here eight years and they have been cleaned three or four times in my time."[5]

In April 1939, J. Henry Ripstra, president of the American Numismatic Association, gave this advice in *The Numismatist:*

> There is no use of coin collectors having tarnished silver coins in their collection any longer, as they can safely remove the tarnish discoloration from an Uncirculated or Proof coin by using the following instructions without any possible danger of injuring the coin whatsoever:
>
> Lay the coin on a small piece of cotton flannel in a saucer. Squeeze lemon juice on the coin, then apply common baking soda on a wad of cotton batting and gently rub the coin. Add lemon juice and soda until the tarnish is removed. Then dip the coin in boiling water and wipe off with a cotton flannel cloth, and you again have a brilliant coin.

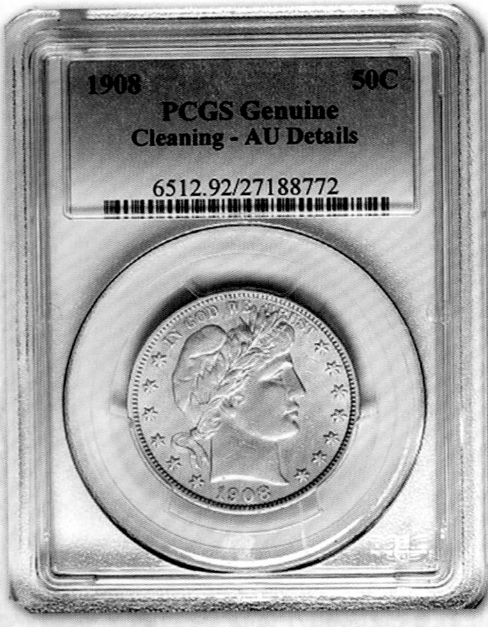

Two of the major grading services will slab and identify improperly cleaned coins, as shown above. Both NGC slabs (shown at left) and PCGS slabs (shown at right) confirm that the coin is not counterfeit and state the grade that would apply if just the details were considered. NGC slabs specifically include the text "Details Grade Does Not Determine Value".

> To properly clean medals of bronze or gold I use common laundry soap and the ordinary household ammonia and scrub well with a bristle brush. Where coins and medals have been lacquered, I remove the lacquer with alcohol. This will not injure the article the least bit. I have demonstrated the above in various parts of the country with absolute success.

The truth is that rubbing coins with baking soda added countless hairlines to their surface. All of a sudden a superb gem Proof could be reduced to below what we would call Proof-65 today.

In January 1949, *The Numismatist* showcased an article, "Let's Keep It Clean!" by G.R.L. Potter. After noting that the advice "don't clean your coins" is sound, especially to the general public, the author noted that it was not necessarily so for numismatists:

> Of the desirability of "clean" coins there can, I think, be no doubt. The most casual scrutiny of catalogues or dealers' lists shows that "brilliant Uncirculated" is the condition commanding the highest price, and it must follow that anything that will maintain or restore such a condition is desirable. It is my contention that such restoration and maintenance is often a very simple matter, and that the procedure is well within the capacity of any collector of average intelligence—which, of course, means all of us!

Potter recommended that numismatists use potassium cyanide. To be sure, he noted that it is a deadly poison, but then he went on to say:

> If the procedure . . . is carefully followed, no contact with the cyanide solution will occur. But accidents will happen, and if you do happen to get any cyanide solution on your skin wash it off immediately in running water until the greasy feel at point of contact has entirely disappeared. Cyanide is like a great many other things in life—fire, electricity, motor cars, or what have you—very dangerous if not properly used, but both safe and useful in careful hands.

For circulated silver coins Potter stated:

> I therefore consider it wisdom to make my worn silver as presentable as possible. First cyanide, then a good silver polish, applied with an old tooth-brush and, if necessary, a final rub with chamois leather and rouge. I think Patrick Henry may as well provide my conclusion: "If this be treason, make the most of it!"

Anyone following Potter's advice ran the definite risk of injury or death to himself or members of his family, and of seriously damaging his coins' value. Many similar articles could be cited. It is no wonder that gem Proofs are in the minority today!

In Summary

In compiling estimates I have added personal experience, especially with regard to high-grade coins. I have had the honor of handling, privately and at auction, some of the finest collections of Barber coins ever formed. Correspondence and conversations with the late David Lawrence have been very valuable as have been the comments in his books.

The estimates are just that: estimates. Any constructive suggestions are welcome and will be considered for future editions of this book. In the meantime I hope estimates will be of use.

Chapter Three

The American Scene 1892–1916

A chronicle of selected national and numismatic events during the era of Barber coinage.

The Year 1892

Current Events. The World's Columbian Exposition dominated the news across America. Construction delays intervened, and the gates were not opened to the general public until the spring of 1893. A "pledge of allegiance" for U.S. schoolchildren to recite on October 12 in commemoration of the discovery of America 400 years prior, composed by socialist and former clergyman Francis Bellamy, appeared in *The Youth's Companion* magazine on September 8. Republican president Benjamin Harrison lost his bid for reelection because of widespread dissatisfaction with the economy. The opposing Democrats campaigned on a platform opposing the McKinley Tariff Act and saw their candidate, former president Grover Cleveland, elected for a second term, four years after his first ended. New York's immigration receiving station moved to Ellis Island in New York Harbor, and over the next 60 years 20 million immigrants would come through the "Golden Door" there.

New arrivals in a detention room on Ellis Island.

The Ohio Supreme Court outlawed John D. Rockefeller's Standard Oil Trust under the 1890 Sherman Act, but Rockefeller retained control of the trust properties through Standard Oil of New Jersey—a new company incorporated under a recent New Jersey holding-company law that permitted companies chartered at Trenton to hold stock in other corporations. In one of the greatest merger and acquisition transactions of all time, General Electric was formed on April 15. H.J. Heinz adopted "57 Varieties" as an advertising slogan.

Detroit machinist Henry Ford road-tested his first motorcar. Abercrombie & Fitch was established by David Abercrombie. Telephone service between New York and Chicago began on October 18. Asa Griggs Candler incorporated the Coca-Cola Company in Georgia. Candler, in 1888, had purchased the formula for Coca-Cola for $550 from its inventor—John Pemberton, a Georgia druggist who created the drink in 1886—and from several other shareholders. Sears, Roebuck & Company used that name for the first time for its growing mail-order business. Juicy Fruit and Spearmint chewing gum were introduced by William Wrigley Jr. (Doublemint gum would be introduced in 1914.)

Chicago surgeon Daniel Hale Williams performed the world's first open-heart surgery, saving the life of a street fighter with a knife wound in an artery near his heart. The Johns Hopkins Medical School and Hospital were founded at the 17-year-old Baltimore University, largely funded by the Garrett family. The new school admitted women on the same basis as men—the first medical school to do so.

The *New York Tribune* published a list of the country's 4,047 millionaires, a number that had grown from fewer than 20 in 1840. Economic gloom was expanding in the United States, the continuing aftermath of unbridled speculation in the 1880s.

THE NUMISMATIC SCENE. Among the leading dealers of the time were S.H. and Henry Chapman, known as the Chapman brothers; Lyman H. Low; David Proskey; and Édouard Frossard. The last boasted that he was the fastest cataloger in the business, having written the 1,200-lot Montagne Collection descriptions within 48 hours of having received the coins.

The *American Journal of Numismatics*, launched in 1866, was published by the American Numismatic and Archaeological Society and contained research articles, news, auction results, and other information. *The Numismatist*, issued in Monroe, Michigan, by editor George F. Heath, M.D., was mailed each month to slightly more than 400 members of the American Numismatic Association, of which Heath had been the primary founder in November 1891. New York City, Philadelphia, and Boston were the main centers of the coin business. There were no useful reference books that gave prices or mintages. Values were determined by reading dealer price lists and auction results.

The market was in a slump and had been since the late 1880s, partly due to a nationwide recession and failures of Western speculators, and partly from a natural consolidation of a decade of unbridled growth. In 1890 Lorin G. Parmelee, who—next to the late T. Harrison Garrett—had the finest private coin collection in America, consigned his collection for sale at auction and realized about $25,000. He reserved many key pieces which he was still trying to sell in 1892.

In *The Numismatist* in February, the first of several numerical grading systems was proposed by Joseph Hooper. Proofs were given numbers I (for unimpaired coins) and II (for coins that had been brushed or harshly cleaned). For circulation strikes the steps were numbered from III Uncirculated to XII (Very Poor). Nothing came of the idea, and it was not until 1949 that Dr. William H. Sheldon's numerical system was adopted by collectors. In the May issue Hooper observed:

> The average collector starts out with very little knowledge of the road to be traveled, being content to gather information along the way, and though often paying dearly, they consider 'experience bought better than experience taught.' Advantage is often taken of the beginner by those having superior knowledge, in buying, selling or exchanging . . .
>
> Knowledge is power, and if used properly is of great value, but if to take advantage of those less favored, is dishonorable. Our advice to all is to get thoroughly posted on your lines of collecting, and to do it as soon as possible. By so doing correct judgments can be formed; to do this, standard works, price sale catalogues and current numismatic literature are indispensable.

The Columbian souvenir (as it was called) half dollar of 1892 for the World's Columbian Exposition.

The first of what was planned to be a series of annual ANA conventions was scheduled for Niagara Falls, New York, on August 16 and 17. Not much publicity was given to it, and only five members turned up. The meeting was opened and then quickly adjourned. Another meeting was set for Pittsburgh on October 1, when 36 members were represented, mostly by proxy.

The first "souvenir" coins, as they were called at the time, were issued for the World's Columbian Exposition. The newspaper coverage of the half dollars was extensive and ranged from complaints about the design and the $1 price to coverage of when the first pieces were struck and issued.

THE YEAR 1893

CURRENT EVENTS. The World's Columbian Exposition opened in May, and millions of visitors thronged the grounds until it closed on October 30. The main attraction was the gigantic Ferris Wheel which cost 50¢ to ride—the same price as admission to the fair. Commemorative stamps of values from 1¢ to $5 were issued, including the 50-cent stamp featuring *The Recall of Columbus*, a painting by Augustus G. Heaton, which was displayed in the Capitol Rotunda in Washington.

The Panic of 1893, as it would be remembered, cast gloom on the financial scene. On May 5 the stock market dropped sharply, and a collapse occurred several weeks later on June 27. A depression was underway, and before the end of the year, over 500 banks failed, 15,000 businesses closed, and 74 railroads were bankrupted. The slump in the economy would last at least through 1897.

Ever since the 1870s the "Silver Question" had been the overwhelming political topic in the country. Western mining interests in particular, joined by agricultural states, were concerned with the falling price of silver, a prime commodity. Its use as the basis of coinage had been discontinued by several European countries. New discoveries in the United States and the opening of more mines increased the supply, driving the market value down. What to do? One result was the passage of the Bland-Allison Act on February 28, 1878, which mandated that Uncle Sam buy from two to four million ounces of silver each month. This was done, and the metal was converted into silver dollars, generating a supply far in excess of commercial demand. Millions piled up in mint and Treasury vaults. By 1893 Democrats favored the unlimited coinage of silver in preference to gold.

Republicans and Eastern financial interests and "old guard" conservatives insisted that gold coins, which were worth full melt-down value, were the standard. Foreign governments, banks, and merchants, fearful that debts would be paid in silver dollars which had a melt value of just 60 cents, drained millions of double eagles from America, resulting in dangerously low reserves on this side of the ocean. This added to the feeling of doom and gloom. The economic outlook was dim. On June 27 prices on the New York Stock Exchange fell precipitately.

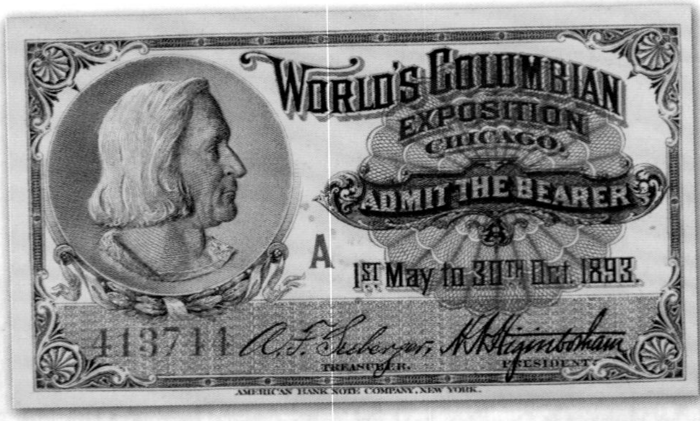

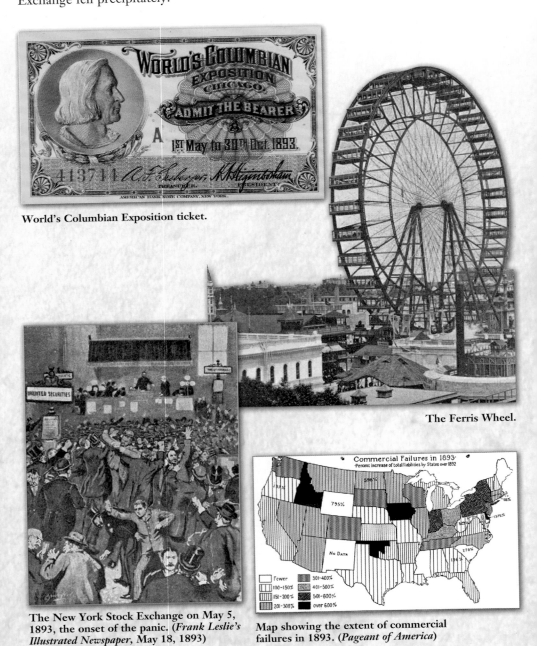

World's Columbian Exposition ticket.

The Ferris Wheel.

The New York Stock Exchange on May 5, 1893, the onset of the panic. (*Frank Leslie's Illustrated Newspaper*, May 18, 1893)

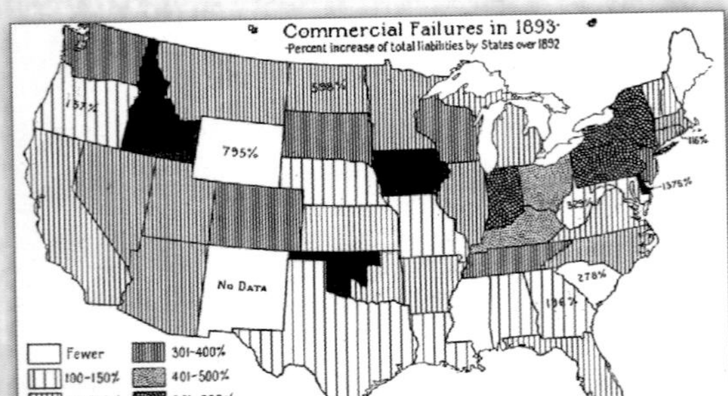

Map showing the extent of commercial failures in 1893. (*Pageant of America*)

Hawaiian annexationists financed by American pineapple and sugar interests overthrew Queen Liliuokalani with support from U.S. minister John Leavitt Stevens. The islands were declared a protectorate of the United States after marines landed there "to protect American interests." A six-million-acre tract in the Oklahoma Territory that had been bought by the government from the Cherokees was officially opened to homesteaders on September 16, 1893. "Sooners" jumped the gun and entered the region before then, but they were allowed to stay. It was estimated that fewer than 1,100 bison survived in the United States, a far cry from the countless millions of a few decades earlier.

Maxwell House coffee, named for a Nashville hotel that served the brew, was marketed. Thomas J. Lipton patented the use of his name as a tea brand. The U.S. Supreme Court declared the tomato to be a vegetable, not a fruit. A nationwide interest in the difficulties experienced by the working class and in the vicissitudes of slum life arose around this time. *Maggie, a Girl of the Streets,* a novel by Stephen Crane, was well received, as were other books, songs, and plays on these subjects. The average worker earned $9.42 per week, and immigrants often received less than $1 per day.

The Numismatic Scene. *Mint Marks* by Augustus G. Heaton was published. With a cover price of $1, it sold well. Heaton, one of the better known numismatists of his day, once served as president of the American Numismatic Association and was a prolific author, a poet, and a professional artist.

The American Numismatic Association had growth problems, and the overall economic conditions, including the slump in the financial market, did not help. In *The Numismatist,* editor Heath assured readers that the ANA was there to stay, but many difficulties loomed ahead, including apathy within the ranks. However, once the Slough of Despond was crossed, the Delectable Mountains lay ahead, Heath proposed. Each member was encouraged to spread the word among friends, acquaintances, and correspondents. Still, there was some doubt of success:

George F. Heath, M.D., founder of the ANA in 1891, was elected president in 1893.

> Stand by the guns! If by any possibility our ship goes down, let it be like the Cumberland, without guns trained and booming and our flag flying. We have set our mark high. If we fail to realize all our hopes and ambitions we shall still be found fighting in a worthy cause; as success crowns our efforts, and we expect nothing else, to our science and Association give the glory.

The annual convention of the ANA was held in Chicago on August 21, at Douglas Hall, at the corner of 35th Street and Cottage Grove Avenue. The program included the presentation of 12 different papers. Fifteen members attended, and an equal number were represented by proxy. George F. Heath was elected president of the association after having been instrumental in its founding in 1891.

An 1887, Indian Head, cent elongated at the Exposition.

Visitors attended the Columbian Exposition, where numismatic attractions included a display of coins from the Mint Cabinet set up by the Treasury Department, various concessions offering coins and other items, and various vendors who rolled out cents and other coins with hand-cranked machines to imprint an exposition message on one side.

In the Electricity Building a seller offered rolled-out old copper large cents.[1] The Scott Stamp & Coin Co. had two exhibits, one in the Anthropological Building and the other in the Plaisance. Commemorative half dollars dated 1892 and 1893 were on sale, as were Isabella quarters.

At year's end the ANA had 177 members.

THE YEAR 1894

CURRENT EVENTS. The slump in silver continued. By 1894 the metal it took to coin a new silver dollar was worth only 49¢. In June the Democratic Silver Convention was held in Omaha, Nebraska, with 1,000 attendees, who listened to William Jennings Bryan extol the virtues of unlimited government purchases of silver. To help stem the drain of stored double eagles to Europe, 1,368,940 more were struck at the Philadelphia Mint and 1,048,560 in San Francisco in 1894. Over the course of the year, importation of gold coins amounted to $30,790,892 face value, and exports amounted to $64,303,840.

"Coxey's Army" arrived in Washington, D.C. on April 30 after a 36-day march by unemployed workers from Massillon, Ohio, led by Jacob S. Coxey. Joined by others in the city, 400 protesters demanded that the government set up public works to provide jobs. Coxey was arrested for walking on the grass near the Capitol. The group dispersed.

When economic conditions forced railroads to reduce their orders for sleeping cars, the Pullman Palace Car Company reduced its workers' wages, but not rents or prices in the company town. In response, the American Railway Union workers, 4,000 strong, staged a wildcat strike that began on May 11. A massive boycott and sympathy strikes ensued which affected most lines west of Detroit. At the action's peak, 250,000 workers in 27 states were involved in related labor actions. Ultimately, the Army was called in by President Cleveland and the ARU dissolved, but not before riots and sabotage caused $80 million in damage and resulted in 30 deaths. In total, some 750,000 U.S. workers went on strike during the year for higher wages and shorter hours.

The first successful cesarean section delivery in America was performed in Boston on a woman with a tiny pelvis who has previously lost two infants. Caramel maker Milton S. Hershey incorporated the Hershey Chocolate Company. Bicycles were the most popular vehicle for personal transportation. In most towns and cities, citizens did not own horses. Streetcar rides cost a nickel in most places.

Popular songs and melodies of the day included "Humoresque," "Sidewalks of New York," and "I've Been Working on the Railroad" (first called the "Levee Song"). Cakewalks and two-steps were popular everywhere. William Sydney Porter (who later used the

Piles of silver ingots at the American Smelter in Leadville, Colorado. A vast oversupply of the metal was a main influence in American politics in the late 1800s.

nom de plume O. Henry) published *The Iconoclast* magazine, which changed its name to *The Rolling Stone* with the April 28 issue and failed in 1895.

The Numismatic Scene. The lingering effects of the Panic of 1893 seem to have had no effect on the coin market, despite the claims in the following opinion piece, which begins on one slant and ends on another. Taken from the March 1894 issue of *The Numismatist:*

> There is no possible doubt but the depressed condition of the times has its effect on the coin market. Coin buying like any other collecting is a luxury, and such luxuries usually come from the surplus over and above the living and ordinary expenses of the purchaser. The result of the stringent times is consequently the dropping to a great extent of luxuries from the list, and numismatics, philately, anthropology, and all the archaeologies and collectings where cash enters as a modicum of exchange have to suffer. One collector who usually puts $500 annually into coins writes that he has made less than one fourth that investment in the past year, and we doubt not but that this proportion of falling off will follow with most collectors.
>
> And yet the dealers say the season has been quite a fair one; that there has not been an appreciable dropping off in trade. This is probably due to two causes: first, the largely increased number of buyers of late, and second, the fact that many of our monied collectors see in these close times many opportunities to invest their surplus cash in standard coins at such prices as will ultimately bring them large returns in their investment.

The annual ANA convention was held in Detroit on August 23 and 24 with meetings in the Museum of Art Building. The convention was attended by 14 members and another 28 were represented by proxy. Absentee member Augustus G. Heaton was later surprised and pleased that he had been elected president. It was reported that 191 people were in good standing as ANA members. Of that number, the division by states was as follows: Massachusetts and Michigan led the pack, each with 24 members; followed by New York with 20; then Pennsylvania, 16; Illinois, 14; Indiana, 10; Rhode Island and New Jersey with 7 each; Wisconsin, 6; Nebraska, 5; Ohio, 4; Connecticut, 4; and, Iowa, North Carolina, New Hampshire, and Virginia with 3 each. Several other states had one or two each, and about two-dozen members were located in foreign countries.

A proposal for the ANA logotype or seal.

By year's end the market for Columbian half dollars collapsed, and large amounts of unsold coins were released into circulation for face value.

The Year 1895

Current Events. By January 1895, Treasury officials and congressmen had endured two years of worrying about the nation's gold reserves. The crisis deepened, with no end in sight. On February 1, 1895, President Cleveland and Secretary of the Treasury John J. Carlisle met with financier J. Pierpont Morgan to attempt to solve the problem. By February 9 only $41,393,212 was held by the Treasury for the redemption of its obligations, which were meant to be payable in gold. Arrangements were quickly made, and J.P. Morgan & Co. and August Belmont & Co. of New York, in cooperation with N.M. Rothschild & Sons of London, organized an offering of securities aimed at foreign investors who held gold. The 30-year bonds, at least half of which were required to be sold in Europe, yielded 4% interest. They sold out in 22 minutes! The Bond Syndicate, as it was known, also promised to use its influence to prevent further "runs" on the Treasury. By March 30 the Treasury reserves had been built back up to $90,000,000, with more gold yet to arrive. The crisis was over. It became popular to say that J.P. Morgan saved the country from bankruptcy.

J.P. Morgan, America's most prominent financier.

Utah adopted a constitution granting women suffrage. Booker T. Washington delivered a speech at the Cotton States and International Exposition in Atlanta, Georgia, and became the first African American to address a racially mixed Southern audience. The Anti-Saloon League of America was formed in Washington, D.C., and would become the leading organization lobbying for prohibition in the United States in the early 1900s. Economic conditions notwithstanding, the Biltmore House at Asheville, North Carolina, was completed for railroad heir George Washington Vanderbilt II at a cost of $4.1 million. The Breakers mansion was completed at Newport for another heir, Cornelius Vanderbilt II. Both of these projects had been started prior to the panic.

The poetry collection *America the Beautiful*, whose eponymous poem was written by Wellesley College professor Katharine Lee Bates after she visited the top of Pikes Peak, was published, and "America the Beautiful" soon became the unofficial national anthem. In 1922 Bates would repurpose many of the poems from the collection in her other notable work, *Yellow Clover: A Book of Remembrance*, which was dedicated to her deceased partner, Katherine Coman. In San Francisco, Adolph Sutro, who had made a fortune building a tunnel in Virginia City, Nevada, to drain mines, opened Sutro Baths next to his French Chateau–style Cliff House. King Camp Gillette developed a new type of razor, but at first was unable to secure backing for it. John Harvey Kellogg introduced the first flaked cereal. A new sport, mintonette, later known as volleyball, was invented. Coca-Cola was first sold in bottles; previously, it was a soda-fountain drink.

In France, Alphonse Mucha popularized the Art Nouveau movement, as on this poster. It soon spread to America.

Photography was all the rage. George Eastman introduced the $5 Kodak camera which became an instant success. George B. Selden was granted the first U.S. patent for an automobile. Later, he filed suits against many other manufacturers, even though the applicability of his patent to certain improvements was questionable, causing headaches as the industry grew.

The Numismatic Scene. The ANA convention was held in Washington, D.C., on September 19 and 20. Heaton, one of four members who lived in that city, was reelected president. The outlook for the association was mixed as enthusiasm had dampened, probably at least partly due to the economy.

In May the National Sculpture Society and the American Numismatic and Archaeological Society held an exhibition in the Fine Arts Building on 57th Street in New York City. Designs for a new goddess of Liberty were on view, with the top two selections awarded prizes of $300 and $200 respectively. Among the artists interested in the project were Augustus Saint-Gaudens and J.Q.A. Ward. Press releases stated that strenuous efforts would be made to have the Treasury Department adopt new motifs. The exhibit was mainly devoted to sculptures and other works of art set among flowers and other decorations. The coin sketches were viewed by some as a farce arranged by private persons, rather than being an integral part of the show. None received any favorable notice from the government.[2]

Sketches for a proposed design to replace the one currently on the silver dollar.

The Year 1896

Current Events. The long-running Silver Question came to a head in 1896. The Republican Party held its nominating convention in St. Louis from June 16 to 18. From the outset, William McKinley, recently retired as the governor of Ohio, was the overwhelming favorite as the presidential candidate. He was nominated forthwith, and Garret Hobart of New Jersey was selected as his running mate. It was the Democrats' turn next, and from July 7 to 11 they met in Chicago. The mood was pro-silver and for the expanded issuance of paper money. President Cleveland, of their own party, was condemned for his anti-silver actions. There was no other obvious candidate. William Jennings Bryan rose to the occasion. Despite an unsuccessful run for the Senate, he was admired as a gifted speaker, and his pro-silver views were unquestioned.

On July 9 at the Democratic National Convention, Bryan mounted the platform and gave his famous Cross of Gold Speech, calling for a silver standard that would be favorable to America's farmers. He stated that if cities were torn down they would spring up again as if by magic, but if farms were demolished, grass would grow in the city streets, concluding with the ringing statement, "You shall not press down upon the brow of labor this crown of thorns, you shall not crucify mankind upon a cross of gold."

On November 3 the voter turnout was very heavy—over 90 percent in some polling places. McKinley carried the day. Silverites had failed to make a convincing case. The Silver Question soon faded away. In Colorado the Cripple Creek Gold District garnered worldwide attention as its mines, opened a few years earlier, continued to deliver large amounts of precious metal.

In the case of *Plessy v. Ferguson* the U.S. Supreme Court upheld an 1890 Louisiana statute mandating racially segregated but equal railroad carriages, ruling that the equal protection clause of the 14th amendment to the U.S. Constitution dealt with political and not social equality. This meant that blacks and whites could be segregated as long as they had equal facilities. This philosophy would remain in effect into the 1960s, when the Civil Rights Act outlawed such discrimination in any public accommodation—although the Supreme Court had already ruled in the 1950s that separate facilities were by definition unequal, and that segregation laws were thereby unconstitutional.

Utah was admitted to the Union as the 45th state after Mormons agreed to give up polygamous marriage. Idaho women gained suffrage through an amendment to the state constitution. Miami was incorporated at Fort Dallas, Florida, which the year before had only three inhabitants. Standard Oil Company director Henry M. Flagler, who extended his Florida East Coast Railway to there, was the catalyst for the city's boom.

The Dow Jones Industrial Average (DJIA) was published for the first time on May 26 to gauge the well-being of the industrial sector. At the time of its creation only 12 industrial stocks were listed on the New York Stock Exchange, including American Cotton, General Electric, American Sugar, and American Tobacco. Other stocks listed included 6 utilities and 53 railroads. Charles H. Dow added up the closing prices of the 12 industrials, divided the figure by 12, and came up with 40.94. Over the years various stocks were switched in and out of the DJIA, making it absolutely worthless for historical comparisons, but most popular writers at that time and later did not know this. However, it became the most closely watched indicator of the movement of common stocks.

On April 20, 1896, a program of films projected by Edison's Vitascope in New York City was the first such showing that attracted national attention in America. The first permanent home for showing movies in the United States was opened in a formerly

In and near Cripple Creek hundreds of mines sold stock to investors, including the Alert Gold Mining Company. Stock exchanges were active in that town as well as in Colorado Springs.

Edison's Vitascope pictures caused a sensation in 1896.

vacant building at 623 Canal Street in New Orleans, where Vitascope Hall offered two shows a day and could accommodate 400 people. Admission was 10¢, and for an extra 10¢, patrons could get a look into the booth where the man was operating the hand-cranked Vitascope. In the meantime, phonograph parlors were all the rage. These consisted of dozens of Edison cylinder phonographs in wooden cases arranged in rows. Upon the deposit of a nickel a patron with earphones could hear a two-minute recording.

The Numismatic Scene. The election campaign spawned a large number of satirical "dollars" criticizing William Jennings Bryan and his advocacy for silver (rather than gold) as the leading coinage metal.

Matters within the ANA were gloomy, correspondence went unanswered, and in *The Numismatist*, the editor despaired in face of the apathy. There was no annual convention. In December Heath stated that his magazine would no longer be connected with the ANA. In contrast, the American Numismatic and Archaeological Society and its *American Journal of Numismatics* were doing well.

In Athens, Greece, the first modern Olympic Games were held. Robert Garrett, a son of the late T. Harrison Garrett, who had formed the largest numismatic collection in private hands by the time of his death in a boating accident in 1886, brought back to America a gold medal for his first-place accomplishment in discus-throwing.

The Year 1897

Current Events. On August 16 or 17 (accounts vary), 1896, gold was discovered in quantity in the Klondike region of the Yukon, in northwestern Canada, close by its border with Alaska. Excitement prevailed in the region, but it was so remote that news of the strike did not reach the United States until the following spring.

Thus was initiated the last great gold rush in North America. The Yukon excitement, the continuing output of Cripple Creek, and optimism resulting from the McKinley election as the president fueled hope that the depression was coming to an end. Ever since 1889, the economy had been in a chill, and the Panic of 1893 had moved it into a

Treasure seekers heading over Chilkoot Pass on the way to the Yukon River.

crisis. Now, in 1897, the specter of debts being paid off in silver dollars worth less than 50 cents in bullion value had passed. The financial community was more secure than it had been in a long while. International commerce was doing well.

At Coney Island, New York, George C. Tilyou opened Steeplechase Park. Eventually, Steeplechase, Dreamland, and Luna Park would constitute the three main sections of America's largest and most famous amusement park. Mail Pouch tobacco was introduced, and for more than half a century farmers were paid for allowing their barns to be used as advertising billboards for the product. Ransom E. Olds and a group of investors established the Olds Motor Vehicle Company. The first Stanley Steamer was introduced into the marketplace, but after several years of good sales it couldn't compete against the convenience of quick-starting gasoline engines. In Washington the Library of Congress was completed to receive books that had been stored for decades in the Capitol.

The Joseph Campbell Preserve Company developed "condensed" soup. Within a year consommé, beefsteak tomato, oxtail, and chicken flavors were offered. Purina cereal was introduced, the name meaning "purity." J.M. Smucker jellies were created on an Ohio farm, and in New York a cough syrup–maker formulated Jell-O. Tennessee distiller Jack Daniel began putting up his whiskey in square bottles to give them a distinctive shape. In New England dairy producer Harvey P. Hood packaged his milk in glass bottles, an improvement over ladling milk from large cans into the pitchers of customers.

The Waldorf-Astoria hotel opened in New York. With 1,000 rooms and 765 private baths, it was the largest and most luxurious hotel in the world. The first underground rapid transit system in the country was opened, a subway line that connected Boston's Public Gardens and Park Street.

New York *Evening Sun* reader Virginia O'Hanlon of 115 West 95th Street wrote to the paper's editor: "I am 8 years old. Some of my little friends say there is no Santa Claus.

In the late 1800s and early 1900s, Coney Island was the foremost amusement area in America.

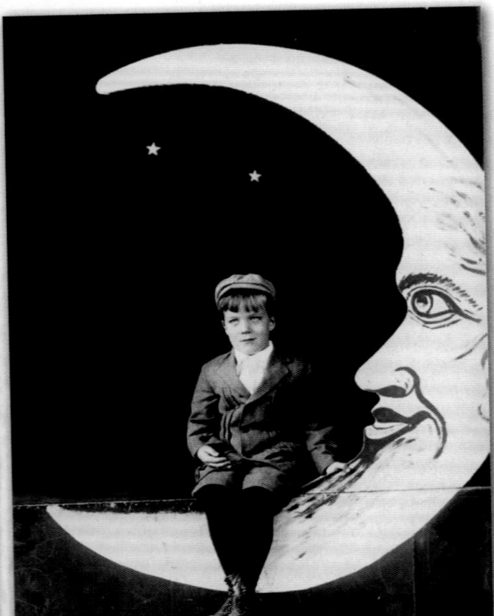

The paper or cardboard moon was a popular prop in amusement-park photo parlors.

Papa says, 'If you see it in *The Sun* it's so.' Please tell me the truth; is there a Santa Claus?" The reply: "Virginia, your little friends are wrong. They have been affected by the skepticism of a skeptical age. They do not believe except they see. . . Yes, Virginia, there is a Santa Claus. He exists as certainly as love and generosity and devotion exist . . . Thank God, he lives, and he lives forever."

The Numismatic Scene. In the summer of the year Heath's interest in the ANA was revived when he received a letter from J.A. Heckelman, president of the Board of Trustees, calling for nominations for officers:

> Vive le Association! Note the call of Brother Heckelman and attend to the matter of nominations at once. The Association must go forward on deeper and broader and stronger lines than ever before. Put good men to the front and let the work go on. From past experience there is doubt as to the successful operation of our Exchange Department in the Association. There is also a doubt in the mind of the editor as to the advisability of this journal resuming its old relation to the Association at the close of the year. It may be best to put the Association dues down to a mere nominal figure and leaving the subscription of this magazine to the discretion of the members individually.

No ANA convention was held.

The Year 1898

Current Events. The *New York Journal* owned by William Randolph Hearst urged readers and Congress to do battle with Spain over perceived repression in Cuba, where many citizens were seeking independence. A few days later a mysterious explosion that destroyed the U.S. battleship *Maine* in Havana harbor on February 15, 1898, was blamed on the Spaniards, with speculators alleging the use of a torpedo. Spain on the other hand claimed the explosion was an internal accident. This was the incident Hearst and others were hoping for. President McKinley initially tried to persuade Spain to adopt a conciliatory policy, but inability to reach a consensus and public outcry led Congress to declare war on April 20. For the next 112 days in the newspapers were jam-packed with action, including Theodore Roosevelt leading his Rough Riders from horseback in the Battle of San Juan Hill and, of particular note, the defeat of the Spanish fleet in Manila Harbor in the Philippines by Rear Admiral George Dewey.

As commander of the new steel fleet that sailed to Manila to avenge the sinking of the *Maine*, Dewey became an instant hero. His name and that of his flagship USS *Olympia* were used on products ranging from cigars to music boxes to slot machines. America became a recognized world power. More American troops died during the war from eating contaminated preserved meat than from battle wounds, and their deaths raised concern for reform of the meat-packing industry.

The USS *Olympia*, Rear Admiral George Dewey's flagship.

The Trans-Mississippi Exposition World's Fair opened in Omaha on June 1, was very successful, and was a marker signifying the increasingly good economic climate. In Wyoming nearly 2.9 million tons of coal were mined. Soon the state would produce more than Pennsylvania, West Virginia, and Kentucky combined. About 1,000 automobiles were manufactured, 10 times as many as in 1897. A Stanley Steamer driven by Francis E. Stanley climbed to the top of Mount Washington in New Hampshire. Goodyear Tire and Rubber Company was established in Akron, Ohio. In New York City the Bronx Zoo opened to visitors. In New Bern, North Carolina, Pepsi-Cola was put on sale. The International Paper Company was created by a merger of nearly 30 United States and Canadian firms. The Marconi Wireless Company was incorporated and would soon be important in radio transmissions.

The last known wild passenger pigeon died—the last member of a species that was once so prolific a flock could take an hour to pass overhead and would darken the sky. Aspirin (acetylsalicylic acid) as a pain killer was perfected by the German chemists of Bayer AG. The United Mine Workers of America was organized to promote the well-being of mine workers who often labored under difficult conditions with little or no safety precautions. Child labor was prevalent across America, again with no safety precautions, and child laborers included workers in mining operations and factories. The Dow Jones Industrial Average dropped 5.57 points (8.7 percent) on December 18 due to interest rates rising with the expansion of the economy.

Hawaii was annexed to the United States, starting a flood of worn 1883-dated Hawaiian dimes, quarters, half dollars, and dollars coming to the mainland to be melted. These had been minted in San Francisco to the extent of $1,000,000 face value to the order of sugar magnate Claus Spreckels.

THE NUMISMATIC SCENE. In *The Numismatist* in February, editor George F. Heath wrote:

> Ye editor is glad to be able to announce that the American Numismatic Association is showing signs of awakening and can confidently announce that measures are being taken to restore it again to its pristine activity and usefulness. Nominations for the various offices are being made and soon will be sent with ballots to all members who have been awaiting a grand rally. From now on *The Numismatist* will take the field in an active, earnest effort to inject vitality into this sleeping old hulk that has already lain too long dormant. Vive le Association!

In April 1898 there were 250 ANA members in good standing. Again, no convention was held. Heath argued that although official conventions are very nice, only a few attend them, so the Association should direct its efforts toward building up local societies instead. His magazine resumed its affiliation with the organization. Joseph Hooper, a long-time columnist for *The Numismatist*, was president of the Association.

THE YEAR 1899

CURRENT EVENTS. With gold streaming in from Cripple Creek, the Klondike, and other scattered areas, and with a large flow-back of double eagles and other coins from Europe, the Treasury had large gold reserves by 1899. During the year the face value of gold coins struck at the mints totaled $111,344,220, setting a record and crossing the $100-million mark for the first time. The economy was robust once again, and few effects lingered from the Panic of 1893.

Old and new methods of transportation at a railroad crossing gate. (*Harper's Weekly*, July 1, 1899)

Carnegie Steel was created in this year. United States copper producers merged to create the American Smelting and Refining Co. trust. Consolidated Edison Co. was created by a merger of New York's Edison Illuminating Co. with Consolidated Gas. American Car and Foundry was founded to compete with the Pullman Palace Car Co., and it would go on to become the world's largest maker of freight cars. William H. Woodin, who would achieve numismatic fame and also become Franklin D. Roosevelt's first secretary of the Treasury in 1933, was an officer and later president.

Scott Joplin's *Maple Leaf Rag*, which took its name from the Maple Leaf Club in Sedalia, Missouri, was published and went on to become the greatest and most famous piano rag. Ragtime, an evolution of two-steps and cakewalks, went on to become the musical sensation of America for the next 15 or so years.

On October 14 the *Literary Digest* stated, "The ordinary horseless carriage is at present a luxury for the wealthy; and although its price will probably fall in the future, it will never, of course, come into as common use as the bicycle."

THE NUMISMATIC SCENE. ANA president Hooper, ruminating on the recent malaise within the organization, blamed stamp collecting: "The interest taken of late years in the science of philately has divested the once earnest attention of a portion of our most valuable membership."[3] There was minimal activity, and no annual convention was held.

One of the hot topics in the hobby was the 1804 silver dollar—how and when were they made, where are they now? To *The Numismatist* issue of May 1899, George W. Rice contributed an article which pointed out differences of the reverse dies among quarter dollars dated 1892. Barber silver coins were hardly ever mentioned in print nor, for that matter, were current coins of other denominations.

THE YEAR 1900

CURRENT EVENTS. On March 14, 1900, Congress passed the Gold Standard Act. Although gold coins had maintained very close to their full weight and intrinsic value since the first federal half eagles were struck in the summer of 1795, gold had not been official as a fixed standard. The new legislation corrected this. The act was a non-event because most citizens thought America had been on such a standard for a long time.

At the Democratic National Convention, Kansas City, Admiral George Dewey sought the presidential nomination, but Democrats did not want him, as he had married a Catholic woman, and that would have impaired his chances of taking the White House. Republican President McKinley won reelection against Democrats William Jennings Bryan and former vice president Adlai E. Stevenson who campaigned on the almost-dead Free Silver platform. Thousands of workers cast their votes for Socialist-party candidate Eugene V. Debs.

Continuing the policy of imperialism that gained it the Philippines and Hawaii, the United States annexed Puerto Rico as a territory. In the meantime, occupation troops in the Philippines suppressed riots and insurrection instigated by Filipinos who resented American rule. America and Great Britain agreed to build a canal through Nicaragua, a much more northern route to connect the Atlantic and the Pacific than the canal planned by the French to cross Panama.

F.W. Woolworth operated 59 stores in which most items were priced from 1¢ to 10¢. The first National Automobile Show opened November 10 in Madison Square Garden in New York City, with 31 exhibitors displaying 159 models. By year's end there were over 13,000 automobiles estimated to be in service in the United States, but only 144 miles of road had hard surfaces.

Electric trolley cars, forbidden in Manhattan, were in use in nearly every city, with 30,000 cars running on 15,000 miles of track. The Kodak Brownie box camera was marketed for just $1, a small amount when compared to the fees to process the film. The Lionel Train Company marketed toy trains powered by small batteries. Hills Bros. of San Francisco introduced ground coffee in vacuum-sealed tin cans.

A campaign poster of 1900.

A trolley line took visitors to and from Canobie Lake Park near Salem, New Hampshire.

On September 8 Galveston, Texas, was hit by a hurricane that killed between 6,000 and 8,000 people and stands today as the deadliest natural disaster recorded in United States history. Property damage was estimated at $17 million. The bison count was down to just a few hundred, while two million or more wild horses roamed the West. The census of the year showed a population of 75,994,575. In the preceding decade 3,688,000 immigrants had come to America. Illiteracy touched a new low of 10.7 percent. One home in 13 had a telephone, and one in seven had a bathtub. Public telephones were available in most railroad stations and hotels. Commercial baths did a good business in larger towns and cities.

The Numismatic Scene. Editor Heath wrote that the new Lafayette commemorative silver dollar offered at $2 was monopolizing the attention of collectors, a good thing, he stated, "For besides being a legal coin, they represent something. In this case, besides being a souvenir, they have a legal value, and the possessor has the satisfaction of knowing that he has contributed so much to a worthy object." A list of active dealers in the United States was published in *The Numismatist:*

> S.H. and H. Chapman, 1348 Pine Street, Philadelphia; Thomas L. Elder, 343 Princeton Place, East Pittsburgh, Pennsylvania; W.S. Greany, 838 Guerrere Street, San Francisco; Lyman H. Low, 4th Ave. and 22nd St., New York City; A.E. Marks, Portland, Maine; Herbert E. Morey, 31 Exchange St., Boston; New York Coin & Stamp Company, 851-853 Broadway, New York City; St. Louis Coin & Stamp Co., 209 No. 8th Street, St. Louis; J.W. Scott & Co., 36 John Street, New York City; Charles Steigerwalt, 130 E. King Street, Lancaster, Pennsylvania; Stevens & Co., 69 Dearborn Street, Chicago; William von Bergen, 89 Court St., Boston; Farran Zerbe, who traded as "Coin Zerbe," in Tyrone, Pennsylvania; and two dealers in paper money: R.L. Deitrick, Lorraine, Virginia, and Luther B. Tuthill, South Creek, North Carolina.

Again there was no annual convention.

The Year 1901

Current Events. On September 6, 1901, President William McKinley was visiting the Pan-American Exposition in Buffalo, New York, taking in the sights of the latest world's fair. At the Temple of Music he paused, and Leon Czolgosz rushed up and fired two shots at close range into his abdomen, wounding him. McKinley was rushed to a nearby house, made comfortable, and hopes and prayers were given for his recovery. Thomas E. Elder of Pittsburgh, who dealt in coins in his spare time, was the professional telegrapher on hand who sent updates to the world concerning the president's condition.[4] McKinley deteriorated, and he slipped away on September 14 from complications of infection. Succeeding him in the White House was Vice President Theodore Roosevelt. Continuing its policy of imperialism, the government demanded that Cuba cede to it an area of land suitable for a naval base and agree for the United States to loosely monitor Cuban government.

The Spindletop gusher came in on January 10, 1901, in Beaumont, Texas, and spouted 110,000 barrels of oil daily for nine days, until it was capped. Texas was thus established as an oil-producing center, and in coming years vast reserves would be found there. The United States Steel Corporation was organized on March 3, 1901, and it was capitalized at $1,402,846,000 under the auspices of J.P. Morgan, who consolidated the Carnegie Steel Company and other firms in a transaction valued at $492 million. Carnegie was personally paid in five percent gold bonds, with a par value of $225 million.

The Victor Talking Machine Co. was founded by Eldredge Johnson. A few years later he offered to sell it to the Regina Music Box Co., but his offer was rejected as representatives of Regina stated that with the pure tone of Regina's products as compared to scratchy-sounding records, music boxes would always be more popular. The Quaker Oats Co. was incorporated. New York became the first state to require license plates on automobiles. Nobel prizes were awarded for the first time, and the first given in physics went to W.C. Röntgen for his discovery of X-rays. The Dow Jones Industrial Average closed on December 31 at 64.56, down from 70.71 at the end of 1900.

The original oil painting entitled *His Master's Voice*, by Englishman Francis Barraud, that was the source for the iconic logo of the Victor Talking Machine Company and its successors.

THE NUMISMATIC SCENE. In the February issue of *The Numismatist*, Augustus G. Heaton advised that the field of collecting branch-mint coins still offered many opportunities as rarities could be found in circulation.

After a lapse of several years the annual (if it could be called that at the time) convention of the ANA was held, this time in Buffalo, New York, on August 22. The venue was the office of Dr. B.P. Wright at 158 Pearl Street. Wright was a specialist in store cards and tokens and for many months had been contributing lengthy serial articles on them for *The Numismatist*. Miss Virginia H. Eaton, one of just two female members of the ANA, was the first to arrive and, embarrassingly, was mistaken for a patient. In all, 17 members attended, and about 50 others were represented by proxy.

"The year 1901 has been a prosperous one for the Association," reported George Heath in an editorial.

> 119 new members have joined our ranks, and if indications point to anything they are a class that may be depended upon to stick by us. Of 112 of this number we have more or less complete data. Their age is an average of about 38½ years. The fascination of our science is no respector of age, it delights the young, and as the years go by it only finds its votaries more firmly bound with its charms. Our youngest this year is 13 and our oldest is 69. Fourteen are 50 or over in years.

The drapery at the elbow of Miss Liberty on Liberty Seated silver coins was the subject of an article by Augustus G. Heaton in the October 1901 issue of *The Numismatist*. Heaton and Heath were polymaths and could write authoritatively on just about any specialty.

In July 1901 the military government of the Philippine Islands was replaced with a civilian administration headed by William Howard Taft, who was a judge at the time. One of his first goals was to devise a new territorial coinage that was compatible with the old Spanish monetary system, but also legally exchangeable for U.S. money at the rate of two Philippine pesos for one American dollar. The coins would debut in 1903.

THE YEAR 1902

CURRENT EVENTS. On a hunting trip in Mississippi, President Roosevelt hoped to bag a bear. His efforts were fruitless, but a backup was provided by helpers who captured a bear cub and chained it to a tree. The November 18, 1902, edition of the *Washington Evening Star* included a cartoon showing the president refusing to shoot it. A bear doll was made by a candy store owner. Publicized, the "Teddy Bear" became an everlasting favorite. The first part of Ida Tarbell's exposé on the Standard Oil Company was published in *McClure's* magazine. Part of *The History of the Standard Oil Company*, which appeared in installments through 1904 and then released in book form, this exposé focused on certain corporate misdeeds of the era and helped inspire the round of trust busting that took place in this decade. Roosevelt, during his administration, would file suit against 43 major corporations viewed as engaging in monopolistic or restrictive practices. On August 22 Theodore Roosevelt became the first president to ride in an automobile when he rode in a Columbia Electric Victoria through Hartford, Connecticut.

The first Rose Bowl football game was played in Pasadena, California, on January 1 as part of the Tournament of Roses held since 1890. Michigan defeated Stanford 49 to 0. On the home entertainment scene, disc-type music boxes were very popular, as were foot-pumped player pianos, and phonographs. Music was important, and a sign of a fine home was a piano in the parlor. Evening activities included games and reading. The Dow Jones Industrial Average ended the year at 62.49, down from 64.56 at the end of 1901.

The Numismatic Scene. In the January issue of *The Numismatist* Heaton took a swipe at the reverse design of the current quarter and half dollar:

> The heraldic eagle on recent dates of silver is but a witless imitation of the two-headed crowned eagles of old and absolute empires of Eastern Europe which typify double or triple sovereignty. What business have we, in our young and united great republic of equality and freedom, with a flayed eagle or with its hints of heraldry and imperialism? If we must needs have the rapacious and autocratic bird as an emblem, let him be restored, as on the dollars of 1838 and 1839, and on the copper-nickel cents, to life and impressive speed and power, or to his natural watchful dignity in repose.

In Chicago, Virgil M. Brand, a wealthy brewer, was in the process of forming the largest collection of coins in private hands in America. By the time of his passing in 1926 it totaled over 350,000 items. William Roderick Sherman, age nine, became the ANA's youngest member. Many coin collectors and dealers issued advertising tokens, responding to advertisements by J. Cranston, who made such pieces to order. Among hot areas of the market were Hard Times tokens, encased postage stamps, colonials, half cents, and large cents. Collector interest in current Proof coins was low, and yearly mintages for silver issues were modest—just 777 sets in 1902, and declining in later years. Mintmarked coins were a very narrow specialty, and hardly anything about them appeared in print. No ANA convention was held. At year's end there were 450 members, an increase of 102 since January—a good sign. The association had a mail-order lending library, but no requests were received in 1902.

The Year 1903

Current Events. In the case of *Giles v. Harris*, the Supreme Court dismissed hearings against a new clause in the Alabama Constitution which required those registering to vote to pass a test that was subjectively administered by election officials—these officials were able to use their control of the testing circumstances to pass whites taking the test while denying blacks who did similarly well. The court did not rule on the constitutionality of the law, but instead dismissed the case because they believed that the plaintiff's request had not met the *amount-in-controversy* threshold necessary for the court to hear the case—the court did not see how a decision registering the black voters who had already applied for voting privileges would sufficiently address the unconstitutionality of the clause in question, were it found unconstitutional.

The U.S. Land Department conveyed title of the Everglades swamp to Florida. The Hay-Herran Treaty signed by Secretary of State John Hay and the foreign minister of Colombia provided for a six-mile strip across the Isthmus of Panama to be leased to the United States for $10 million, plus annual payments of $250,000, plus $40 million to buy out French investors who had been underway in a canal project. The idea of a cross-Nicaraguan canal was dropped.

The Ford Motor Company was incorporated with a capital of $28,000 raised by 12 stockholders. A Packard automobile arrived in New York, having spent 52 days travelling from San Francisco—the first recorded transcontinental automobile trip. The Ford Motor Company was incorporated. The Harley-Davidson motorcycle was introduced.

The Wright brothers made the first sustained manned flight in a controlled gasoline-powered aircraft and stayed aloft for 59 seconds at Kitty Hawk, North Carolina. Milton Hershey broke ground for what would become his vast chocolate factory and town not far from Harrisburg, Pennsylvania.

A short film produced by Thomas Edison, *The Great Train Robbery*, was all the rage in theatres. The first World Series game was played when the American League and National League champions met in a post-season playoff in a best-of-nine contest in November. The winners were the Boston Red Sox (originally called the Red Stockings).

The monetary situation remained stable during the year. The commercial and banking sectors of the economy were prosperous, and no significant problems were reported. The New York Stock Exchange Building was completed. The Dow Jones Industrial Average ended the year at 49.11, down from 62.49 at the end of 1902.

THE NUMISMATIC SCENE. "Brilliant is best" was the rallying cry for nearly all collectors of and dealers in silver coins. The Mint Cabinet collection silver coins had been cleaned recently by an attendant who bought silver polish in a department store to do so. Farran Zerbe on a visit there asked an employee about this questionable practice and was told, "That is nothing. I have been here eight years and they have been cleaned three or four times in my time."[5] (See page 34.)

On another front, Zerbe, an entrepreneur, somehow arranged for Congress to authorize 250,000 commemorative gold dollars, half with the portrait of Thomas Jefferson and half with McKinley, in connection with his concession and the forthcoming Louisiana Purchase Exposition. These were promoted at $3 each, causing much controversy. They proved to be a market failure, and only 17,500 of each were sold, with the rest melted.[6]

The Wright brothers' first sustained powered flight at Kitty Hawk, North Carolina, in 1903.

The Philadelphia and San Francisco mints began striking special coins for the Philippine Islands, including copper and silver denominations. The coins were designed by Filipino sculptor, engraver, and silversmith Melecio Figueroa. Philippine Proof sets, of which a remarkable 2,558 were made, were offered for $2 each. In contrast, just 755 silver Proof sets of United States coins were struck.

In the December issue of *The Numismatist* B. Max Mehl, of Fort Worth, Texas, placed his first advertisement. From that point his career went onward and upward. By the time of his passing in 1957 he had handled more "name" collections than any other dealer.

The Year 1904

Current Events. The presidential election of the year pitted incumbent Theodore Roosevelt against Democratic candidate Alton B. Parker. Roosevelt, who had achieved great popularity with the general public, won in a landslide. In a 5 to 4 decision, the Supreme Court ruled that the Northern Securities Company was in violation of the Sherman Act of 1890 and ordered dissolution of the railroad trust. Reformers organized the National Child Labor Committee. Bethlehem Steel Company was founded, furnishing strong competition to U.S. Steel, which had formed in 1901. In New York City the first subway tube was excavated under the Hudson River.

In this year Cripple Creek gold output was valued at $22,220,680, making it the greatest gold camp in the world. It was time for another "rush," or so it seemed.

In 1902 gold had been discovered in a remote area in south central Nevada. Word spread, many fortune seekers traveled to Tonopah and Goldfield—hastily erected boom towns attracting miners from all directions and thousands of investors in stock. The excitement faded within a few years.

On February 7 a fire broke out in the warehouse of the John E. Hurst Co. in downtown Baltimore at the intersection of German and Sharp streets. A series of explosions followed, and by nightfall nearly 10 blocks had been leveled. Cy Young pitched the first perfect American League game in history on May 5 for the team that would become the Boston Red Sox, throwing to 27 batters in nine innings without a single one reaching first base.

Goldfield, Nevada, was a boom town in the first decade of the 20th century.

THE NUMISMATIC SCENE. On October 15 the ANA held a convention in St. Louis. In attendance were 17 members and three spouses. Albert R. Frey was elected president. Attendees visited the Louisiana Purchase Exposition (which opened on April 30 and would close in December). One attraction was the same Ferris Wheel that had been at the World's Columbian Exposition in 1893. Farran Zerbe had his Money of the World concession and offered various items for sale, including 1903-dated commemorative gold dollars. The average age of a new member joining in 1904 was 37 years and eight months. No further conventions were held until 1907.

The latest commemorative coin was a gold dollar for the Lewis & Clark Exposition held in Portland, Oregon. These were offered for $2 each. Additional coins were made in 1905 with that date. The mintage of Morgan-design silver dollars ended this year, as the supply of earmarked bullion for them had been exhausted.

In the Philippines, it became evident that the little bronze half-centavo coin was too small a denomination to be popular in commerce. The Philadelphia Mint in 1903 and early 1904 had produced nearly 18 million of the unnecessary coins, millions of which sat in Philippine Treasury vaults until 1908.

Attendees at the 1904 ANA convention in St. Louis. George F. Heath is standing at the left. In the front row left, near Heath, is Farran Zerbe, who had his Money of the World concession at the world's fair.

A souvenir postcard from the Louisiana Purchase Exposition in St. Louis.

The Year 1905

Current Events. Discrimination was widespread in America, and targets included Chinese-Americans, African-Americans, Catholics, and recent immigrants. Child labor was widely practiced, with youngsters at work in textile mills and coal mines. The Massachusetts Legislature rejected a bill that would have required patent medicine bottles to carry labels showing their ingredients. At the time, many medicines contained cocaine, morphine, and up to 40 percent alcohol. The first Rotary Club was organized in Chicago on February 23, beginning a rise in men's philanthropic luncheon clubs. Years later coin dealer B. Max Mehl would be elected international president of that organization.

Outside of all cities and many towns in America were amusement parks connected to the communities by trolley lines. The carousel with its music and flying horses was always a center of attention.

Tiffany & Co. sold a pearl necklace for $1 million—the most expensive item ever, and a store record that would stand for the rest of the century. Pearls led fashion and were showcased more than diamonds in jewelry offerings. Popular songs included "In My Merry Oldsmobile," "Wait Till the Sun Shines Nellie," "Daddy's Little Girl," "My Gal Sal," "In the Shade of the Old Apple Tree," and "What You Gonna Do When the Rent Comes Round?" Vaudeville star Eva Tanguay became known as the "I Don't Care" Girl, from her notable song of the same name. The books *Adventures of Huckleberry Finn* and *The Adventures of Tom Sawyer* were banned from the Brooklyn Public Library as they set a "bad example."

On March 17 President Theodore Roosevelt had the honor of giving away his cousin Eleanor Roosevelt, who would become a noted humanitarian and political speaker, when she married her fifth cousin once removed, Columbia Law School student and future president Franklin Delano Roosevelt, age 23. Because of Franklin's polio-related health problems, Eleanor would assist him heavily on the campaign trail leading to the White House, often speaking in his stead.

In the biological sciences, the structure of chlorophyll was identified—the biomolecule which allows plants to absorb energy from light during photosynthesis. The National Association of Audubon Societies for the Protection of Wild Birds and Animals was founded in the United States.

An ornate carousel.

In 1905 the main domestic sources for newly mined silver were Montana, with 14.6 million ounces; Colorado, 14.3; Utah, 12.4; Idaho, 7.8; Arizona, 2.7; and Nevada, 2.7. The production of Nevada's Comstock Lode, so important during the 1860s and 1870s, had diminished sharply by this time.

THE NUMISMATIC SCENE. In April D.M. Averill & Company of Portland, Oregon, ran a quarter page advertisement stating that only 25,028 commemorative gold dollars of 1904 were minted and "these are nearly exhausted." This was a lie, as only 10,000 were ever sold. Thomas L. Elder, who had moved his business from Pittsburgh to New York City, conducted his first auction in September. In the next three decades he would become the leading coin auctioneer there. S.H. and Henry Chapman wrote advertisements claiming "Philadelphia—the Mint City from the foundation of the government—is the Best Coin Market." New York and Philadelphia were the main numismatic centers, with Boston and Chicago furnishing strong competition.

In October it was reported that the ANA had 418 members, of whom 351 lived in the United States. President Theodore Roosevelt, who had been impressed with the artistry of ancient Greek coins on display at the Smithsonian Institution, determined to upgrade the designs of American issues. He commissioned sculptor Augustus Saint-Gaudens, whose studio was in Cornish, New Hampshire, to redesign all denominations from the cent to the double eagle. The artist was in failing health, and before his death in 1907 had completed just the $10 and $20 values.

Following the discontinuation of the silver dollar, the Mint began selling Proof sets with the cent and nickel for 8 cents, sets with the three silver denominations dime to half dollar for $1.50, and Proof gold coins for 25 cents more than their face value.

THE YEAR 1906

CURRENT EVENTS. At 5:13 in the morning of April 18 a severe earthquake struck the city of San Francisco. The shock broke the mains of the Spring Valley Water Company. For a short time citizens milled about assessing the situation. There had been structural damage, but otherwise most buildings remained intact and repairable. Within a short time, however, fire broke out in several areas of the city. Without water, firemen and others were helpless as it spread. Crews used dynamite to level some buildings in the path of the flames, but the effort was of no use. Three days later, when the conflagration ended, the central part of the city was a scene of 28,000 burned-out buildings, fallen and partially standing brick walls, and rubble everywhere.

San Francisco ablaze.

Congress passed the Hepburn Act, which extended jurisdiction of the Interstate Commerce Commission and gave the ICC powers to set railroad rates. Upton Sinclair's exposé of Chicago stock yards, *The Jungle*, was published and attracted great interest, exposing filthy conditions in the meatpacking industry and the terrible circumstances under which laborers worked. The Pure Food and Drug Act became a reality and would be implemented on January 1, 1907, essentially ending the era of medically worthless patent medicines. Radio broadcasts became a reality, and broadcasts could be picked up at a range of several hundred miles by those having the proper equipment (popular commercial radio would not arrive until the early 1920s). In the meantime, nearly all instant communications were by telegraph and telephone. On January 12, 1906, the Dow Jones Industrial Average closed above 100 for the first time. By year's end it had slipped to 94.35.

The Numismatic Scene. The Harlan P. Smith specimen of the 1822 half eagle, a coin of which only three are known, crossed the auction block at $2,163, setting a record for the most valuable United States coin. Records were made to be broken, the market was strong, and in the next few years this price was topped many times. The Chapman brothers, partners in business since 1878, dissolved their partnership. Each went his own way, and successfully so.

Although the San Francisco Mint produced more than 200,000 peso coins for the Philippines in 1906, nearly all of them were held back from circulation because of the rising price of silver. Most were later sold as bullion and melted, resulting in the rarity of surviving 1906-S pesos.

The Year 1907

Current Events. Commerce and the economy were robust for most of 1907. It was an era of investment in new facilities and businesses, of rapid growth of the automobile industry, and more.

President Roosevelt wanted to impress other countries with America's naval strength. The Great White Fleet, comprised of 16 battleships, left for an around-the-world cruise and returned one year and 68 days later. Oklahoma, carved out of the Oklahoma and

Celebrating the return of the Great White Fleet.

Indian territories, was admitted to the Union as the 46th state. Long-distance swimmer Annette Kellerman was arrested for indecent exposure at Boston's Revere Beach when she appeared in a one-piece bathing suit lacking a skirt. Nearly 1.29 million immigrants entered the United States, a record that would endure for the rest of the century.

In San Francisco the beautifully ornate French chateau–style Cliff House built by Adolph Sutro in 1897 burned to the ground. The building had been a tourist destination and social venue, a must-see for visitors.

The Panic of 1907 took place late in the year. Unlike other panics such as in 1857 and 1893, this one was mainly confined to financial circles and did not affect everyday life in America. It severely affected stocks. On December 31 the Dow Jones Industrial Average closed at 58.75, down sharply from 94.35 at the end of 1906. Within a couple of years the panic was forgotten.

The loss of the Cliff House on September 7, 1907.
Seal Rocks and the expanse of the Pacific Ocean are in the distance.

DISAPPOINTED DEPOSITORS BESIEGING KNICKERBOCKER TRUST CO.'S BUILDING AFTER BANK HAD CLOSED ITS DOORS.

KNICKERBOCKER TRUST REPORTED AS READY TO ASK FOR A RECEIVER

President Higgins Appeals in Vain to Heads of Other Trust Companies. Att'y-General Jackson in Town to Consult with Bank Superintendent.

CORTELYOU ISSUES A REASSURING STATEMENT

Scene from the Panic of 1907. (*New York American*, October 23, 1907)

The Numismatic Scene. The yearly ANA convention resumed, and President Albert R. Frey stated that it would be held in Columbus, Ohio, for several days beginning on September 22. The Neil House, which charged $1 to $3 per day, was set as the convention headquarters. In addition, nominations for a new slate of ANA officers were solicited.

Matthew A. Stickney, who had visited the Mint in 1843, obtaining a rare 1804 dollar, and who built one of the finest collections ever held of issues through the year 1873, died on August 14, 1894. In 1906 Henry Chapman bought the collection intact from Stickney's heirs. Auctioned in 1907 via a 224-page catalog describing 3,026 lots, the event created a sensation. Over 1,000 bidders took part. The prices totaled $37,859.21—the highest amount ever for a rare coin sale.[7]

In the Philippines, the rising price of silver made it profitable for speculators to remove the large Philippine pesos from circulation and melt them for their precious-metal value. In response, in 1907 the U.S. Mint lowered the fineness of the Philippine peso from .900 to .800 and reduced its diameter from 38 mm to 35 mm. With one-third less silver than the U.S./Philippine pesos of 1903 to 1906, the new coins were safe from silver speculators and stayed in circulation.

The new $10 Indian Head eagles by Augustus Saint-Gaudens were released in the autumn, followed by his MCMVII double eagles in December. The latter created nationwide interest, and almost immediately the coins commanded a premium. Saint-Gaudens's model for a new cent was not approved by the Mint.

On September 1 the membership of the ANA stood at 421, not much change from two years earlier. The convention convened in Columbus, Ohio, at the Neil House hotel beginning on September 22 with 28 members present. At the final session, on the 24th, Farran Zerbe was elected president. Among the entertainment was George F. Heath's offering of recited limericks describing many of the people in attendance. A good time was had by all. "So great was the enthusiasm, that without doubt conventions will be held yearly after this," Heath wrote in his report of the event.

Convention Group, A. N. A. Columbus, O.

First row: Messrs. Gies, Wright, Heath, Zerbe, Wood, King, Frey, Green, Leon.
Second row: Messrs. Yawger, Schwartz, S. H. & H. Chapman, Granberg.
Third row: Messrs. Ginn, Elder, Duffield, Williams, Misner.
Back row: Messrs. Clark, Coover, Marcuson, Keech, Walworth, Mitchelson, Buck, Whitsett, Henderson.

Attendees at the 1907 ANA Convention in Columbus, Ohio.

THE YEAR 1908

CURRENT EVENTS. President Theodore Roosevelt declined to run for a third term. His secretary of war, William Howard Taft, secured the Republican nomination. William Jennings Bryan, who ran for the third time on the Democratic ticket, was easily defeated in November, gaining only 162 electoral votes to Taft's 321. Former president Grover Cleveland died at Princeton, New Jersey, on June 24 at age 71. In retirement he had spent much of his summer months at a vacation house in Tamworth, New Hampshire. The Bureau of Investigation, later known as the Federal Bureau of Investigation, was established under the Department of Justice to fight crime, but in many instances its efforts were directed toward labor organizers.

Henry Ford manufactured his first Model T. Produced until the Model A replaced it in 1927, the Model T became the world's best-selling automobile. In the meantime horsepower in the literal sense was still very much in evidence in towns, cities, and resorts.

Tea bags made of Chinese silk were introduced by New York merchant Thomas Sullivan and soon became a sensation. General Electric introduced the first commercially successful electric toaster, but sales were limited by the fact that only about 10 percent of American homes were wired for electricity. The first electric typewriter was introduced. Most offices in larger towns and cities had electrical service.

In Chelsea, Massachusetts, a raging fire destroyed about a third of this Boston suburb. The Grand Canyon National Monument was so designated, keeping it forever in the public domain. The economy had recovered most of its losses from the Panic of 1907. The Dow Jones Industrial Average closed on December 30, 1908, at 86.15, up from 58.75 at the end of 1907.

THE NUMISMATIC SCENE. The MCMVII double eagle of 1907 inspired great praise in the public and numismatic press in early 1908—unprecedented acclaim for a new American coin design. Unfortunately it required three blows of the coining press to bring up the high relief design properly, and the Roman numerals were not easily decoded by the public. The result was that Chief Engraver Charles E. Barber, the nemesis of the late Saint-Gaudens, flattened the relief and changed the design to use regular

Model T Ford automobiles awaiting shipment.

The Tally Ho Stage with summer tourists in the White Mountains of New Hampshire.

numerals. In contrast, the new 1908 quarter eagle and half eagle design by Bela Lyon Pratt was widely condemned after its release in November.

In April 1908 James Francis Smith, governor-general of the Philippines, secured permission to ship 7,565,400 of the colony's 1903 and 1904–dated bronze half centavos to the San Francisco Mint, to be re-coined into the more popular one-centavo pieces. They were transported in June.

A 1903 half-centavo coin of the Philippines, struck at the Philadelphia Mint. Millions would be shipped back to the United States to be melted and re-coined in 1908. (1.5x actual size)

On June 16 Dr. George F. Heath, founder of the ANA in 1891 and of *The Numismatist* in 1888, died peacefully at his home in Monroe, Michigan, after feeling uncomfortable for just a few hours. This marked the end of an era.

In a quiet move ANA president Farran Zerbe went to Monroe and met with Heath's widow and purchased *The Numismatist*, not for the ANA, but for himself. He later announced that this was beneficial to all involved, as it would result in the magazine being continued without interruption. Notably absent from his explanation was any offer to turn the publication over to the ANA.

The annual convention was held in Philadelphia. Early arrivals were welcomed on Saturday, September 26, by Mr. and Mrs. Henry Chapman, who acted as host and hostess throughout the event, which included events in their spacious home. Henry's brother, S. Hudson Chapman, was ill at the time. Early birds visited Fairmount Park and the Museum of Art on Sunday, followed by dinner that evening at the Hotel Majestic. The convention was called to order on Tuesday at the Hotel Stenton, the official headquarters. It was reported that 556 active and 6 honorary members belonged to the association. Zerbe was reelected president.

In one of the presentations, veteran dealer John W. Haseltine reminisced about his life in coins. He told of his father-in-law, William K. Idler, who had close connections to Mint officials and whose estate included many previously unknown patterns and special pieces. Unsaid was that Haseltine and his current business partner Stephen K. Nagy had been selling many of these in recent times, some of which were sold in publicized sales and others of which were disposed of quietly. The event closed on October 1. The next day Henry Chapman and invited guests took the electric railway to Atlantic City to enjoy the attractions there. Others went to New York City, where, on Monday evening, Thomas L. Elder hosted a banquet at the Café Martin, as a precursor to his sale of the Wilson Collection from the 5th to the 7th.

In New York City on October 6, the magnificent new building and museum of the American Numismatic Society (which had recently dropped "and Archaeological" from its name) was opened in Audubon Terrace at 155th Street and Broadway. Railroad scion Archer Huntington had donated the money to build it.

The new headquarters of the American Numismatic Society.

The New York Numismatic Club was organized on the evening of December 11 at Keen's Old English Chop House at 36th Street and Sixth Avenue, New York City. The group would prosper.

Organized in 1908, the New York Numismatic Club went on to be important for many years, remaining so today.

The Year 1909

Current Events. In early 1909, just before President Theodore Roosevelt was scheduled to leave the White House to make way for the incoming president William Howard Taft, he met with well-known film producer Colonel William Selig. One of the first things the president hoped to do after leaving office was to go big-game hunting in Africa. Of course, this was a natural opportunity for Selig, whose offer to come along and film the trip seems to have been accepted. Something went wrong with the arrangements, and while the Smithsonian Institution—the sponsor of the trip—sent a cameraman, no one from Selig's company was invited. Undeterred, in their Chicago studio Selig's company produced *Hunting Big Game in Africa* using a tired lion, some local black citizens hired as extras, and an actor made up to look like Roosevelt. The former president was not mentioned in the publicity for the film, but the public assumed the pictures were really from Roosevelt's trip.

The salary of the president of the United States was raised to $75,000 per year, which it would remain until 1949. In another act of American imperialism, the government sent marines to Nicaragua to oust dictator José Santos Zelaya, who feared United States domination in the area. The construction of the Panama Canal continued, frustrated at times by outbreaks of malaria and problems with the workers. The latest version of the Wright brothers' airplane passed tests by the United States Army. The brothers signed a contract to make a plane that could carry two men, fly for 60 minutes, and reach a speed of 40 miles per hour, and they formed the American Wright Co. to do so.

The National Association for the Advancement of Colored People (NAACP) was established to combat the effects of institutionalized racism on communities of color. At the time, Jim Crow laws enforced segregation, denying black Americans the right to use the same facilities as whites; voting rights in some areas were severely restricted for people of color; and black communities were further threatened by acts of violence directed at them by whites. Sadly, lynchings were common. The Japanese faced their share of prejudice as well, and in 1908 Congress had decreed that no

Theodore Roosevelt on his big game–hunting trip. More images from his trip can be found in the Smithsonian Institution Archives.

more Japanese people could enter the United States. In the 19th century, iterations of the Chinese Exclusion Act had posed similar limits on Asian immigration. To a much lesser extent Catholics and other European immigrants endured prejudice.

Popular songs included "I Wonder Who's Kissing Her Now," "Put on Your Old Grey Bonnet," "Meet Me Tonight in Dreamland," "The Whiffenpoof Song," "Casey Jones," and "On Wisconsin!" Dreamland was a section of Coney Island, America's most popular amusement park. The Kewpie doll illustrated and patented by Rose O'Neill rivaled the Teddy Bear's popularity. The Dow Jones Industrial Average closed on December 31 at 99.05, up from 86.15 at the end of 1908.

The Numismatic Scene. The January issue of *The Numismatist* bore a profusion of line illustrations (by numismatist Howland Wood) and halftone plates, as well as decorative capital letters, which began each article. The overall effect was one of artistic improvement from what had been done before, initiating a new era of graphics excellence. Clearly, as the new owner and editor, Zerbe was firmly on the right track. His knowledge of virtually every numismatic discipline, from the shadowy days of the first ancient coinage right down to the latest issues, stood him well in his capacity as editor. Edgar H. Adams, America's preeminent numismatic scholar, conducted a column which covered many subjects, especially pattern coins, a special interest.

In the vaults of the Philadelphia Mint, millions of double eagles were stored with no intention of releasing them into circulation. They were to be held in reserve as backing for Gold Certificates.

At an unknown time in 1909, dies for Barber silver coins were made with the date first incorporated into the master die, and then transferred to the working die.[8] After this practice was implemented, there were no more variations in date positions.

C.W. Cowell, a Colorado numismatist, reported:

> Collectors who are interested in mintmark gold should endeavor to fill their sets as rapidly as possible. During the recent bank panic a great deal of gold was drawn out of Southern banks and C and D mintmarks may now be easily found, and usually in Fine condition.[9]

Unlike previous years, a sharp contest for the presidency of the ANA emerged in the early summer. On one side was contender Francis C. Higgins of New York City, and on the other was Dr. J.M. Henderson of Columbus, Ohio, who was strongly backed by Farran Zerbe. Thomas L. Elder, Higgins, and certain other members of the American Numismatic Association, particularly those in the dealer community, took exception to Zerbe's ownership of *The Numismatist*, and this exception extended to his endorsement of Henderson for president.

Zerbe, as owner of the magazine, had the last word and wrote that Higgins "has rendered practically no service to the organization. His campaign methods now characterize his unfitness for the office." Elder distributed a leaflet that called Zerbe a fraud and cited examples of his dishonest behavior. In response, the ever clever Zerbe solicited new members to enroll in the ANA at a reduced rate for just six months instead of a year, temporarily bolstering the ranks of his supporters.

In the meantime, the new Lincoln cent was released in August and created its own controversy when some objected to designer Victor D. Brenner's initials (V.D.B.) appearing on the reverse, and they were subsequently removed. This antagonism against Brenner's initials defied logic as current Barber coins had the designer's initial on the obverse and the double eagles had Saint-Gaudens' monogram.

The annual convention was held in Montreal, Canada, from August 9 to 14. More than 50 members attended in person and about 450 others were represented by proxy, including a host of Zerbe's six-month enrollees. Before the event started, representatives of the Higgins and Henderson factions met, realized that Zerbe and his associates held so many proxies that Henderson would win regardless, and agreed to make peace rather than disrupt the convention. *The Numismatist*, still owned by Zerbe, gave a glowing account of the meeting. ANA membership, including the six-monthers, totaled 621. Later, Thomas L. Elder was heard to remark that the whole election affair was reminiscent of the New York City politics of Boss Tweed and Tammany Hall. The sordid election left scars for years to come.

THE YEAR 1910

CURRENT EVENTS. Halley's Comet brightened the night skies, and there was fear of what might happen when Earth passed through its tail. These worries proved themselves inconsequential when the Earth accomplished the feat without incident on May 18. The Boy Scouts of America was established, building on British roots. Theodore Roosevelt, back from a successful trip to Africa, took a ride in an airplane, becoming the first president to do so. Automobiles were a common sight all across America, although horses were still used for most local freight delivery. The economy was strong, and many companies expanded their business. Unemployment stood at 5.9 percent.

Going to the movies gained in popularity, becoming America's favorite entertainment. Films were usually one reel in length, running for about 12 minutes. A dozen or more production companies, mostly located in New York and New Jersey, turned out a constant stream of subjects. Nickelodeon theatres, whose fronts were usually ornamented with many light bulbs, typically charged 5¢ admission. Penny arcades were everywhere—in every amusement park as well as year round in downtown areas. Coin-operated pianos were widely distributed as well. It took a nickel to hear the latest ragtime tune. The Dow Jones Industrial Average closed on December 31 at 81.36, down from 99.05 at the end of 1909.

The Acme Theater on a snowy day in Eastport, Maine.

The Numismatic Scene. Interest in minute die differences in modern coins attracted the attention of several numismatists, Charles E. McKirk prominent among them, who pointed out that the placement of the S on cents of 1909 varied and there were slight differences in date positions on Indian cents of 1871. In *The Numismatist*, February 1910, a three-page article by Fred. G. McKean, "Certain Defects on Recent Quarter Dollars," described die cracks, areas of weakness, and date position variations seen on coins from 1892 onward.

The annual ANA convention was held in New York City with headquarters at the Park Avenue Hotel. The first meeting was held on Tuesday, September 6, in the building of the American Numismatic Society. Dr. J.M. Henderson was reelected president. A resolution was passed to send a request to the director of the Mint to cease making gold Proof coins in the present style and return to mirrored fields and frosted high areas (this fell on deaf ears). Lyman Low made an alternative suggestion, stating that the surfaces of the current gold coins were not suitable for mirrored fields, and that, instead, coins made for collectors should have SPECIMEN lettered on their edges and that those for circulation should have reeded edges. A mini-scandal arose when a photographer hired to take a group photo of attendees collected $1 each from various members and then disappeared without a trace.

Zerbe, tiring of running *The Numismatist*, stated that the ANA could buy the publication for his cost and expenses, his offer including about 10,000 back issues and 2,000 illustration blocks. An angel in the form of W.W.C. Wilson stepped in, bought it back from Zerbe, and presented it as a gift to the ANA.

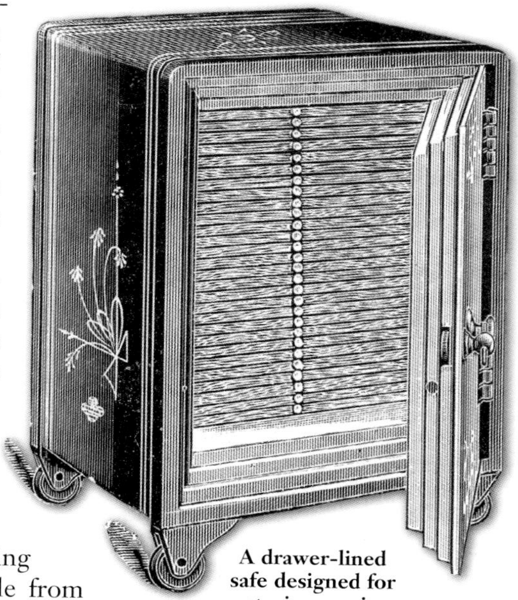

A drawer-lined safe designed for storing a coin collection.

Coin collections and inventories were usually kept in paper envelopes measuring 2x2 inches square, pill envelopes available from drugstores, cabinets, or drawer-lined safes. There were no albums or folders, and there would not be any until the late 1920s.

The Year 1911

Current Events. In California women were given the right to vote. Women's suffrage was in place in scattered other states, but not nationally. Eugene B. Ely landed his airplane on the deck of the USS *Pennsylvania* in San Francisco Bay, a first for aviation. The Hope Diamond, the world's most famous gem, was sold by Pierre Cartier to 25-year-old heiress Evalyn Walsh McLean for a record $180,000. In New York City a fire at the Triangle Shirtwaist factory trapped many workers on upper floors and killed 145, calling national attention to poor safety conditions in manufacturing establishments. Also in New York City, the Atlantic Garden in the Bowery, a famous German beer hall, was razed. In Spring Green, Wisconsin, architect Frank Lloyd Wright completed Taliesin, a wide-ranging house that integrated many natural features.

The nickel was king. Coin-operated pianos, vending devices, and arcade machines were popular all over America. Race car driver Louis Chevrolet joined with W.C. Durant to form the Chevrolet Motor Co. Automobiles were produced by dozens of different companies from small to large. The first Indianapolis 500-mile race was run, starting more than a century of tradition.

John D. Rockefeller's Standard Oil Company trust was broken by a Supreme Court ruling. Divisions of the company remained in business separately, usually retaining *Standard Oil* in their names, as did the company Standard Oil of California.

On April 17 a one-day record was set at Ellis Island in New York Harbor when 11,745 immigrants arrived. The Golden Door continued to beckon to many immigrants, Europeans in particular, who were prone to settle in cities.

Many students dropped out of school after eighth grade. Fewer than five percent of men graduating from high school went to college, and for women the rate was even lower. The Dow Jones Industrial Average closed on December 30 at 81.68, not much of a change from 81.36 at the end of 1910.

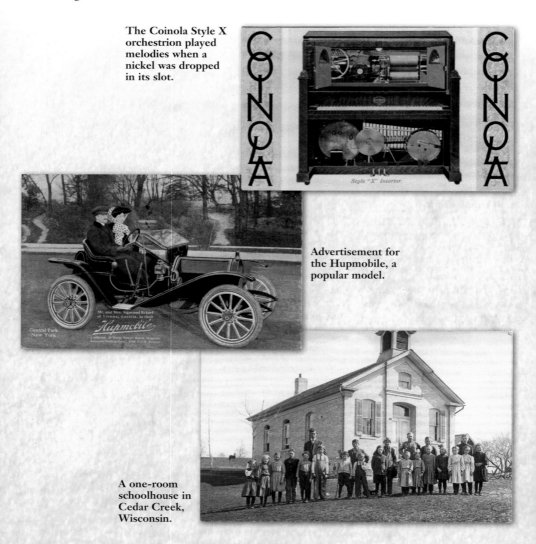

The Coinola Style X orchestrion played melodies when a nickel was dropped in its slot.

Advertisement for the Hupmobile, a popular model.

A one-room schoolhouse in Cedar Creek, Wisconsin.

The Numismatic Scene. As of January *The Numismatist* suffered a setback. No longer did the publication have a single editor. Now it was run by a committee, with Albert R. Frey as general editor, assisted by Edgar H. Adams and George H. Blake—certainly three well-qualified individuals. The appearance of graphics within the publication deteriorated, and gone were the interesting illustrations used to start columns, along with other typographical fillers which Zerbe had peppered throughout each issue. The publication was now rather bland looking, reminiscent of the pre-Zerbe era, but with a few more illustrations. The editorial content continued to be as good as ever.

For many years collectors knew of the 1879, Flowing Hair, $4 gold Stella. In February 1911, they were made aware of three other varieties—Coiled Hair coins of 1879 and 1880 and a Flowing Hair $4 gold piece of 1880—illustrated for the first time in *The Numismatist.* The source of these coins was not disclosed, but the estate of William K. Idler with its secret treasures would seem to be a good possibility.

The annual convention was held in Chicago from August 29 to 31 at the LaSalle Hotel, with some meetings held at the Art Institute. About 50 members were on hand. ANA President Henderson gave remarks which included this question: "Has the ANA progressed or retrograded? There has been a net loss in membership; that is, we now have fewer names in our books, but we have more than doubled the number of interested members." This net loss was not a real loss, as most of Zerbe's six-months members simply had not renewed. Judson Brenner of DeKalb, Illinois, was elected as the new president without controversy.

By 1911 speculators and profiteers in the Philippines had pulled nearly all of the U.S. colony's large, heavy pesos (those of 1903 to 1906) from circulation, to be melted for their higher-than-face-value silver content. An official report of June 30 stated that fewer than 10 percent of the old coins still remained in the Philippines. Meanwhile, the San Francisco Mint continued to produce the newer, smaller silver pesos for circulation.

The Year 1912

Current Events. New Mexico became the 47th state on January 6 and Arizona became the 48th on February 14. To recognize these additions, two more stars were added to the obverse border of the double eagle. The Union would remain at 48 states until 1959. On the night of April 14, on its maiden voyage, the RMS *Titanic* of the White Star Line hit an iceberg and sank 375 miles southeast of Newfoundland. Of the 2,224 people aboard, 1,513 died.

Theodore Roosevelt, with several years of travel and other recreational activities behind him, decided to toss his hat in the political ring and seek the Republican nomination for president. The incumbent Republican, William Howard Taft, also sought reelection. Roosevelt was the landslide winner in the primaries, but at the nomination convention the attendees were loyal to Taft and chose him. Not to be deterred, Roosevelt organized the Progressive Party and became its candidate. Wounded by a would-be assassin in Wisconsin in October, Roosevelt said he remained as fit as a bull moose, after which his party was nicknamed the Bull Moose Party. The Republicans were split in their votes, and the election went to Woodrow Wilson, an educator and the former governor of New Jersey.

Federal employees were granted an eight-hour work day. In the private sectors most workers were at their jobs 10 to 12 hours a day, six days a week. On Sundays most citizens attended church.

Juliette Gordon Low founded the Girl Guides of America in her native city of Savannah, Georgia.

The Girl Guides of America was established, and in the next year would change its name to the Girl Scouts of America. The Boston Red Sox won the World Series 4 to 3 against the New York Giants. In football the official dimensions of the playing field were standardized, and the value of a touchdown was raised from five to six points. The wife of the Japanese ambassador together with First Lady Helen Taft headed a ceremony to plant 3,020 cherry trees on the shore of the Tidal Basin in Washington, D.C. Leon Lenwood Bean founded L.L. Bean, Inc., in Freeport, Maine, and offered hunting shoes at $4 to $5.50 per pair. The economy was good, and unemployment was only 4.6 percent. The Dow Jones Industrial Average closed on December 31 at 87.87, up from 81.68 at the end of 1911.

THE NUMISMATIC SCENE. The January 1912 issue of *The Numismatist* was produced under the editorship of Edgar H. Adams, a prolific writer whose output had included some of the most important articles printed in the journal in recent times. Earlier, Adams had been an associate editor to Frey, who resigned, complaining that he had been "misunderstood."

In 1912 long-time ANA member Congressman William Ashbrook of Ohio succeeded in having the association awarded a *federal* charter—a very rare distinction and honor.

The annual ANA convention was headquartered at the Hotel Rochester in upstate New York. Rates were given as follows: a room with running water cost $1.50, a room with a shower cost $2 and up, a front room with a private bath cost $2.50 and up, and a suite cost $5 per day and up. The three-day event opened on Monday, August 26, with 55 members registered.

Edgar H. Adams stated the event was undoubtedly the most successful convention in the organization's history. Controversies which marred the conventions of years earlier were set aside, "and each member was actuated with a single desire to bring about complete harmony, and these efforts have been eminently successful." The annual election was conducted by mail in this year, and the results were not available during the convention. In December it was announced that President Judson Brenner was unopposed in his bid for reelection, and the same was true for the other officers.

THE YEAR 1913

CURRENT EVENTS. On March 3 a parade of 5,000 suffragists marched down Pennsylvania Avenue, this the day before Woodrow Wilson was inaugurated as president. Wilson proved to be against universal suffrage, and he also had other prejudices, including against African Americans, whom he claimed were an inferior race. The great social movement of the time other than women's suffrage was for prohibition of the sale of alcoholic beverages, and a number of states had passed such laws, pioneered by Maine in 1855. In such areas liquor continued to be sold widely, if clandestinely.

The 16th Amendment to the Constitution provided for graduated income taxes for those earning more than $3,000 per year, but there were enough loopholes that most wealthy people were not negatively affected. J.P. Morgan, the most famous financier, died in Rome on March 31 at the age of 75. It was estimated that the United States accounted for about 40 percent of world manufacturing. The Underwood-Simmons Tariff Act, which was passed on May 8, lowered import duties on many items, and the act was viewed as a threat to domestic industry. Membership in the American Federation of Labor crossed the two-million mark. There were strikes and other signs of labor unrest throughout the country. The Federal Reserve System was established, with 12 branch banks and 25 smaller banks, and it would revolutionize the flow of money and the distribution of coins and currency.

Aeroplanes or, as they were sometimes called, flying machines were popular all across the country, and many "barnstormers" appeared at county fairs and other events, often allowing interested bystanders to pay for a ride aloft. This was a dangerous sport.

The Ford Motor Co. introduced the first moving assembly line in automobile manufacturing. The Erector Set was marketed and inspired ensuing generations of youngsters to build miniature versions of metal bridges, cranes, and other devices. Grand Central Station opened in New York City. Trains were the main way to travel from city to city with accommodations ranging from minimal facilities to luxurious Pullman coaches with bedrooms. Electric interurban railways were a rapid growth industry linking shorter runs from city to city. The first "word cross" or crossword puzzle was published in the *New York World.*

Parcel Post service was started by the United States Post Office, to the opposition of Adams Express, American Express, Wells Fargo, United States Express, and other private companies. Parcel Post proved to be a boon to Sears, Roebuck & Co., Montgomery Ward, and other mail order companies.

Seized illegal liquor in the "Rum Room" of the Portland, Maine, City Hall. Prohibition was one of the great social causes of the early 1900s.

Aviator George Schmidt, on September 2, 1913, set for an exhibition flight in Vermont. Two hundred feet above the Rutland fairgrounds the plane turned turtle and crashed, killing Schmidt and injuring his passenger, laywer J. Dyer Spellman. Schmidt had been flying for five years.

The Dow Jones Industrial Average closed on December 31 at 78.78, down from 87.87 at the end of 1912. The limited number of stocks in the average did not correctly reflect the economy, which was in a strong growth stage. Unemployment was only 4.3 percent.

THE NUMISMATIC SCENE. On the editorial page in January, Edgar H. Adams noted that *The Numismatist* was self-supporting for the first time in its history and had enough income from advertising and subscriptions to cover all expenses.

Coinage of the new "Buffalo" nickel commenced on February 17 at the Philadelphia Mint on a press that turned out 120 coins a minute. It earned a negative review in *The Numismatist.*

The annual ANA convention was held at the Hotel Pontchartrain in Detroit from August 23 to 27 with 56 members in attendance. The American Numismatic Society in New York City suspended the publication of the *American Journal of Numismatics* and invited its members to sign up for *The Numismatist*, which thenceforth contained expanded news about the ANS. This increased the subscription base by about 400 names, more than making up for those who did not renew. Now there were 618 members.

For the second year, the election was held by mail. Ballots opened on November 5 revealed that Frank G. Duffield was elected president with 298 votes, against 124 votes for Carl Wurtzbach.

THE YEAR 1914

CURRENT EVENTS. According to some accounts, the first few months of 1914 were dull in commerce, which many blamed on President Woodrow Wilson and the recent tariff. Others, especially those in the labor force, held that the economy was strong, catalyzing strikes for higher wages. Violence and deaths pervaded certain Western mining districts, most notably in Ludlow, Colorado, where security personnel from John D. Rockefeller Jr.'s mine, along with Colorado National Guard forces, stormed a strikers' camp, killing two-dozen men, women, and children. Henry Ford, whose workers resented the pressure of working on the assembly line, were restive, and there was a constant turnover. In an effort to remedy this he offered wages of $5 per day, or twice the national average and a sum equal to what a worker in Great Britain earned in a week. Those who accepted the enticement learned that pay was $2.60 per day, plus a $2.40 per day bonus to be paid if they were still on the job at the end of a year. Ford's strategy was successful. During the year Ford built 240,700 Model T cars as part of an overall United States production of 543,679 cars. About a million automobiles were in service, but fewer than 100,000 trucks, most of which were used for small deliveries.

It was a year for war. There were hostile acts against Americans in Mexico, and on April 21 President Wilson dispatched a fleet with 3,000 marines to Veracruz. That country was in turmoil and would continue to be as insurrectionists claimed power in various districts. President Huerta resigned on July 15. In the meantime, on June 18, in a place no one had heard of—Sarajevo—the presumed heir to the Austro-Hungarian throne, Archduke Franz Ferdinand, and his wife Sophie, would be shot dead by a 16-year-old high school student who had been hired as an assassin by Serbian anarchists. Austria-Hungary was in turmoil. In response to a cry for help from Serbia, Russia mobilized forces, while German troops readied to help Austria. France supported Russia, and Great Britain supported France. The Great War, later known as World War I, began when Germany declared war on Russia on August 1 and France on August 3. The United States declared neutrality, but many citizens sided with Great Britain and were against Germany. The conflict engendered great uncertainty on this side of the Atlantic, investors became very cautious, and commerce, already with problems, suffered further. Accurate statistics were scarce, and most laborers felt that their wages were low even though capitalists were earning record amounts.

Wooden Tinkertoy kits were introduced and competed with metal Erector Sets for the attention of the younger set. *Tarzan of the Apes*, by Edgar Rice Burroughs, was published, launching the popular series of novels, and subsequently films, that would capture the imagination of generations. Clarence Birdseye popularized the freezing of fish, and the public learned that when thawed, even months later, the fish tasted fresh.

What was later known as the Greyhound bus line began this year as the Mesabi Transportation Co. in Hibbing, Minnesota, when Carl Eric Wickman ran a Hupmobile vehicle on a regular schedule to nearby Alice to transport iron mine workers. The first red and green electric traffic light was installed in Cleveland. The Gulf Oil Co. distributed the first automobile road maps—a practice that quickly caught on with other gasoline purveyors when they realized that maps encouraged driving long distances. Motoring parties were all the rage, and across the country various groups would take scenic tours to destination hotels, most of which maintained garages and limited automobile repair facilities.

A bookplate featuring the characters of Edgar Rice Burroughs, designed for him by his nephew. Tarzan is holding the planet Mars.

Suffragists marched on the Capitol on June 28 and a representative presented Wilson with a petition for women's right to vote. The president was indifferent to their cause, and later during his administration suffragettes in the nation's capital would be jailed.

Suffragettes General Rosalie Jones, Jessie Stubbs, and Colonel Ida Craft pose with the American flag and advertisements for upcoming suffrage meetings.

In Alaska the city of Anchorage was established at the head of Cook Inlet to serve as headquarters of the 538-mile Alaska Railroad under construction. In August the Panama Canal opened its 50.7-mile waterway to shipping. This cut about 8,000 nautical miles of travel from the route around Cape Horn at the southern tip of South America. The cost, including both the money expended by the United States and that spent in earlier efforts by France, was over $500 million.

The 12 Federal Reserve Banks established in 1913 opened for business on November 16, 1914, and proved to be an effective system for monetary stability. Still, national banks and other institutions, while audited yearly, had little in the way of oversight when things went wrong, and when they failed, stockholders and depositors lost. The Federal Trade Commission was established by Congress.

The unemployment rate was at 7.9 percent as manufacturers and some others cut back in view of the uncertainty of the outcome of the war, which was worsening with every news account. On July 30 the decision was made to close down the New York Stock Exchange due to apprehension concerning the economy as the war spread in Europe. At the time the Dow Jones Industrial Average was at 71.42. The Exchange was reopened four and one half months later. The index closed on December 31 at 54.58, down from 78.78 at the end of 1913. For many, the economic outlook was dim.

THE NUMISMATIC SCENE. ANA president Duffield stated that it was about time to establish an official grading system, as the subject had been debated many times (this would not happen until the late 1970s!). He estimated that there were at least 5,000 active coin collectors in the United States and Canada, and another 5,000 who were interested in the subject but who were not active. Fewer than 700 of these 10,000 people were members of the ANA, he lamented.

A memorable event was the exhibition of United States coins held at the American Numismatic Society in New York City from January 17 through February 18, 1914. A beautiful catalog was prepared illustrating the rarest of the rare. Bauman L. Belden organized the exhibit. William H. Woodin, Charles C. Gregory, H.O. Granberg, Dr. George

AUCTION SALE OF THE WILLIAM F. GABLE COLLECTION, MAY 27, 28, AND 29, 1914.

From left to right: William B. Hale, Robert Gable, William Pukall, G. Kraft, Henry Chapman, B. Max Mehl, Dr. J. H. Cornell, W. W. Garrabrant, J. A. Clouser, unknown, Dr. R. M. Scott, Thomas L. Elder, Jas. A. Walker, Clarence S. Bement, Hillyer Ryder, Elmer S. Sears, (back of S. H. Chapman,) William L. Fisher, J. P. Hale Jenkins, Dr. H. W. Beckwith, E. H. Adams, Gus Egolf. In front, Robert L. Moore, and S. H. Chapman. (The photograph given was taken on May 29, and there were several other collectors present upon other days who were not there on the day the photograph was taken.)

Bidders and buyers at the Gable Collection sale as photographed on May 29, 1914.

P. French, Hillyer Ryder, Carl Wurtzbach, Judson Brenner, and Howard Newcomb were among those who loaned coins to the exhibition. Newcomb's offering consisted of a marvelous collection of mintmarked pieces.

In May 1914 S. Hudson Chapman auctioned the William F. Gable Collection for record prices. During this era there was a continuing parade of old-time collections being sold to those who were in the process of building their own holdings. The market was very strong.

The annual convention was held in Springfield, Massachusetts, and headquartered at the Hotel Kimball, which was said to be the only absolutely fireproof hotel in the city. Rooms with running water and free use of a bath (presumably located somewhere other than the room) were available for $1.50, while a suite for two persons cost $9 upward. The event opened on August 22 and ran for four days with 68 registered attendees. There were no nominations for new officers, and no ballots were mailed out. The incumbents remained in place.

The Year 1915

Current Events. The sluggish economy of 1914 shifted into high gear in 1915 as American factories supplied large quantities of munitions and other items to Britain and France. There were great debates as to whether the United States should enter the Great War as a combatant. President Wilson called for "preparedness." The war worsened, and at the second Battle of Ypres the Germans used poison gas. On May 7, 1915, the RMS *Lusitania*, with many American passengers aboard, was sunk by German U-boats with a loss of 1,198 lives. Many pacifists changed their views.

The brokerage firm of Merrill Lynch was formed when former semipro baseball player Charles Merrill joined Johns Hopkins graduate Edmund C. Lynch. In time the firm would become America's most famous brokerage house and would finance many projects. New Jersey, the most permissive state for regulating corporate charters, changed when many practices considered abusive were terminated. Delaware, seizing an opportunity, became the nation's leading center for charters, as it remains to this day.

The one millionth Ford automobile was manufactured, half a million having been manufactured in 1915 alone. Gil Anderson at the wheel of a Stutz set an automobile speed record at 102.6 miles per hour. The first long-distance rail service between San Francisco and New York City was established.

In San Francisco the Panama-Pacific International Exposition opened its gates to reveal a wonderland of attractions. Its twin themes were to celebrate the completion of the Panama Canal and the rebuilding of San Francisco after the earthquake and fire. In San Diego the Panama-California Exposition opened, but furnished little competition for San Francisco's affair. Rocky Mountain National Park was established, comprising 262,000 acres in Colorado with 107 peaks above 10,000 feet in elevation.

A souvenir postcard for the Panama-Pacific International Exposition in San Francisco.

D.W. Griffith adapted the novel *The Clansman* into a film spectacle, *The Birth of a Nation*, which became a sensation in theatres across the country. The film traced the genesis of the Ku Klux Klan—a hate group which targets African Americans and other minorities—and has been condemned as racist propaganda rationalizing violence against black communities by portraying black men as animalistic sexual predators. At a special preview held in Los Angeles, actors dressed in white Ku Klux Klan outfits were in the street outside, and at the official premiere in Atlanta, real Klansmen were present. Unfortunately, the Klan's attitudes were embraced by many Americans at the time, and efforts by the NAACP to elicit an official government condemnation of the film fell on deaf ears. In fact, projected as one of the subtitles on the screen was this quotation from *History of the American People*, written by the sitting president of the United States:

> The white men were roused by a mere instinct of self-preservation . . . until at last there had sprung into existence a great Ku Klux Klan, a veritable empire of the South, to protect the Southern country. —Woodrow Wilson.

The film set off a wave of enthusiasm for the KKK that resulted in dozens of new chapters being formed. The organization continued as a national force until the late 1920s, by which time it was generally recognized as not being patriotic, but being prejudicial. It still exists today.

Audrey Munson, by that time having modeled for several sculptors, including for a Panama-Pacific International Exposition medal, played a model who posed nude in the Thanhouser film *Inspiration*, the first non-pornographic depiction of female nudity in American film.

THE NUMISMATIC SCENE. In his monthly message in the January issue of *The Numismatist*, editor Edgar H. Adams called upon collectors to support the movement to improve the designs of United States coins. He also said that Sand Blast Proof gold coins, which were disliked by most collectors, should be replaced with mirrored fields that would necessitate a design modification. Interest in all Proof coins had been dropping sharply, and the production of sets was discontinued this year, except for minor coin sets with the cent and nickel in 1916. Proof sets would be offered again until 1936.

In the March issue of *The Numismatist* an article by Thomas L. Elder included this:

> I would strongly recommend also that all the numismatic societies interest themselves in a movement to improve the present United States silver coinage of the regular issues. These include the half dollar, quarter, and dime, a type adopted in 1892. The designs may be changed without act of Congress in 1917, when the 25 years of issue shall have elapsed. These coins are almost unparalleled in modern issues for ugliness, and they are in no way indicative of the power and progress of the United States, in fact they should be considered unacceptable to the smallest islands of the seas. In this movement art alliances and sculptor societies should lend their aid and influence . . .

In August Edgar H. Adams announced his resignation as editor of *The Numismatist*. Frank G. Duffield became his successor. Although members in attendance at the 1914 convention had discussed where the 1915 event should be held and voted overwhelmingly against the suggestion of San Francisco, in early 1915 the ANA Board of Governors ignored this. Attendees who arrived early took a tour of Golden Gate Park, the Cliff House, and other attractions on Sunday, August 29. The event opened on August 30 and lasted for three days. The Hotel Stewart served as headquarters. The gathering set a new low record for attendance of members, and it was reported that the entire body

contribute. Response was low, as most collectors did not want to reveal their holdings. George R. Ross continued his serial study of half cents, noting that from 1793 to 1857 he had identified 122 different varieties. Unrelated to Ross, *The United States Half Cents From the First Year of Issue, 1793, to the Year When Discontinued, 1857. All Dates and Varieties Described and Illustrated*, by Ebenezer Gilbert, was published by Thomas L. Elder. On May 16 Elder held the first of what would be many auction sales. He also issued medals condemning pacifists such as Henry Ford and William Jennings Bryan.

Much space in *The Numismatist* was devoted to the forthcoming new designs for silver coins. Mercury dimes were released in October and garnered wide favorable reviews. Although Standing Liberty quarters and Liberty Walking half dollars were struck late in this year they were not released until January 1917. The war in Europe had spawned the creation of many medals, mostly by Germans. From this time, and continuing for the next several years, these medals were a prime focus of *The Numismatist.*

In 1916 the San Francisco Mint continued to strike bronze, copper-nickel, and silver coinage for the Philippines, but the ongoing world war interfered with regular shipments to the islands. (In February 1918 the Philippine Legislature would appropriate money to begin constructing its own new mint facility in Manila, which would open in 1920.)

The San Francisco Mint struck 1,435,000 silver 20-centavo coins for the Philippines in 1916. (1.5x actual size)

San Francisco was revealed as being the only city in the United States where gold coins were seen more often than paper money in general commerce. "A silver dollar of 1794, the first standard dollar ever coined by the United States, was received at the United States Sub-Treasury Wednesday from a Louisville bank, and it was redeemed with a $1 Silver Certificate," per a notice in the Cincinnati *Times-Star*, April 20, 1916.

Beginning on September 23 the annual convention of the American Numismatic Association was held in Baltimore. It was reported that membership totaled 482. Members attending the show numbered 38. H.O. Granberg, the Wisconsin owner of a particularly large collection, was elected president for the coming year. In recent times the Philadelphia Mint had been indifferent to the interests of collectors desiring to order Proof coins, and because of this a special resolution was made and passed by the convention:

> Resolved, That this national organization respectfully petitions the Honorable Director of the U.S. Mints to order Proof specimens of all the authorized coins of the United States for the current and subsequent years to be struck according to precedent at the U.S. Mint at Philadelphia and placed on sale with the medal clerk as heretofore, at the usual premium, as has been the rule for upwards of 60 years.
>
> It is also requested that the coins for this year, 1916, of the design used from 1892 to 1915, and for which dies have been made, be ordered struck and put on sale as aforesaid, and should the dies be ready in 1916 of the contemplated new designs, that they, too, be struck in Proof and also placed on sale; continuing to the end of 1916 to have both sets on sale . . .

This did not happen, and Matte Proofs of the Lincoln cent and Buffalo nickel were the only special coins made in 1916, after which Proof coinage for collectors was entirely discontinued, not to resume until 1936.

Chapter Four

BARBER DIMES 1892–1916

THE DESIGN OF THE NEW DIME

The Barber-type dime minted from 1892 to 1916 features on the obverse Miss Liberty facing right, her hair in a Phrygian cap, and wearing a laurel wreath, with the word LIBERTY in tiny letters in a band above her forehead. This word is in the area of highest relief, with the result that it wore away quickly, as noted in chapter 2. The inscription UNITED STATES OF AMERICA surrounds, and the date is below.

The reverse was adapted by Charles E. Barber from James B. Longacre's cereal wreath design, which was used on the Liberty Seated dimes of 1860 to 1891. Close examination will reveal slight differences. The design features a large wreath enclosing ONE DIME. The original version of the wreath was conceived in 1859 "to allow perfect striking of the Seated Liberty obverse," as Mint Director James Ross Snowden wrote in a letter to Secretary of the Treasury Howell Cobb. Snowden called it "Newlin's wreath of cereals," perhaps suggesting that local numismatist Harold Newlin had suggested it.[1] Patterns of the cereal wreath were made by Chief Engraver James B. Longacre in 1859 for Liberty Seated dimes and half dimes and several varieties of half dollars, the last of which sported "French Liberty Head" obverses.

Pattern 1859 half dollar (Judd-241) cereal wreath reverse. The dies were only partially finished, with the result that there are countless tiny raised lines.

There was no room for the motto IN GOD WE TRUST on the coin, so it was omitted. The obverse design of the dime, with UNITED STATES OF AMERICA around the border, differs from that of the quarter and half dollar in that the latter denominations have stars around the obverse periphery. This difference is not generally known.

THE PATTERN DIME OF 1891

One pattern is known for the Barber dime. During the development process most pattern activity was directed to the half dollar. Dated 1891, the obverse very closely follows the adopted design of 1892. Differences are very minor and include some adjustments of the border letters and where the ribbon touches the left upright of the N of UNITED. The only existing example is in the National Numismatic Collection in the Smithsonian Institution.

Pattern 1891 dime (J-1760).

MINTAGES AND DISTRIBUTION

Barber dimes were first released into circulation in January 1892. Although Barber coins in general received many reviews in the popular press, the dime was never singled out as being the most worthy of criticism, nor was the quarter. That questionable honor belongs to the half dollar, as given in chapter 2.

Barber dimes were minted each year from 1892 to 1916, the quantities depending on the call for the denomination in circulation. Far more Barber dimes were minted than the number of Barber quarters and half dollars combined.

MINTAGES OF BARBER DIMES

Mintages of Barber dimes from highest to lowest, by issue, are as follows:

1907: 22,220,000
1902: 21,380,000
1906: 19,957,731
1913: 19,760,000
1899: 19,580,000
1903: 19,500,000
1912: 19,350,000
1911: 18,870,000
1901: 18,859,665
1916: 18,490,000
1900: 17,600,000
1914: 17,360,250
1898: 16,320,000
1904: 14,600,357
1905: 14,551,623
1892: 12,120,000
1914-D: 11,908,000
1912-D: 11,760,000
1910: 11,520,000
1911-D: 11,209,000
1897: 10,868,533
1908: 10,600,000
1909: 10,240,000
1903-O: 8,180,000
1908-D: 7,490.000
1905-S: 6,855,199
1916-S: 5,820,000
1915: 5,620,000
1901-O: 5,620,000
1900-S: 5,168,270
1907-O: 5,058,000
1902-O: 4,500,000
1907-D: 4,080,000
1906-D: 4,060,000
1892-O: 3,841,700
1911-S: 3,520,000
1910-D: 3,490,000
1912-S: 3,420,000
1905-O: 3,400,000
1893: 3,340,000
1908-S: 3,220,000
1907-S: 3,178,470
1906-S: 3,136,640
1899-O: 2,650,000
1906-O: 2,610,000
1893-S: 2,491,401
1909-O: 2,287,000
1898-O: 2,130,000
1914-S: 2,100,000
1902-S: 2,070,000
1900-O: 2,010,000
1896: 2,000,000
1899-S: 1,867,493
1908-O: 1,789,000
1893-O: 1,760,000
1898-S: 1,702,507
1897-S: 1,342,844
1894: 1,330,000
1910-S: 1,240,000
1895-S: 1,120,000
1909-S: 1,000,000
1892-S: 990,710
1915-S: 960,000
1909-D: 954,000
1894-O: 720,000
1895: 690,000
1897-O: 666,000
1903-S: 613,500
1896-O: 610,000
1901-S: 593,022
1896-S: 575,056
1913-S: 510,000
1895-O: 440,000
1894-S: 24

HUB CHANGES

In 1901 a new obverse hub die was introduced in the Barber dime series. The differences between the new and the old are very subtle and require magnification to detect. On the old, the ribbon touches the left upright of the N of UNITED, and a leaf tip is distant from the second S of STATES. On the new, the ribbon is clear of the N, and the leaf is very close to the S. This alteration seems to have lowered the relief slightly, almost imperceptibly, with the result that dimes with this obverse did not have the word LIBERTY wear away as quickly, perhaps adding a year, or two, or three, to the life of a dime before this happened.

In 1901 a new reverse hub die was introduced in the Barber dime series. The differences between the new and the old are very subtle. On the old, the right wreath ribbon is lighter than it is on the new.

Neither of the two hub changes has ever gained traction with numismatists as a variety.

Collecting Barber Dimes

Of the three Barber coin denominations, the dime is most widely collected today. That has been true for past years as well, dating back to the 1930s when Wayte Raymond's National coin albums and other coin albums were widely sold, and these made it convenient to store and display coins at the same time. Whitman folders entered the scene, were inexpensive, and did much to boost interest. Even though the Depression pervaded the country, the face value of a dime was not a deterrent to hobbyists. All Barber coins were available in circulation, dating back to 1892, but most were of 20th-century dates. The design of all three denominations is such that, even with only a modest amount of wear, most of LIBERTY on the obverse disappeared. Amazingly, by 1935 many Barber coins made only 20 years earlier had been worn down to G-4 condition, or even lower.

Today, to qualify as grade VG-8 some letters in LIBERTY must be visible. To merit the Fine-12 designation all letters need to be readable, although those in highest relief can be weak. By the 1930s, typical grades for dimes dated in the 1890s were Abt. Good (AG-3) to Good (G-4), and, for those dated in the early 20th century, Good. The only exceptions to the rule of well-worn Barber coins were the occasional pieces that had been set aside by choice or by chance in the early years. Today we have the situation that perhaps 90 percent of the Barber coins in collectors' hands are well worn. This is unique to the Barber coin series.

The 1894-S dime, of which just 24 were struck and only eight can be confirmed today, is non-collectible and can be put in this special category, just as Dr. William H. Sheldon did with early coppers in his *Early American Cents* book in 1949, designating them as NC. This point of philosophy enables you to ignore the 1894-S and have an otherwise complete collection of available issues. Alternatively, many collectors ignore the 1894-S because it was not a regular issue intended for general circulation.

Detail of Obverse Hub I on an 1892 dime. Note the shape of the leaf tip and its distance from the second S in STATES.

Detail of the same area of Obverse Hub II on a 1911 dime. Note the shape of the leaf tip and its closeness to the second S in STATES.

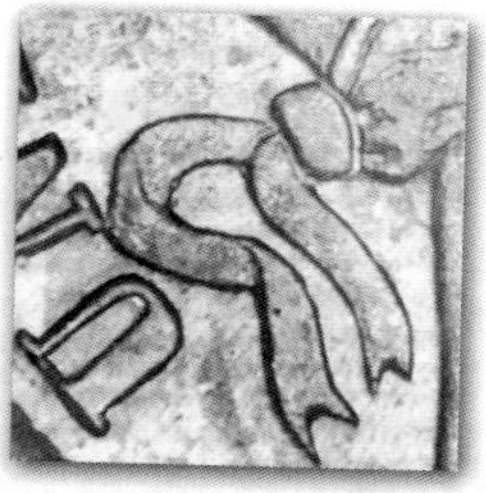

Another detail of Obverse Hub I, shown on an 1897 dime. The ribbon touches the left upright of the N of UNITED.

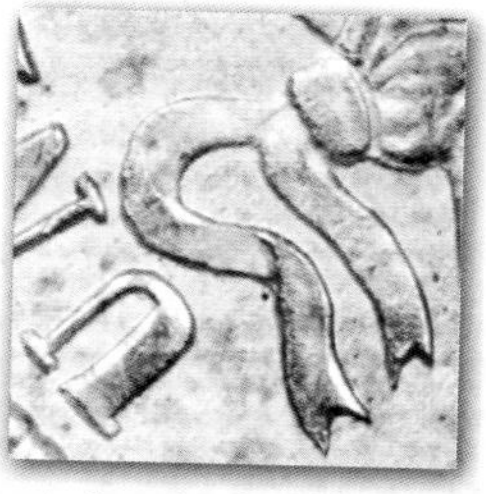

A detail of the same area on Obverse Hub II, this on a 1913 dime. The ribbon is clear of the left upright of the N of UNITED.

Detail of Reverse Hub I on an 1897-O dime. The right wreath ribbon is light.

Detail of Hub Reverse Hub II on a 1913 dime. The right wreath ribbon is heavier than on the earlier type.

In the grades of AG-3 and G-4, the most elusive issues are those that combine the two factors of low mintages and early dates, this category representing most of the mint-marked issues of the 1890s, as well as the 1895 Philadelphia issue. For Mint State coins the same rules for rarity can be applied in general, except that for coins having the same mintage range, San Francisco and New Orleans pieces in Mint State range are generally harder to find. More than those from other mints, New Orleans dimes sometimes show weak striking. Remarkably, there is no record of any cache or hoard yielding a significant number of Mint State dimes.

The Complete Guide to Barber Dimes, by David Lawrence, is *the* key reference and is recommended as a comprehensive source. Kevin Flynn's *Authoritative Reference on Barber Dimes* features many close-up illustrations of repunched dates and mintmarks, along with other information.

PRICES IN 1946

The first edition of *A Guide Book of United States Coins* was issued in 1946 with a cover date of 1947. The most expensive Barber dime was the 1894-S priced at $2,000 in Uncirculated grade. In Fine grade, the cheapest price for a common variety was 50¢, and for Uncirculated, $2.00. Most Proofs were $4.00 each.

Ranked in descending order the top 20 Uncirculated prices in the series from the 1946 *Guide Book* are given below. These prices can be compared to Barber dime values today. In modern times pricing is influenced by much more information from population reports and studies by specialists.

The Top 20 Barber Dime Prices in 1946

1. 1894-S: $2,000	6. 1895-S: $17.50	11. 1897-S: $12.50	16. 1903-S: $12.50
2. 1895-O: $30.00	7. 1913-S: $16.00	12. 1899-O: $12.50	17. 1904-S: $12.50
3. 1901-S: $27.50	8. 1902-S: $15.00	13. 1899-S: $12.50	18. 1894-O: $9.00
4. 1896-S: $18.50	9. 1898-O: $13.50	14. 1900-O: $12.50	19. 1893-S: $8.50
5. 1897-O: $20.00	10. 1892-S: $12.50	15. 1900-S: $12.50	20. 1901-O: $8.50

DIE VARIETIES AMONG BARBER DIMES

The 1905-O Micro o is the major die variety in the Barber dime series and is easily collectible. Beyond that, there are many repunched date varieties from 1892 through 1908, and across the entire series minor variations in mintmark placement and orientation can be found.

A number of misplaced dates (MPDs) are found in the form of traces of date numerals hidden in the denticles. These are believed to have been caused when the workman about to enter the date logotype touched it lightly on the edge of the die to evaluate the hardness of the metal.

ASPECTS OF STRIKING

Circulation-strike Barber dimes were struck at high speed on knuckle-action presses with no thought given to making their appearance ideal for collectors. A typical die would last for 200,000 to 300,000 impressions. Earlier strikings from such dies tended to be sharper, and the fields, more lustrous. Some early strikes were highly prooflike, the famous 1894-S dime being an example. It is popular for certification services to label some of these as "branch-mint Proofs," although no records have been found of any special ceremonies or striking events for mirrorlike coins.

In the early years of the series few numismatists were interested in circulation strikes at all. Collecting Proofs satisfied the need to get one dime of each date. After Augustus G. Heaton's *Mint Marks* was published in 1893, interest in branch-mint coins rose. Collectors accepted examples of whatever striking quality or sharpness came to hand. There is no record of weakly struck coins causing any complaints. A later generation of collectors, with David Lawrence and his books taking the lead, began to pay attention to such features. Now we know that in the Barber dime series the New Orleans issues are often weakly struck in areas, while the San Francisco issues are usually quite sharp, the weakly struck 1909-S being a notable exception. Philadelphia coins are usually quite sharp. Unlike the quarter and half dollar, in which series many circulation strikes from all mints have weakness on the right side of the reverse, the dime, with its traditional cereal-wreath style dating from the 1860s, there is no consistent problem point.

Proof Barber Dimes

Proofs were struck of each year from 1892 to 1915, inclusive, for the numismatic trade. None were made in 1916. Proofs of 1901 to 1904 typically have lightly polished portraits in the die and are not "cameo" or deeply frosted like the Proofs of other years. The popularity of Proofs with collectors declined over a long period, with the result that the last two years, 1914 and 1915, have the lowest mintages.

Apart from collector apathy, a reason for this is that Lincoln cents, first minted in 1909, were struck with matte rather than mirror Proof surfaces. Matte Proofs were not popular with collectors, and this disaffection extended to other series as well. By 1913 and 1914 Proofs of the Lincoln cent, the Buffalo nickel, and all of the gold coins were issued with matte surfaces, leaving just the three silver coins—the Barber dime, quarter, and half dollar—with the traditional mirror fields. Mintage figures and collector interest plummeted. Today, Matte Proofs are highly desired and are very expensive. However, in their own era they were shunned by many.

It is not generally known that the majority of Proof denominations of the 1901 to 1904 years have Miss Liberty's head slightly polished *in the die.* This is in contrast to the cameo or frost seen on most other issues. In any case, a set of 24 Proof Barber dimes makes an attractive display. A gallery of Proof Barber dimes can be found on page 167.

Grading Barber Dimes

1897-O. Graded MS-65.

MS-60 to 70 (Mint State). ***Obverse:*** At MS-60, some abrasion and contact marks are evident, most noticeably on the cheek and the obverse field to the right. Luster is present, but may be dull or lifeless. Many Barber coins have been cleaned, especially those of the earlier dates. At MS-63, contact marks are very few; abrasion still is evident, but less than at lower levels. An MS-65 coin may have minor abrasion on the cheek, but contact marks are so minute as to require magnification. Luster should be full and rich. ***Reverse:*** Comments apply as for the obverse, except that in lower–Mint State grades abrasion and contact marks are most noticeable on the highest parts of the leaves and the ribbon, though less so on ONE DIME. At MS-65 or higher, there are no marks visible to the unaided eye. The field is mainly protected by design elements and does not show abrasion as much as does the obverse on a given coin.

Illustrated coin: This is a lustrous coin, with scattered areas of toning.

1907-S. Graded AU-50.

AU-50, 53, 55, 58 (About Uncirculated). ***Obverse:*** Light wear is seen on the head, especially on the forward hair under LIBERTY. At AU-58, the luster is extensive, but incomplete, especially on the higher parts and in the right field. At AU-50 and 53, luster is less. ***Reverse:*** Wear is seen on the leaves and ribbon. An AU-58 coin will have nearly full luster, more so than on the obverse, as the design elements protect the small field areas. At AU-50 and 53, there still is significant luster.

1895-O. Graded EF-40.

EF-40, 45 (Extremely Fine). ***Obverse:*** Further wear is seen on the head. The hair above the forehead lacks most detail. LIBERTY shows wear but still is strong. ***Reverse:*** Further wear is seen on all areas, most noticeably at the wreath and ribbon. Leaves retain excellent details except on the higher areas.

1914-S. Graded VF-30.

VF-20, 30 (Very Fine). ***Obverse:*** The head shows more wear, now with nearly all detail gone in the hair above the forehead. LIBERTY shows wear, but is complete. The leaves on the head all show wear, as does the upper part of the cap. ***Reverse:*** Wear is more extensive. The details in the highest leaves are weak or missing, but in lower levels the leaf details remain strong.

1901-S. Graded F-12.

F-12, 15 (Fine). ***Obverse:*** The head shows extensive wear. LIBERTY, the key place to check, is weak, especially at ER, but is fully readable. The ANA grading standards and *Photograde* adhere to this. PCGS suggests that lightly struck coins "may have letters partially missing." Traditionally, collectors insist on a full LIBERTY. ***Reverse:*** Much detail of the leaves in the higher areas is gone. The rim remains bold.

Illustrated coin: LIBERTY is readable, but letters ER are light.

1895-O. Graded VG-8.

VG-8, 10 (Very Good). ***Obverse:*** A net of three letters in LIBERTY must be readable. Traditionally LI is clear, and after that there is a partial letter or two. ***Reverse:*** Further wear has made the wreath flat; now only in outline form with only a few traces of details. The rim is complete.

1892-S. Graded G-4.

G-4, 6 (Good). ***Obverse:*** The head is in outline form, with the center flat. Most of the rim is there. All letters and the date are full. ***Reverse:*** The leaves are all combined and in outline form. The rim is weak in areas.

1908-S. Graded AG-3.

AG-3 (About Good). ***Obverse:*** The lettering is readable, but the parts near the border may be worn away. The date is clear. ***Reverse:*** The wreath and interior letters are partially worn away. The rim is weak.

1911. Graded PF-67 Deep Cameo.

PF–60 to 70 (Proof). ***Obverse and Reverse:*** Proofs that are extensively cleaned and have many hairlines, or that are dull and grainy, are lower level, such as PF–60 to 62. These are not widely desired, save for the rare (in any grade) year of 1895, and even so most collectors would rather have a lustrous MS-60 than a dull PF-60. With medium hairlines and good reflectivity, an assigned grade of PF-64 is indicated. Tiny horizontal lines on Miss Liberty's cheek, known as *slide marks*, from National and other album slides scuffing the relief of the cheek, are endemic among Barber silver coins. With noticeable marks of this type, the highest grade assignable is PF-64. With relatively few hairlines, a rating of PF-65 can be given. PF-66 should have hairlines so delicate that magnification is needed to see them. Above that, a Proof should be free of any hairlines or other problems.

Illustrated coin: Proof dimes of 1911 are rare (only 543 minted), but one with a Deep Cameo finish, as displayed by this coin, is *extremely* rare. The coin is fully struck on both sides, and has neither a blemish nor a trace of toning.

Being a Smart Buyer

As most Barber dimes are well struck, finding choice examples is easier than it is for the quarters and half dollars. Points to check on the dime are the high parts of the hair and leaves on the obverse and the wreath leaves on the reverse. When weakly struck coins are found, most likely they are New Orleans Mint issues. That mint spaced the dies slightly farther apart than the other mints did.

Among grades from AG-3 to VG-8, avoid those with marks or digs. Occasionally one is seen with an arc or circle on the center of the obverse, the result of a mechanical coin dispensing device used on trolley cars and elsewhere. The typical color of a well-circulated Barber dime is light gray. Coins that have been cleaned by dipping (not by an abrasive process) can generally acquire natural toning over a period of time.

For Mint State and Proof coins seek pieces that are sharply struck and have excellent eye appeal. A pleasing PF-63 is more desirable to own than a dark or stained MS-65. Some coins that were stored for a long time in Wayte Raymond's National holders have pleasing, light, iridescent toning around the borders caused by sulphur in the folders interacting with the coin. Most coins with intense rainbow toning are artificially colored.

1892 DIME

Circulation-strike mintage: 12,120,000
Proof mintage: 1,245

AVAILABILITY IN MINT STATE: Easy to find due to a combination of the novelty of the first year of issue and a very high mintage. Such a coin is an ideal candidate for a type set. Thousands exist. ***Estimated number MS-65 or higher:*** 600 to 750.

AVAILABILITY IN CIRCULATED GRADES: 60,000 to 80,000. Most are AG-3 or G-4.

CHARACTERISTICS OF STRIKING: Usually well struck.

AVAILABILITY IN PROOF FORMAT: ***Proof–60 to 64:*** 600 to 800. ***Proof-65 or better:*** 100 to 120.

This is by far the record Proof mintage for the type. Many were sold to the general public who did not handle them carefully. Gems are rare in proportion to the mintage.

NOTES: Some of these were rolled out as souvenirs at the World's Columbian Exposition.

MARKET VALUES – CIRCULATION STRIKES

G-4	VG-8	F-12	VF-20	EF-40	AU-50
$7	$7.50	$18	$25	$30	$80

MS-60	MS-62	MS-63	MS-64	MS-65
$135	$175	$240	$375	$650

MARKET VALUES – PROOF STRIKES

PF-60	PF-63	PF-64	PF-65	PF-65Cam	PF-66	PF-66Cam	PF-67
$275	$575	$925	$1,500	$1,700	$2,000	$2,250	$3,500

CERTIFIED POPULATIONS – CIRCULATION STRIKES

Fair	AG	G	VG	F	VF	EF	AU	MS-60
0	0	2	1	1	8	12	147	5

MS-61	MS-62	MS-63	MS-64	MS-65	MS-66	MS-67	MS-68	MS-69	MS-70
74	191	260	342	139	68	23	0	0	0

CERTIFIED POPULATIONS – PROOF STRIKES

PF-50	PF-60	PF-61	PF-62	PF-63	PF-64
0	0	10	15	40	79
PF-65	**PF-66**	**PF-67**	**PF-68**	**PF-69**	**PF-70**
58	57	34	0	0	0

1892-O Dime

Circulation-strike mintage: 3,841,700

Availability in Mint State: The public did save these as novelties as the first year of issue, and probably well over 1,000 coins survive at levels from MS–60 to 64. Probably as a combination of being jostled during the distribution process and careless handling later, most are at lower levels. David Lawrence considered this to be very common across lower–Mint State ranges. In view of the rarity of MS-65 coins, this suggests that MS–63 and 64 coins are a good option. ***Estimated number MS-65 or higher:*** 75 to 90.

Availability in circulated grades: 15,000 to 18,000. Most are AG-3 or G-4.

Characteristics of striking: Usually well struck.

Notes: Some of these were rolled out as souvenirs at the World's Columbian Exposition. Such coins are fairly scarce. The vast majority of such coins are cents, in particular, and nickels. Most rolled-out dimes are Philadelphia issues. Those from other mints are rarities.

An 1892-O rolled out at the World's Columbian Exposition.

MARKET VALUES – CIRCULATION STRIKES

G-4	VG-8	F-12	VF-20	EF-40	AU-50
$12	$15	$35	$50	$75	$95

MS-60	MS-62	MS-63	MS-64	MS-65
$175	$225	$300	$500	$1,250

CERTIFIED POPULATIONS – CIRCULATION STRIKES

Fair	AG	G	VG	F	VF	EF	AU	MS-60
0	0	2	2	5	5	5	39	2

MS-61	MS-62	MS-63	MS-64	MS-65	MS-66	MS-67	MS-68	MS-69	MS-70
20	28	38	68	14	7	2	0	0	0

1892-S DIME

Circulation-strike mintage: 990,710

AVAILABILITY IN MINT STATE: Not many were saved as the first year of issue. In 1991 David Lawrence estimated a range of 76 to 200 coins known in grades from MS-60 upward. There may be a few more than that, based on later studies, but the 1892-S still remains hard to find. ***Estimated number MS-65 or higher:*** 50 to 60.

AVAILABILITY IN CIRCULATED GRADES: 3,000 to 4,000. Most are AG-3 or G-4. David Lawrence stated that this is one of the 12 scarcest Barber dimes in grades G-4 to VG-8, and also that this is one of the 11 scarcest Barber dimes in grades F-12 to VF-35.

CHARACTERISTICS OF STRIKING: Usually well struck.

VARIETIES: There is a large S mintmark, apparently from the same punch used to create the 1892-S silver dollar (per Walter Breen). This general style continues through the year 1898.

The so-called "thin date" examples result from the date logotype being punched lightly into the die. Although Walter Breen describes this variety as "rare," for most collectors it falls into the "who cares?" category; thus, there is little premium attached should you find one.

Varieties of the 1892-S exist with double-punched mintmark.

One variety has a chip out of the die, causing a "cut" to connect the top of the 2 to the neck truncation above.

Notes: Some of these were rolled out as souvenirs at the World's Columbian Exposition.

MARKET VALUES – CIRCULATION STRIKES

G-4	VG-8	F-12	VF-20	EF-40	AU-50
$65	$120	$190	$240	$280	$330

MS-60	MS-62	MS-63	MS-64	MS-65
$425	$600	$775	$1,500	$3,500

CERTIFIED POPULATIONS – CIRCULATION STRIKES

Fair	AG	G	VG	F	VF	EF	AU	MS-60
2	4	11	2	5	6	6	23	0

MS-61	MS-62	MS-63	MS-64	MS-65	MS-66	MS-67	MS-68	MS-69	MS-70
4	22	9	50	3	2	0	0	0	0

1893 Dime

Circulation-strike mintage: 3,340,000
Proof mintage: 792

Availability in Mint State: Common in grades from MS–60 to 63, less so in 64. As a general rule, but excepting 1894 and 1895, Philadelphia Mint Barber dimes are very easy to find at lower–Mint State levels. ***Estimated number MS-65 or higher:*** 200 to 240.

Availability in circulated grades: 12,000 to 15,000. Most are AG-3 or G-4.

Characteristics of striking: Usually well struck.

Availability in Proof format: ***Proof–60 to 64:*** 280 to 330. ***Proof-65 or better:*** 65 to 80.

MARKET VALUES – CIRCULATION STRIKES

G-4	VG-8	F-12	VF-20	EF-40	AU-50
$8	$12	$20	$30	$45	$75

MS-60	MS-62	MS-63	MS-64	MS-65
$150	$200	$250	$350	$950

MARKET VALUES – PROOF STRIKES

PF-60	PF-63	PF-64	PF-65	PF-65Cam	PF-66	PF-66Cam	PF-67
$275	$575	$925	$1,500	$1,700	$2,000	$2,250	$3,500

CERTIFIED POPULATIONS – CIRCULATION STRIKES

Fair	AG	G	VG	F	VF	EF	AU	MS-60
1	1	9	0	1	4	2	32	1

MS-61	MS-62	MS-63	MS-64	MS-65	MS-66	MS-67	MS-68	MS-69	MS-70
11	43	53	58	47	18	5	0	0	0

CERTIFIED POPULATIONS – PROOF STRIKES

PF-50	PF-60	PF-61	PF-62	PF-63	PF-64
1	1	1	13	32	52
PF-65	**PF-66**	**PF-67**	**PF-68**	**PF-69**	**PF-70**
59	60	35	14	1	0

VARIETIES: ***So-called "1893, 3 Over 2" dime:*** At one time, as in the 1988 reference *Walter Breen's Complete Encyclopedia of U.S. and Colonial Coins*, the field embraced the idea of an 1893, 3 Over 2, dime. Although close examination shows a raised area in the lower part of the 3, it is not considered to be an overdate by modern experts. John Dannreuther, the well-known expert on die varieties, reported: "I overlaid these a few years ago. It is an 1893/1893 as the diagonal of the 3 lines up perfectly. The first punching was down to the right, so the other digits are pretty well aligned."[2] This variety was purported to have been discovered by Walter Breen in February 1960, and was first publicized in *Coin World*, March 16, 1961. The same researcher noted that at least four dies were overdated, three for "business strikes" (his term for circulation strikes) and one for Proofs. The supposed variety caught on, and many were listed in auction catalogs, certified, and otherwise offered to the collecting public.

MARKET VALUES – CIRCULATION STRIKES

G-4	VG-8	F-12	VF-20	EF-40	AU-50
$140	$150	$160	$175	$200	$300

MS-60	MS-62	MS-63	MS-64	MS-65
$700	$1,200	$1,800	$3,000	$5,500

1893-O Dime

Circulation-strike mintage: 1,760,000

Availability in Mint State: In Mint State this is another rarity from the 19th century. Covering a wider range of Uncirculated grades, this issue is still slightly scarce in lower–Mint State grades. Hand-selected MS–63 and 64 coins offer a good value. ***Estimated number MS-65 or higher:*** 60 to 70.

Availability in circulated grades: 5,000 to 6,000. Most are AG-3 or G-4. David Lawrence stated that this is one of the 12 scarcest Barber dimes in grades of G-4 to VG-8.

Characteristics of striking: Often occurs with areas of light striking, including the hair above the forehead. Patiently hunt for quality.

Notes: David Lawrence mentions that a hoard was assembled by a Western dealer-collector; I know nothing more than this.

MARKET VALUES – CIRCULATION STRIKES

G-4	VG-8	F-12	VF-20	EF-40	AU-50
$30	$45	$120	$150	$190	$230

MS-60	MS-62	MS-63	MS-64	MS-65
$325	$450	$650	$1,250	$2,250

CERTIFIED POPULATIONS – CIRCULATION STRIKES

Fair	AG	G	VG	F	VF	EF	AU	MS-60
0	2	4	5	4	14	10	17	1

MS-61	MS-62	MS-63	MS-64	MS-65	MS-66	MS-67	MS-68	MS-69	MS-70
5	18	24	44	10	5	3	0	0	0

1893-S DIME

Circulation-strike mintage: 2,491,401

AVAILABILITY IN MINT STATE: Covering a wider range of Uncirculated grades, this issue is still slightly scarce in lower–Mint State grades. MS-63 to MS-64 coins offer a collecting option at less cost than MS-65 prices. ***Estimated number MS-65 or higher:*** 55 to 65.

AVAILABILITY IN CIRCULATED GRADES: 7,000 to 9,000. Most are AG-3 or G-4.

CHARACTERISTICS OF STRIKING: Usually well struck.

MARKET VALUES – CIRCULATION STRIKES

G-4	VG-8	F-12	VF-20	EF-40	AU-50
$15	$25	$37	$60	$85	$150

MS-60	MS-62	MS-63	MS-64	MS-65
$290	$425	$700	$1,500	$3,000

CERTIFIED POPULATIONS – CIRCULATION STRIKES

Fair	AG	G	VG	F	VF	EF	AU	MS-60
0	1	7	4	4	4	10	24	1

MS-61	MS-62	MS-63	MS-64	MS-65	MS-66	MS-67	MS-68	MS-69	MS-70
8	21	20	28	17	1	0	0	0	0

VARIETIES: ***1893-S, Repunched Mintmark (Fivaz-Stanton–501):*** This variety displays a very strong repunched mintmark to the right. As a caveat, many of this variety also exhibit strike doubling to the left, but this is a *doubled* mintmark, not tripled. At least several hundred exist in various grades.

1893-S, Large S Over Small S: In *The Numismatic Scrapbook Magazine*, May 1938, Chuck Franzen, a Montana collector, reported owning an 1893-S dime with a large S over a small s. Not listed in any modern texts seen.

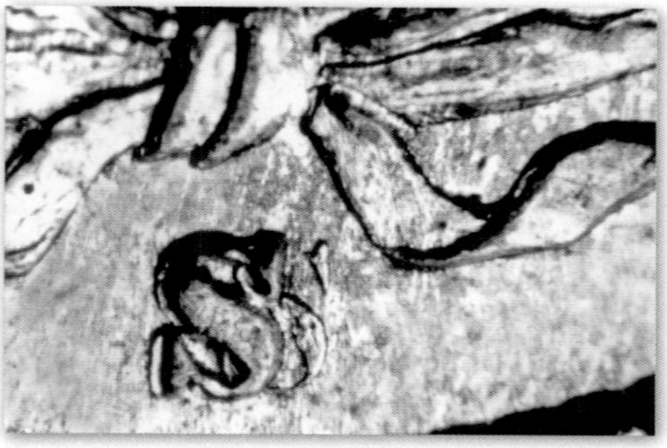

Detail of 1893-S, Repunched Mintmark (Fivaz-Stanton–501).

So-called "1893-S, 3-S Over 2-S" dime: *Walter Breen's Complete Encyclopedia of U.S. and Colonial Coins*, 1988, lists this as his number 3485, called there "extremely rare," with the citation being the sale of a VF piece in the 1977 ANA auction, lot 624, which realized $250. This variety has been dismissed by modern experts.

1894 Dime

Circulation-strike mintage: 1,330,000
Proof mintage: 972

Availability in Mint State: This issue is quite scarce in the context of Philadelphia Mint Barber dimes. The population is probably in the mid-hundreds. ***Estimated number MS-65 or higher:*** 80 to 95. A key issue at this level.

Availability in circulated grades: 4,000 to 5,000. Most are AG-3 or G-4. Considered to be a scarcer date among Philadelphia dimes despite the high mintage.

Characteristics of striking: Usually well struck.

Availability in Proof format: ***Proof–60 to 64:*** 450 to 600. ***Proof-65 or better:*** 125 to 150.

Notes: One variety has a sharply repunched date, with the original figures being slightly lower than the final ones.

MARKET VALUES – CIRCULATION STRIKES

G-4	VG-8	F-12	VF-20	EF-40	AU-50
$30	$45	$120	$160	$180	$220

MS-60	MS-62	MS-63	MS-64	MS-65
$325	$400	$500	$700	$1,200

MARKET VALUES – PROOF STRIKES

PF-60	PF-63	PF-64	PF-65	PF-65Cam	PF-66	PF-66Cam	PF-67
$275	$575	$925	$1,500	$1,700	$2,000	$2,250	$3,500

CERTIFIED POPULATIONS – CIRCULATION STRIKES

Fair	AG	G	VG	F	VF	EF	AU	MS-60
1	7	15	4	6	4	10	28	1

MS-61	MS-62	MS-63	MS-64	MS-65	MS-66	MS-67	MS-68	MS-69	MS-70
4	22	24	35	26	12	4	0	0	0

CERTIFIED POPULATIONS – PROOF STRIKES

PF-50	PF-60	PF-61	PF-62	PF-63	PF-64
0	1	5	6	30	101
PF-65	**PF-66**	**PF-67**	**PF-68**	**PF-69**	**PF-70**
64	64	37	11	0	0

1894-O DIME

Circulation-strike mintage: 720,000

AVAILABILITY IN MINT STATE: David Lawrence stated that this is one of the handful of top rarities among Barber dimes in grades MS–60 to 64. At *any* Mint State level an 1894-O is a prize. ***Estimated number MS-65 or higher:*** 25 to 30. A gem 1894-O is a landmark coin.

AVAILABILITY IN CIRCULATED GRADES: 2,000 to 2,500. Examples are scarce and in strong demand. David Lawrence stated that this is one of the 11 scarcest Barber dimes in grades F-12 to VF-35 and that it is among the dozen scarcest Barber dimes in grades EF-40 to AU-58.

CHARACTERISTICS OF STRIKING: Usually well struck.

NOTES: The 1894-O is elusive in all high grades, particularly in Mint State, but as the number of buyers of Barber dimes by date and Mint is relatively small, little fame or publicity has been attached to the issue.

MARKET VALUES – CIRCULATION STRIKES

G-4	VG-8	F-12	VF-20	EF-40	AU-50
$70	$95	$200	$275	$425	$600

MS-60	MS-62	MS-63	MS-64	MS-65
$1,450	$2,000	$2,500	$5,500	$12,500

CERTIFIED POPULATIONS – CIRCULATION STRIKES

Fair	AG	G	VG	F	VF	EF	AU	MS-60
0	8	26	14	11	12	13	17	0

MS-61	MS-62	MS-63	MS-64	MS-65	MS-66	MS-67	MS-68	MS-69	MS-70
2	3	12	4	1	0	1	0	0	0

1894-S Dime

Circulation-strike mintage: 24

Availability in Mint State: Of the 8 known, all but two are Mint State. ***Estimated number MS-65 or higher:*** 6

Availability in circulated grades: Two known, both well worn.

Characteristics of striking: Very sharp.

Availability in Proof format: None were struck in this format, but most high-grade coins are prooflike. Some have been cataloged and certified as Proofs based on their appearance.

Notes: The entire mintage of the 1894-S dime consists of just 24 coins struck June 9, 1894, to balance an account.

Of the 24 1894-S dimes struck, only eight can be traced today. Six are in varying levels of Mint State, typically with prooflike surfaces, and the remaining two are well worn. For a long time the 1894-S dime has been the most famous rarity in the entire Barber silver series. In October 2007, an example graded PF-64 sold at auction for $1,552,500. Certification services typically grade this issue using Proof grades, despite the fact that it is a circulation strike. See appendix II for "The Story of the 1894-S Dime."

MARKET VALUES

PF-63
$1,500,000

CERTIFIED POPULATIONS

PF-50	PF-60	PF-61	PF-62	PF-63	PF-64
0	0	0	1	1	0

PF-65	PF-66	PF-67	PF-68	PF-69	PF-70
2	2	0	0	0	0

1895 DIME

Circulation-strike mintage: 690,000
Proof mintage: 880

AVAILABILITY IN MINT STATE: Though this issue exists in a wider range of grades, David Lawrence estimated that fewer than 500 coins are known in grades from MS-60 to 64. In all grades, this is the most elusive Philadelphia Mint Barber dime. ***Estimated number MS-65 or higher:*** 70 to 85. The 1895 is the key date among Philadelphia Mint Barber dimes.

AVAILABILITY IN CIRCULATED GRADES: 2,000 to 2,500. Most are AG-3 or G-4. The low mintage made this a date to look for in the 1930s when many were still in circulation. David Lawrence stated that this is one of the 12 scarcest Barber dimes in grades of G-4 to VG-8, is one of the 11 scarcest Barber dimes in grades F-12 to VF-35, and is among the dozen scarcest Barber dimes in grades EF-40 to AU-58. In other words, in *any* grade this is a key issue.

CHARACTERISTICS OF STRIKING: Usually well struck.

AVAILABILITY IN PROOF FORMAT: ***Proof-60 to 64:*** 400 to 500. ***Proof-65 or better:*** 95 to 115. Proofs are sometimes seen with irregular rough areas on the neck.

MARKET VALUES – CIRCULATION STRIKES

G-4	VG-8	F-12	VF-20	EF-40	AU-50
$80	$160	$325	$475	$550	$625

MS-60	MS-62	MS-63	MS-64	MS-65
$725	$850	$1,000	$1,750	$2,500

MARKET VALUES – PROOF STRIKES

PF-60	PF-63	PF-64	PF-65	PF-65Cam	PF-66	PF-66Cam	PF-67
$275	$575	$925	$1,600	$1,800	$2,250	$2,500	$3,750

CERTIFIED POPULATIONS – CIRCULATION STRIKES

Fair	AG	G	VG	F	VF	EF	AU	MS-60
2	2	24	5	8	16	7	20	1

MS-61	MS-62	MS-63	MS-64	MS-65	MS-66	MS-67	MS-68	MS-69	MS-70
6	10	18	34	10	1	1	1	0	0

CERTIFIED POPULATIONS – PROOF STRIKES

PF-50	PF-60	PF-61	PF-62	PF-63	PF-64
0	0	7	8	32	92
PF-65	**PF-66**	**PF-67**	**PF-68**	**PF-69**	**PF-70**
66	55	43	14	0	0

1895-O Dime

Circulation-strike mintage: 440,000

Availability in Mint State: David Lawrence stated that this is one of the four top rarities among Barber dimes in grades MS-60 or higher. Even an MS-60 coin is notable. ***Estimated number MS-65 or higher:*** 15 to 18. The 1895-O is far and away the rarest Barber dime at the gem level, except for the 1894-S. Very few gems have appeared in even the finest collections.

Availability in circulated grades: 1,000 to 1,200. Most are AG-3 or G-4. David Lawrence stated that this is one of the 12 scarcest Barber dimes in grades of G-4 to VG-8, is one of the 11 scarcest Barber dimes in grades F-12 to VF-35, and that this is one of the two rarest Barber dimes in grades EF-40 to AU-58.

Characteristics of striking: Variable, but usually quite sharp.

Notes: This is the key issue to the series, excepting the 1894-S. Examples are highly desired in all grades.

MARKET VALUES – CIRCULATION STRIKES

G-4	VG-8	F-12	VF-20	EF-40	AU-50
$375	$550	$850	$1,250	$2,400	$3,400

MS-60	MS-62	MS-63	MS-64	MS-65
$6,000	$7,000	$10,000	$15,000	$25,000

CERTIFIED POPULATIONS – CIRCULATION STRIKES

Fair	AG	G	VG	F	VF	EF	AU	MS-60
11	38	72	29	13	35	20	17	0

MS-61	MS-62	MS-63	MS-64	MS-65	MS-66	MS-67	MS-68	MS-69	MS-70
1	5	5	9	6	1	0	0	0	0

VARIETIES: Several minor die variations exist. On some the O mintmark is quite weak from the die having been partially filled with grease or grime.

1895-S DIME

Circulation-strike mintage: 1,120,000

AVAILABILITY IN MINT STATE: All Mint State coins are elusive. David Lawrence estimated a range of 76 to 200 coins are known in grades from MS-60 upward. MS–63 and 64 coins offer a viable alternative to MS-65 for careful buyers. ***Estimated number MS-65 or higher:*** 27 to 32. Very few exist in this rarefied category.

AVAILABILITY IN CIRCULATED GRADES: 3,000 to 3,500. Most are AG-3 or G-4. This issue is scarce and desirable. David Lawrence stated that this is one of the 12 scarcest Barber dimes in grades of G-4 to VG-8. Fine to AU coins are even more elusive.

CHARACTERISTICS OF STRIKING: Usually very sharp.

MARKET VALUES – CIRCULATION STRIKES

G-4	VG-8	F-12	VF-20	EF-40	AU-50
$42	$60	$135	$190	$240	$310

MS-60	MS-62	MS-63	MS-64	MS-65
$500	$700	$1,100	$2,000	$6,000

CERTIFIED POPULATIONS – CIRCULATION STRIKES

Fair	AG	G	VG	F	VF	EF	AU	MS-60
0	3	25	6	7	11	4	33	3

MS-61	MS-62	MS-63	MS-64	MS-65	MS-66	MS-67	MS-68	MS-69	MS-70
8	27	26	50	4	2	0	0	0	0

VARIETIES: Several varieties exist, the most notable possibly being with the last two date digits repunched and with the S doubled. However, little premium is attached to this variety despite its rarity.

1896 DIME

Circulation-strike mintage: 2,000,000
Proof mintage: 762

AVAILABILITY IN MINT STATE: Considering all Barber dimes in Mint State levels from MS-60 upward, the 1896 is among the easiest of the early dates to find. ***Estimated number MS-65 or higher:*** 75 to 95.

AVAILABILITY IN CIRCULATED GRADES: 7,000 to 9,000. Most are AG-3 or G-4.

CHARACTERISTICS OF STRIKING: Usually well struck.

AVAILABILITY IN PROOF FORMAT: ***Proof–60 to 64:*** 375 to 525. ***Proof-65 or better:*** 85 to 100.

MARKET VALUES – CIRCULATION STRIKES

G-4	VG-8	F-12	VF-20	EF-40	AU-50
$10	$22	$50	$75	$100	$120

MS-60	MS-62	MS-63	MS-64	MS-65
$175	$300	$500	$650	$1,150

MARKET VALUES – PROOF STRIKES

PF-60	PF-63	PF-64	PF-65	PF-65Cam	PF-66	PF-66Cam	PF-67
$275	$575	$925	$1,500	$1,700	$2,000	$2,250	$3,500

CERTIFIED POPULATIONS – CIRCULATION STRIKES

Fair	AG	G	VG	F	VF	EF	AU	MS-60
0	1	4	3	3	4	4	15	0

MS-61	MS-62	MS-63	MS-64	MS-65	MS-66	MS-67	MS-68	MS-69	MS-70
7	25	14	28	17	9	0	0	0	0

CERTIFIED POPULATIONS – PROOF STRIKES

PF-50	PF-60	PF-61	PF-62	PF-63	PF-64
1	0	4	9	19	69
PF-65	**PF-66**	**PF-67**	**PF-68**	**PF-69**	**PF-70**
49	69	29	4	0	0

1896-O Dime

Circulation-strike mintage: 610,000

Availability in Mint State: The 1896-O is one of the handful of top rarities among Barber dimes in grades MS-60 or higher. At any Mint State level an 1896-O dime is a keeper. ***Estimated number MS-65 or higher:*** 40 to 50. One of the standard rarities among gem early Barber dimes.

Availability in circulated grades: 3,000 to 3,500. Most are AG-3 or G-4. David Lawrence stated that this is one of the 12 scarcest Barber dimes in grades of G-4 to VG-8, is one of the 11 scarcest Barber dimes in grades F-12 to VF-35, and is among the dozen scarcest Barber dimes in grades EF-40 to AU-58. Such coins are hard to find all across the grading spectrum.

Characteristics of striking: Variable, but some are quite sharp. Take time to find a well-struck example.

MARKET VALUES – CIRCULATION STRIKES

G-4	VG-8	F-12	VF-20	EF-40	AU-50
$80	$160	$290	$350	$450	$650

MS-60	MS-62	MS-63	MS-64	MS-65
$1,000	$1,600	$2,400	$4,500	$7,500

CERTIFIED POPULATIONS – CIRCULATION STRIKES

Fair	AG	G	VG	F	VF	EF	AU	MS-60
1	2	25	12	10	15	11	9	0

MS-61	MS-62	MS-63	MS-64	MS-65	MS-66	MS-67	MS-68	MS-69	MS-70
2	2	3	8	5	4	2	0	0	0

VARIETIES: Walter Breen describes a variety known as the "extra heavy date," noting that it was discovered by Dr. Charles R. Ruby. Breen's description reads: "Date repeatedly repunched but extra outlines blurred. Serifs thick, 96 closed — knobs joined loops."

1896-S DIME

Circulation-strike mintage: 575,056

AVAILABILITY IN MINT STATE: Probably no more than 200 or so are known in grades MS–60 to 64. ***Estimated number MS-65 or higher:*** 45 to 55.

AVAILABILITY IN CIRCULATED GRADES: 1,500 to 1,800. Most are AG-3 or G-4. David Lawrence stated that this is one of the 12 scarcest Barber dimes in grades of G-4 to VG-8, is one of the 11 scarcest Barber dimes in grades F-12 to VF-35, and is one of the 11 scarcest Barber dimes in grades EF-40 to AU-58. This issue is rare on all counts. As demonstrated by certain inventories published in chapter 2, key Barber dimes of the 1890s had all but disappeared from circulation by the 1930s.

CHARACTERISTICS OF STRIKING: Usually sharp.

NOTES: This date has always been a classic scarcity in the series, a fact that is generally overlooked in the marketplace.

MARKET VALUES – CIRCULATION STRIKES

G-4	VG-8	F-12	VF-20	EF-40	AU-50
$80	$150	$280	$335	$400	$550

MS-60	MS-62	MS-63	MS-64	MS-65
$850	$1,100	$1,500	$3,000	$4,500

CERTIFIED POPULATIONS – CIRCULATION STRIKES

Fair	AG	G	VG	F	VF	EF	AU	MS-60
2	5	29	6	6	7	7	10	1

MS-61	MS-62	MS-63	MS-64	MS-65	MS-66	MS-67	MS-68	MS-69	MS-70
4	10	6	21	13	20	0	0	0	0

1897 DIME

Circulation-strike mintage: 10,868,533
Proof mintage: 731

AVAILABILITY IN MINT STATE: Common in lower–Mint State grades. ***Estimated number MS-65 or higher:*** 200 to 240.

AVAILABILITY IN CIRCULATED GRADES: 35,000 to 40,000. Most are AG-3 or G-4.

CHARACTERISTICS OF STRIKING: Usually very sharp.

AVAILABILITY IN PROOF FORMAT: ***Proof–60 to 64:*** 400 to 500. ***Proof-65 or better:*** 95 to 115.

MARKET VALUES – CIRCULATION STRIKES

G-4	VG-8	F-12	VF-20	EF-40	AU-50
$4	$5	$8	$15	$32	$75

MS-60	MS-62	MS-63	MS-64	MS-65
$135	$175	$240	$375	$625

MARKET VALUES – PROOF STRIKES

PF-60	PF-63	PF-64	PF-65	PF-65Cam	PF-66	PF-66Cam	PF-67
$275	$575	$925	$1,500	$1,700	$2,000	$2,250	$3,500

CERTIFIED POPULATIONS – CIRCULATION STRIKES

Fair	AG	G	VG	F	VF	EF	AU	MS-60
0	0	1	1	2	5	4	50	0

MS-61	MS-62	MS-63	MS-64	MS-65	MS-66	MS-67	MS-68	MS-69	MS-70
28	69	79	110	53	32	7	0	0	0

CERTIFIED POPULATIONS – PROOF STRIKES

PF-50	PF-60	PF-61	PF-62	PF-63	PF-64
1	3	9	18	20	55

PF-65	PF-66	PF-67	PF-68	PF-69	PF-70
43	51	37	11	0	0

Varieties: Varieties with repunched dates occur but have attracted little attention.

1897, Repunched Date (FS-301): This is the most dramatic repunched date for this year. The original digits are visible to the left of the correctly placed digits.

MARKET VALUES – CIRCULATION STRIKES

EF-40	AU-50	MS-60
$80	$120	$200

1897-O Dime

Circulation-strike mintage: 666,000

Availability in Mint State: Probably fewer than 500 coins are known in grades from MS–60 to 64. MS–63 and 64 coins are a good alternative to MS-65. ***Estimated number MS-65 or higher:*** 50 to 60.

Availability in circulated grades: 1,800 to 2,200. Most are AG-3 or G-4. David Lawrence stated that this is one of the 12 scarcest Barber dimes in grades of G-4 to VG-8, is one of the 11 scarcest Barber dimes in grades F-12 to VF-35, and is among the dozen scarcest Barber dimes in grades EF-40 to AU-58.

Characteristics of striking: Variable, but examples are often found well struck.

Notes: Walter Breen mentions a "Bar joins 97" variety, noting that it is extremely rare and was first published in *The Numisma,* May 5, 1957 (this was the journal of the New Netherlands Coin Co., Inc., New York City, operated by Charles M. Wormser and John J. Ford Jr.). Most if not all of the Barber dime information in Breen's 1988 *Complete Encyclopedia of U.S. and Colonial Coins* has been superseded by David Lawrence's 1991 book.

The 1897-O is well-known as a key date. Examples are elusive at all levels.

MARKET VALUES – CIRCULATION STRIKES

G-4	VG-8	F-12	VF-20	EF-40	AU-50
$65	$115	$280	$375	$475	$600

MS-60	MS-62	MS-63	MS-64	MS-65
$900	$1,300	$1,700	$2,500	$4,000

CERTIFIED POPULATIONS – CIRCULATION STRIKES

Fair	AG	G	VG	F	VF	EF	AU	MS-60
1	5	20	5	7	16	7	8	0

MS-61	MS-62	MS-63	MS-64	MS-65	MS-66	MS-67	MS-68	MS-69	MS-70
3	8	4	18	10	4	3	0	0	0

1897-S DIME

Circulation-strike mintage: 1,342,844

AVAILABILITY IN MINT STATE: MS–60 to 64 1897-S dimes are hard to find, but they still offer a more attainable alternative to MS-65 pieces. ***Estimated number MS-65 or higher:*** 65 to 75.

AVAILABILITY IN CIRCULATED GRADES: 4,000 to 5,000. Most are AG-3 or G-4. David Lawrence rated the 1897-S as scarce in any grade.

CHARACTERISTICS OF STRIKING: Usually well struck.

MARKET VALUES – CIRCULATION STRIKES

G-4	VG-8	F-12	VF-20	EF-40	AU-50
$18	$35	$90	$120	$175	$260

MS-60	MS-62	MS-63	MS-64	MS-65
$450	$650	$1,000	$2,000	$3,750

CERTIFIED POPULATIONS – CIRCULATION STRIKES

Fair	AG	G	VG	F	VF	EF	AU	MS-60
0	1	5	1	9	6	8	18	0

MS-61	MS-62	MS-63	MS-64	MS-65	MS-66	MS-67	MS-68	MS-69	MS-70
4	6	11	22	7	1	1	0	0	0

1898 Dime

Circulation-strike mintage: 16,320,000
Proof mintage: 735

Availability in Mint State: Common in lower–Mint State grades. ***Estimated number MS-65 or higher:*** 300 to 360.

Availability in circulated grades: 60,000 to 80,000. Most are AG-3 or G-4. There are enough examples around that EF and AU coins can be easily found.

Characteristics of striking: Usually very sharp.

Availability in Proof format: ***Proof–60 to 64:*** 475 to 525. ***Proof-65 or better:*** 80 to 95.

Notes: Walter Breen describes an "overdate," noting that there is a "curved line within a loop of final 8, not matching any curve of another 8, most likely the middle stroke of a 2," further noting that there was one in the Gilhousen sale, lot 494. Could this simply be a repunching? Many of Breen's "overdates" in various series have been dismissed by modern scholars.

MARKET VALUES – CIRCULATION STRIKES

G-4	VG-8	F-12	VF-20	EF-40	AU-50
$4	$5	$8	$12	$26	$75

MS-60	MS-62	MS-63	MS-64	MS-65
$115	$150	$220	$350	$675

MARKET VALUES – PROOF STRIKES

PF-60	PF-63	PF-64	PF-65	PF-65Cam	PF-66	PF-66Cam	PF-67
$275	$575	$925	$1,500	$1,700	$2,000	$2,250	$3,500

CERTIFIED POPULATIONS – CIRCULATION STRIKES

Fair	AG	G	VG	F	VF	EF	AU	MS-60
0	0	1	0	1	4	5	63	1

MS-61	MS-62	MS-63	MS-64	MS-65	MS-66	MS-67	MS-68	MS-69	MS-70
15	69	91	119	68	20	7	1	0	0

CERTIFIED POPULATIONS – PROOF STRIKES

PF-50	PF-60	PF-61	PF-62	PF-63	PF-64
1	0	1	13	29	66
PF-65	**PF-66**	**PF-67**	**PF-68**	**PF-69**	**PF-70**
48	54	58	20	0	0

1898-O DIME

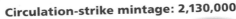

Circulation-strike mintage: 2,130,000

AVAILABILITY IN MINT STATE: While it seems unlikely given the generous mintage of the 1898-O, this is one of the handful of top rarities among Barber dimes in grades MS-60 or higher. This is amazing. ***Estimated number MS-65 or higher:*** 35 to 40. Although the mintage of the 1898-O dime crossed the two-million mark, relatively few gems survived. This is one of the most elusive issues in the series.

AVAILABILITY IN CIRCULATED GRADES: 6,000 to 8,000. Most are AG-3 or G-4. David Lawrence stated that this is one of the 11 scarcest Barber dimes in grades EF-40 to AU-58.

CHARACTERISTICS OF STRIKING: Variable. Some are weak on the hair above the forehead and the higher wreath details. Sharp examples exist.

NOTES: Walter Breen describes an "extra heavy date" resulting from the logotype punch being impressed more deeply than normal into the dies.

MARKET VALUES – CIRCULATION STRIKES

G-4	VG-8	F-12	VF-20	EF-40	AU-50
$12	$26	$85	$140	$190	$280

MS-60	MS-62	MS-63	MS-64	MS-65
$450	$650	$1,200	$1,750	$3,000

CERTIFIED POPULATIONS – CIRCULATION STRIKES

Fair	AG	G	VG	F	VF	EF	AU	MS-60
0	0	0	1	2	17	5	9	0

MS-61	MS-62	MS-63	MS-64	MS-65	MS-66	MS-67	MS-68	MS-69	MS-70
5	5	16	9	15	1	0	1	0	0

1898-S Dime

Circulation-strike mintage: 1,702,507

Availability in Mint State: Several hundred lower-level Mint State coins exist. ***Estimated number MS-65 or higher:*** 45 to 55.

Availability in circulated grades: 2,000 to 2,500. Most are AG-3 or G-4.

Characteristics of striking: Usually well struck.

Notes: Some or most of this mintage was shipped to the Philippine Islands after the Spanish-American War ended in the summer of the year. As a result, such dimes were scarce in domestic circulation.

Walter Breen describes a variety as an "overdate," possibly 1898-S, 8 Over 6, and notes that he has seen three. However, I am skeptical of his examples' overdate status.

MARKET VALUES – CIRCULATION STRIKES

G-4	VG-8	F-12	VF-20	EF-40	AU-50
$8	$15	$32	$45	$80	$150

MS-60	MS-62	MS-63	MS-64	MS-65
$375	$600	$1,200	$2,000	$3,500

CERTIFIED POPULATIONS – CIRCULATION STRIKES

Fair	AG	G	VG	F	VF	EF	AU	MS-60
0	0	2	0	2	4	4	13	1

MS-61	MS-62	MS-63	MS-64	MS-65	MS-66	MS-67	MS-68	MS-69	MS-70
4	8	8	6	5	3	0	0	0	0

1899 DIME

Circulation-strike mintage: 19,580,000
Proof mintage: 846

AVAILABILITY IN MINT STATE: Common in lower–Mint State grades. ***Estimated number MS-65 or higher:*** 125 to 140.

AVAILABILITY IN CIRCULATED GRADES: 100,000 to 125,000. Most are AG-3 or G-4. Easily found in all circulated grades.

CHARACTERISTICS OF STRIKING: Usually sharp.

AVAILABILITY IN PROOF FORMAT: ***Proof–60 to 64:*** 450 to 600. ***Proof-65 or better:*** 75 to 90.

MARKET VALUES – CIRCULATION STRIKES

G-4	VG-8	F-12	VF-20	EF-40	AU-50
$4	$5	$8	$12	$25	$75

MS-60	MS-62	MS-63	MS-64	MS-65
$130	$165	$240	$375	$650

MARKET VALUES – PROOF STRIKES

PF-60	PF-63	PF-64	PF-65	PF-65Cam	PF-66	PF-66Cam	PF-67
$275	$575	$925	$1,500	$1,700	$2,000	$2,250	$3,500

CERTIFIED POPULATIONS – CIRCULATION STRIKES

Fair	AG	G	VG	F	VF	EF	AU	MS-60
0	0	3	2	1	5	6	50	1

MS-61	MS-62	MS-63	MS-64	MS-65	MS-66	MS-67	MS-68	MS-69	MS-70
12	48	73	85	43	6	4	0	0	0

CERTIFIED POPULATIONS – PROOF STRIKES

PF-50	PF-60	PF-61	PF-62	PF-63	PF-64
1	3	3	11	28	63
PF-65	**PF-66**	**PF-67**	**PF-68**	**PF-69**	**PF-70**
43	48	37	3	0	0

1899-O Dime

Circulation-strike mintage: 2,650,000

Availability in Mint State: MS–60 to 63 coins are available easily enough. MS-64 examples are scarce. ***Estimated number MS-65 or higher:*** 45 to 55. This issue is inexplicably rare at the gem level.

Availability in circulated grades: 10,000 to 12,000. Most are AG-3 or G-4.

Characteristics of striking: Variable. Many are weak in areas. Keep your eyes out for a sharp one.

MARKET VALUES – CIRCULATION STRIKES

G-4	VG-8	F-12	VF-20	EF-40	AU-50
$10	$18	$65	$95	$140	$225

MS-60	MS-62	MS-63	MS-64	MS-65
$400	$600	$1,150	$2,500	$4,000

CERTIFIED POPULATIONS – CIRCULATION STRIKES

Fair	AG	G	VG	F	VF	EF	AU	MS-60
0	2	2	3	5	21	9	14	0

MS-61	MS-62	MS-63	MS-64	MS-65	MS-66	MS-67	MS-68	MS-69	MS-70
5	17	11	13	8	3	2	0	0	0

1899-S DIME

Circulation-strike mintage: 1,867,493

AVAILABILITY IN MINT STATE: Fewer than 500 coins are estimated to exist in lower–Mint State ranges. ***Estimated number MS-65 or higher:*** 80 to 95.

AVAILABILITY IN CIRCULATED GRADES: 3,500 to 4,000. Most are AG-3 or G-4.

CHARACTERISTICS OF STRIKING: Usually sharp.

NOTES: Much of this coinage was shipped to the Philippine Islands for circulation there.

MARKET VALUES – CIRCULATION STRIKES

G-4	VG-8	F-12	VF-20	EF-40	AU-50
$8.50	$16	$32	$35	$45	$110

MS-60	MS-62	MS-63	MS-64	MS-65
$300	$550	$750	$1,750	$2,750

CERTIFIED POPULATIONS – CIRCULATION STRIKES

Fair	AG	G	VG	F	VF	EF	AU	MS-60
0	0	1	0	1	4	5	18	1

MS-61	MS-62	MS-63	MS-64	MS-65	MS-66	MS-67	MS-68	MS-69	MS-70
10	20	18	15	4	3	2	0	0	0

1900 Dime

Circulation-strike mintage: 17,600,000
Proof mintage: 912

Availability in Mint State: Easy to find in lower–Mint State grades, this being true of all turn-of-the-century Philadelphia Barber dimes. ***Estimated number MS-65 or higher:*** 90 to 110.

Availability in circulated grades: 125,000 to 150,000. Most are G-4.

Characteristics of striking: Usually sharp.

Availability in Proof format: ***Proof–60 to 64:*** 350 to 450. ***Proof-65 or better:*** 65 to 80.

MARKET VALUES – CIRCULATION STRIKES

G-4	VG-8	F-12	VF-20	EF-40	AU-50
$4	$5	$8	$12	$25	$75

MS-60	MS-62	MS-63	MS-64	MS-65
$125	$160	$240	$380	$850

MARKET VALUES – PROOF STRIKES

PF-60	PF-63	PF-64	PF-65	PF-65Cam	PF-66	PF-66Cam	PF-67
$275	$575	$925	$1,500	$1,700	$2,000	$2,250	$3,500

CERTIFIED POPULATIONS – CIRCULATION STRIKES

Fair	AG	G	VG	F	VF	EF	AU	MS-60
0	0	0	1	2	4	6	35	1

MS-61	MS-62	MS-63	MS-64	MS-65	MS-66	MS-67	MS-68	MS-69	MS-70
12	34	47	57	34	13	4	0	0	0

CERTIFIED POPULATIONS – PROOF STRIKES

PF-50	PF-60	PF-61	PF-62	PF-63	PF-64
0	0	1	19	33	62
PF-65	**PF-66**	**PF-67**	**PF-68**	**PF-69**	**PF-70**
34	36	34	11	0	0

1900-O Dime

Circulation-strike mintage: 2,010,000

Availability in Mint State: The 1900-O dime is surprisingly rare in view of its mintage. Survival was more a matter of chance than of numismatic intent. ***Estimated number MS-65 or higher:*** 75 to 90.

Availability in circulated grades: 12,000 to 15,000. Most are AG-3 or G-4. David Lawrence stated that this is one of the 12 scarcest Barber dimes in grades of G-4 to VG-8, is one of the 11 scarcest Barber dimes in grades F-12 to VF, and is among the dozen scarcest Barber dimes in grades EF-40 to AU-58.

Characteristics of striking: Variable. Many have areas of weakness. Take time to find a sharp one.

Notes: Walter Breen notes that different mintmarks vary greatly in their position, and that a specimen in the Gilhousen collection sale, lot 502, had O leaning crazily to the left. This example has not been seen by the present writer.

MARKET VALUES – CIRCULATION STRIKES

G-4	VG-8	F-12	VF-20	EF-40	AU-50
$18	$38	$110	$160	$220	$360

MS-60	MS-62	MS-63	MS-64	MS-65
$650	$775	$1,150	$2,750	$5,000

CERTIFIED POPULATIONS – CIRCULATION STRIKES

Fair	AG	G	VG	F	VF	EF	AU	MS-60
1	0	2	6	6	14	14	13	1

MS-61	MS-62	MS-63	MS-64	MS-65	MS-66	MS-67	MS-68	MS-69	MS-70
0	6	10	12	9	6	1	0	0	0

1900-S Dime

Circulation-strike mintage: 5,168,270

Availability in Mint State: Easy to find in lower–Mint State levels. As for most Barber dimes, MS-63 and MS-64 coins are very affordable and, if hand-picked for strike and eye appeal, can be more worthwhile to own than certified MS-65 coins that are unattractive (of which many exist). ***Estimated number MS-65 or higher:*** 90 to 110.

Availability in circulated grades: 40,000 to 50,000. Most are AG-3 or G-4.

Characteristics of striking: Usually well struck. Mint State coins are typically seen with rich luster.

MARKET VALUES – CIRCULATION STRIKES

G-4	VG-8	F-12	VF-20	EF-40	AU-50
$5	$6	$12	$20	$30	$75

MS-60	MS-62	MS-63	MS-64	MS-65
$175	$300	$425	$700	$1,800

CERTIFIED POPULATIONS – CIRCULATION STRIKES

Fair	AG	G	VG	F	VF	EF	AU	MS-60
0	2	0	0	3	5	6	53	2

MS-61	MS-62	MS-63	MS-64	MS-65	MS-66	MS-67	MS-68	MS-69	MS-70
4	18	18	27	10	5	0	0	0	0

1901 Dime

Circulation-strike mintage: 18,859,665
Proof mintage: 813

Availability in Mint State: Common in lower–Mint State categories. ***Estimated number MS-65 or higher:*** 150 to 180.

Availability in circulated grades: 125,000 to 150,000. Most are G-4. Easy to find in any circulated grade desired.

Characteristics of striking: Usually sharp.

Availability in Proof format: ***Proof–60 to 64:*** 350 to 450. ***Proof-65 or better:*** 65 to 80.

Proofs of this year of all denominations were made with the portrait features lightly polished in the die, instead of frosted or cameo. This continued through 1904 for most coins. Walter Breen notes that about 5% of the Proofs of this date have the last two digits slightly doubled.

Notes: New obverse and reverse hubs were introduced this year. All 1901 Philadelphia Mint dimes have Obverse Hub II. Both reverses I and II were used in conjunction with the new obverse.

MARKET VALUES – CIRCULATION STRIKES

G-4	VG-8	F-12	VF-20	EF-40	AU-50
$4	$5	$7	$10	$26	$75

MS-60	MS-62	MS-63	MS-64	MS-65
$125	$160	$240	$375	$625

MARKET VALUES – PROOF STRIKES

PF-60	PF-63	PF-64	PF-65	PF-65Cam	PF-66	PF-66Cam	PF-67
$275	$575	$925	$1,500	$1,700	$2,000	$2,250	$3,500

CERTIFIED POPULATIONS – CIRCULATION STRIKES

Fair	AG	G	VG	F	VF	EF	AU	MS-60
0	0	0	0	1	2	4	46	0

MS-61	MS-62	MS-63	MS-64	MS-65	MS-66	MS-67	MS-68	MS-69	MS-70
21	44	61	84	26	6	4	0	0	0

CERTIFIED POPULATIONS – PROOF STRIKES

PF-50	PF-60	PF-61	PF-62	PF-63	PF-64
0	0	8	15	22	69
PF-65	**PF-66**	**PF-67**	**PF-68**	**PF-69**	**PF-70**
51	57	21	2	0	0

1901-O Dime

Circulation-strike mintage: 5,620,000

Availability in Mint State: It is incredible that so few examples exist in Mint State considering the high mintage of this variety. The population of coins from MS–60 to 64 is probably fewer than 250. ***Estimated number MS-65 or higher:*** 45 to 55.

Availability in circulated grades: 30,000 to 40,000. Most are G-4.

Characteristics of striking: Often weak in areas. As is generally true for New Orleans Barber dimes, close examination and taking your time will pay dividends as some sharp examples do exist.

Notes: The 1901-O has the new hub obverse but the old Reverse Hub I (Reverse Hub II was used beginning with 1902-O).

MARKET VALUES – CIRCULATION STRIKES

G-4	VG-8	F-12	VF-20	EF-40	AU-50
$4	$5.50	$16	$28	$75	$180

MS-60	MS-62	MS-63	MS-64	MS-65
$450	$650	$950	$2,500	$3,800

CERTIFIED POPULATIONS – CIRCULATION STRIKES

Fair	AG	G	VG	F	VF	EF	AU	MS-60
0	2	1	1	2	9	11	30	1

MS-61	MS-62	MS-63	MS-64	MS-65	MS-66	MS-67	MS-68	MS-69	MS-70
5	11	12	21	8	6	0	0	0	0

Varieties: ***1901-O, O Over Horizontal O (FS-501):*** This variety shows the O mintmark horizontally punched at the inside top and bottom of the prime O mintmark. This reverse was used with two different obverse dies.[3] These can be found in all grades, but Mint State coins are elusive.

1901-S Dime

Circulation-strike mintage: 593,022

Availability in Mint State: Probably fewer than 200 exist in grades from MS–60 to 64. In any Mint State grade the 1901-S is in demand, perhaps some of this demand reflecting the aura from the 1901-S quarter's rarity. ***Estimated number MS-65 or higher:*** 45 to 55.

Availability in circulated grades: 2,500 to 3,000. Most are G-4. David Lawrence stated that this is one of the 12 scarcest Barber dimes in grades of G-4 to VG-8.

Characteristics of striking: Usually sharp.

Notes: The 1901-S, with its low mintage, has long been considered a key date in the Barber dime series, and rightfully so. Specimens are elusive at all levels.

MARKET VALUES – CIRCULATION STRIKES

G-4	VG-8	F-12	VF-20	EF-40	AU-50
$80	$150	$350	$450	$550	$675

MS-60	MS-62	MS-63	MS-64	MS-65
$1,050	$1,250	$1,800	$2,300	$5,500

CERTIFIED POPULATIONS – CIRCULATION STRIKES

Fair	AG	G	VG	F	VF	EF	AU	MS-60
3	6	20	10	11	12	17	18	0

MS-61	MS-62	MS-63	MS-64	MS-65	MS-66	MS-67	MS-68	MS-69	MS-70
1	4	10	9	5	4	0	1	0	0

1902 Dime

Circulation-strike mintage: 21,380,000
Proof mintage: 777

Availability in Mint State: Lower-range Mint State coins are very common due to the huge number produced. ***Estimated number MS-65 or higher:*** 100 to 120. Gems are amazingly elusive for a Philadelphia Mint issue with such a huge mintage! A numismatic mystery.

Availability in circulated grades: 200,000 to 250,000. Most are G-4. Although most are in lower grades as noted, for specialists it is easy enough to find higher-grade coins as desired, as many exist in proportion to the demand for them.

Characteristics of striking: Usually sharp.

Availability in Proof format: ***Proof–60 to 64:*** 400 to 500. ***Proof-65 or better:*** 50 to 60.

MARKET VALUES – CIRCULATION STRIKES

G-4	VG-8	F-12	VF-20	EF-40	AU-50
$4	$5	$6	$8	$25	$75

MS-60	MS-62	MS-63	MS-64	MS-65
$125	$160	$240	$375	$660

MARKET VALUES – PROOF STRIKES

PF-60	PF-63	PF-64	PF-65	PF-65Cam	PF-66	PF-66Cam	PF-67
$275	$575	$925	$1,500	$1,700	$2,000	$2,250	$3,500

CERTIFIED POPULATIONS – CIRCULATION STRIKES

Fair	AG	G	VG	F	VF	EF	AU	MS-60
0	1	2	1	3	10	9	42	1

MS-61	MS-62	MS-63	MS-64	MS-65	MS-66	MS-67	MS-68	MS-69	MS-70
11	31	36	49	16	11	0	0	0	0

CERTIFIED POPULATIONS – PROOF STRIKES

PF-50	PF-60	PF-61	PF-62	PF-63	PF-64
0	4	6	16	29	74
PF-65	**PF-66**	**PF-67**	**PF-68**	**PF-69**	**PF-70**
34	24	15	1	0	0

1902-O Dime

Circulation-strike mintage: 4,500,000

Availability in Mint State: Probably fewer than 200 exist in grades from MS–60 to 64. ***Estimated number MS-65 or higher:*** 25 to 30. In gem Mint State the 1902-O is one of the key issues in the Barber dime series—surprising in view of the multimillion coin mintage.

Availability in circulated grades: 30,000 to 40,000. Most are G-4. Very common when well worn. Scarce to rare in any grade in which LIBERTY is readable.

Characteristics of striking: Often weak in areas, but sharp examples can be found.

MARKET VALUES – CIRCULATION STRIKES

G-4	VG-8	F-12	VF-20	EF-40	AU-50
$4	$6	$15	$32	$65	$150

MS-60	MS-62	MS-63	MS-64	MS-65
$400	$650	$1,000	$1,500	$4,000

CERTIFIED POPULATIONS – CIRCULATION STRIKES

Fair	AG	G	VG	F	VF	EF	AU	MS-60
0	0	1	1	1	12	8	26	0

MS-61	MS-62	MS-63	MS-64	MS-65	MS-66	MS-67	MS-68	MS-69	MS-70
3	16	11	38	7	3	1	0	0	0

1902-S Dime

Circulation-strike mintage: 2,070,000

Availability in Mint State: It is thought that in grades from MS–60 to 64 fewer than 250 1902-S dimes exist. ***Estimated number MS-65 or higher:*** 45 to 55. One of the rarer issues of the era, yet another numismatic surprise.

Availability in circulated grades: 12,000 to 15,000. Most are G-4.

Characteristics of striking: Usually sharp.

MARKET VALUES – CIRCULATION STRIKES

G-4	VG-8	F-12	VF-20	EF-40	AU-50
$9	$20	$55	$80	$140	$200

MS-60	MS-62	MS-63	MS-64	MS-65
$400	$650	$1,000	$1,500	$4,000

CERTIFIED POPULATIONS – CIRCULATION STRIKES

Fair	AG	G	VG	F	VF	EF	AU	MS-60
0	1	3	1	7	9	5	14	1

MS-61	MS-62	MS-63	MS-64	MS-65	MS-66	MS-67	MS-68	MS-69	MS-70
6	8	13	9	8	3	2	0	0	0

1903 DIME

Circulation-strike mintage: 19,500,000
Proof mintage: 755

AVAILABILITY IN MINT STATE: Readily available in grades from MS–60 to 64 with the population estimated in the high hundreds. ***Estimated number MS-65 or higher:*** 120 to 140.

AVAILABILITY IN CIRCULATED GRADES: 200,000 to 250,000. Most are G-4. Easy to locate in any desired grade.

CHARACTERISTICS OF STRIKING: Usually sharp.

AVAILABILITY IN PROOF FORMAT: ***Proof–60 to 64:*** 375 to 475. ***Proof-65 or better:*** 80 to 95.

MARKET VALUES – CIRCULATION STRIKES

G-4	VG-8	F-12	VF-20	EF-40	AU-50
$4	$5	$6	$8	$25	$75

MS-60	MS-62	MS-63	MS-64	MS-65
$125	$160	$240	$375	$1,000

MARKET VALUES – PROOF STRIKES

PF-60	PF-63	PF-64	PF-65	PF-65Cam	PF-66	PF-66Cam	PF-67
$275	$575	$925	$1,500	$1,700	$2,000	$2,250	$3,500

CERTIFIED POPULATIONS – CIRCULATION STRIKES

Fair	AG	G	VG	F	VF	EF	AU	MS-60
0	1	1	3	0	6	6	28	1

MS-61	MS-62	MS-63	MS-64	MS-65	MS-66	MS-67	MS-68	MS-69	MS-70
9	23	29	32	16	8	0	0	0	0

CERTIFIED POPULATIONS – PROOF STRIKES

PF-50	PF-60	PF-61	PF-62	PF-63	PF-64
0	1	3	17	27	69
PF-65	**PF-66**	**PF-67**	**PF-68**	**PF-69**	**PF-70**
45	36	14	1	0	0

1903-O Dime

Circulation-strike mintage: 8,180,000

Availability in Mint State: Covering a wider range of Mint State grades, probably fewer than 500 coins are known in grades from MS–60 to 64. Again, MS–63 and 64 coins offer a good alternative to MS-65 coins and can be more attractive overall—if cherrypicked for quality (which only a tiny percentage of buyers take the time to do). ***Estimated number MS-65 or higher:*** 45 to 55. The rarity at the gem level of 1903-O is generally reflective of New Orleans dimes with high mintages. Probably no more than a few dozen collectors sought such pieces at the time of issue. When coins were found again they were often below the MS-65 grade.

Availability in circulated grades: 60,000 to 80,000. Most are G-4.

Characteristics of striking: Usually sharp.

Notes: The 1903-O uses the anachronistic Obverse Hub I in combination with the usual Reverse Hub II of this era.

MARKET VALUES – CIRCULATION STRIKES

G-4	VG-8	F-12	VF-20	EF-40	AU-50
$5	$6	$14	$25	$55	$110

MS-60	MS-62	MS-63	MS-64	MS-65
$275	$400	$550	$1,000	$4,500

CERTIFIED POPULATIONS – CIRCULATION STRIKES

Fair	AG	G	VG	F	VF	EF	AU	MS-60
0	0	1	0	1	6	16	63	1

MS-61	MS-62	MS-63	MS-64	MS-65	MS-66	MS-67	MS-68	MS-69	MS-70
13	18	13	29	5	0	1	0	0	0

1903-S DIME

Circulation-strike mintage: 613,500

AVAILABILITY IN MINT STATE: Probably fewer than 250 are known in lower–Mint State levels, all being of an elusive nature. ***Estimated number MS-65 or higher:*** 55 to 65.

AVAILABILITY IN CIRCULATED GRADES: 2,000 to 2,500. Most are G-4. David Lawrence stated that this is one of the 12 scarcest Barber dimes in grades of G-4 to VG-8, one of the 11 scarcest Barber dimes in grades F-12 to VF-35, and one of the 11 scarcest Barber dimes in grades EF-40 to AU-58.

CHARACTERISTICS OF STRIKING: Usually sharp.

NOTES: Old reverse hubs were used.

MARKET VALUES – CIRCULATION STRIKES

G-4	VG-8	F-12	VF-20	EF-40	AU-50
$85	$130	$350	$475	$700	$850

MS-60	MS-62	MS-63	MS-64	MS-65
$1,200	$1,400	$1,800	$2,250	$3,500

CERTIFIED POPULATIONS – CIRCULATION STRIKES

Fair	AG	G	VG	F	VF	EF	AU	MS-60
3	5	13	6	15	18	9	18	0

MS-61	MS-62	MS-63	MS-64	MS-65	MS-66	MS-67	MS-68	MS-69	MS-70
1	6	1	12	1	7	2	0	0	0

1904 Dime

Circulation-strike mintage: 14,600,357
Proof mintage: 670

Availability in Mint State: Lower–Mint State grades are quite common. ***Estimated number MS-65 or higher:*** 150 to 180. Another Barber dime that is surprisingly scarce at this level.

Availability in circulated grades: 120,000 to 140,000. Most are G-4. Similar to other Philadelphia dimes of the era, the 1904 can be found easily in any desired grade.

Characteristics of striking: Usually sharp.

Availability in Proof format: ***Proof–60 to 64***: 350 to 450. ***Proof-65 or better:*** 75 to 90.

MARKET VALUES – CIRCULATION STRIKES

G-4	VG-8	F-12	VF-20	EF-40	AU-50
$4	$5	$6	$9	$25	$70

MS-60	MS-62	MS-63	MS-64	MS-65
$110	$160	$240	$385	$1,400

MARKET VALUES – PROOF STRIKES

PF-60	PF-63	PF-64	PF-65	PF-65Cam	PF-66	PF-66Cam	PF-67
$275	$575	$925	$1,500	$1,700	$2,000	$2,250	$3,500

CERTIFIED POPULATIONS – CIRCULATION STRIKES

Fair	AG	G	VG	F	VF	EF	AU	MS-60
0	0	0	1	0	3	5	23	1

MS-61	MS-62	MS-63	MS-64	MS-65	MS-66	MS-67	MS-68	MS-69	MS-70
6	27	47	60	7	7	0	0	0	0

CERTIFIED POPULATIONS – PROOF STRIKES

PF-50	PF-60	PF-61	PF-62	PF-63	PF-64
0	2	7	20	36	61

PF-65	PF-66	PF-67	PF-68	PF-69	PF-70
43	34	16	2	0	0

1904-S DIME

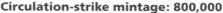

Circulation-strike mintage: 800,000

AVAILABILITY IN MINT STATE: Fewer than 400 coins are known in grades from MS–60 to 64. ***Estimated number MS-65 or higher:*** 35 to 40. Not often seen in the marketplace.

AVAILABILITY IN CIRCULATED GRADES: 4,000 to 5,000. Most are G-4. David Lawrence stated that this is one of the 12 scarcest Barber dimes in grades of G-4 to VG-8.

CHARACTERISTICS OF STRIKING: Usually sharp.

NOTES: This is a key issue among 20th-century Barber dimes and is rarer than the mintage would indicate. San Francisco dimes are as a class harder to find than are those of Philadelphia and New Orleans, because San Francisco Dimes survive in lower percentages of their original mintages.

MARKET VALUES – CIRCULATION STRIKES

G-4	VG-8	F-12	VF-20	EF-40	AU-50
$45	$75	$160	$235	$325	$475

MS-60	MS-62	MS-63	MS-64	MS-65
$800	$1,000	$1,500	$3,000	$4,000

CERTIFIED POPULATIONS – CIRCULATION STRIKES

Fair	AG	G	VG	F	VF	EF	AU	MS-60
5	3	12	4	10	12	12	19	1

MS-61	MS-62	MS-63	MS-64	MS-65	MS-66	MS-67	MS-68	MS-69	MS-70
3	18	7	16	5	2	0	0	0	0

1905 Dime

Circulation-strike mintage: 14,551,623
Proof mintage: 727

Availability in Mint State: Common in lower–Mint State ranges. ***Estimated number MS-65 or higher:*** 100 to 120.

Availability in circulated grades: 100,000 to 125,000. Most are G-4. Easy to find in any grade desired.

Characteristics of striking: Usually sharp.

Availability in Proof format: ***Proof–60 to 64:*** 350 to 450. ***Proof-65 or better:*** 95 to 115.

MARKET VALUES – CIRCULATION STRIKES

G-4	VG-8	F-12	VF-20	EF-40	AU-50
$4	$5	$6	$10	$25	$75

MS-60	MS-62	MS-63	MS-64	MS-65
$125	$160	$240	$375	$660

MARKET VALUES – PROOF STRIKES

PF-60	PF-63	PF-64	PF-65	PF-65Cam	PF-66	PF-66Cam	PF-67
$275	$575	$925	$1,500	$1,700	$2,000	$2,250	$3,500

CERTIFIED POPULATIONS – CIRCULATION STRIKES

Fair	AG	G	VG	F	VF	EF	AU	MS-60
0	0	1	1	4	2	5	36	3

MS-61	MS-62	MS-63	MS-64	MS-65	MS-66	MS-67	MS-68	MS-69	MS-70
5	26	36	41	23	3	2	0	0	0

CERTIFIED POPULATIONS – PROOF STRIKES

PF-50	PF-60	PF-61	PF-62	PF-63	PF-64
0	0	6	11	31	57

PF-65	PF-66	PF-67	PF-68	PF-69	PF-70
40	40	21	9	0	0

1905-O Dime

Circulation-strike mintage: Most of 3,400,000

Availability in Mint State: Easy to find in lower–Mint State grades. ***Estimated number MS-65 or higher:*** 110 to 120.

Availability in circulated grades: 40,000 to 50,000. Most are G-4.

Characteristics of striking: Often with areas of weakness. Patience is required to find a sharp example.

MARKET VALUES – CIRCULATION STRIKES

G-4	VG-8	F-12	VF-20	EF-40	AU-50
$5	$10	$35	$60	$100	$150

MS-60	MS-62	MS-63	MS-64	MS-65
$300	$400	$500	$700	$1,350

CERTIFIED POPULATIONS – CIRCULATION STRIKES

Fair	AG	G	VG	F	VF	EF	AU	MS-60
0	1	7	3	1	9	4	19	0

MS-61	MS-62	MS-63	MS-64	MS-65	MS-66	MS-67	MS-68	MS-69	MS-70
6	20	29	43	12	7	4	0	0	0

1905-o, Micro o, Dime

Circulation-strike mintage: Smaller part of 3,400,000

Availability in Mint State: Mint State examples appear now and then.

Availability in circulated grades: Unlike the 1892-O, Micro o, half dollar, the Micro o dime is readily available in most circulated grades below EF-40.

Notes: This is one of the most popular issues in the Barber series and is on nearly every want list. Two different obverse dies were used with this reverse.

Mehl's Numismatic Monthly, March 1910, included this comment sent by S.E. Young, M.D., of Baywood, Virginia:

> Noticing reference to a new mint mark found on 1905 dime from New Orleans Mint set me to looking at mint marks generally. I was to find one dime with the microscopic 'O' as described by your correspondent, after looking through all the dimes in two or three post-offices and two banks. This seems to indicate that the 1905 small 'O' variety occurs on about one of each 1,000 dimes made at New Orleans since 1900.

The above seems to overstate the rarity, but the variety is very elusive.

MARKET VALUES – CIRCULATION STRIKES

G-4	VG-8	F-12	VF-20	EF-40	AU-50	MS-60	MS-62	MS-63
$25	$50	$110	$160	$175	$275	$600	$1,500	$3,500

CERTIFIED POPULATIONS – CIRCULATION STRIKES

Fair	AG	G	VG	F	VF	EF	AU	MS-60
0	1	3	2	2	12	3	6	1

MS-61	MS-62	MS-63	MS-64	MS-65	MS-66	MS-67	MS-68	MS-69	MS-70
0	1	0	3	0	0	0	0	0	0

1905-S DIME

Circulation-strike mintage: 6,855,199

AVAILABILITY IN MINT STATE: Easy to find in grades from MS–60 to 64, a comment that applies to the vast majority of 20th century Barber dimes. ***Estimated number MS-65 or higher:*** 90 to 110.

AVAILABILITY IN CIRCULATED GRADES: 30,000 to 40,000. Most are G-4.

CHARACTERISTICS OF STRIKING: Usually sharp.

NOTES: John McCloskey reported that 1905-S normally is seen with Hub II for the obverse and reverse, but a rare combination with the usual Obverse Hub II and the anachronistic Reverse Hub I exists.

MARKET VALUES – CIRCULATION STRIKES

G-4	VG-8	F-12	VF-20	EF-40	AU-50
$4	$6	$9	$20	$40	$95

MS-60	MS-62	MS-63	MS-64	MS-65
$250	$285	$325	$600	$950

CERTIFIED POPULATIONS – CIRCULATION STRIKES

Fair	AG	G	VG	F	VF	EF	AU	MS-60
0	3	1	1	1	6	9	48	0

MS-61	MS-62	MS-63	MS-64	MS-65	MS-66	MS-67	MS-68	MS-69	MS-70
8	29	33	28	13	1	1	0	0	0

1906 Dime

Circulation-strike mintage: 19,957,731
Proof mintage: 675

Availability in Mint State: Common in lower–Mint State levels. ***Estimated number MS-65 or higher:*** 150 to 180.

Availability in circulated grades: 200,000 to 250,000. Most are G-4. Finding a 1906 dime in any grade desired is easy to do.

Characteristics of striking: Usually sharp.

Availability in Proof format: ***Proof–60 to 64:*** 300 to 400. ***Proof-65 or better:*** 55 to 65.

MARKET VALUES – CIRCULATION STRIKES

G-4	VG-8	F-12	VF-20	EF-40	AU-50
$4	$5	$6	$10	$25	$75

MS-60	MS-62	MS-63	MS-64	MS-65
$125	$160	$240	$375	$625

MARKET VALUES – PROOF STRIKES

PF-60	PF-63	PF-64	PF-65	PF-65Cam	PF-66	PF-66Cam	PF-67
$275	$575	$925	$1,500	$1,700	$2,000	$2,250	$3,500

CERTIFIED POPULATIONS – CIRCULATION STRIKES

Fair	AG	G	VG	F	VF	EF	AU	MS-60
0	1	0	6	2	3	8	54	3

10	54	62	99	46	4	4	0	0	0
26	29	29	4	3	1	2	6	88	0

CERTIFIED POPULATIONS – PROOF STRIKES

PF-50	PF-60	PF-61	PF-62	PF-63	PF-64
0	1	2	10	29	61

PF-65	PF-66	PF-67	PF-68	PF-69	PF-70
37	22	23	4	0	0

1906-D Dime

Circulation-strike mintage: 4,060,000

Availability in Mint State: This issue is easily enough available in lower–Mint State range, but not among the most common. ***Estimated number MS-65 or higher:*** 75 to 90.

Availability in circulated grades: 30,000 to 40,000. Most are G-4. This is a slightly scarcer issue in F-12 or higher grades.

Characteristics of striking: Usually sharp.

Notes: The 1906-D represents the first year of coinage operation at the new Denver mint. A number of repunched varieties exist, none of which brings a significant premium.

MARKET VALUES – CIRCULATION STRIKES

G-4	VG-8	F-12	VF-20	EF-40	AU-50
$4	$5	$8	$15	$35	$80

MS-60	MS-62	MS-63	MS-64	MS-65
$175	$300	$400	$850	$1,500

CERTIFIED POPULATIONS – CIRCULATION STRIKES

Fair	AG	G	VG	F	VF	EF	AU	MS-60
0	1	1	2	4	4	3	10	0

MS-61	MS-62	MS-63	MS-64	MS-65	MS-66	MS-67	MS-68	MS-69	MS-70
3	13	17	22	21	6	0	0	0	0

1906-O Dime

Circulation-strike mintage: 2,610,000

Availability in Mint State: Probably well over 1,000 exist, in Mint State grades up to MS-64. ***Estimated number MS-65 or higher:*** 150 to 180.

Availability in circulated grades: 20,000 to 25,000. Most are G-4. Elusive in EF and AU grades.

Characteristics of striking: Usually better than average for a New Orleans dime, but care is advised to be sure you buy a sharp one.

MARKET VALUES – CIRCULATION STRIKES

G-4	VG-8	F-12	VF-20	EF-40	AU-50
$6	$14	$45	$75	$110	$130

MS-60	MS-62	MS-63	MS-64	MS-65
$200	$250	$325	$650	$1,100

CERTIFIED POPULATIONS – CIRCULATION STRIKES

Fair	AG	G	VG	F	VF	EF	AU	MS-60
1	0	1	1	4	4	4	7	1

MS-61	MS-62	MS-63	MS-64	MS-65	MS-66	MS-67	MS-68	MS-69	MS-70
2	16	14	45	19	12	9	1	0	0

1906-S Dime

Circulation-strike mintage: 3,136,640

Availability in Mint State: Although the 1906-S is not among the most common Barber dimes, in grades of MS–60 to 64, there are more than enough to supply the demand. ***Estimated number MS-65 or higher:*** 125 to 140.

Availability in circulated grades: 25,000 to 30,000. Most are G-4. Relatively scarce in F-12 and higher grades.

Characteristics of striking: Usually sharp.

MARKET VALUES – CIRCULATION STRIKES

G-4	VG-8	F-12	VF-20	EF-40	AU-50
$4	$6	$13	$25	$45	$110

MS-60	MS-62	MS-63	MS-64	MS-65
$275	$325	$550	$850	$1,250

CERTIFIED POPULATIONS – CIRCULATION STRIKES

Fair	AG	G	VG	F	VF	EF	AU	MS-60
0	0	0	1	4	5	4	15	0

MS-61	MS-62	MS-63	MS-64	MS-65	MS-66	MS-67	MS-68	MS-69	MS-70
11	19	10	27	14	9	2	0	0	0

Varieties: One variety has a triple-punched 6 in the date. Another variety has the S mintmark over an inverted S, as distinguished under magnification.

1907 Dime

Circulation-strike mintage: 22,220,000
Proof mintage: 575

Availability in Mint State: Common in lower–Mint State grades. ***Estimated number MS-65 or higher:*** 220 to 260.

Availability in circulated grades: 125,000 to 150,000. Most are G-4. Readily available in any grade desired.

Characteristics of striking: Usually sharp.

Availability in Proof format: ***Proof–60 to 64:*** 290 to 340. ***Proof-65 or better:*** 70 to 80. At the gem level this is one of the scarcer Proofs of the denomination.

Notes: This is the issue with the largest circulation-strike mintage in the entire Barber silver series.

MARKET VALUES – CIRCULATION STRIKES

G-4	VG-8	F-12	VF-20	EF-40	AU-50
$4	$5	$6	$10	$25	$75

MS-60	MS-62	MS-63	MS-64	MS-65
$125	$160	$240	$375	$625

MARKET VALUES – PROOF STRIKES

PF-60	PF-63	PF-64	PF-65	PF-65Cam	PF-66	PF-66Cam	PF-67
$275	$575	$925	$1,500	$1,700	$2,000	$2,250	$3,500

CERTIFIED POPULATIONS – CIRCULATION STRIKES

Fair	AG	G	VG	F	VF	EF	AU	MS-60
0	0	2	2	3	11	9	58	3

MS-61	MS-62	MS-63	MS-64	MS-65	MS-66	MS-67	MS-68	MS-69	MS-70
16	49	98	94	46	46	0	0	0	0

CERTIFIED POPULATIONS – PROOF STRIKES

PF-50	PF-60	PF-61	PF-62	PF-63	PF-64
0	2	4	6	23	59
PF-65	**PF-66**	**PF-67**	**PF-68**	**PF-69**	**PF-70**
33	34	25	1	0	0

1907-D Dime

Circulation-strike mintage: 4,080,000

Availability in Mint State: Scarce in lower–Mint State ranges despite a generous mintage. ***Estimated number MS-65 or higher:*** 45 to 55. This is far rarer than the mintage would suggest. It is thought by some that three or four barrels of freshly minted coins were lost in a wagon wreck.[4]

Availability in circulated grades: 20,000 to 25,000. Most are G-4.

Characteristics of striking: Usually sharp.

MARKET VALUES – CIRCULATION STRIKES

G-4	VG-8	F-12	VF-20	EF-40	AU-50
$4	$5	$10	$20	$45	$110

MS-60	MS-62	MS-63	MS-64	MS-65
$300	$450	$900	$1,600	$2,250

CERTIFIED POPULATIONS – CIRCULATION STRIKES

Fair	AG	G	VG	F	VF	EF	AU	MS-60
0	0	1	1	1	2	3	14	1

MS-61	MS-62	MS-63	MS-64	MS-65	MS-66	MS-67	MS-68	MS-69	MS-70
3	9	10	16	12	6	1	1	0	0

1907-O Dime

Circulation-strike mintage: 5,058,000

Availability in Mint State: Easy to find in lower ranges of Mint State. ***Estimated number MS-65 or higher:*** 90 to 110.

Availability in circulated grades: 40,000 to 50,000. Most are G-4. Somewhat scarce in EF and AU grades.

Characteristics of striking: Most are notoriously weak in areas, including the hair above the forehead. Finding a sharp one will be a challenge.

MARKET VALUES – CIRCULATION STRIKES

G-4	VG-8	F-12	VF-20	EF-40	AU-50
$4	$7	$30	$45	$70	$110

MS-60	MS-62	MS-63	MS-64	MS-65
$200	$250	$375	$450	$1,200

CERTIFIED POPULATIONS – CIRCULATION STRIKES

Fair	AG	G	VG	F	VF	EF	AU	MS-60
0	0	1	3	2	6	6	20	1

MS-61	MS-62	MS-63	MS-64	MS-65	MS-66	MS-67	MS-68	MS-69	MS-70
0	18	38	35	18	14	2	0	0	0

1907-S DIME

Circulation-strike mintage: 3,178,470

AVAILABILITY IN MINT STATE: Scarce in any Mint State grade. Compare to the other two 1907-S, Barber, denominations. ***Estimated number MS-65 or higher:*** 35 to 40. Why the 1907-S is very rare at the gem level is a puzzle. Whatever the reason, this is a key among 20th-century Barber dimes.

AVAILABILITY IN CIRCULATED GRADES: 25,000 to 30,000. Most are G-4. These are very common.

CHARACTERISTICS OF STRIKING: Usually well struck.

MARKET VALUES – CIRCULATION STRIKES

G-4	VG-8	F-12	VF-20	EF-40	AU-50
$4	$6	$15	$27	$75	$150

MS-60	MS-62	MS-63	MS-64	MS-65
$400	$500	$750	$1,500	$2,500

CERTIFIED POPULATIONS – CIRCULATION STRIKES

Fair	AG	G	VG	F	VF	EF	AU	MS-60
0	1	0	0	2	6	6	30	1

MS-61	MS-62	MS-63	MS-64	MS-65	MS-66	MS-67	MS-68	MS-69	MS-70
5	15	13	12	6	1	0	0	0	0

1908 Dime

Circulation-strike mintage: 10,600,000
Proof mintage: 545

Availability in Mint State: Common in grades from MS–60 to 64. ***Estimated number MS-65 or higher:*** 200 to 240.

Availability in circulated grades: 80,000 to 100,000. Most are G-4. Readily available in any desired grade.

Characteristics of striking: Usually sharp.

Availability in Proof format: ***Proof–60 to 64:*** 280 to 330. ***Proof-65 or better:*** 50 to 60.

Notes: Walter Breen cites an "overdate" for this year, occurring among Proofs, with "uncertain digit within 8, possibly a 6." Modern students do not agree.

In 1908 thousands of counterfeit dimes of this date were circulated from the Boston area.[5]

MARKET VALUES – CIRCULATION STRIKES

G-4	VG-8	F-12	VF-20	EF-40	AU-50
$4	$5	$6	$10	$25	$75

MS-60	MS-62	MS-63	MS-64	MS-65
$125	$160	$240	$375	$625

MARKET VALUES – PROOF STRIKES

PF-60	PF-63	PF-64	PF-65	PF-65Cam	PF-66	PF-66Cam	PF-67
$275	$575	$925	$1,500	$1,700	$2,000	$2,250	$3,500

CERTIFIED POPULATIONS – CIRCULATION STRIKES

Fair	AG	G	VG	F	VF	EF	AU	MS-60
0	0	5	2	2	4	6	28	1

MS-61	MS-62	MS-63	MS-64	MS-65	MS-66	MS-67	MS-68	MS-69	MS-70
13	37	72	89	38	17	4	0	0	0

CERTIFIED POPULATIONS – PROOF STRIKES

PF-50	PF-60	PF-61	PF-62	PF-63	PF-64
0	1	4	7	25	50
PF-65	**PF-66**	**PF-67**	**PF-68**	**PF-69**	**PF-70**
44	32	21	6	0	0

1908-D DIME

Circulation-strike mintage: 7,490,000

AVAILABILITY IN MINT STATE: Very common in lower–Mint State categories. ***Estimated number MS-65 or higher:*** 60 to 70. Another "believe it or not" coin—how can a dime with such a high mintage be so rare in gem Mint State? Perhaps bagged coins were jostled a lot while being transported from the Denver Mint.

AVAILABILITY IN CIRCULATED GRADES: 60,000 to 80,000. Most are G-4. Easy enough to find in any desired grade.

CHARACTERISTICS OF STRIKING: Usually sharp.

MARKET VALUES – CIRCULATION STRIKES

G-4	VG-8	F-12	VF-20	EF-40	AU-50
$4	$5	$6	$10	$28	$75

MS-60	MS-62	MS-63	MS-64	MS-65
$130	$175	$300	$750	$1,000

CERTIFIED POPULATIONS – CIRCULATION STRIKES

Fair	AG	G	VG	F	VF	EF	AU	MS-60
0	0	4	2	3	7	10	41	0

MS-61	MS-62	MS-63	MS-64	MS-65	MS-66	MS-67	MS-68	MS-69	MS-70
6	27	31	32	18	8	3	0	0	0

VARIETIES: ***1908-D, 0 Over 8, Repunched Date (FS-303):*** Among 1908-D dimes there are quite a few repunched dates illustrated by Kevin Flynn in his *Authoritative Reference on Barber Dimes.* Most are relatively minor. This unusual one has been selected by Bill Fivaz and J.T. Stanton for inclusion in *The Cherrypickers' Guide to Rare Die Varieties,* which also illustrates multiple varieties. On this repunched date, the 0 in 1908 is over a previous 8, probably the result of the 1908 logotype having been punched in too far to the left, then mostly effaced except for the 8, and then repunched in the correct position. The center arcs of the earlier 8 show clearly inside the center of the 0. This variety is rare at all grade levels.

1908-O DIME

Circulation-strike mintage: 1,789,000

AVAILABILITY IN MINT STATE: Slightly scarce in lower–Mint State grades. ***Estimated number MS-65 or higher:*** 100 to 120.

AVAILABILITY IN CIRCULATED GRADES: 12,000 to 15,000. Most are G-4. John Frost commented: "While this issue is not technically scarce as a date, this is a surprisingly tough coin. Often when a collector is building a set, this date is one of the last of the non-keys that they find, especially above VG."[6]

CHARACTERISTICS OF STRIKING: Usually with some light areas.

MARKET VALUES – CIRCULATION STRIKES

G-4	VG-8	F-12	VF-20	EF-40	AU-50
$6	$12	$45	$65	$95	$150

MS-60	MS-62	MS-63	MS-64	MS-65
$300	$450	$600	$850	$1,250

CERTIFIED POPULATIONS – CIRCULATION STRIKES

Fair	AG	G	VG	F	VF	EF	AU	MS-60
0	0	1	1	2	8	4	13	0

MS-61	MS-62	MS-63	MS-64	MS-65	MS-66	MS-67	MS-68	MS-69	MS-70
3	5	20	28	9	13	4	0	0	0

1908-S DIME

Circulation-strike mintage: 3,220,000

AVAILABILITY IN MINT STATE: Slightly scarce in lower–Mint State ranges. ***Estimated number MS-65 or higher:*** 120 to 140.

AVAILABILITY IN CIRCULATED GRADES: 25,000 to 30,000. Most are G-4.

CHARACTERISTICS OF STRIKING: Usually sharp.

MARKET VALUES – CIRCULATION STRIKES

G-4	VG-8	F-12	VF-20	EF-40	AU-50
$4	$6	$15	$25	$45	$170

MS-60	MS-62	MS-63	MS-64	MS-65
$350	$500	$800	$1,250	$1,500

CERTIFIED POPULATIONS – CIRCULATION STRIKES

Fair	AG	G	VG	F	VF	EF	AU	MS-60
1	0	0	0	1	4	11	21	0

MS-61	MS-62	MS-63	MS-64	MS-65	MS-66	MS-67	MS-68	MS-69	MS-70
1	10	14	15	8	7	0	0	0	0

1909 DIME

Circulation-strike mintage: 10,240,000
Proof mintage: 650

Availability in Mint State: Common in lower–Mint State grades. ***Estimated number MS-65 or higher:*** 100 to 120.

Availability in circulated grades: 80,000 to 100,000. Most are G-4. Common in higher grades in relation to the number of collectors seeking them.

Characteristics of striking: Usually sharp.

Availability in Proof format: ***Proof–60 to 64:*** 350 to 450. ***Proof-65 or better:*** 75 to 90.

MARKET VALUES – CIRCULATION STRIKES

G-4	VG-8	F-12	VF-20	EF-40	AU-50
$4	$5	$6	$10	$25	$75

MS-60	MS-62	MS-63	MS-64	MS-65
$125	$160	$240	$375	$625

MARKET VALUES – PROOF STRIKES

PF-60	PF-63	PF-64	PF-65	PF-65Cam	PF-66	PF-66Cam	PF-67
$275	$575	$925	$1,500	$1,700	$2,000	$2,250	$3,500

CERTIFIED POPULATIONS – CIRCULATION STRIKES

Fair	AG	G	VG	F	VF	EF	AU	MS-60
0	0	1	2	4	4	1	35	1

MS-61	MS-62	MS-63	MS-64	MS-65	MS-66	MS-67	MS-68	MS-69	MS-70
18	38	59	82	31	10	0	0	0	0

CERTIFIED POPULATIONS – PROOF STRIKES

PF-50	PF-60	PF-61	PF-62	PF-63	PF-64
2	1	2	16	35	71

PF-65	PF-66	PF-67	PF-68	PF-69	PF-70
46	50	28	5	0	0

1909-D Dime

Circulation-strike mintage: 954,000

AVAILABILITY IN MINT STATE: Somewhat scarce in lower–Mint State categories. ***Estimated number MS-65 or higher:*** 30 to 40, if indeed that many.

AVAILABILITY IN CIRCULATED GRADES: 4,000 to 5,000. Most are G-4. Very scarce in EF and AU grades.

CHARACTERISTICS OF STRIKING: Usually sharp.

MARKET VALUES – CIRCULATION STRIKES

G-4	VG-8	F-12	VF-20	EF-40	AU-50
$8	$20	$60	$90	$140	$225

MS-60	MS-62	MS-63	MS-64	MS-65
$500	$650	$1,000	$1,400	$2,500

CERTIFIED POPULATIONS – CIRCULATION STRIKES

Fair	AG	G	VG	F	VF	EF	AU	MS-60
0	0	3	2	5	4	8	13	0

MS-61	MS-62	MS-63	MS-64	MS-65	MS-66	MS-67	MS-68	MS-69	MS-70
2	7	13	35	15	3	2	0	0	0

1909-O DIME

Circulation-strike mintage: 2,287,000

AVAILABILITY IN MINT STATE: Slightly scarce in lower–Mint State grades. ***Estimated number MS-65 or higher:*** 80 to 95.

AVAILABILITY IN CIRCULATED GRADES: 20,000 to 25,000. Most are G-4.

CHARACTERISTICS OF STRIKING: Typically weak in areas. Sharply struck coins exist, but they take some searching to find.

NOTES: A variety earlier known as 1909-O, O Over Inverted D Mintmark, has been discredited by modern scholars.

MARKET VALUES – CIRCULATION STRIKES

G-4	VG-8	F-12	VF-20	EF-40	AU-50
$5	$8	$13	$25	$70	$150

MS-60	MS-62	MS-63	MS-64	MS-65
$250	$375	$575	$1,100	$1,500

CERTIFIED POPULATIONS – CIRCULATION STRIKES

Fair	AG	G	VG	F	VF	EF	AU	MS-60
0	0	3	1	1	6	5	16	0

MS-61	MS-62	MS-63	MS-64	MS-65	MS-66	MS-67	MS-68	MS-69	MS-70
8	8	19	22	15	3	2	0	0	0

1909-S Dime

Circulation-strike mintage: 1,000,000

Availability in Mint State: Slightly scarce in lower–Mint State grades. ***Estimated number MS-65 or higher:*** 45 to 55. Another 20th-century rarity.

Availability in circulated grades: 8,000 to 10,000. Most are G-4. David Lawrence stated that this is one of the 11 scarcest Barber dimes in grades F-12 to VF-35 and is one of the 11 scarcest Barber dimes in grades EF-40 to AU-58.

Characteristics of striking: Usually sharp.

MARKET VALUES – CIRCULATION STRIKES

G-4	VG-8	F-12	VF-20	EF-40	AU-50
$9	$20	$80	$130	$180	$310

MS-60	MS-62	MS-63	MS-64	MS-65
$550	$700	$1,400	$1,750	$2,800

CERTIFIED POPULATIONS – CIRCULATION STRIKES

Fair	AG	G	VG	F	VF	EF	AU	MS-60
0	0	0	4	7	11	2	9	0

MS-61	MS-62	MS-63	MS-64	MS-65	MS-66	MS-67	MS-68	MS-69	MS-70
4	13	9	31	9	3	0	0	0	0

1910 DIME

Circulation-strike mintage: 11,520,000
Proof mintage: 551

AVAILABILITY IN MINT STATE: Easily located in all Mint State grades. ***Estimated number MS-65 or higher:*** 300 to 360.

AVAILABILITY IN CIRCULATED GRADES: 80,000 to 100,000. Most are G-4.

CHARACTERISTICS OF STRIKING: Usually sharp.

AVAILABILITY IN PROOF FORMAT: ***Proof–60 to 64:*** 300 to 350. ***Proof-65 or better:*** 50 to 60. Surprisingly rare at the gem level.

MARKET VALUES – CIRCULATION STRIKES

G-4	VG-8	F-12	VF-20	EF-40	AU-50
$4	$5	$6	$10	$25	$75

MS-60	MS-62	MS-63	MS-64	MS-65
$125	$160	$240	$365	$625

MARKET VALUES – PROOF STRIKES

PF-60	PF-63	PF-64	PF-65	PF-65Cam	PF-66	PF-66Cam	PF-67
$275	$575	$925	$1,500	$1,700	$2,000	$2,250	$3,500

CERTIFIED POPULATIONS – CIRCULATION STRIKES

Fair	AG	G	VG	F	VF	EF	AU	MS-60
0	0	1	1	0	11	7	41	0

MS-61	MS-62	MS-63	MS-64	MS-65	MS-66	MS-67	MS-68	MS-69	MS-70
22	64	85	128	64	28	6	0	0	0

CERTIFIED POPULATIONS – PROOF STRIKES

PF-50	PF-60	PF-61	PF-62	PF-63	PF-64
0	0	4	8	30	59
PF-65	**PF-66**	**PF-67**	**PF-68**	**PF-69**	**PF-70**
51	38	21	7	0	0

1910-D Dime

Circulation-strike mintage: 3,490,000

Availability in Mint State: Lower-level Mint State coins are available readily enough. ***Estimated number MS-65 or higher:*** 60 to 70. Another instance of a late-date rarity in gem Mint State.

Availability in circulated grades: 25,000 to 30,000. Most are G-4.

Characteristics of striking: Often with some weakness and dull surfaces. Check the hair above the forehead first.

MARKET VALUES – CIRCULATION STRIKES

G-4	VG-8	F-12	VF-20	EF-40	AU-50
$4	$5	$10	$20	$48	$95

MS-60	MS-62	MS-63	MS-64	MS-65
$220	$300	$450	$650	$1,500

CERTIFIED POPULATIONS – CIRCULATION STRIKES

Fair	AG	G	VG	F	VF	EF	AU	MS-60
0	0	1	2	1	3	3	13	0

MS-61	MS-62	MS-63	MS-64	MS-65	MS-66	MS-67	MS-68	MS-69	MS-70
4	11	17	27	3	3	1	0	0	0

1910-S DIME

Circulation-strike mintage: 1,240,000

AVAILABILITY IN MINT STATE: Slightly scarce in lower–Mint State grades. ***Estimated number MS-65 or higher:*** 90 to 110.

AVAILABILITY IN CIRCULATED GRADES: 10,000 to 12,000. Most are G-4.

CHARACTERISTICS OF STRIKING: Usually sharp.

MARKET VALUES – CIRCULATION STRIKES

G-4	VG-8	F-12	VF-20	EF-40	AU-50
$6	$9	$50	$70	$110	$180

MS-60	MS-62	MS-63	MS-64	MS-65
$425	$550	$700	$1,100	$2,250

CERTIFIED POPULATIONS – CIRCULATION STRIKES

Fair	AG	G	VG	F	VF	EF	AU	MS-60
0	0	1	2	3	4	8	8	0

MS-61	MS-62	MS-63	MS-64	MS-65	MS-66	MS-67	MS-68	MS-69	MS-70
1	8	8	13	7	2	2	0	0	0

1911 Dime

Circulation-strike mintage: 18,870,000
Proof mintage: 543

Availability in Mint State: Easily found in lower–Mint State grades. ***Estimated number MS-65 or higher:*** 600 to 750.

Availability in circulated grades: 200,000 to 250,000. Most are G-4. Easily available in higher grades.

Characteristics of striking: Usually sharp.

Availability in Proof format: ***Proof–60 to 64:*** 290 to 340. ***Proof-65 or better:*** 65 to 80.

Proof dimes have a raised ridge, almost like a thin extra leaf, extending from the left ribbon to a denticle.

Notes: In this year there was a great scarcity of dimes in circulation in the East and Midwest. To provide metal for coinage, the Treasury Department purchased silver bullion in bulk for the first time in two years.[7]

MARKET VALUES – CIRCULATION STRIKES

G-4	VG-8	F-12	VF-20	EF-40	AU-50
$4	$5	$6	$10	$25	$75

MS-60	MS-62	MS-63	MS-64	MS-65
$125	$160	$240	$365	$625

MARKET VALUES – PROOF STRIKES

PF-60	PF-63	PF-64	PF-65	PF-65Cam	PF-66	PF-66Cam	PF-67
$275	$575	$925	$1,500	$1,700	$2,000	$2,250	$3,500

CERTIFIED POPULATIONS – CIRCULATION STRIKES

Fair	AG	G	VG	F	VF	EF	AU	MS-60
0	1	6	4	2	11	11	92	0

MS-61	MS-62	MS-63	MS-64	MS-65	MS-66	MS-67	MS-68	MS-69	MS-70
41	127	183	246	138	49	11	2	0	0

CERTIFIED POPULATIONS – PROOF STRIKES

PF-50	PF-60	PF-61	PF-62	PF-63	PF-64
0	1	3	12	12	75
PF-65	**PF-66**	**PF-67**	**PF-68**	**PF-69**	**PF-70**
54	35	28	12	2	0

1911-D Dime

Circulation-strike mintage: 11,209,000

Availability in Mint State: One of the most common Barber silver coins at the gem level. ***Estimated number MS-65 or higher:*** 600 to 750.

Availability in circulated grades: 80,000 to 100,000. Most are G-4. Easy to find in all grades.

Characteristics of striking: Usually sharp, but some examples are weak.

MARKET VALUES – CIRCULATION STRIKES

G-4	VG-8	F-12	VF-20	EF-40	AU-50
$4	$5	$6	$10	$25	$75

MS-60	MS-62	MS-63	MS-64	MS-65
$125	$160	$240	$365	$625

CERTIFIED POPULATIONS – CIRCULATION STRIKES

Fair	AG	G	VG	F	VF	EF	AU	MS-60
0	1	1	2	6	2	9	38	2

MS-61	MS-62	MS-63	MS-64	MS-65	MS-66	MS-67	MS-68	MS-69	MS-70
12	25	28	62	40	25	7	0	0	0

1911-S Dime

Circulation-strike mintage: 3,520,000

Availability in Mint State: Easy to find in any desired Mint State level. ***Estimated number MS-65 or higher:*** 275 to 325.

Availability in circulated grades: 25,000 to 30,000. Most are G-4.

Characteristics of striking: Usually sharp.

MARKET VALUES – CIRCULATION STRIKES

G-4	VG-8	F-12	VF-20	EF-40	AU-50
$4	$5	$10	$20	$40	$100

MS-60	MS-62	MS-63	MS-64	MS-65
$200	$275	$400	$750	$1,000

CERTIFIED POPULATIONS – CIRCULATION STRIKES

Fair	AG	G	VG	F	VF	EF	AU	MS-60
0	1	0	1	1	0	4	22	0

MS-61	MS-62	MS-63	MS-64	MS-65	MS-66	MS-67	MS-68	MS-69	MS-70
12	19	29	34	31	25	5	1	0	0

1912 Dime

Circulation-strike mintage: 19,350,000
Proof mintage: 700

AVAILABILITY IN MINT STATE: Easy to find in lower–Mint State ranges, the 1912 is among the commonest issues. ***Estimated number MS-65 or higher:*** 500 to 600.

AVAILABILITY IN CIRCULATED GRADES: 200,000 to 250,000. Most are G-4. Common in all circulated grades.

CHARACTERISTICS OF STRIKING: Variable, which is unusual for a Philadelphia Mint Barber dime. A sharp coin is easily found.

AVAILABILITY IN PROOF FORMAT: ***Proof–60 to 64:*** 300 to 400. ***Proof-65 or better:*** 65 to 80.

MARKET VALUES – CIRCULATION STRIKES

G-4	VG-8	F-12	VF-20	EF-40	AU-50
$4	$5	$6	$10	$25	$75

MS-60	MS-62	MS-63	MS-64	MS-65
$110	$135	$220	$325	$600

MARKET VALUES – PROOF STRIKES

PF-60	PF-63	PF-64	PF-65	PF-65Cam	PF-66	PF-66Cam	PF-67
$275	$575	$925	$1,500	$1,700	$2,000	$2,250	$3,500

CERTIFIED POPULATIONS – CIRCULATION STRIKES

Fair	AG	G	VG	F	VF	EF	AU	MS-60
0	0	2	3	5	12	18	101	1

MS-61	MS-62	MS-63	MS-64	MS-65	MS-66	MS-67	MS-68	MS-69	MS-70
38	117	206	251	153	38	9	0	0	0

CERTIFIED POPULATIONS – PROOF STRIKES

PF-50	PF-60	PF-61	PF-62	PF-63	PF-64
0	0	5	9	32	50

PF-65	PF-66	PF-67	PF-68	PF-69	PF-70
41	27	14	5	0	0

1912-D DIME

Circulation-strike mintage: 11,760,000

Availability in Mint State: Lower–Mint State grades are plentiful in the marketplace. ***Estimated number MS-65 or higher:*** 150 to 180.

Availability in circulated grades: 80,000 to 100,000. Easy to find in all grades.

Characteristics of striking: Variable. Take time to find a sharp one.

MARKET VALUES – CIRCULATION STRIKES

G-4	VG-8	F-12	VF-20	EF-40	AU-50
$4	$5	$6	$10	$25	$75

MS-60	MS-62	MS-63	MS-64	MS-65
$125	$160	$240	$365	$625

CERTIFIED POPULATIONS – CIRCULATION STRIKES

Fair	AG	G	VG	F	VF	EF	AU	MS-60
0	0	8	8	4	13	11	62	1

MS-61	MS-62	MS-63	MS-64	MS-65	MS-66	MS-67	MS-68	MS-69	MS-70
23	38	58	76	27	6	1	0	0	0

1912-S Dime

Circulation-strike mintage: 3,420,000

Availability in Mint State: Common in lower–Mint State ranges. ***Estimated number MS-65 or higher:*** 75 to 90. A poster example of another late-date dime that is curiously rare in MS-65 or higher grades.

Availability in circulated grades: 30,000 to 40,000. Most are G-4.

Characteristics of striking: Usually sharp.

MARKET VALUES – CIRCULATION STRIKES

G-4	VG-8	F-12	VF-20	EF-40	AU-50
$4	$5	$6	$12	$35	$90

MS-60	MS-62	MS-63	MS-64	MS-65
$170	$225	$300	$500	$850

CERTIFIED POPULATIONS – CIRCULATION STRIKES

Fair	AG	G	VG	F	VF	EF	AU	MS-60
0	0	3	0	1	2	2	35	1

MS-61	MS-62	MS-63	MS-64	MS-65	MS-66	MS-67	MS-68	MS-69	MS-70
7	19	26	34	38	6	2	0	0	0

1913 DIME

Circulation-strike mintage: 19,760,000
Proof mintage: 622

AVAILABILITY IN MINT STATE: Very common in lower–Mint State ranges. ***Estimated number MS-65 or higher:*** 400 to 480.

AVAILABILITY IN CIRCULATED GRADES: 200,000 to 250,000. Most are G-4. More of this issue (47 examples) were found than any other in the Schneider holding formed in 1937 and 1938 (see page 28).

CHARACTERISTICS OF STRIKING: Varies, but many are quite sharp.

AVAILABILITY IN PROOF FORMAT: ***Proof–60 to 64:*** 300 to 400. ***Proof-65 or better:*** 50 to 60.

NOTES: Dimes of this year from Philadelphia and San Francisco each have minor details added in the master die to three of the five leaves directly over the word LIBERTY in the form of light lines at the centers as shown above.[8]

Detail showing light lines added to the centers of the leaves for this issue.

MARKET VALUES – CIRCULATION STRIKES

G-4	VG-8	F-12	VF-20	EF-40	AU-50
$4	$5	$6	$10	$25	$75

MS-60	MS-62	MS-63	MS-64	MS-65
$125	$160	$240	$365	$625

MARKET VALUES – PROOF STRIKES

PF-60	PF-63	PF-64	PF-65	PF-65Cam	PF-66	PF-66Cam	PF-67
$275	$575	$975	$1,500	$1,700	$2,000	$2,250	$3,500

CERTIFIED POPULATIONS – CIRCULATION STRIKES

Fair	AG	G	VG	F	VF	EF	AU	MS-60
0	0	5	1	10	8	15	101	3

MS-61	MS-62	MS-63	MS-64	MS-65	MS-66	MS-67	MS-68	MS-69	MS-70
31	105	192	213	83	18	4	0	0	0

CERTIFIED POPULATIONS – PROOF STRIKES

PF-50	PF-60	PF-61	PF-62	PF-63	PF-64
0	1	5	22	36	69

PF-65	PF-66	PF-67	PF-68	PF-69	PF-70
24	21	15	2	1	0

1913-S Dime

Circulation-strike mintage: 510,000

Availability in Mint State: Slightly scarce in lower–Mint State levels. The low mintage has called much attention to this issue. ***Estimated number MS-65 or higher:*** 120 to 140.

Availability in circulated grades: 3,000 to 4,000. Most are G-4. Scarce in EF and AU grades.

Characteristics of striking: Usually well struck.

Notes: In 1991 David Lawrence considered the issue to be "over-rated because of high survivorship." John Frost stated that in the most recent BCCS population census (2008) there was certainly a level of hoarding of this date. One member reported 74 examples, mostly in low grades, and numerous others had 10 to 20 of them.[9]

MARKET VALUES – CIRCULATION STRIKES

G-4	VG-8	F-12	VF-20	EF-40	AU-50
$35	$55	$125	$190	$250	$320

MS-60	MS-62	MS-63	MS-64	MS-65
$500	$600	$800	$1,000	$1,500

CERTIFIED POPULATIONS – CIRCULATION STRIKES

Fair	AG	G	VG	F	VF	EF	AU	MS-60
0	11	33	19	11	23	7	19	0

MS-61	MS-62	MS-63	MS-64	MS-65	MS-66	MS-67	MS-68	MS-69	MS-70
3	10	21	23	21	7	1	0	0	0

1914 DIME

Circulation-strike mintage: 17,360,250
Proof mintage: 425

AVAILABILITY IN MINT STATE: Easy to find in any Mint State level desired. ***Estimated number MS-65 or higher:*** 600 to 750. One of the most common Barber silver coins at the gem level.

AVAILABILITY IN CIRCULATED GRADES: 125,000 to 150,000. Most are G-4. Such coins were common in circulation into the late 1940s.

CHARACTERISTICS OF STRIKING: Variable, but most examples are sharp.

AVAILABILITY IN PROOF FORMAT: ***Proof–60 to 64:*** 250 to 300. ***Proof-65 or better:*** 50 to 60.

Only 425 Proofs were minted, the smallest Proof production of any Barber dime.

MARKET VALUES – CIRCULATION STRIKES

G-4	VG-8	F-12	VF-20	EF-40	AU-50
$4	$5	$6	$10	$25	$75

MS-60	MS-62	MS-63	MS-64	MS-65
$125	$160	$240	$365	$625

MARKET VALUES – PROOF STRIKES

PF-60	PF-63	PF-64	PF-65	PF-65Cam	PF-66	PF-66Cam	PF-67
$275	$575	$925	$1,500	$1,700	$2,000	$2,250	$3,500

CERTIFIED POPULATIONS – CIRCULATION STRIKES

Fair	AG	G	VG	F	VF	EF	AU	MS-60
0	1	3	3	5	22	10	79	2

MS-61	MS-62	MS-63	MS-64	MS-65	MS-66	MS-67	MS-68	MS-69	MS-70
15	75	154	276	143	43	1	0	0	0

CERTIFIED POPULATIONS – PROOF STRIKES

PF-50	PF-60	PF-61	PF-62	PF-63	PF-64
0	0	4	6	33	46

PF-65	PF-66	PF-67	PF-68	PF-69	PF-70
38	25	13	2	0	0

1914-D Dime

Circulation-strike mintage: 11,908,000

Availability in Mint State: Very common in any Mint State grade desired. ***Estimated number MS-65 or higher:*** 175 to 200.

Availability in circulated grades: 180,000 to 100,000. Most are G-4. Easy to find in any grade desired.

Characteristics of striking: Usually sharp.

MARKET VALUES – CIRCULATION STRIKES

G-4	VG-8	F-12	VF-20	EF-40	AU-50
$4	$5	$6	$10	$20	$75

MS-60	MS-62	MS-63	MS-64	MS-65
$110	$135	$220	$325	$600

CERTIFIED POPULATIONS – CIRCULATION STRIKES

Fair	AG	G	VG	F	VF	EF	AU	MS-60
0	0	5	3	9	20	12	84	2

MS-61	MS-62	MS-63	MS-64	MS-65	MS-66	MS-67	MS-68	MS-69	MS-70
28	85	91	111	43	14	8	0	0	0

1914-S DIME

Circulation-strike mintage: 2,100,000

AVAILABILITY IN MINT STATE: Easy to find in any desired Mint State level. ***Estimated number MS-65 or higher:*** 110 to 130.

AVAILABILITY IN CIRCULATED GRADES: 15,000 to 18,000. Most are G-4.

CHARACTERISTICS OF STRIKING: Variable, but most are sharp.

MARKET VALUES – CIRCULATION STRIKES

G-4	VG-8	F-12	VF-20	EF-40	AU-50
$4	$5	$10	$18	$40	$80

MS-60	MS-62	MS-63	MS-64	MS-65
$175	$225	$350	$700	$1,400

CERTIFIED POPULATIONS – CIRCULATION STRIKES

Fair	AG	G	VG	F	VF	EF	AU	MS-60
0	2	2	0	2	6	3	20	0

MS-61	MS-62	MS-63	MS-64	MS-65	MS-66	MS-67	MS-68	MS-69	MS-70
7	16	31	41	21	9	1	0	0	0

1915 Dime

Circulation-strike mintage: 5,620,000
Proof mintage: 450

Availability in Mint State: Common in all Mint State levels. ***Estimated number MS-65 or higher:*** 200 to 240.

Availability in circulated grades: 50,000 to 60,000. Most are G-4. Easy to find in any grade desired.

Detail of crudely cut date.

Characteristics of striking: Variable, but most examples are sharp.

Availability in Proof format: ***Proof–60 to 64:*** 275 to 325. ***Proof-65 or better:*** 30 to 40. This is probably the rarest Proof Barber dime at the gem level.

Notes: The digits on the logotype for this year are somewhat crudely done for an unknown reason—a curiosity.

MARKET VALUES – CIRCULATION STRIKES

G-4	VG-8	F-12	VF-20	EF-40	AU-50
$4	$5	$6	$10	$25	$75

MS-60	MS-62	MS-63	MS-64	MS-65
$125	$160	$240	$365	$625

MARKET VALUES – PROOF STRIKES

PF-60	PF-63	PF-64	PF-65	PF-65Cam	PF-66	PF-66Cam	PF-67
$275	$575	$925	$1,500	$1,700	$2,000	$2,250	$3,500

CERTIFIED POPULATIONS – CIRCULATION STRIKES

Fair	AG	G	VG	F	VF	EF	AU	MS-60
0	0	1	2	2	4	4	38	0

MS-61	MS-62	MS-63	MS-64	MS-65	MS-66	MS-67	MS-68	MS-69	MS-70
14	43	65	102	42	9	0	0	0	0

CERTIFIED POPULATIONS – PROOF STRIKES

PF-50	PF-60	PF-61	PF-62	PF-63	PF-64
1	1	6	8	17	49
PF-65	**PF-66**	**PF-67**	**PF-68**	**PF-69**	**PF-70**
27	13	20	1	0	0

1915-S DIME

Circulation-strike mintage: 960,000

AVAILABILITY IN MINT STATE: Slightly scarce in lower–Mint State grades. ***Estimated number MS-65 or higher:*** 80 to 95.

AVAILABILITY IN CIRCULATED GRADES: 10,000 to 12,000. Most are G-4.

CHARACTERISTICS OF STRIKING: Usually sharp.

MARKET VALUES – CIRCULATION STRIKES

G-4	VG-8	F-12	VF-20	EF-40	AU-50
$7	$12	$35	$50	$70	$140

MS-60	MS-62	MS-63	MS-64	MS-65
$275	$325	$475	$675	$1,400

CERTIFIED POPULATIONS – CIRCULATION STRIKES

Fair	AG	G	VG	F	VF	EF	AU	MS-60
0	0	1	1	3	5	10	25	0

MS-61	MS-62	MS-63	MS-64	MS-65	MS-66	MS-67	MS-68	MS-69	MS-70
6	13	16	40	13	7	5	0	0	0

1916 Dime

Circulation-strike mintage: 18,490,000

Availability in Mint State: Easy to find in any desired Mint State grade. ***Estimated number MS-65 or higher:*** 500 to 600.

Availability in circulated grades: 125,000 to 150,000. Most are or G-4.

Characteristics of striking: Often weak, but sharp examples can be found with diligent searching.

MARKET VALUES – CIRCULATION STRIKES

G-4	VG-8	F-12	VF-20	EF-40	AU-50
$4	$5	$6	$10	$25	$75

MS-60	MS-62	MS-63	MS-64	MS-65
$125	$160	$240	$365	$625

CERTIFIED POPULATIONS – CIRCULATION STRIKES

Fair	AG	G	VG	F	VF	EF	AU	MS-60
0	0	9	8	9	17	12	159	4

MS-61	MS-62	MS-63	MS-64	MS-65	MS-66	MS-67	MS-68	MS-69	MS-70
69	199	257	316	141	40	8	0	0	0

1916-S DIME

Circulation-strike mintage: 5,820,000

AVAILABILITY IN MINT STATE: Common in grades from MS-60 to MS-64. ***Estimated number MS-65 or higher:*** 200 to 240.

AVAILABILITY IN CIRCULATED GRADES: 40,000 to 55,000. Most are G-4.

CHARACTERISTICS OF STRIKING: Variable. Take time to find a sharp one.

MARKET VALUES – CIRCULATION STRIKES

G-4	VG-8	F-12	VF-20	EF-40	AU-50
$4	$5	$6	$10	$25	$75

MS-60	MS-62	MS-63	MS-64	MS-65
$125	$160	$240	$350	$650

CERTIFIED POPULATIONS – CIRCULATION STRIKES

Fair	AG	G	VG	F	VF	EF	AU	MS-60
0	0	2	0	0	9	5	50	2

MS-61	MS-62	MS-63	MS-64	MS-65	MS-66	MS-67	MS-68	MS-69	MS-70
15	40	60	69	39	30	0	0	0	0

A Gallery of Barber Dime Proof Coinage

Proof dimes were struck of each year from 1892 to 1915, inclusive, for the numismatic trade. None were made in 1916. See page 87 for a longer discussion. This is not a complete showing of Barber dime Proofs.

1892, Proof, dime.

1893, Proof, dime.

1894, Proof, dime.

1895, Proof, dime.

1897, Proof, dime.

1898, Proof, dime.

1899, Proof, dime.

1900, Proof, dime.

1902, Proof, dime.

1904, Proof, dime.

1905, Proof, dime.

1906, Proof, dime.

1907, Proof, dime.

1909, Proof, dime.

1910, Proof, dime.

1911, Proof, dime.

1912, Proof, dime.

1914, Proof, dime.

Chapter Five

Barber Quarters 1892–1916

The Design of the Barber Quarter

Charles E. Barber's Liberty Head motif, commonly referred to as the "Barber" style, was used on quarter dollars from 1892 through 1916. The obverse motif of Liberty is similar to that found on the dime and half dollar and features her facing to the right, her hair in a Phrygian cap, wearing a laurel wreath, with LIBERTY on a small band above her forehead. Six stars are to the left and seven to the right, IN GOD WE TRUST is above, and the date is below.

The reverse is an adaptation of the Great Seal of the United States and depicts a heraldic eagle holding in its talons an olive branch and arrows, although the branch and arrows are transposed from the position used on quarter coinage (and other silver and gold issues) of nearly a century earlier. Above the eagle is a galaxy of 13 stars. UNITED STATES OF AMERICA and QUARTER DOLLAR surround the design.

Pattern 1891 quarter, Judd-1761. The reverse mainly differs in having clouds and a different arrangement of the stars.

Pattern Coin

Only one pattern is known for the Barber quarter. Dated 1891, the obverse very closely follows the adopted design of 1892, but with slight differences. These include adjustments of the border letters, the details of the ribbon and its relationship to the stars, and the position of the stars in relation to the portrait and lettering.

The only existing example is in the National Numismatic Collection in the Smithsonian Institution. The reason no more quarter varieties were made is that the half dollar was used to try out various ideas, with the thought that whatever was adopted for the half dollar could be used on the quarter as well.

Mintages and Distribution

It is recorded that the first Barber quarters were struck at the Philadelphia Mint on Saturday, January 2, 1892, at 9:00 a.m. Coins reached circulation soon afterward. The Treasury Department paid out large quantities from its building in Washington and also by shipments to banks, individuals, businesses, and others requesting them.

As evidenced by the fairly strong mintage quantities from 1892 onward, demand for and use of Barber quarters was strong. There was no particular effort to retire worn coins from circulation, with the result that into the 1930s and 1940s such pieces were common in pocket change, though usually worn down to grades of About Good and Good. By the early 1950s, scattered coins were still seen, and by the end of the decade they were all gone.

Mintages of Barber Quarters

Mintages of Barber quarters from highest to lowest, by issue, are as follows:

1899: 12,624,000	1902-O: 4,748,000	1894-S: 2,648,821	1907-S: 1,360,000
1902: 12,196,967	1907-O: 4,560,000	1899-O: 2,644,000	1909-S: 1,348,000
1898: 11,100,000	1895: 4,440,000	1907-D: 2,484,000	1905-O: 1,230,000
1900: 10,016,000	1912: 4,400,000	1904-O: 2,456,000	1903-S: 1,036,000
1903: 9,669,309	1908: 4,232,000	1910: 2,244,000	1898-S: 1,020,592
1904: 9,588,143	1896: 3,874,000	1906-O: 2,056,000	1911-S: 988,000
1909: 9,268,000	1911: 3,720,000	1905-S: 1,884,000	1911-D: 933,600
1892, Types 1 & II: 8,236,000	1915-D: 3,694,000	1898-O: 1,868,000	1908-S: 784,000
1897: 8,140,000	1906: 3,655,760	1900-S: 1,858,585	1909-O: 712,000
1907: 7,192,000	1903-O: 3,500,000	1916: 1,788,000	1912-S: 708,000
1916-D: 6,540,800	1915: 3,480,000	1895-S: 1,764,681	1899-S: 708,000
1914: 6,244,250	1894: 3,432,000	1901-O: 1,612,000	1915-S: 704,000
1908-O: 6,244,000	1900-O: 3,416,000	1893-S: 1,545,535	1897-S: 542,229
1908-D: 5,788,000	1893-O: 3,396,000	1902-S: 1,524,612	1913: 484,000
1893: 5,444,023	1906-D: 3,280,000	1910-D: 1,500,000	1914-S: 264,000
1909-D: 5,114,000	1914-D: 3,046,000	1896-O: 1,484,000	1896-S: 188,039
1905: 4,967,523	1894-O: 2,852,000	1913-D: 1,450,800	1901-S: 72,664
	1895-O: 2,816,000	1897-O: 1,414,800	1913-S: 40,000

Barber Quarter Hub Changes

In early 1892 it was found that the quarters did not stack properly. To correct this, Barber made slight adjustments to both sides. The engraver wrote to Mint Director Edward O. Leech to say that on the obverse he had increased the width of the border and had decreased the radius circle that contained the words IN GOD WE TRUST.[1] These obverse differences are subtle and can best be seen by studying the distance of the stars and letters to the denticles. On the earlier dies the spacing is ever so slightly farther away.

The changes to the reverse were obvious. The two different Barber quarter dollar reverse hubs of 1892 were first described in *The Numismatist* by George W. Rice in May 1899. Changes to the obverse are less well known.[2]

Obverse Hub I was used from 1892 through 1900, and Obverse Hub II, from 1900 to the end of the series in 1916. The differences are slight. On Obverse Hub II the relief is imperceptibly lower, the denticles are longer and slightly more widely spaced, and Liberty's inner ear has more detail. The differences are best seen by comparing two coins under magnification. The lowering of the relief resulted in LIBERTY not wearing away as quickly in circulation, but still most examples were AG-3 or G-4 by the mid-1930s.

The alterations worked. A stack of 21 of the new coins introduced in 1900 was equal in height to a stack of 20 of the earlier type.

In 1900 Reverse Hub III was introduced with slight changes. In that year coins from all three mints were made with both II and III reverses. William Cowburn in his study of quarter dollar reverses gave these estimates for 1900 coinage:

1900 Philadelphia: 44% Reverse Hub II and 56% III.

1900 Proofs: Type II.

1900 New Orleans: 50% Reverse Hub II and 50% III.

1900 San Francisco: 61% Reverse Hub II and 39% III.[3]

The earliest Barber quarters from all three mints have the Type I reverse, from Reverse Hub I. This can be distinguished at a glance by looking at the E in UNITED at the upper left. On Type I part of the crossbar of the letter can be seen above the eagle's wing, while on Type II, from Reverse Hub II, the wing covers this feature completely. Upon close inspection, there are many differences between the Reverse Hub I and II. Overall, the Reverse Hub II eagle and other features are slightly smaller, permitting a wider space between the letters and the denticles. The stars above the eagle are slightly different on each. For quick reference see below ST of STATES.[4]

These differences were ignored by collectors for many years. In recent decades they have become popular, and nearly all specialists endeavor to obtain one of each reverse for the three date and mintmark varieties of 1892.

The Type II hub was used from partway through 1892 into 1900 in which year the Type III hub was introduced. On Reverse Hub III, the wings extend farther than on Hub II. This is most easily seen on the E of UNITED, where the left wing now protrudes beyond the top of the E. The letters on this reverse are also closer to the denticles than the letters on the Type II reverse.

For the Obverse Hub and Reverse Hub combinations in the transitional year of 1900 Steve Hustad listed these:

1900 Philadelphia: Obverse Hub I / Reverse Hub II and II/III.

1900 Proofs: I/II.

1900 New Orleans: II/II and II/III.

1900 San Francisco: I/II and II/III.[5]

Detail of Reverse Hub I showing part of the crossbar of E of UNITED visible above the wing.

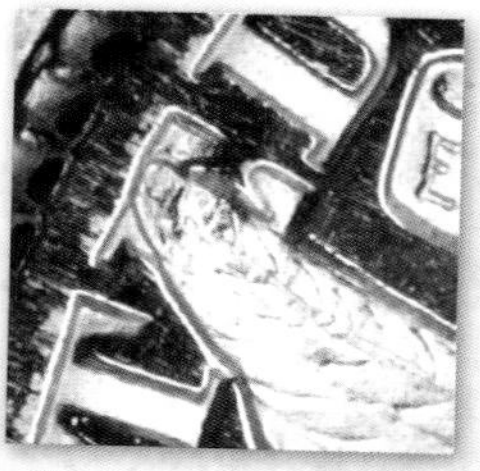

Detail of Reverse Hub II with the crossbar not visible and with the wing of the eagle not protruding through the top of the E. This hub was used through part of the year 1900.

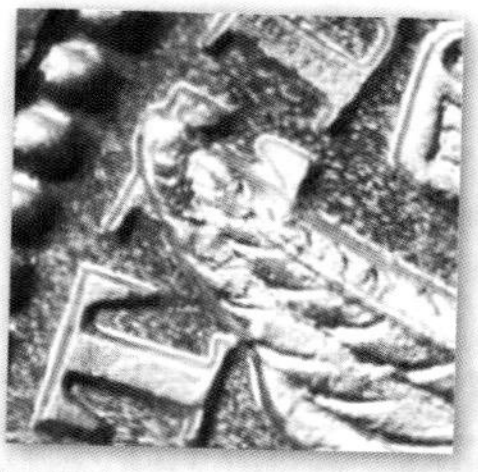

Detail of Reverse Hub III with the crossbar not visible and with the wing of the eagle protruding slightly through the top of the E. The wing on the right (not shown) also extends farther than on Hub II. The letters are slightly closer to the denticles than on Hub II. Hub III was used from part of the year 1900 through 1916.

Collecting Barber Quarters

The Barber quarter series is eminently collectible. There are no "impossible" rarities—although the 1896-S, 1901-S, and 1913-S, all of which are remarkable for their low mintages, are the three keys. Of these three, the 1896-S is probably a bit more elusive in gem state than the lower-mintage 1901-S, with the 1913-S being the most available of the three in gem state, although still a notable rarity. All three of these key dates are also very challenging to find in higher circulated grades. Interestingly, whereas the 1913-S is the least rare of the three in Mint State, it is perhaps the most difficult of the three to find in EF and AU grades.[6] As noted in chapter 2, interest in collecting mintmarks did not begin until 1893, when Augustus G. Heaton published his study, *Mint Marks*. However, it was not until after August 1909, when the 1909-S V.D.B. cent made its debut, that mintmarks gained interest, but even then interest in mintmarks was moderate for the Barber quarters. By the time the Barber series came to a close in 1916, relatively few mintmarked issues had been set aside.

The survival of New Orleans, San Francisco, and Denver Mint Barber quarters in Mint State is primarily a matter of chance, this being particularly so for the years prior to 1909. This is especially true of coins at MS-63 and higher levels. David Lawrence, whose *Complete Guide to Barber Quarters* book is an essential reference, commented to me:

> As a rule, New Orleans quarters are far scarcer than their mintages suggest, led in rarity by the 1909-O and 1901-O, followed by the 1905-O, 1896-O, 1898-O, 1903-O, 1904-O, 1897-O, 1902-O, and 1900-O. Many of these are surprisingly hard to find even in low–Mint State grades. In fact, only the 1892-O, 1893-O, 1907-O, and 1908-O are readily available.
>
> At the turn of the century large numbers of 1898-S, 1899-S, and 1900-S quarters were sent to the Philippines. Today, these are surprisingly rare in Mint State.

I recall a conversation with the late Ray Byrne, the well-known Pittsburgh collector, who commented that, after quite a few years of trying to put together an Uncirculated collection of Barber quarters, he gave up, simply because the quality wasn't there. Despite intense searching, he was not able to find gems for even certain dates that were supposed to be "common." Of course, any specialist in Barber quarters reading this today will recognize the situation.

When it comes to analyzing the availability of high-grade Barber quarters, historic auction listings are of little help, as quality is not factored in. Moreover, I know from having attended many sales that coins described as "Uncirculated" often had light friction, this being especially true of auctions held from the 1950s through the 1970s, before the advent of third-party grading. Somewhat more useful in calculating rarity today are the population reports produced by PCGS and NGC, but even so these treat only the numerical grades without addressing aesthetic value.

The design of the pieces is such that even a slight amount of handling will result in scuffing and marking of the cheek of Miss Liberty. Most probably, pieces freshly put into commercial channels from bank bags were what collectors today would call MS-63, or even less.

It is also worth noting that although it is common practice to give a *single* number to the grading of a Barber quarter, some will display a reverse that is a point or two finer than the obverse. This is because the intricacies of the reverse design tended to protect the fields from abrasions.

Among branch-mint Barber coins, while some can be found in such grades as MS-60 through MS-63, all are scarce in gem condition, and many are very rare, as David Lawrence has noted.

Prices in 1946

The first edition of *A Guide Book of United States Coins* was issued in 1946 with a cover date of 1947. The most expensive Barber quarter was the 1894-S, priced at $2,000 in Uncirculated grade. Ranked in descending order the top 20 1946 Uncirculated prices are given below. A number of issues are tied with the same prices. In 1946 the true rarity of certain issues was guesswork. In 2015 there is more information from population reports and studies by specialists:

The Top 20 Barber Quarter Prices in 1946

1. 1901-S: $325.00	6. 1897-S: $22.50	11. 1892-S: $15.00	16. 1907-S: $15.00
2. 1896-S: $100.00	7. 1895-O: $20.00	12. 1898-S: $15.00	17. 1894-O: $12.50
3. 1913-S: $100.00	8. 1896-O: $20.00	13. 1899-S: $15.00	18. 1902-S: $12.50
4. 1901-O: $50.00	9. 1909-O: $20.00	14. 1900-S: $15.00	19. 1905-S: $12.50
5. 1912-S: $50.00	10. 1897-O: $16.00	15. 1903-O: $15.00	20. 1903-S: $11.00[7]

Die Varieties

Reverse Hub I and Reverse Hub II of 1892, explained earlier in this chapter, created the most important die issues in the series. The Reverse Hub III coins of 1900 are easy enough to discern, but these are not widely collected. Beyond these varieties, there are many repunched date varieties from 1892 through 1908, and across the entire series minor variations in mintmark placement and orientation can be found.

A number of misplaced dates (MPDs) are found in the form of traces of date numerals hidden in the denticles. These are believed to have been caused when the workman about to enter the date logotype touched it lightly on the edge of the die to evaluate the hardness of the metal. These and other curiosities can be found in *The Cherrypicker's Guide to Rare Die Varieties* by Bill Fivaz and J.T. Stanton.

Mehl's Numismatic Monthly, March 1910, included this comment from S.E. Young, M.D., of Baywood, Virginia, who enjoyed issues in an era in which most collectors did not notice them:

> Another discovery is in regard to quarters made at the New Orleans Mint. I have examined quite a few of the present style quarters made from 1891 to date, and find mint mark "O" placed in four distinct positions as regards letters and eagle's tail.
>
> First, I find the great majority of these quarters placed about midway between the last R of QUARTER, about one-half millimeter below the eagle's tail.
>
> Second, I find the "O" just about one-half mm to left of D of DOLLAR and same distance from eagle's tail.
>
> Third, I find the "O" about the same distance from R of quarter and same distance from eagle's tail.
>
> Fourth, I find on quarter of 1892 the "O" directly over last R of QUARTER and no space between it and eagle's tail—in fact the eagle's tail had to be "bobbed" to make room for it. This seems to be the rarest of the "O" quarters, as I have only found one and that dated 1892. The others seem to be common.
>
> *S.E. Young, M.D.*

ASPECTS OF STRIKING

Grading numbers do not consider the quality or sharpness of the strike, which for some coins can be weak in areas. Key points to look for: on the obverse check the hair directly above Liberty's forehead; on the right side of the reverse check where the wing meets the shield, and also check the eagle's talons.

David Lawrence further commented that New Orleans Barber quarters are notoriously weakly struck, but coins from Philadelphia and San Francisco can be very weak as well, especially on Miss Liberty's hair and the eagle's talons on the right. These weaknesses are especially evident on issues after the hub change in 1900. "Basically, the later the date after 1900, the poorer the strike," he concluded. Further, while some early circulation-strike issues are encountered with prooflike surfaces, in general this mirrorlike finish is unusual among Barber quarters. Attractive pieces are especially prized by collectors.

PROOF BARBER QUARTERS

During the first year Proof half dollars were struck to the amount of 1,245 pieces, sold as part of silver sets. Most 1892 quarters had the Type II reverse. It is not certain that all of these were distributed, and, in fact, probably many were not. No doubt they were intended to be sold at the World's Columbian Exposition which, as it turned out, did not open its gates until 1893. In 1893 the Proof mintage dropped to a more reasonable level, from a marketing viewpoint, when 792 were struck. Proofs of 1901 to 1904 typically have lightly polished portraits in the die and are not "cameo" or deeply frosted like Proofs of other years. Among Philadelphia issues in the Barber quarter series, Proofs were struck each year from 1892 through 1915. The last year, 1916, did not see a Proof coinage.

After about 1909, when the new Matte Proof format introduced with the Lincoln cent became unpopular with numismatists, and especially after 1913 when the same format was introduced on the Buffalo nickel, overall Proof mintages dropped sharply across all denominations. By 1914 and 1915 Proof mintages were lower than at any time in the previous several decades. In the latter year production was terminated. Today, Proof Barber quarters are available in approximate proportion to their original mintages, as they were sold to collectors at a premium and were specifically saved. However, quality varies on a time line, and earlier dates are proportionally more elusive in high grades than are later dates.

A gallery of Proof Barber quarters can be found on page 255.

1894. Graded PF-63.

PF–60 to 70 (Proof). ***Obverse and Reverse:*** Proofs that are extensively cleaned and have many hairlines, or that are dull and grainy, are lower level, such as PF–60 to 62. These are not widely desired by collectors. With medium hairlines and good reflectivity, an assigned grade of PF-64 is appropriate. Tiny horizontal lines on Miss Liberty's cheek, known as slide marks, from National and other album slides scuffing the relief of the cheek, are endemic on all Barber silver coins. With noticeable marks of this type, the highest grade assignable is PF-64. With relatively few hairlines, a rating of PF-65 can be given. PF-66 should have hairlines so delicate that magnification is needed to see them. Above that, a Proof should be free of any hairlines or other problems.

Illustrated coin: Light gray and lilac toning combine to create a beautiful coin.

A Note From David Lawrence on Grading Barber Quarters

David Lawrence has added:

> Quarters from the later Obverse Hub II lack the sharp detail found in the early dates and must be graded differently. It is not uncommon to find full EF coins without a sharp band under the word LIBERTY and AU coins without much three-dimensionality on the hair over the forehead.
>
> Coins from 1901 onward are more difficult to grade in EF and AU than the early dates. Pay attention to the wear—or lack of wear—on the laurel wreath and the degree of rubbing on Liberty's cheek.
>
> One additional step in confirming that a later-date Barber quarter is a full EF despite not having the complete and sharp band under LIBERTY is to look at the reverse, to ensure that all of the eagle's feathers are separated.

Being a Smart Buyer

The guidelines for being a smart or savvy buyer of Barber quarters parallel those for dimes and half dollars. For well-circulated examples avoid any with scratches, digs, stains, or other detractions.

For Mint State coins, seek those that are sharply struck. These are in the *minority*, believe it or not! On the obverse, check the star centers and the hair above Liberty's forehead. The first place to look on the reverse is on the right side. Points of weakness are mainly where the eagle's wing joins the shield and on the eagle's talons. As there are no nicknames for sharply struck coins (such as Full Details), and as the certification services make no notice of such, you have the advantage that a sharp coin when found will cost no more than a weakly struck coin of the same grade.

Eye appeal is important. Many coins are dark brown, stained, or otherwise unattractive. Pick ones that are brilliant with rich luster or have light, iridescent toning. Again you have an advantage here, as the certification services have graded a lot of ugly coins as MS-65 and higher, and you can avoid these.

For Proof coins, Proof-64 and higher grades are desirable, again cherrypicking for quality. Many Proof-64 coins are nicer than those graded 65.

1892, Type I Reverse, Quarter

Circulation-strike mintage: Smaller part of 8,236,000
Proof mintage: 100 estimated

Availability in Mint State: Common in the context of Mint State Barber quarters of the early 1890s. ***Estimated number MS-65 or higher:*** 250 to 300.

Availability in circulated grades: 15,000 to 18,000. Most are AG-3 or G-4. There are many in higher circulated grades from having been saved as the first year of issue.

Characteristics of striking: Usually found well struck.

Availability in Proof format: ***Proof-60 to 64:*** 55 to 65. ***Proof-65 or better:*** 5 to 10.

Of the 1,245 Proofs struck this year, the vast majority have the Type II reverse. The Type I is very rare. The good news is that few seek one of each of the types, so when found a Type I is likely to cost no more than a Type II.

Notes: The first examples of the Barber quarter were struck at the Philadelphia Mint on Saturday, January 2, 1892, at 9:00 a.m. Many were saved as souvenirs by the public. A few examples of this issue were rolled out as souvenirs at the World's Columbian Exposition.

An inventive counterfeiting scheme was also developed, as related in this 1892 clipping from *Numismatica Miscellanea:*

> **A Quarter to Ten. Edward Wolcott's Gold Plating Scheme Raises Money Rapidly.** Sioux City, IA, July 29.—Edward Wolcott, a young man from Omaha, was arrested here yesterday for counterfeiting. He took the new silver quarters, cut out the letters "quar," and changed the last 'r' to n, making it read 'ten dollars.' The coins were then neatly plated with gold. He went to stores and bought 5 and 10 cent articles to get the change.

Pricing is given for the 1892, Type II Reverse, quarter—which is more common—at the end of that entry. Certified populations for both types are given there as well.

1892, Type II Reverse, Quarter

Circulation-strike mintage: Larger part of 8,236,000
Proof mintage: Part of 1,245

Availability in Mint State: Very common in the context of Mint State Barber quarters of the early 1890s. ***Estimated number MS-65 or higher:*** 500 to 600.

Availability in circulated grades: 35,000 to 40,000. Most are AG-3 or G-4. Similar to the situation for Type I, this issue is readily available in high circulated grades, as many were saved as the first year of issue.

Characteristics of striking: Usually found well struck.

Availability in Proof format: ***Proof-60 to 64:*** 550 to 750. ***Proof-65 or better:*** 70 to 85. Quite rare in relation to the record mintage. Likely, many sets were sold as souvenirs, and the coins were spent or mishandled.

Notes: A few of these were rolled out as souvenirs at the World's Columbian Exposition. One is illustrated at right.

An 1892, Type II Reverse, rolled out for the World's Columbian Exposition.

MARKET VALUES – CIRCULATION STRIKES

G-4	VG-8	F-12	VF-20	EF-40	AU-50	MS-60	MS-63	MS-65
$9	$10	$26	$45	$75	$130	$235	$440	$1,100

MARKET VALUES – PROOF STRIKES

PF-60	PF-63	PF-65	PF-65Cam
$450	$800	$1,900	$2,300

CERTIFIED POPULATIONS – CIRCULATION STRIKES

Fair	AG	G	VG	F	VF	EF	AU	MS-60
1	3	6	6	1	10	30	368	5

MS-61	MS-62	MS-63	MS-64	MS-65	MS-66	MS-67	MS-68	MS-69	MS-70
92	221	279	359	171	92	23	7	0	0

CERTIFIED POPULATIONS – PROOF STRIKES

PF-50	PF-60	PF-61	PF-62	PF-63	PF-64
2	1	11	24	50	112

PF-65	PF-66	PF-67	PF-68	PF-69	PF-70
64	53	45	22	1	0

1892-O, TYPE I REVERSE, QUARTER

Circulation-strike mintage: Part of 2,640,000

AVAILABILITY IN MINT STATE: Readily found in lower–Mint State grades. ***Estimated number MS-65 or higher:*** 50 to 60. Elusive at this level.

AVAILABILITY IN CIRCULATED GRADES: 4,000 to 5,000. Most are AG-3 or G-4.

CHARACTERISTICS OF STRIKING: Variable, but often quite sharp.

NOTES: The 1892-O, Type I, quarter is significantly rarer than the Type II, just the opposite of the situation for the 1892-S.

Having the mintmark O centered over the opening at the letter R, and below the center tail feather, constitutes the "normal" position (for 1892 only). In subsequent years the mintmark was moved to between the R and the D or over the D.

A few of these were rolled out as souvenirs at the World's Columbian Exposition.

Pricing is given for the 1892-O, Type II Reverse, quarter—which is more common—at the end of that entry. Certified populations for both types are given there as well.

1892-O, Type II Reverse, Quarter

Circulation-strike mintage: Part of 2,640,000

Availability in Mint State: Lower-level Mint State examples are easily found. ***Estimated number MS-65 or higher:*** 100 to 120. Somewhat scarce.

Availability in circulated grades: 6,000 to 8,000 can be found in grades AG-3 to VF-35. Most are AG-3 or G-4.

Characteristics of striking: Usually sharp, but there are exceptions.

Notes: A few of these were rolled out as souvenirs at the World's Columbian Exposition.

MARKET VALUES – CIRCULATION STRIKES

G-4	VG-8	F-12	VF-20	EF-40	AU-50	MS-60	MS-63	MS-65
$15	$20	$45	$60	$95	$160	$300	$475	$1,550

CERTIFIED POPULATIONS – CIRCULATION STRIKES

Fair	AG	G	VG	F	VF	EF	AU	MS-60
0	1	1	2	3	5	6	124	3

MS-61	MS-62	MS-63	MS-64	MS-65	MS-66	MS-67	MS-68	MS-69	MS-70
28	63	85	74	28	6	1	1	0	0

1892-S, Type I Reverse, Quarter

Circulation-strike mintage: Part of 964,079

Availability in Mint State: Scarce but not particularly hard to find in lower–Mint State grades. ***Estimated number MS-65 or higher:*** 12 to 15. A rarity.

Availability in circulated grades: 1,200 to 1,400. Most are AG-3 or G-4. One of the scarcer issues. In high circulated grades these are rare.

Characteristics of striking: The obverse is deeply basined on some (e.g. the Eliasberg sale 1997 lot 1548).

Notes: Having the mintmark S centered over the opening at the letter R, and below the center tail feather, constitutes the "normal" position (for 1892 only). In subsequent years the mintmark was moved to between the R and the D or over the D.

A few of these were rolled out as souvenirs at the World's Columbian Exposition.

Varieties: ***1892-S, Strongly Doubled Mintmark (FS-501):*** The mintmark on this variety is doubled strongly to the north. Around 30 examples are estimated to exist.

Pricing is given for the 1892-S, Type II Reverse, quarter—which is more common—at the end of that entry. Certified populations for both types are given there as well.

1892-S, Type II Reverse, Quarter

Circulation-strike mintage: Part of 964,079

Availability in Mint State: Grades such as MS–63 and 64 are more available than gems, but on an absolute basis even these are scarce.

Availability in circulated grades: 1,600 to 2,000. Most are AG-3 or G-4. One of the scarcer issues. In high circulated grades such coins are rare in proportion to the demand for them.

Characteristics of striking: Variable. Be on the lookout for a sharp example.

Notes: A few of these were rolled out as souvenirs at the World's Columbian Exposition.

MARKET VALUES – CIRCULATION STRIKES

G-4	VG-8	F-12	VF-20	EF-40	AU-50	MS-60	MS-63	MS-65
$30	$50	$80	$130	$200	$300	$475	$1,050	$4,000

CERTIFIED POPULATIONS – CIRCULATION STRIKES

Fair	AG	G	VG	F	VF	EF	AU	MS-60
0	7	9	3	0	7	5	25	2

MS-61	MS-62	MS-63	MS-64	MS-65	MS-66	MS-67	MS-68	MS-69	MS-70
5	16	17	17	6	2	1	0	0	0

1893 Quarter

Circulation-strike mintage: 5,444,023
Proof mintage: 792

Availability in Mint State: Readily available in lower–Mint State grades. ***Estimated number MS-65 or higher:*** 100 to 120. Slightly scarce.

Availability in circulated grades: 10,000 to 12,000. Most are AG-3 or G-4.

Characteristics of striking: Usually well struck.

Availability in Proof format: ***Proof-60 to 64:*** 425 to 525. ***Proof-65 or better:*** 100 to 120.

MARKET VALUES – CIRCULATION STRIKES

G-4	VG-8	F-12	VF-20	EF-40	AU-50	MS-60	MS-63	MS-65
$9	$10	$26	$45	$75	$130	$235	$440	$1,400

MARKET VALUES – PROOF STRIKES

PF-60	PF-63	PF-65	PF-65Cam
$450	$775	$1,900	$2,300

CERTIFIED POPULATIONS – CIRCULATION STRIKES

Fair	AG	G	VG	F	VF	EF	AU	MS-60
0	1	1	4	1	11	9	64	1

MS-61	MS-62	MS-63	MS-64	MS-65	MS-66	MS-67	MS-68	MS-69	MS-70
15	39	56	69	28	4	2	0	0	0

CERTIFIED POPULATIONS – PROOF STRIKES

PF-50	PF-60	PF-61	PF-62	PF-63	PF-64
1	2	3	13	19	88

PF-65	PF-66	PF-67	PF-68	PF-69	PF-70
60	65	39	18	3	0

1893-O QUARTER

Circulation-strike mintage: 3,396,000

AVAILABILITY IN MINT STATE: Many exist in grades MS–60 to 64. ***Estimated number MS-65 or higher:*** 75 to 90. Somewhat scarce.

AVAILABILITY IN CIRCULATED GRADES: 12,000 to 14,000. Most are AG-3 or G-4.

CHARACTERISTICS OF STRIKING: The striking for this issue is of average quality, making this issue conform to the rule, not the exception, for New Orleans quarters.

MARKET VALUES – CIRCULATION STRIKES

G-4	VG-8	F-12	VF-20	EF-40	AU-50	MS-60	MS-63	MS-65
$10	$14	$30	$60	$110	$170	$275	$500	$2,000

CERTIFIED POPULATIONS – CIRCULATION STRIKES

Fair	AG	G	VG	F	VF	EF	AU	MS-60
0	1	4	1	1	5	10	49	2

MS-61	MS-62	MS-63	MS-64	MS-65	MS-66	MS-67	MS-68	MS-69	MS-70
25	25	21	30	20	6	3	1	0	0

1893-S Quarter

Circulation-strike mintage: 1,454,535

Availability in Mint State: For some reason not known today, the 1893-S in any Mint State grade is elusive. David Lawrence called this issue one of 17 Barber quarter issues considered to be "very scarce" in any Mint State category. ***Estimated number MS-65 or higher:*** 45 to 55.

Availability in circulated grades: 4,000 to 5,000. Most are AG-3 or G-4.

Characteristics of striking: Usually sharp.

Notes: In Édouard Frossard's June 1894 sale of the William M. Friesner Collection, two 1893-S quarters were offered, one listed with the S mintmark over D and the other listed with the S between R and D—a very early listing of mintmark positions.

MARKET VALUES – CIRCULATION STRIKES

G-4	VG-8	F-12	VF-20	EF-40	AU-50	MS-60	MS-63	MS-65
$20	$35	$60	$110	$175	$300	$425	$1,000	$6,000

CERTIFIED POPULATIONS – CIRCULATION STRIKES

Fair	AG	G	VG	F	VF	EF	AU	MS-60
0	2	8	3	2	6	5	16	1

MS-61	MS-62	MS-63	MS-64	MS-65	MS-66	MS-67	MS-68	MS-69	MS-70
8	8	18	22	8	1	1	0	0	0

1894 Quarter

Circulation-strike mintage: 3,432,000
Proof mintage: 972

Availability in Mint State: Easier to find in lower grades. ***Estimated number MS-65 or higher:*** 80 to 95.

Availability in circulated grades: 12,000 to 15,000. Most are AG-3 or G-4.

Characteristics of striking: Variable.

Availability in Proof format: ***Proof-60 to 64:*** 600 to 700. ***Proof-65 or better:*** 80 to 95.

MARKET VALUES – CIRCULATION STRIKES

G-4	VG-8	F-12	VF-20	EF-40	AU-50	MS-60	MS-63	MS-65
$9	$10	$35	$50	$95	$150	$240	$450	$1,200

MARKET VALUES – PROOF STRIKES

PF-60	PF-63	PF-65	PF-65Cam
$450	$800	$1,900	$2,300

CERTIFIED POPULATIONS – CIRCULATION STRIKES

Fair	AG	G	VG	F	VF	EF	AU	MS-60
0	1	1	2	1	6	3	27	0

MS-61	MS-62	MS-63	MS-64	MS-65	MS-66	MS-67	MS-68	MS-69	MS-70
11	26	23	42	22	5	2	0	0	0

CERTIFIED POPULATIONS – PROOF STRIKES

PF-50	PF-60	PF-61	PF-62	PF-63	PF-64
0	3	4	19	30	99
PF-65	**PF-66**	**PF-67**	**PF-68**	**PF-69**	**PF-70**
78	60	41	5	1	0

1894-O Quarter

Circulation-strike mintage: 2,852,000

Availability in Mint State: Not common in lower–Mint State grades, but readily available in proportion to the number of specialists seeking them. ***Estimated number MS-65 or higher:*** 60 to 70.

Availability in circulated grades: 6,000 to 8,000. Most are AG-3 or G-4.

Characteristics of striking: Variable.

MARKET VALUES – CIRCULATION STRIKES

G-4	VG-8	F-12	VF-20	EF-40	AU-50	MS-60	MS-63	MS-65
$10	$20	$45	$70	$130	$230	$325	$725	$2,000

CERTIFIED POPULATIONS – CIRCULATION STRIKES

Fair	AG	G	VG	F	VF	EF	AU	MS-60
0	0	4	5	5	4	1	31	1

MS-61	MS-62	MS-63	MS-64	MS-65	MS-66	MS-67	MS-68	MS-69	MS-70
8	19	20	36	7	7	1	0	0	0

1894-S Quarter

Circulation-strike mintage: 2,648,821

Availability in Mint State: Same comment as preceding. ***Estimated number MS-65 or higher:*** 50 to 60.

Availability in circulated grades: 2,000 to 2,500. Most are AG-3 or G-4.

Characteristics of striking: Usually well struck.

MARKET VALUES – CIRCULATION STRIKES

G-4	VG-8	F-12	VF-20	EF-40	AU-50	MS-60	MS-63	MS-65
$10	$15	$40	$60	$120	$210	$325	$725	$2,500

CERTIFIED POPULATIONS – CIRCULATION STRIKES

Fair	AG	G	VG	F	VF	EF	AU	MS-60
0	1	2	0	1	6	7	35	1

MS-61	MS-62	MS-63	MS-64	MS-65	MS-66	MS-67	MS-68	MS-69	MS-70
12	36	28	59	11	3	0	0	0	0

1895 QUARTER

Circulation-strike mintage: 4,440,000
Proof mintage: 880

AVAILABILITY IN MINT STATE: Easy to find in lower–Mint State grades. The number of people building a set of Barber quarters in MS-63 or higher grades is not high at any given time, so prices rarity-for-rarity are much less for Barber coins than in the successor Standing Liberty quarter series (1916–1930). ***Estimated number MS-65 or higher:*** 100 to 120.

AVAILABILITY IN CIRCULATED GRADES: 15,000 to 20,000. Most are AG-3 or G-4.

CHARACTERISTICS OF STRIKING: Average strikes are the rule, but sharp examples can be found.

AVAILABILITY IN PROOF FORMAT: ***Proof-60 to 64:*** 500 to 600. ***Proof-65 or better:*** 65 to 80.

MARKET VALUES – CIRCULATION STRIKES

G-4	VG-8	F-12	VF-20	EF-40	AU-50	MS-60	MS-63	MS-65
$10	$14	$30	$45	$80	$140	$250	$500	$1,600

MARKET VALUES – PROOF STRIKES

PF-60	PF-63	PF-65	PF-65Cam
$450	$800	$1,900	$2,300

CERTIFIED POPULATIONS – CIRCULATION STRIKES

Fair	AG	G	VG	F	VF	EF	AU	MS-60
1	1	5	5	2	3	7	38	1

MS-61	MS-62	MS-63	MS-64	MS-65	MS-66	MS-67	MS-68	MS-69	MS-70
8	32	37	46	20	10	5	0	0	0

CERTIFIED POPULATIONS – PROOF STRIKES

PF-50	PF-60	PF-61	PF-62	PF-63	PF-64
2	1	7	18	29	61

PF-65	PF-66	PF-67	PF-68	PF-69	PF-70
48	44	33	29	1	0

1895-O Quarter

Circulation-strike mintage: 2,816,000

Availability in Mint State: David Lawrence called this issue one of 17 Barber quarter issues considered to be "very scarce" in any Mint State category. MS–63 and 64 coins are more available than higher grades, but they are not easy to find. ***Estimated number MS-65 or higher:*** 30 to 35. At the gem level the 1895-O is among the rarer Barber quarters, despite its generous mintage.

Availability in circulated grades: 6,000 to 8,000. Most are AG-3 or G-4.

Characteristics of striking: Often weak in areas.

MARKET VALUES – CIRCULATION STRIKES

G-4	VG-8	F-12	VF-20	EF-40	AU-50	MS-60	MS-63	MS-65
$12	$20	$50	$70	$140	$230	$400	$900	$2,600

CERTIFIED POPULATIONS – CIRCULATION STRIKES

Fair	AG	G	VG	F	VF	EF	AU	MS-60
0	2	3	1	5	7	6	23	0

MS-61	MS-62	MS-63	MS-64	MS-65	MS-66	MS-67	MS-68	MS-69	MS-70
4	17	12	20	11	2	3	0	0	0

1895-S Quarter

Circulation-strike mintage: 1,764,681

Availability in Mint State: MS–63 and 64 coins are available as an alternative to the hard-to-find and expensive gem pieces. As noted earlier, with cherrypicking it is possible to find certified MS-64 coins that are more attractive and more desirable (in my opinion) than MS-65 quarters with a so-so appearance. ***Estimated number MS-65 or higher:*** 27 to 32. One of the rarer Barber quarters at the gem level, surprisingly so in view of the generous mintage.

Availability in circulated grades: 5,000 to 7,000. Most are AG-3 or G-4.

Characteristics of striking: Some from relapped dies are highly prooflike.

MARKET VALUES – CIRCULATION STRIKES

G-4	VG-8	F-12	VF-20	EF-40	AU-50	MS-60	MS-63	MS-65
$20	$32	$70	$120	$170	$275	$420	$1,050	$3,500

CERTIFIED POPULATIONS – CIRCULATION STRIKES

Fair	AG	G	VG	F	VF	EF	AU	MS-60
0	2	11	4	3	6	3	27	0

MS-61	MS-62	MS-63	MS-64	MS-65	MS-66	MS-67	MS-68	MS-69	MS-70
4	10	12	18	7	3	0	2	0	0

Varieties: ***Large S Over Small s:*** The Eliasberg coin description from one of the Eliasberg sales:

> On the reverse the S is sharply doubled, with a 'ghost S,' slightly smaller in size, appearing to the left of the larger S, the latter being centered over the upright of the D. Quite possibly a mintmark punch one size too small was at first used, then corrected. This appears to be the same as David Lawrence's No. 101, clearly illustrated by him, but without the size difference mentioned (although it is readily noticeable in his photograph). This variety can be found with some looking, and is often cherrypicked without paying a premium price.

1896 Quarter

Circulation-strike mintage: 3,874,000
Proof mintage: 762

Availability in Mint State: Lower-level Mint State coins are easy to find. ***Estimated number MS-65 or higher:*** 100 to 120.

Availability in circulated grades: 15,000 to 20,000. Most are AG-3 or G-4.

Characteristics of striking: Variable.

Availability in Proof format: ***Proof-60 to 64:*** 400 to 500. ***Proof-65 or better:*** 70 to 80.

MARKET VALUES – CIRCULATION STRIKES

G-4	VG-8	F-12	VF-20	EF-40	AU-50	MS-60	MS-63	MS-65
$10	$14	$30	$45	$80	$135	$250	$425	$1,250

MARKET VALUES – PROOF STRIKES

PF-60	PF-63	PF-65	PF-65Cam
$450	$800	$1,900	$2,300

CERTIFIED POPULATIONS – CIRCULATION STRIKES

Fair	AG	G	VG	F	VF	EF	AU	MS-60
1	0	3	1	2	6	6	19	2

MS-61	MS-62	MS-63	MS-64	MS-65	MS-66	MS-67	MS-68	MS-69	MS-70
15	26	41	39	19	8	3	0	0	0

CERTIFIED POPULATIONS – PROOF STRIKES

PF-50	PF-60	PF-61	PF-62	PF-63	PF-64
0	1	1	10	31	75

PF-65	PF-66	PF-67	PF-68	PF-69	PF-70
49	58	55	37	5	0

1896-O Quarter

Circulation-strike mintage: 1,484,000

Availability in Mint State: After the 1901-S, David Lawrence considered this to be one of the six next-rarest Barber quarters in various Mint State levels. Choice MS–63 and 64 coins are special. ***Estimated number MS-65 or higher:*** 25 to 30. Such coins are few and far between in the marketplace.

Availability in circulated grades: 3,000 to 4,000. Most are AG-3 or G-4.

Characteristics of striking: This coin often comes very softly struck, and many coins have mushy denticles. Well-struck coins are scarce.

Notes: The 1896-O, years ago, was considered to be one of the great key issues of the series, but since then it has dropped from view somewhat, due no doubt to the paucity of examples on the market. There is simply not enough opportunity to showcase them. However, the appreciation for this issue may be returning. David Lawrence commented that the 1896-O is the first of the New Orleans Mint Barber quarters that is truly scarce in all grades.

MARKET VALUES – CIRCULATION STRIKES

G-4	VG-8	F-12	VF-20	EF-40	AU-50	MS-60	MS-63	MS-65
$55	$85	$200	$320	$550	$800	$1,000	$2,000	$6,500

CERTIFIED POPULATIONS – CIRCULATION STRIKES

Fair	AG	G	VG	F	VF	EF	AU	MS-60
4	9	20	5	4	17	8	23	2

MS-61	MS-62	MS-63	MS-64	MS-65	MS-66	MS-67	MS-68	MS-69	MS-70
2	8	6	28	10	5	1	0	0	0

1896-S QUARTER

Circulation-strike mintage: 188,039

AVAILABILITY IN MINT STATE: Any Mint State coin from 60 up is rare and important. After the 1901-S, David Lawrence considered this to be one of the six next-rarest Barber quarters in various Mint State levels. ***Estimated number MS-65 or higher:*** 10 to 15. At the gem level the 1896-S has always been a rarity.

AVAILABILITY IN CIRCULATED GRADES: 1,600 to 1,800. Most are AG-3 or G-4. These are rarer than the lower-mintage 1901-S in terms of *certified* coins, but among "raw" coins the 1896-S is more often found.[8] David Lawrence considered this to be one of the five hardest-to-find quarters in EF and AU grades. While the 1896-S is rarer than 1901-S and 1913-S at the gem level, in all circulated grades, it is the number 3 coin of the Big 3, *i.e.*, it is the most available of the three.

CHARACTERISTICS OF STRIKING: Both pairs of dies clashed early in their production runs, leaving horizontal lines within Liberty's ear, transferred from the reverse shield. The majority of, but certainly not all of, 1896-S quarters have them, which can aid in authentication.[9]

NOTES: The 1896-S, with a mintage of just 188,039, ranks today as one of the three great classics in the Barber quarter series, its companions being the 1901-S and 1913-S. At the gem level the 1896-S is significantly rarer than the lower-mintage 1913-S. David Lawrence commented to the writer in 1997, after viewing the Eliasberg coin: "I have sold three gem 1901-S quarters, but not a single 1896-S higher than MS-64! I have only *seen* one MS-65 offered, and it had a large spot on the reverse. The 1896-S is highly underrated in MS-65 or higher grades. Recall that your Norweb Collection coin graded MS-64."

MARKET VALUES – CIRCULATION STRIKES

G-4	VG-8	F-12	VF-20	EF-40	AU-50	MS-60	MS-63	MS-65
$900	$1,500	$2,400	$3,800	$5,000	$7,000	$10,000	$17,500	$50,000

CERTIFIED POPULATIONS – CIRCULATION STRIKES

Fair	AG	G	VG	F	VF	EF	AU	MS-60
21	104	185	40	19	9	10	14	1

MS-61	MS-62	MS-63	MS-64	MS-65	MS-66	MS-67	MS-68	MS-69	MS-70
0	4	6	14	7	2	1	0	0	0

1897 Quarter

Circulation-strike mintage: 8,140,000
Proof mintage: 731

Availability in Mint State: Many exist from MS–60 to 64. Typically, Mint State coins have good eye appeal. ***Estimated number MS-65 or higher:*** 100 to 120. Easy to find in the context of the early series, but more elusive than the mintage suggests.

Availability in circulated grades: 30,000 to 35,000. Most are AG-3 or G-4.

Characteristics of striking: Usually well struck.

Availability in Proof format: ***Proof-60 to 64:*** 400 to 500. ***Proof-65 or better:*** 70 to 85.

MARKET VALUES – CIRCULATION STRIKES

G-4	VG-8	F-12	VF-20	EF-40	AU-50	MS-60	MS-63	MS-65
$9	$14	$26	$40	$70	$120	$240	$450	$1,400

MARKET VALUES – PROOF STRIKES

PF-60	PF-63	PF-65	PF-65Cam
$450	$800	$1,900	$2,300

CERTIFIED POPULATIONS – CIRCULATION STRIKES

Fair	AG	G	VG	F	VF	EF	AU	MS-60
0	1	4	3	3	6	11	48	1

MS-61	MS-62	MS-63	MS-64	MS-65	MS-66	MS-67	MS-68	MS-69	MS-70
21	42	48	52	23	10	1	0	0	0

CERTIFIED POPULATIONS – PROOF STRIKES

PF-50	PF-60	PF-61	PF-62	PF-63	PF-64
1	1	7	16	34	69

PF-65	PF-66	PF-67	PF-68	PF-69	PF-70
44	52	31	18	0	0

1897-O QUARTER

Circulation-strike mintage: 1,414,800

AVAILABILITY IN MINT STATE: David Lawrence thought this to be one of 17 Barber quarter issues considered "very scarce" in any Mint State category. ***Estimated number MS-65 or higher:*** 50 to 60.

AVAILABILITY IN CIRCULATED GRADES: 4,000 to 5,000. Most are AG-3 or G-4. In circulated grades VF and up, it is almost as hard to find as the better-known 1897-S.

CHARACTERISTICS OF STRIKING: Usually with moderate lightness of strike on the right side of the reverse, at the upper right of the shield and adjacent wing, and, more pronounced, on the eagle's talons.

MARKET VALUES – CIRCULATION STRIKES

G-4	VG-8	F-12	VF-20	EF-40	AU-50	MS-60	MS-63	MS-65
$40	$65	$180	$340	$385	$600	$850	$1,800	$3,250

CERTIFIED POPULATIONS – CIRCULATION STRIKES

Fair	AG	G	VG	F	VF	EF	AU	MS-60
0	5	17	9	6	13	8	17	0

MS-61	MS-62	MS-63	MS-64	MS-65	MS-66	MS-67	MS-68	MS-69	MS-70
6	4	3	14	6	5	4	0	0	0

1897-S Quarter

Circulation-strike mintage: 542,229

Availability in Mint State: After the 1901-S, David Lawrence considered this to be one of the six next-rarest Barber quarters in various Mint State levels. Mint State coins usually have good eye appeal. ***Estimated number MS-65 or higher:*** 60 to 70.

Availability in circulated grades: 2,000 to 2,500. Most are AG-3 or G-4. David Lawrence considered this to be one of the five hardest-to-find quarters in AU grades.

Characteristics of striking: Usually well struck.

Notes: This is the last year in the Barber quarter series in which some branch-mint coins have the mintmark over the D of DOLLAR.

Varieties: All but one reverse die had the mintmark far to the right, over the D of DOLLAR. The variety from the one reverse with the mintmark between the R and D (known as the "center mintmark") is very scarce and highly collected by knowledgeable collectors, and generally is offered with a substantial premium by those who recognize it.[10]

MARKET VALUES – CIRCULATION STRIKES

G-4	VG-8	F-12	VF-20	EF-40	AU-50	MS-60	MS-63	MS-65
$120	$150	$300	$550	$825	$1,000	$1,600	$1,900	$6,000

CERTIFIED POPULATIONS – CIRCULATION STRIKES

Fair	AG	G	VG	F	VF	EF	AU	MS-60
1	12	36	15	9	8	11	14	0

MS-61	MS-62	MS-63	MS-64	MS-65	MS-66	MS-67	MS-68	MS-69	MS-70
2	3	8	18	10	1	2	1	0	0

1898 QUARTER

Circulation-strike mintage: 11,100,000
Proof mintage: 735

AVAILABILITY IN MINT STATE: Lower-level Mint State coins are common in relation to the demand for them. ***Estimated number MS-65 or higher:*** 150 to 180.

AVAILABILITY IN CIRCULATED GRADES: 30,000 to 35,000. Most are AG-3 or G-4, although higher circulated grades are easy to find.

CHARACTERISTICS OF STRIKING: Usually well struck.

AVAILABILITY IN PROOF FORMAT: ***Proof-60 to 64:*** 400 to 500. ***Proof-65 or better:*** 60 to 70.

MARKET VALUES – CIRCULATION STRIKES

G-4	VG-8	F-12	VF-20	EF-40	AU-50	MS-60	MS-63	MS-65
$9	$10	$26	$45	$70	$125	$225	$425	$1,200

MARKET VALUES – PROOF STRIKES

PF-60	PF-63	PF-65	PF-65Cam
$450	$775	$1,900	$2,300

CERTIFIED POPULATIONS – CIRCULATION STRIKES

Fair	AG	G	VG	F	VF	EF	AU	MS-60
0	0	7	4	6	7	11	74	1

MS-61	MS-62	MS-63	MS-64	MS-65	MS-66	MS-67	MS-68	MS-69	MS-70
15	40	53	65	26	21	3	3	0	0

CERTIFIED POPULATIONS – PROOF STRIKES

PF-50	PF-60	PF-61	PF-62	PF-63	PF-64
1	1	3	13	26	51

PF-65	PF-66	PF-67	PF-68	PF-69	PF-70
58	59	59	46	11	0

1898-O Quarter

Circulation-strike mintage: 1,868,000

Availability in Mint State: As is true of so many Barber silver coins, even advanced collectors with well-fortified bank accounts usually settle for an MS–63 or 64. The 1898-O is not traditionally recognized as a rarity in the same class as the branch-mint coins of 1896 and 1897. However, David Lawrence suggested that in Mint State the 1898-O is rarer than the 1896-O, and, who knows, it may be. Estimating rarity is hard to do, and ideas change. In any event, both the more famous 1896-O and the 1898-O are rare at this level, and they are even more so if in the gem class. ***Estimated number MS-65 or higher:*** 30 to 35. Seldom seen in the marketplace.

Availability in circulated grades: 4,000 to 5,000. Most are AG-3 or G-4. Very hard to find in EF and AU grades.

Characteristics of striking: The striking usually has some lightness on the right side of the reverse.

MARKET VALUES – CIRCULATION STRIKES

G-4	VG-8	F-12	VF-20	EF-40	AU-50	MS-60	MS-63	MS-65
$15	$28	$70	$140	$300	$390	$625	$1,500	$8,750

CERTIFIED POPULATIONS – CIRCULATION STRIKES

Fair	AG	G	VG	F	VF	EF	AU	MS-60
0	2	4	2	3	11	4	16	0

MS-61	MS-62	MS-63	MS-64	MS-65	MS-66	MS-67	MS-68	MS-69	MS-70
3	14	9	9	3	3	0	1	0	0

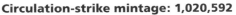

1898-S QUARTER

Circulation-strike mintage: 1,020,592

AVAILABILITY IN MINT STATE: Surprise! In connection with reviewing the Eliasberg coins, David Lawrence commented that the 1898-S is "truly scarce in Mint State as most, if not all, of the mintage went to the Philippines, and coins were not saved in high grades." He considered this to be one of the six next-rarest Barber quarters in various Mint State levels from MS-60 upward, after the 1901-S. See John Frost's comment under notes. ***Estimated number MS-65 or higher:*** 10 to 15.

AVAILABILITY IN CIRCULATED GRADES: 2,000 to 2,500. Most are AG-3 or G-4. Many VF and EF coins have been cleaned. Many cleaned VF pieces were repatriated from the Philippines.

CHARACTERISTICS OF STRIKING: Usually well struck, some with exceptional eye appeal. Rarely prooflike.

NOTES: As noted earlier, some or most of this mintage was shipped to the Philippine Islands after the Spanish-American War ended in the summer of the year. As a result, such quarters were scarce in domestic circulation.

John Frost commented:

> From my personal experience 1898-S in Mint State comes nice, with most examples offered being MS-64 and higher, and thus resulting in a higher percentage of gems than normally expected. There are very few low Mint State grade examples. An additional problem is that many, even most of the certified examples in MS–60 to 62 are not Mint State at all, but would be considered by experienced specialists to be AU-58s at best. I've seen several *cleaned* AU coins in major service holders calling them MS–61 and 62. Like the 1904-S Barber half, this issue is considerably rarer in true Mint State than the population reports would have you believe. In his book David Lawrence called the 1898-S in any Mint State grade the 'best kept secret in the Barber quarter series' and I agree. After passing on three obviously not-new 'Mint State' slabbed examples, I paid quadruple bid for a raw MS-62 in an old R.M. Smythe auction and thought I stole it. Knowledgeable collectors know this coin's true rarity, and if they cannot afford one of the occasionally-offered gems, they will pay through the nose to get a lower grade, but still actually a Mint State example.[11]

MARKET VALUES – CIRCULATION STRIKES

G-4	VG-8	F-12	VF-20	EF-40	AU-50	MS-60	MS-63	MS-65
$11	$25	$40	$55	$100	$200	$400	$1,400	$7,500

CERTIFIED POPULATIONS – CIRCULATION STRIKES

Fair	AG	G	VG	F	VF	EF	AU	MS-60
0	0	5	3	0	4	7	15	0

MS-61	MS-62	MS-63	MS-64	MS-65	MS-66	MS-67	MS-68	MS-69	MS-70
2	7	8	8	8	2	2	0	0	0

1899 Quarter

Circulation-strike mintage: 12,624,000
Proof mintage: 846

Availability in Mint State: Common in lower–Mint State levels in relation to the number of collectors seeking such pieces. ***Estimated number MS-65 or higher:*** 125 to 140.

Availability in circulated grades: 50,000 to 60,000. Most are AG-3 or G-4, sometimes VG. More of this issue (73 examples) were found than any others in the Schneider holding formed in 1937 and 1938. The runners up were 1907 and 1916-D (tied with 54 examples), 1914 (50 examples), and 1908-O (49 examples). (See page 28.)

Characteristics of striking: Usually well struck.

Availability in Proof format: ***Proof-60 to 64:*** 500 to 600. ***Proof-65 or better:*** 60 to 70.

Notes: This is the largest circulation-strike mintage in the Barber quarter series, edging out 1902 by a small margin. The same situation occurred for half dollars.

Varieties: ***Doubled Die Reverse:*** With strong doubling at QUARTER DOLLAR and the arrows, doubling varies elsewhere. This very rare variety is thought to be the most prominent doubled die in the entire Barber series.[12]

MARKET VALUES – CIRCULATION STRIKES

G-4	VG-8	F-12	VF-20	EF-40	AU-50	MS-60	MS-63	MS-65
$9	$10	$26	$45	$75	$125	$225	$400	$1,100

MARKET VALUES – PROOF STRIKES

PF-60	PF-63	PF-65	PF-65Cam
$450	$800	$1,900	$2,300

CERTIFIED POPULATIONS – CIRCULATION STRIKES

Fair	AG	G	VG	F	VF	EF	AU	MS-60
0	1	5	4	4	20	13	67	0

MS-61	MS-62	MS-63	MS-64	MS-65	MS-66	MS-67	MS-68	MS-69	MS-70
14	52	54	79	20	7	1	0	0	0

CERTIFIED POPULATIONS – PROOF STRIKES

PF-50	PF-60	PF-61	PF-62	PF-63	PF-64
1	1	7	12	18	47

PF-65	PF-66	PF-67	PF-68	PF-69	PF-70
33	39	31	11	1	0

1899-O QUARTER

Circulation-strike mintage: 2,644,000

AVAILABILITY IN MINT STATE: Lower-level Mint State coins are easy enough to find. ***Estimated number MS-65 or higher:*** 40 to 50. Seldom seen.

AVAILABILITY IN CIRCULATED GRADES: 10,000 to 12,000. Most are AG-3 or G-4.

CHARACTERISTICS OF STRIKING: Usually well struck, which is rare for a New Orleans quarter of the decade. There are exceptions, however.

MARKET VALUES – CIRCULATION STRIKES

G-4	VG-8	F-12	VF-20	EF-40	AU-50	MS-60	MS-63	MS-65
$11	$18	$35	$70	$120	$260	$400	$800	$2,500

CERTIFIED POPULATIONS – CIRCULATION STRIKES

Fair	AG	G	VG	F	VF	EF	AU	MS-60
0	0	1	0	3	9	3	21	0

MS-61	MS-62	MS-63	MS-64	MS-65	MS-66	MS-67	MS-68	MS-69	MS-70
4	9	13	25	10	2	1	0	0	0

1899-S Quarter

Circulation-strike mintage: 708,000

Availability in Mint State: David Lawrence called this one of 17 Barber quarter issues considered to be "very scarce" in any Mint State category. ***Estimated number MS-65 or higher:*** 60 to 70.

Availability in circulated grades: 1,500 to 1,800. Most are AG-3 or G-4. Occasionally repatriated coins from the Philippines are found in VF or so grade, cleaned, but not as often as for 1898-S. Nice EF and AU coins are seldom seen.

Characteristics of striking: Usually well struck. Some high-grade pieces are prooflike.

Notes: David Lawrence noted that, like the 1898-S, most 1899-S quarters were shipped to the Philippines. For the collector endeavoring to put together a Mint State set of Barber quarters this is a "stopper," he commented—an unappreciated rarity.

MARKET VALUES – CIRCULATION STRIKES

G-4	VG-8	F-12	VF-20	EF-40	AU-50	MS-60	MS-63	MS-65
$27	$40	$95	$110	$140	$270	$425	$1,400	$3,500

CERTIFIED POPULATIONS – CIRCULATION STRIKES

Fair	AG	G	VG	F	VF	EF	AU	MS-60
0	0	1	1	1	0	5	20	0

MS-61	MS-62	MS-63	MS-64	MS-65	MS-66	MS-67	MS-68	MS-69	MS-70
2	3	3	5	8	3	5	0	0	0

1900 QUARTER

Circulation-strike mintage: 10,016,000
Proof mintage: 912

AVAILABILITY IN MINT STATE: Lower-level Mint State coins are common. ***Estimated number MS-65 or higher:*** 150 to 180.

AVAILABILITY IN CIRCULATED GRADES: 50,000 to 60,000. Most are G-4.

CHARACTERISTICS OF STRIKING: Usually well struck.

AVAILABILITY IN PROOF FORMAT: ***Proof-60 to 64:*** 450 to 600. ***Proof-65 or better:*** 65 to 80.

NOTES: All Proofs and a small percentage of circulation strikes are from Type I Obverse Hub, Type II Reverse Hub. Most circulation strikes are Type II Obverse Hub, Type III Reverse Hub.[13]

MARKET VALUES – CIRCULATION STRIKES

G-4	VG-8	F-12	VF-20	EF-40	AU-50	MS-60	MS-63	MS-65
$9	$10	$26	$45	$75	$125	$240	$425	$1,250

MARKET VALUES – PROOF STRIKES

PF-60	PF-63	PF-65	PF-65Cam
$450	$800	$1,900	$2,300

CERTIFIED POPULATIONS – CIRCULATION STRIKES

Fair	AG	G	VG	F	VF	EF	AU	MS-60
0	0	2	3	4	6	10	44	0

MS-61	MS-62	MS-63	MS-64	MS-65	MS-66	MS-67	MS-68	MS-69	MS-70
11	23	44	96	34	6	3	1	0	0

CERTIFIED POPULATIONS – PROOF STRIKES

PF-50	PF-60	PF-61	PF-62	PF-63	PF-64
0	0	8	13	29	72

PF-65	PF-66	PF-67	PF-68	PF-69	PF-70
46	51	37	13	0	0

1900-O Quarter

Circulation-strike mintage: 3,416,000

Availability in Mint State: Easy enough to find in lower–Mint State grades. ***Estimated number MS-65 or higher:*** 60 to 70.

Availability in circulated grades: 20,000 to 25,000. Most are G-4.

Characteristics of striking: Usually lightly struck on the right side of the reverse. Exceptions can be found and are elusive.

Notes: Type I Obverse Hub, Type II Reverse Hub and Type II Obverse Hub, Type II Reverse Hub, hub combinations are standard.

MARKET VALUES – CIRCULATION STRIKES

G-4	VG-8	F-12	VF-20	EF-40	AU-50	MS-60	MS-63	MS-65
$12	$26	$65	$110	$150	$310	$525	$850	$3,500

CERTIFIED POPULATIONS – CIRCULATION STRIKES

Fair	AG	G	VG	F	VF	EF	AU	MS-60
0	0	2	2	7	7	9	18	0

MS-61	MS-62	MS-63	MS-64	MS-65	MS-66	MS-67	MS-68	MS-69	MS-70
3	12	12	28	8	3	2	1	0	0

1900-S QUARTER

Circulation-strike mintage: 1,858,585

AVAILABILITY IN MINT STATE: David Lawrence called this one of 17 Barber quarter issues considered to be "very scarce" in any Mint State category. This issue is slightly scarce in Mint State, but quite available at lower–Mint State levels. ***Estimated number MS-65 or higher:*** 45 to 55. Seldom offered for sale.

AVAILABILITY IN CIRCULATED GRADES: 9,000 to 14,000. Most are G-4. Nice VF and EF coins can be found with some searching, but original-surface AU coins are very difficult to locate.

CHARACTERISTICS OF STRIKING: Usually sharply struck. In rare instances, examples can be somewhat prooflike.

NOTES: Type I Obverse Hub, Type II Reverse Hub and Type II Obverse Hub, Type II Reverse Hub, hub combinations are standard.

MARKET VALUES – CIRCULATION STRIKES

G-4	VG-8	F-12	VF-20	EF-40	AU-50	MS-60	MS-63	MS-65
$10	$15	$35	$55	$80	$130	$350	$1,000	$4,500

CERTIFIED POPULATIONS – CIRCULATION STRIKES

Fair	AG	G	VG	F	VF	EF	AU	MS-60
0	0	4	0	2	9	11	56	0

MS-61	MS-62	MS-63	MS-64	MS-65	MS-66	MS-67	MS-68	MS-69	MS-70
2	9	6	12	4	4	3	0	0	0

1901 Quarter

Circulation-strike mintage: 8,892,000
Proof mintage: 813

Availability in Mint State: Lower-level Mint State coins plentiful. ***Estimated number MS-65 or higher:*** 100 to 120.

Availability in circulated grades: 50,000 to 60,000. Most are G-4. A slightly better Philadelphia coin in VG and higher grades.

Characteristics of striking: Usually well struck.

Availability in Proof format: ***Proof-60 to 64:*** 290 to 340. ***Proof-65 or better:*** 60 to 70.

Notes: Obverse Hub II is used from this year forward.

MARKET VALUES – CIRCULATION STRIKES

G-4	VG-8	F-12	VF-20	EF-40	AU-50	MS-60	MS-63	MS-65
$9	$10	$26	$45	$80	$135	$240	$425	$1,350

MARKET VALUES – PROOF STRIKES

PF-60	PF-63	PF-65	PF-65Cam
$450	$800	$1,900	$2,300

CERTIFIED POPULATIONS – CIRCULATION STRIKES

Fair	AG	G	VG	F	VF	EF	AU	MS-60
10	7	4	3	7	19	7	44	2

MS-61	MS-62	MS-63	MS-64	MS-65	MS-66	MS-67	MS-68	MS-69	MS-70
9	40	38	65	18	5	0	0	0	0

CERTIFIED POPULATIONS – PROOF STRIKES

PF-50	PF-60	PF-61	PF-62	PF-63	PF-64
2	3	4	18	26	52

PF-65	PF-66	PF-67	PF-68	PF-69	PF-70
50	39	44	12	0	0

1901-O QUARTER

Circulation-strike mintage: 1,612,000

AVAILABILITY IN MINT STATE: David Lawrence called this one of 17 Barber quarter issues considered to be "very scarce" in any Mint State category. ***Estimated number MS-65 or higher:*** Only 30 to 35 are estimated to exist. The 1901-O is another Barber quarter rarity in gem preservation.

AVAILABILITY IN CIRCULATED GRADES: 6,000 to 7,500. Most are G-4. This issue is underrated in higher circulated grades, and VF to AU coins are very scarce. This coin is often one of the last issues a collector needs to complete a set, excluding the 1896-S, 1901-S, and 1913-S.[14]

CHARACTERISTICS OF STRIKING: Variable. Take time to find a sharp one.

MARKET VALUES – CIRCULATION STRIKES

G-4	VG-8	F-12	VF-20	EF-40	AU-50	MS-60	MS-63	MS-65
$40	$60	$140	$275	$550	$750	$950	$1,850	$5,500

CERTIFIED POPULATIONS – CIRCULATION STRIKES

Fair	AG	G	VG	F	VF	EF	AU	MS-60
5	3	8	6	8	10	9	9	0

MS-61	MS-62	MS-63	MS-64	MS-65	MS-66	MS-67	MS-68	MS-69	MS-70
1	3	2	5	6	1	0	0	0	0

1901-S Quarter

Circulation-strike mintage: 72,664

Availability in Mint State: The 1901-S is the runaway key to the Barber quarter series in terms of demand at all levels. Any Mint State coin from 60 onward is rare. ***Estimated number MS-65 or higher:*** 8 to 12.

Availability in circulated grades: 1,800 to 2,200. Most are AG-3 and G-4. Well over 1,000 have been certified by PCGS and NGC—many more than for any other quarter in the Barber series. This is because even in G-4 the 1901-S sells for multiple thousands of dollars. While this coin is available in grades up to VG, examples Fine to AU are rarely seen. The rarity of 1901-S became widely recognized in the 1930s when, for the first time, the *Standard Catalogue of United States Coins* listed mintage figures in addition to values. Accordingly, in relation to the mintage a higher *percentage* of 1901-S quarters survive than do other issues of the era. In terms of actual survivors this is far and away the rarest Barber quarter.

Characteristics of striking: Usually well struck.

Notes: Even though the 1913-S quarter has a lower mintage than the 1901-S, in the days when examples of both could be found in circulation the 1901-S was at least twice as rare.

Mint State 1901-S quarters are, indeed, notable rarities. So far as is known, none were saved in roll or other quantities. The contention that A.C. Gies of Pittsburgh, Pennsylvania, had a roll of this date and also of other Barber quarters has been dismissed for reasons examined in detail (including notes from John J. Ford Jr.) in another book by the writer, *Lost and Found Coin Hoards and Treasures*. In essence, rumors of rolls of Barber quarters dating before 1909 which would have been held by Gies, Pukall, Raymond, and others are simply fantasy. Rolls that were put away by these gentlemen were primarily of lower denominations such as cents and nickels.

The 1901-S is also the most faked Barber coin. Many G and VG coins exist with added mintmarks, so care must be taken when buying in these grades. Either try to acquire a certified example, or learn the diagnostics of both pairs of dies used to strike this coin.[15]

MARKET VALUES – CIRCULATION STRIKES

G-4	VG-8	F-12	VF-20	EF-40	AU-50	MS-60	MS-63	MS-65
$5,250	$10,000	$16,500	$23,000	$30,000	$32,500	$37,500	$45,000	$75,000

CERTIFIED POPULATIONS – CIRCULATION STRIKES

Fair	AG	G	VG	F	VF	EF	AU	MS-60
70	116	64	20	6	7	3	9	0

MS-61	MS-62	MS-63	MS-64	MS-65	MS-66	MS-67	MS-68	MS-69	MS-70
0	1	1	4	3	2	2	0	0	0

1902 QUARTER

Circulation-strike mintage: 12,196,967
Proof mintage: 777

AVAILABILITY IN MINT STATE: Easy to find in all lower–Mint State levels. ***Estimated number MS-65 or higher:*** 150 to 180.

AVAILABILITY IN CIRCULATED GRADES: 80,000 to 100,000. Most are G-4.

CHARACTERISTICS OF STRIKING: Usually well struck.

AVAILABILITY IN PROOF FORMAT: ***Proof-60 to 64:*** 400 to 500. ***Proof-65 or better:*** 60 to 70.

NOTES: Some 967 coins of the 12,196,967 production have the notation "Porta [Puerto] Rican" in the records of the Philadelphia Mint. The meaning of this entry is unknown.[16]

MARKET VALUES – CIRCULATION STRIKES

G-4	VG-8	F-12	VF-20	EF-40	AU-50	MS-60	MS-63	MS-65
$9	$10	$26	$45	$65	$120	$240	$425	$1,200

MARKET VALUES – PROOF STRIKES

PF-60	PF-63	PF-65	PF-65Cam
$450	$800	$1,900	$2,300

CERTIFIED POPULATIONS – CIRCULATION STRIKES

Fair	AG	G	VG	F	VF	EF	AU	MS-60
0	2	1	4	7	16	18	68	0

MS-61	MS-62	MS-63	MS-64	MS-65	MS-66	MS-67	MS-68	MS-69	MS-70
8	38	54	47	24	6	1	0	0	0

CERTIFIED POPULATIONS – PROOF STRIKES

PF-50	PF-60	PF-61	PF-62	PF-63	PF-64
1	4	5	20	41	60
PF-65	**PF-66**	**PF-67**	**PF-68**	**PF-69**	**PF-70**
30	41	20	5	0	0

1902-O QUARTER

Circulation-strike mintage: 4,748,000

AVAILABILITY IN MINT STATE: David Lawrence called this one of 17 Barber quarter issues considered to be "very scarce" in any Mint State category. Easily available at lower–Mint State levels. ***Estimated number MS-65 or higher:*** 60 to 70.

AVAILABILITY IN CIRCULATED GRADES: 25,000 to 30,000. Most are G-4.

CHARACTERISTICS OF STRIKING: Usually with lightness on the right side of the reverse. Some are sharper than others, and thus being patient when looking for an example is worthwhile.

MARKET VALUES – CIRCULATION STRIKES

G-4	VG-8	F-12	VF-20	EF-40	AU-50	MS-60	MS-63	MS-65
$10	$16	$50	$85	$140	$225	$475	$1,300	$3,750

CERTIFIED POPULATIONS – CIRCULATION STRIKES

Fair	AG	G	VG	F	VF	EF	AU	MS-60	
0	1	2	3	1	14	7	28	0	
MS-61	**MS-62**	**MS-63**	**MS-64**	**MS-65**	**MS-66**	**MS-67**	**MS-68**	**MS-69**	**MS-70**
6	7	10	21	3	2	0	1	0	0

1902-S QUARTER

Circulation-strike mintage: 1,524,612

AVAILABILITY IN MINT STATE: MS-63 and 64 coins form an alternative to MS-65 for a high-level collection. A high-level MS-64 can be a better coin than an unattractive MS-65. ***Estimated number MS-65 or higher:*** 55 to 65.

AVAILABILITY IN CIRCULATED GRADES: 6,000 to 7,500. Most are G-4. Coins grading VF to AU are more difficult to find than the mintage figure might suggest.

CHARACTERISTICS OF STRIKING: Usually well struck, this being a general rule for the San Francisco quarters.

MARKET VALUES – CIRCULATION STRIKES

G-4	VG-8	F-12	VF-20	EF-40	AU-50	MS-60	MS-63	MS-65
$14	$22	$55	$90	$160	$240	$500	$950	$3,200

CERTIFIED POPULATIONS – CIRCULATION STRIKES

Fair	AG	G	VG	F	VF	EF	AU	MS-60
0	2	1	2	3	5	4	28	2

MS-61	MS-62	MS-63	MS-64	MS-65	MS-66	MS-67	MS-68	MS-69	MS-70
6	11	12	16	9	4	1	1	0	0

1903 Quarter

Circulation-strike mintage: 9,669,309
Proof mintage: 755

Availability in Mint State: Lower-range Mint State coins are easily enough found. ***Estimated number MS-65 or higher:*** 50 to 60. Amazingly rare considering the very high mintage.

Availability in circulated grades: 60,000 to 80,000. Most are G-4. Among circulated Philadelphia Mint quarters of this era, the 1903 is one of the scarcer issues in Fine or better.

Characteristics of striking: Usually sharp.

Availability in Proof format: ***Proof-60 to 64:*** 400 to 500. ***Proof-65 or better:*** 85 to 100.

MARKET VALUES – CIRCULATION STRIKES

G-4	VG-8	F-12	VF-20	EF-40	AU-50	MS-60	MS-63	MS-65
$9	$10	$26	$45	$65	$120	$240	$450	$2,000

MARKET VALUES – PROOF STRIKES

PF-60	PF-63	PF-65	PF-65Cam
$450	$775	$1,900	$2,300

CERTIFIED POPULATIONS – CIRCULATION STRIKES

Fair	AG	G	VG	F	VF	EF	AU	MS-60
0	0	1	0	5	8	9	32	2

MS-61	MS-62	MS-63	MS-64	MS-65	MS-66	MS-67	MS-68	MS-69	MS-70
7	20	18	20	3	3	0	0	0	0

CERTIFIED POPULATIONS – PROOF STRIKES

PF-50	PF-60	PF-61	PF-62	PF-63	PF-64
0	1	7	12	23	56

PF-65	PF-66	PF-67	PF-68	PF-69	PF-70
69	47	53	19	1	0

1903-O QUARTER

Circulation-strike mintage: 3,500,000

AVAILABILITY IN MINT STATE: In MS-63 and 64 grades it is elusive. ***Estimated number MS-65 or higher:*** 30 to 35. In the second edition of his book, David Lawrence considered the 1903-O and the 1896-S quarter to be the rarest of all pieces in the Barber series at the gem level. Things have a way of changing when more information becomes available, and many more have since been certified, but the 1903-O in gem Mint State certainly is a rarity.

AVAILABILITY IN CIRCULATED GRADES: 20,000 to 25,000. Most are G-4.

CHARACTERISTICS OF STRIKING: Usually fairly well struck—an exception among New Orleans quarters.

MARKET VALUES – CIRCULATION STRIKES

G-4	VG-8	F-12	VF-20	EF-40	AU-50	MS-60	MS-63	MS-65
$10	$12	$40	$60	$120	$275	$425	$1,200	$4,500

CERTIFIED POPULATIONS – CIRCULATION STRIKES

Fair	AG	G	VG	F	VF	EF	AU	MS-60
1	1	1	1	4	6	7	30	0

MS-61	MS-62	MS-63	MS-64	MS-65	MS-66	MS-67	MS-68	MS-69	MS-70
4	9	11	8	6	1	0	0	0	0

1903-S Quarter

Circulation-strike mintage: 1,036,000

Availability in Mint State: Scarce but quite available in lower–Mint State categories. ***Estimated number MS-65 or higher:*** 75 to 90.

Availability in circulated grades: 5,000 to 6,000. Most are G-4.

Characteristics of striking: Usually well struck. Most Mint State coins have excellent eye appeal.

MARKET VALUES – CIRCULATION STRIKES

G-4	VG-8	F-12	VF-20	EF-40	AU-50	MS-60	MS-63	MS-65
$15	$25	$45	$85	$150	$275	$425	$850	$2,200

CERTIFIED POPULATIONS – CIRCULATION STRIKES

Fair	AG	G	VG	F	VF	EF	AU	MS-60
0	2	0	2	1	3	6	11	0

MS-61	MS-62	MS-63	MS-64	MS-65	MS-66	MS-67	MS-68	MS-69	MS-70
2	12	11	17	18	2	0	0	0	0

1904 QUARTER

Circulation-strike mintage: 9,588,143
Proof mintage: 670

AVAILABILITY IN MINT STATE: Readily available in Mint State grades below the gem level. As is true for all Barber coins that are not especially valuable in circulated grades or lower–Mint State levels, such coins are not often certified, thus giving them the undeserved appearance of rarities in population reports. ***Estimated number MS-65 or higher:*** 75 to 90.

AVAILABILITY IN CIRCULATED GRADES: 60,000 to 80,000. Most are G-4.

CHARACTERISTICS OF STRIKING: Usually sharp.

AVAILABILITY IN PROOF FORMAT: ***Proof-60 to 64:*** 350 to 450. ***Proof-65 or better:*** 80 to 95.

MARKET VALUES – CIRCULATION STRIKES

G-4	VG-8	F-12	VF-20	EF-40	AU-50	MS-60	MS-63	MS-65
$9	$10	$26	$45	$70	$120	$225	$400	$1,200

MARKET VALUES – PROOF STRIKES

PF-60	PF-63	PF-65	PF-65Cam
$450	$800	$1,900	$2,300

CERTIFIED POPULATIONS – CIRCULATION STRIKES

Fair	AG	G	VG	F	VF	EF	AU	MS-60
0	0	1	2	4	7	7	42	0

MS-61	MS-62	MS-63	MS-64	MS-65	MS-66	MS-67	MS-68	MS-69	MS-70
7	12	23	34	18	4	1	0	0	0

CERTIFIED POPULATIONS – PROOF STRIKES

PF-50	PF-60	PF-61	PF-62	PF-63	PF-64
1	0	3	20	33	56

PF-65	PF-66	PF-67	PF-68	PF-69	PF-70
64	42	38	6	1	0

1904-O QUARTER

Circulation-strike mintage: 2,456,000

AVAILABILITY IN MINT STATE: David Lawrence called this one of 17 Barber quarter issues considered to be "very scarce" in any Mint State category. ***Estimated number MS-65 or higher:*** 70 to 85.

AVAILABILITY IN CIRCULATED GRADES: 12,000 to 15,000. Most are G-4.

CHARACTERISTICS OF STRIKING: In his book, David Lawrence reported that this issue is usually poorly struck and "often with some depression on the face." A few, including our illustrated Mint State coin, are sharply struck and problem free, but these are very rare. The positive aspect is that if a sharply struck coin is found there will probably be no premium charged for it.

MARKET VALUES – CIRCULATION STRIKES

G-4	VG-8	F-12	VF-20	EF-40	AU-50	MS-60	MS-63	MS-65
$30	$40	$85	$150	$240	$450	$800	$1,300	$3,000

CERTIFIED POPULATIONS – CIRCULATION STRIKES

Fair	AG	G	VG	F	VF	EF	AU	MS-60
0	2	5	0	7	12	11	30	1

MS-61	MS-62	MS-63	MS-64	MS-65	MS-66	MS-67	MS-68	MS-69	MS-70
2	7	11	20	8	7	1	0	0	0

1905 QUARTER

Circulation-strike mintage: 4,967,523
Proof mintage: 727

AVAILABILITY IN MINT STATE: Easy to find in any Mint State grade desired. ***Estimated number MS-65 or higher:*** 100 to 120.

AVAILABILITY IN CIRCULATED GRADES: 30,000 to 35,000. Most are AG-3 or G-4.

CHARACTERISTICS OF STRIKING: Usually well struck, but there are scattered exceptions.

AVAILABILITY IN PROOF FORMAT: ***Proof-60 to 64:*** 350 to 450. ***Proof-65 or better:*** 95 to 115.

MARKET VALUES – CIRCULATION STRIKES

G-4	VG-8	F-12	VF-20	EF-40	AU-50	MS-60	MS-63	MS-65
$30	$35	$50	$65	$70	$120	$240	$440	$1,300

MARKET VALUES – PROOF STRIKES

PF-60	PF-63	PF-65	PF-65Cam
$450	$800	$1,900	$2,300

CERTIFIED POPULATIONS – CIRCULATION STRIKES

Fair	AG	G	VG	F	VF	EF	AU	MS-60
1	4	4	2	9	13	5	32	1

MS-61	MS-62	MS-63	MS-64	MS-65	MS-66	MS-67	MS-68	MS-69	MS-70
8	21	27	40	11	7	0	1	0	0

CERTIFIED POPULATIONS – PROOF STRIKES

PF-50	PF-60	PF-61	PF-62	PF-63	PF-64
0	0	4	11	36	66

PF-65	PF-66	PF-67	PF-68	PF-69	PF-70
52	43	27	7	0	0

1905-O Quarter

Circulation-strike mintage: 1,230,000

Availability in Mint State: David Lawrence called this one of 17 Barber quarter issues considered to be "very scarce" in any Mint State category. ***Estimated number MS-65 or higher:*** 50 to 60.

Availability in circulated grades: 6,000 to 7,500. Most are G-4. Coins in all grades above VG are in great demand, and EF and AU coins are very scarce.

Characteristics of striking: Variable. Sharp examples can be found.

Notes: David Lawrence, whose enthusiasm for the Eliasberg Collection paralleled the present author's sentiments, commented in a letter in 1996: "The 1905-O is another coin on everyone's want list in *any* Mint State grade. This is a 'magic' date to those who know the series. It is the easiest of all Barber quarters to sell to collectors building sets, for it is significantly undervalued in all price guides."

MARKET VALUES – CIRCULATION STRIKES

G-4	VG-8	F-12	VF-20	EF-40	AU-50	MS-60	MS-63	MS-65
$40	$60	$120	$220	$260	$350	$475	$1,250	$5,500

CERTIFIED POPULATIONS – CIRCULATION STRIKES

Fair	AG	G	VG	F	VF	EF	AU	MS-60
0	1	4	5	6	7	5	12	1

MS-61	MS-62	MS-63	MS-64	MS-65	MS-66	MS-67	MS-68	MS-69	MS-70
3	6	11	14	2	2	1	0	0	0

1905-S QUARTER

Circulation-strike mintage: 1,884,000

AVAILABILITY IN MINT STATE: David Lawrence called this one of 17 Barber quarter issues considered to be "very scarce" in any Mint State category. ***Estimated number MS-65 or higher:*** 45 to 55. A 20th-century rarity despite its high mintage.

AVAILABILITY IN CIRCULATED GRADES: 9,000 to 14,000. Most are G-4.

CHARACTERISTICS OF STRIKING: Usually well struck, but some have lightness in the usual places on the reverse.

MARKET VALUES – CIRCULATION STRIKES

G-4	VG-8	F-12	VF-20	EF-40	AU-50	MS-60	MS-63	MS-65
$30	$40	$75	$100	$105	$225	$350	$1,000	$3,500

CERTIFIED POPULATIONS – CIRCULATION STRIKES

Fair	AG	G	VG	F	VF	EF	AU	MS-60
0	2	4	4	2	9	8	23	0

MS-61	MS-62	MS-63	MS-64	MS-65	MS-66	MS-67	MS-68	MS-69	MS-70
1	9	10	19	7	5	2	0	0	0

1906 Quarter

Circulation-strike mintage: 3,655,760
Proof mintage: 675

Availability in Mint State: Readily available in any Mint State grade desired. ***Estimated number MS-65 or higher:*** 220 to 265.

Availability in circulated grades: 25,000 to 30,000. Most are G-4. Easy to find in any grade desired.

Characteristics of striking: Usually well struck, but there are exceptions.

Availability in Proof format: ***Proof-60 to 64:*** 350 to 450. ***Proof-65 or better:*** 90 to 110.

MARKET VALUES – CIRCULATION STRIKES

G-4	VG-8	F-12	VF-20	EF-40	AU-50	MS-60	MS-63	MS-65
$9	$10	$26	$45	$70	$120	$240	$425	$1,100

MARKET VALUES – PROOF STRIKES

PF-60	PF-63	PF-65	PF-65Cam
$450	$800	$1,900	$2,300

CERTIFIED POPULATIONS – CIRCULATION STRIKES

Fair	AG	G	VG	F	VF	EF	AU	MS-60
0	0	2	3	2	2	2	27	1

MS-61	MS-62	MS-63	MS-64	MS-65	MS-66	MS-67	MS-68	MS-69	MS-70
9	25	34	54	34	4	3	0	0	0

CERTIFIED POPULATIONS – PROOF STRIKES

PF-50	PF-60	PF-61	PF-62	PF-63	PF-64
1	2	2	14	20	42

PF-65	PF-66	PF-67	PF-68	PF-69	PF-70
36	48	28	12	0	0

1906-D Quarter

Circulation-strike mintage: 3,280,000

Availability in Mint State: Not hard to find in any desired grade MS-60 upward. *Estimated number MS-65 or higher:* 75 to 90.

Availability in circulated grades: 20,000 to 25,000. Most are G-4.

Characteristics of striking: Often weakly struck in areas.

Notes: This is the first year of Denver Mint quarters. The first of this denomination were struck in February of this year.

MARKET VALUES – CIRCULATION STRIKES

G-4	VG-8	F-12	VF-20	EF-40	AU-50	MS-60	MS-63	MS-65
$9	$10	$30	$50	$70	$145	$250	$450	$1,450

CERTIFIED POPULATIONS – CIRCULATION STRIKES

Fair	AG	G	VG	F	VF	EF	AU	MS-60
0	0	2	1	0	3	0	21	0

MS-61	MS-62	MS-63	MS-64	MS-65	MS-66	MS-67	MS-68	MS-69	MS-70
11	14	17	34	17	1	0	0	0	0

1906-O Quarter

Circulation-strike mintage: 2,056,000

Availability in Mint State: Easy enough to find in any desired Mint State category. ***Estimated number MS-65 or higher:*** 175 to 200.

Availability in circulated grades: 9,000 to 14,000. Most are G-4. Due to poor strike (see characteristics of striking), finding VF and EF coins is a challenge; they often look more worn than they actually are.

Characteristics of striking: On average, the 1906-O is the most weakly struck coin in the series. On the obverse, even AU coins may not have a full band under LIBERTY. Usually examples are lightly struck where the upper right of the shield joins the wing and on the eagle's talons—the usual places—but some are sharper than others. Again, take time to find a sharp one. If you are lucky enough to find one of the few well-struck examples, it will have been well worth the search.

MARKET VALUES – CIRCULATION STRIKES

G-4	VG-8	F-12	VF-20	EF-40	AU-50	MS-60	MS-63	MS-65
$9	$10	$40	$60	$100	$200	$300	$550	$1,450

CERTIFIED POPULATIONS – CIRCULATION STRIKES

Fair	AG	G	VG	F	VF	EF	AU	MS-60
0	0	1	2	0	4	3	20	0

MS-61	MS-62	MS-63	MS-64	MS-65	MS-66	MS-67	MS-68	MS-69	MS-70
4	10	16	40	23	11	4	1	0	0

1907 QUARTER

Circulation-strike mintage: 7,192,000
Proof mintage: 575

AVAILABILITY IN MINT STATE: Easy to find at all Mint State levels. ***Estimated number MS-65 or higher:*** 150 to 180.

AVAILABILITY IN CIRCULATED GRADES: 50,000 to 60,000. Most are G-4. Easy to find in high circulated grades.

CHARACTERISTICS OF STRIKING: Usually well struck.

AVAILABILITY IN PROOF FORMAT: ***Proof-60 to 64:*** 250 to 300. ***Proof-65 or better:*** 40 to 50. The 1907 and 1915 are the rarest Barber quarters at the gem level.

MARKET VALUES – CIRCULATION STRIKES

G-4	VG-8	F-12	VF-20	EF-40	AU-50	MS-60	MS-63	MS-65
$9	$10	$26	$40	$65	$120	$225	$400	$1,100

MARKET VALUES – PROOF STRIKES

PF-60	PF-63	PF-65	PF-65Cam
$450	$800	$1,900	$2,300

CERTIFIED POPULATIONS – CIRCULATION STRIKES

Fair	AG	G	VG	F	VF	EF	AU	MS-60
0	0	6	4	3	7	12	77	2

MS-61	MS-62	MS-63	MS-64	MS-65	MS-66	MS-67	MS-68	MS-69	MS-70
14	58	63	73	28	13	2	1	0	0

CERTIFIED POPULATIONS – PROOF STRIKES

PF-50	PF-60	PF-61	PF-62	PF-63	PF-64
0	3	4	14	33	70

PF-65	PF-66	PF-67	PF-68	PF-69	PF-70
43	90	34	18	1	0

1907-D Quarter

Circulation-strike mintage: 2,484,000

Availability in Mint State: Lower–Mint State coins are easy to find. ***Estimated number MS-65 or higher:*** 45 to 55. By all logic the 1907-D with its high mintage should be readily available in gem Mint State, but the reality is otherwise.

Availability in circulated grades: 15,000 to 18,000. Most are G-4. Surprisingly elusive in high circulated grades.

Characteristics of striking: Often weak, but sharp coins can be found with some searching.

MARKET VALUES – CIRCULATION STRIKES

G-4	VG-8	F-12	VF-20	EF-40	AU-50	MS-60	MS-63	MS-65
$9	$10	$26	$48	$70	$175	$250	$650	$2,250

CERTIFIED POPULATIONS – CIRCULATION STRIKES

Fair	AG	G	VG	F	VF	EF	AU	MS-60
0	1	2	4	3	2	4	16	1

MS-61	MS-62	MS-63	MS-64	MS-65	MS-66	MS-67	MS-68	MS-69	MS-70
3	7	26	28	6	3	0	0	0	0

Varieties: A minor doubled-die obverse exists, with doubling seen in the ribbons to the left of Liberty's neck.

1907-O Quarter

Circulation-strike mintage: 4,560,000

AVAILABILITY IN MINT STATE: Slightly scarce at lower–Mint State levels. ***Estimated number MS-65 or higher:*** 70 to 85.

AVAILABILITY IN CIRCULATED GRADES: 25,000 to 30,000. Most are G-4.

CHARACTERISTICS OF STRIKING: David Lawrence noted that the 1907-O was "the poorest struck coin in the series," with some pieces having distortions, scars, and other problems. Moreover, he suggested that the 1907-O is "undervalued in all Mint State grades and in AU as well." I second this. Does even one sharp coin exist? John Frost commented: "The 1907-O is considered the *poorest and most unusually struck* coin in the series, versus the 1906-O which is the *weakest strike*, but without the oddities found on the 1907-O coins, such as 'mumps' (distortions on neck and jaw), scars, etc."[17]

MARKET VALUES – CIRCULATION STRIKES

G-4	VG-8	F-12	VF-20	EF-40	AU-50	MS-60	MS-63	MS-65
$9	$10	$26	$45	$70	$135	$275	$500	$1,850

CERTIFIED POPULATIONS – CIRCULATION STRIKES

Fair	AG	G	VG	F	VF	EF	AU	MS-60
0	0	4	1	5	5	7	32	2

MS-61	MS-62	MS-63	MS-64	MS-65	MS-66	MS-67	MS-68	MS-69	MS-70
6	27	28	38	17	8	1	1	0	0

1907-S Quarter

Circulation-strike mintage: 1,360,000

Availability in Mint State: David Lawrence called this one of 17 Barber quarter issues considered to be "very scarce" in any Mint State category. See comments under the 1907-S dime and half dollar. For some reason all are scarcer than might be expected. ***Estimated number MS-65 or higher:*** 95 to 115.

Availability in circulated grades: 6,000 to 8,000. Most are G-4. Very difficult to locate in grades above VF.

Characteristics of striking: Usually well struck with a nice appearance.

MARKET VALUES – CIRCULATION STRIKES

G-4	VG-8	F-12	VF-20	EF-40	AU-50	MS-60	MS-63	MS-65
$10	$18	$45	$70	$140	$280	$475	$1,200	$5,000

CERTIFIED POPULATIONS – CIRCULATION STRIKES

Fair	AG	G	VG	F	VF	EF	AU	MS-60
0	0	1	3	2	6	4	4	0

MS-61	MS-62	MS-63	MS-64	MS-65	MS-66	MS-67	MS-68	MS-69	MS-70
3	8	8	22	8	5	1	0	0	0

1908 QUARTER

Circulation-strike mintage: 4,232,000
Proof mintage: 545

AVAILABILITY IN MINT STATE: Easily found in Mint State. ***Estimated number MS-65 or higher:*** 150 to 180.

AVAILABILITY IN CIRCULATED GRADES: 25,000 to 30,000. Most are G-4. Strangely enough, while G to VF and also AU coins are all extremely common, EF coins are surprisingly hard to find. There seems to be no explanation for this oddity.[18]

CHARACTERISTICS OF STRIKING: Usually sharp.

AVAILABILITY IN PROOF FORMAT: ***Proof-60 to 64:*** 290 to 340. ***Proof-65 or better:*** 50 to 60.

MARKET VALUES – CIRCULATION STRIKES

G-4	VG-8	F-12	VF-20	EF-40	AU-50	MS-60	MS-63	MS-65
$9	$10	$26	$45	$70	$120	$240	$425	$1,100

MARKET VALUES – PROOF STRIKES

PF-60	PF-63	PF-65	PF-65Cam
$450	$775	$1,900	$2,300

CERTIFIED POPULATIONS – CIRCULATION STRIKES

Fair	AG	G	VG	F	VF	EF	AU	MS-60
0	1	1	2	4	1	3	46	0

MS-61	MS-62	MS-63	MS-64	MS-65	MS-66	MS-67	MS-68	MS-69	MS-70
9	42	42	64	13	2	3	0	0	0

CERTIFIED POPULATIONS – PROOF STRIKES

PF-50	PF-60	PF-61	PF-62	PF-63	PF-64
0	0	5	12	27	43

PF-65	PF-66	PF-67	PF-68	PF-69	PF-70
32	31	31	7	1	0

1908-D Quarter

Circulation-strike mintage: 5,788,000

Availability in Mint State: Readily available at lower–Mint State levels. ***Estimated number MS-65 or higher:*** 100 to 120. Rare in relation to the generous mintage.

Availability in circulated grades: 35,000 to 42,500. Most are G-4. Easy to find in higher circulated grades as well.

Characteristics of striking: Usually fairly well struck.

MARKET VALUES – CIRCULATION STRIKES

G-4	VG-8	F-12	VF-20	EF-40	AU-50	MS-60	MS-63	MS-65
$9	$10	$26	$45	$70	$120	$240	$425	$1,250

CERTIFIED POPULATIONS – CIRCULATION STRIKES

Fair	AG	G	VG	F	VF	EF	AU	MS-60
1	0	4	5	11	16	9	52	0

MS-61	MS-62	MS-63	MS-64	MS-65	MS-66	MS-67	MS-68	MS-69	MS-70
10	33	28	51	19	3	3	1	0	0

1908-O QUARTER

Circulation-strike mintage: 6,244,000

AVAILABILITY IN MINT STATE: Easily available in grades from MS–60 to 64. ***Estimated number MS-65 or higher:*** 140 to 170.

AVAILABILITY IN CIRCULATED GRADES: 25,000 to 30,000. Most are G-4.

CHARACTERISTICS OF STRIKING: Usually weak in areas and sometimes with lumps on the neck.

MARKET VALUES – CIRCULATION STRIKES

G-4	VG-8	F-12	VF-20	EF-40	AU-50	MS-60	MS-63	MS-65
$9	$10	$26	$45	$65	$120	$240	$425	$1,200

CERTIFIED POPULATIONS – CIRCULATION STRIKES

Fair	AG	G	VG	F	VF	EF	AU	MS-60
1	2	5	5	2	8	13	28	2

MS-61	MS-62	MS-63	MS-64	MS-65	MS-66	MS-67	MS-68	MS-69	MS-70
10	25	37	66	21	5	2	0	0	0

1908-S QUARTER

Circulation-strike mintage: 784,000

Availability in Mint State: David Lawrence called this one of 17 Barber quarter issues considered to be "very scarce" in any Mint State category. ***Estimated number MS-65 or higher:*** 50 to 60.

Availability in circulated grades: 4,000 to 5,000. Most are G-4. Very hard to find in VF and higher grades.

Characteristics of striking: Usually well struck and quite attractive.

MARKET VALUES – CIRCULATION STRIKES

G-4	VG-8	F-12	VF-20	EF-40	AU-50	MS-60	MS-63	MS-65
$18	$38	$85	$165	$325	$465	$750	$1,200	$4,500

CERTIFIED POPULATIONS – CIRCULATION STRIKES

Fair	AG	G	VG	F	VF	EF	AU	MS-60
0	1	6	7	7	5	4	14	0

MS-61	MS-62	MS-63	MS-64	MS-65	MS-66	MS-67	MS-68	MS-69	MS-70
3	17	5	26	13	7	2	0	0	0

1909 Quarter

Circulation-strike mintage: 9,268,000
Proof mintage: 650

Availability in Mint State: Another readily available date. ***Estimated number MS-65 or higher:*** 175 to 200.

Availability in circulated grades: 60,000 to 80,000. Most are G-4. Easy to find in higher grades.

Characteristics of striking: Usually sharp.

Availability in Proof format: ***Proof-60 to 64:*** 350 to 450. ***Proof-65 or better:*** 75 to 90.

MARKET VALUES – CIRCULATION STRIKES

G-4	VG-8	F-12	VF-20	EF-40	AU-50	MS-60	MS-63	MS-65
$9	$10	$26	$45	$65	$120	$240	$425	$1,100

MARKET VALUES – PROOF STRIKES

PF-60	PF-63	PF-65	PF-65Cam
$450	$800	$1,900	$2,300

CERTIFIED POPULATIONS – CIRCULATION STRIKES

Fair	AG	G	VG	F	VF	EF	AU	MS-60
0	2	2	7	12	16	13	94	2

MS-61	MS-62	MS-63	MS-64	MS-65	MS-66	MS-67	MS-68	MS-69	MS-70
19	65	87	129	33	11	2	0	0	0

CERTIFIED POPULATIONS – PROOF STRIKES

PF-50	PF-60	PF-61	PF-62	PF-63	PF-64
0	1	8	14	34	67

PF-65	PF-66	PF-67	PF-68	PF-69	PF-70
47	51	37	13	0	0

1909-D QUARTER

Circulation-strike mintage: 5,114,000

AVAILABILITY IN MINT STATE: Easy to find in any desired grade. ***Estimated number MS-65 or higher:*** 150 to 180.

AVAILABILITY IN CIRCULATED GRADES: 30,000 to 35,000. Most are G-4. Higher-grade circulated coins are common in relation to the demand for them.

CHARACTERISTICS OF STRIKING: Usually well struck.

MARKET VALUES – CIRCULATION STRIKES

G-4	VG-8	F-12	VF-20	EF-40	AU-50	MS-60	MS-63	MS-65
$9	$10	$26	$45	$85	$150	$240	$425	$1,100

CERTIFIED POPULATIONS – CIRCULATION STRIKES

Fair	AG	G	VG	F	VF	EF	AU	MS-60
0	0	8	9	16	10	13	64	3

MS-61	MS-62	MS-63	MS-64	MS-65	MS-66	MS-67	MS-68	MS-69	MS-70
14	33	45	46	15	4	1	0	0	0

1909-O Quarter

Circulation-strike mintage: 712,000

Availability in Mint State: MS–63 and 64 coins can be a compromise for a high-level set if an MS-65 coin cannot be found or is considered to be too expensive. David Lawrence called this one of 17 Barber quarter issues considered to be "very scarce" in any Mint State category. ***Estimated number MS-65 or higher:*** 20 to 24. At the gem level the 1909-O is a remarkable challenge for a late-date Barber quarter.

Availability in circulated grades: 4,000 to 5,000. Most are G-4. Coins grading VF to AU are seldom seen. David Lawrence considered this to be one the five hardest-to-find quarters in AU grades.

Characteristics of striking: The swan song New Orleans quarter is usually found with weakness in the usual places, but there are scattered exceptions that have fairly decent details.

Notes: The 1909-O is quite scarce in all high grades, even in EF and AU, the latter grade being one of the hardest in the series to locate, per David Lawrence's book. Further, this note came from Lawrence in a letter: "The 1909-O is the scarcest of all the New Orleans Mint Barber quarters in most grades, especially if with a decent strike. It is on the want list of just about everyone who wants to build a Mint State set."

MARKET VALUES – CIRCULATION STRIKES

G-4	VG-8	F-12	VF-20	EF-40	AU-50	MS-60	MS-63	MS-65
$42	$100	$400	$650	$1,000	$1,800	$3,000	$4,000	$10,000

CERTIFIED POPULATIONS – CIRCULATION STRIKES

Fair	AG	G	VG	F	VF	EF	AU	MS-60
0	2	8	10	3	6	1	5	0

MS-61	MS-62	MS-63	MS-64	MS-65	MS-66	MS-67	MS-68	MS-69	MS-70
1	5	9	18	5	1	1	0	0	0

1909-S Quarter

Circulation-strike mintage: 1,348,000

Availability in Mint State: Readily available. ***Estimated number MS-65 or higher:*** 100 to 120. Easy to find and usually with nice eye appeal.

Availability in circulated grades: 25,000 to 30,000. Most are G-4. Scarce in higher circulated grades.

Characteristics of striking: Usually sharp.

MARKET VALUES – CIRCULATION STRIKES

G-4	VG-8	F-12	VF-20	EF-40	AU-50	MS-60	MS-63	MS-65
$9	$10	$35	$55	$90	$185	$285	$750	$2,000

CERTIFIED POPULATIONS – CIRCULATION STRIKES

Fair	AG	G	VG	F	VF	EF	AU	MS-60
0	0	6	4	5	8	4	8	1

MS-61	MS-62	MS-63	MS-64	MS-65	MS-66	MS-67	MS-68	MS-69	MS-70
2	5	13	26	8	14	3	0	0	0

1910 Quarter

Circulation-strike mintage: 2,244,000
Proof mintage: 551

Availability in Mint State: Another quarter that is easy to find and usually has nice eye appeal. ***Estimated number MS-65 or higher:*** 150 to 180.

Availability in circulated grades: 12,000 to 15,000. Most are G-4. Higher-grade circulated coins are common.

Characteristics of striking: Variable, but sharp coins can be found.

Availability in Proof format: ***Proof-60 to 64:*** 275 to 325. ***Proof-65 or better:*** 55 to 65.

MARKET VALUES – CIRCULATION STRIKES

G-4	VG-8	F-12	VF-20	EF-40	AU-50	MS-60	MS-63	MS-65
$9	$10	$26	$45	$80	$140	$240	$425	$1,100

MARKET VALUES – PROOF STRIKES

PF-60	PF-63	PF-65	PF-65Cam
$450	$800	$1,900	$2,300

CERTIFIED POPULATIONS – CIRCULATION STRIKES

Fair	AG	G	VG	F	VF	EF	AU	MS-60
0	0	2	3	5	5	2	21	1

MS-61	MS-62	MS-63	MS-64	MS-65	MS-66	MS-67	MS-68	MS-69	MS-70
12	22	29	44	28	10	0	0	0	0

CERTIFIED POPULATIONS – PROOF STRIKES

PF-50	PF-60	PF-61	PF-62	PF-63	PF-64
1	0	1	15	33	63
PF-65	**PF-66**	**PF-67**	**PF-68**	**PF-69**	**PF-70**
39	46	47	22	3	0

1910-D QUARTER

Circulation-strike mintage: 1,500,000

AVAILABILITY IN MINT STATE: Lower-grade Mint State coins are widely available. ***Estimated number MS-65 or higher:*** 55 to 65. Examples are surprisingly rare at this level for a late-date quarter with a mintage well over a million.

AVAILABILITY IN CIRCULATED GRADES: 6,000 to 7,500. Most are G-4.

CHARACTERISTICS OF STRIKING: Variable. Take time to find a sharp one.

NOTES: From David Lawrence in a 1997 letter: "The 1910-D is an underrated date and is never around when needed. In fact, even EF coins are rare."

MARKET VALUES – CIRCULATION STRIKES

G-4	VG-8	F-12	VF-20	EF-40	AU-50	MS-60	MS-63	MS-65
$10	$11	$45	$70	$125	$240	$350	$900	$1,600

CERTIFIED POPULATIONS – CIRCULATION STRIKES

Fair	AG	G	VG	F	VF	EF	AU	MS-60
0	2	1	4	4	6	6	21	1

MS-61	MS-62	MS-63	MS-64	MS-65	MS-66	MS-67	MS-68	MS-69	MS-70
6	15	16	18	16	6	0	0	0	0

1911 Quarter

Circulation-strike mintage: 3,720,000
Proof mintage: 543

Availability in Mint State: Easy to find. ***Estimated number MS-65 or higher:*** 180 to 220.

Availability in circulated grades: 20,000 to 25,000. Most are G-4. Common in all grades.

Characteristics of striking: Variable. Take time to find a sharp one.

Availability in Proof format: ***Proof-60 to 64:*** 280 to 330. ***Proof-65 or better:*** 70 to 85.

MARKET VALUES – CIRCULATION STRIKES

G-4	VG-8	F-12	VF-20	EF-40	AU-50	MS-60	MS-63	MS-65
$9	$10	$26	$45	$70	$125	$240	$425	$1,100

MARKET VALUES – PROOF STRIKES

PF-60	PF-63	PF-65	PF-65Cam
$450	$800	$1,900	$2,300

CERTIFIED POPULATIONS – CIRCULATION STRIKES

Fair	AG	G	VG	F	VF	EF	AU	MS-60
0	1	3	1	3	3	7	54	0

MS-61	MS-62	MS-63	MS-64	MS-65	MS-66	MS-67	MS-68	MS-69	MS-70
8	31	57	83	23	5	0	0	0	0

CERTIFIED POPULATIONS – PROOF STRIKES

PF-50	PF-60	PF-61	PF-62	PF-63	PF-64
0	1	4	6	17	55

PF-65	PF-66	PF-67	PF-68	PF-69	PF-70
54	47	26	29	2	0

1911-D QUARTER

Circulation-strike mintage: 933,600

AVAILABILITY IN MINT STATE: David Lawrence called this one of 17 Barber quarter issues considered to be "very scarce" in any Mint State category. ***Estimated number MS-65 or higher:*** 20 to 24. At the gem level this is a major rarity.

AVAILABILITY IN CIRCULATED GRADES: 4,000 to 5,000. Most are G-4. Common in low grades. In Fine or better preservation 1911-D quarters are surprisingly hard to find.

CHARACTERISTICS OF STRIKING: Variable. Once again, take time to find a sharp one.

MARKET VALUES – CIRCULATION STRIKES

G-4	VG-8	F-12	VF-20	EF-40	AU-50	MS-60	MS-63	MS-65
$30	$40	$150	$300	$400	$600	$850	$1,300	$5,500

CERTIFIED POPULATIONS – CIRCULATION STRIKES

Fair	AG	G	VG	F	VF	EF	AU	MS-60
1	0	7	3	7	18	6	15	0

MS-61	MS-62	MS-63	MS-64	MS-65	MS-66	MS-67	MS-68	MS-69	MS-70
5	11	14	16	4	0	0	0	0	0

1911-S Quarter

Circulation-strike mintage: 988,000

Availability in Mint State: Plentiful in relation to the demand for them. ***Estimated number MS-65 or higher:*** 220 to 260.

Availability in circulated grades: 4,000 to 5,000. Most are G-4. High-grade coins are elusive, but not as much so as for the 1911-D.

Characteristics of striking: Usually sharp.

MARKET VALUES – CIRCULATION STRIKES

G-4	VG-8	F-12	VF-20	EF-40	AU-50	MS-60	MS-63	MS-65
$9	$10	$55	$85	$165	$280	$375	$750	$1,500

CERTIFIED POPULATIONS – CIRCULATION STRIKES

Fair	AG	G	VG	F	VF	EF	AU	MS-60
1	0	1	2	2	9	5	17	0

MS-61	MS-62	MS-63	MS-64	MS-65	MS-66	MS-67	MS-68	MS-69	MS-70
4	11	13	17	22	80	8	1	0	0

1912 QUARTER

Circulation-strike mintage: 4,400,000
Proof mintage: 700

AVAILABILITY IN MINT STATE: One of the more available issues in any Mint State level. ***Estimated number MS-65 or higher:*** 300 to 360.

AVAILABILITY IN CIRCULATED GRADES: 25,000 to 35,000. Most are G-4. Common in higher grades.

CHARACTERISTICS OF STRIKING: Variable, but sharp coins can be found.

AVAILABILITY IN PROOF FORMAT: ***Proof-60 to 64:*** 500 to 550. ***Proof-65 or better:*** 65 to 80.

MARKET VALUES – CIRCULATION STRIKES

G-4	VG-8	F-12	VF-20	EF-40	AU-50	MS-60	MS-63	MS-65
$9	$10	$26	$45	$70	$120	$240	$425	$1,100

MARKET VALUES – PROOF STRIKES

PF-60	PF-63	PF-65	PF-65Cam
$450	$800	$1,900	$2,300

CERTIFIED POPULATIONS – CIRCULATION STRIKES

Fair	AG	G	VG	F	VF	EF	AU	MS-60
0	2	2	5	7	7	10	55	2

MS-61	MS-62	MS-63	MS-64	MS-65	MS-66	MS-67	MS-68	MS-69	MS-70
12	66	72	138	39	6	1	0	0	0

CERTIFIED POPULATIONS – PROOF STRIKES

PF-50	PF-60	PF-61	PF-62	PF-63	PF-64
0	0	9	9	29	60

PF-65	PF-66	PF-67	PF-68	PF-69	PF-70
53	29	20	8	1	0

1912-S Quarter

Circulation-strike mintage: 708,000

Availability in Mint State: David Lawrence called this one of 17 Barber quarter issues considered to be "very scarce" in any Mint State category. ***Estimated number MS-65 or higher:*** 55 to 65.

Availability in circulated grades: 4,000 to 5,000. Most are G-4. Hard to find VF or better.

Characteristics of striking: Variable, as is so often the case with late-date Barber quarters. Careful searching will yield a sharp one.

MARKET VALUES – CIRCULATION STRIKES

G-4	VG-8	F-12	VF-20	EF-40	AU-50	MS-60	MS-63	MS-65
$20	$30	$65	$90	$125	$220	$400	$900	$1,500

CERTIFIED POPULATIONS – CIRCULATION STRIKES

Fair	AG	G	VG	F	VF	EF	AU	MS-60
0	1	2	1	2	8	5	13	0

MS-61	MS-62	MS-63	MS-64	MS-65	MS-66	MS-67	MS-68	MS-69	MS-70
3	8	15	19	16	2	2	1	0	0

1913 QUARTER

Circulation-strike mintage: 484,000
Proof mintage: 613

AVAILABILITY IN MINT STATE: Readily available despite its relatively low mintage. ***Estimated number MS-65 or higher:*** 120 to 140.

AVAILABILITY IN CIRCULATED GRADES: 2,500 to 3,000. Most are G-4. Although its circulation-strike mintage is the same as the famous 1909-S, V.D.B., cent, the quarter is much rarer in high circulated grades.[19]

CHARACTERISTICS OF STRIKING: Variable. Repeating a theme, this is another Barber quarter for which careful hunting will pay dividends.

AVAILABILITY IN PROOF FORMAT: ***Proof-60 to 64:*** 290 to 340. ***Proof-65 or better:*** 75 to 90.

MARKET VALUES – CIRCULATION STRIKES

G-4	VG-8	F-12	VF-20	EF-40	AU-50	MS-60	MS-63	MS-65
$22	$35	$100	$180	$400	$525	$900	$1,200	$4,000

MARKET VALUES – PROOF STRIKES

PF-60	PF-63	PF-65	PF-65Cam
$450	$850	$1,900	$2,500

CERTIFIED POPULATIONS – CIRCULATION STRIKES

Fair	AG	G	VG	F	VF	EF	AU	MS-60
0	4	3	4	7	11	9	23	2

MS-61	MS-62	MS-63	MS-64	MS-65	MS-66	MS-67	MS-68	MS-69	MS-70
3	5	19	27	19	1	2	0	0	0

CERTIFIED POPULATIONS – PROOF STRIKES

PF-50	PF-60	PF-61	PF-62	PF-63	PF-64
1	0	11	20	36	60

PF-65	PF-66	PF-67	PF-68	PF-69	PF-70
39	42	24	10	1	0

1913-D Quarter

Circulation-strike mintage: 1,450,800

Availability in Mint State: Many nice coins exist. In lower–Mint State levels they are plentiful in relation to the demand for them. ***Estimated number MS-65 or higher:*** 120 to 140.

Availability in circulated grades: 6,000 to 7,500. Most are G-4. Coins grading VF or higher are elusive.

Characteristics of striking: Often soft on the usual reverse places. Some nice strikes exist, however.

MARKET VALUES – CIRCULATION STRIKES

G-4	VG-8	F-12	VF-20	EF-40	AU-50	MS-60	MS-63	MS-65
$12	$15	$35	$60	$85	$175	$275	$450	$1,150

CERTIFIED POPULATIONS – CIRCULATION STRIKES

Fair	AG	G	VG	F	VF	EF	AU	MS-60
0	0	2	6	6	11	5	33	0

MS-61	MS-62	MS-63	MS-64	MS-65	MS-66	MS-67	MS-68	MS-69	MS-70
2	24	24	37	17	8	2	0	0	0

1913-S QUARTER

Circulation-strike mintage: 40,000

AVAILABILITY IN MINT STATE: Of the three key issues in the Barber quarter series, the 1896-S, 1901-S, and 1913-S the last is much more available in Mint State than are the other two. The reason for this is not clear. A.C. Gies, long-time (born 1855) Pittsburgh collector, is known to have saved bank-wrapped rolls of coins beginning with the year 1901, and from time to time has been cited as the source for most 1913-S Barber quarters surviving today in Mint State. It is believed that most of his rolls were of minor denominations, there is no record of him or anyone else having dispersed a roll quantity of the 1913-S. David Lawrence called this one of 17 Barber quarter issues considered to be "very scarce" in any Mint State category. ***Estimated number MS-65 or higher:*** 60 to 70.

AVAILABILITY IN CIRCULATED GRADES: 1,000 to 1,200. Most are AG-3 to G-4. Many of these were plucked from circulation in the 1930s, mostly AG-3 and G-4, when collectors took note of the low mintage figure. Nice VG coins are usually available, and occasionally in Fine, but in VF and above, it is a vastly different story. High circulated grades are almost never seen, as apparently very few people saved them once they entered circulation. In fact, there are more Mint state examples known of the 1913-S than VF, EF, and AU combined. There are likely only a dozen or so known in EF, and probably 15 to 20 known in AU. Some collectors building AU or even EF sets end up buying a Mint State 1913-S because they are far easier to locate, and not that much more money.[20]

CHARACTERISTICS OF STRIKING: The 1913-S has a striking peculiarity most people don't know about, which can aid in authentication. Every example seems to be unevenly struck, with weakness most easily seen on the left side of the obverse. This is true on coins struck from either of the two pairs of dies used for this issue. On AG-3 and G-4 coins, the left obverse rim will be barely present or absent, while the right rim is strong. This uneven strike is also seen on high-grade coins, although it is less obvious to the unaided eye. If a low-grade purported 1913-S quarter looks evenly struck, approach with caution, as it may be an altered coin with an added mintmark.[21]

NOTES: The 1913-S quarter mintage of 40,000 coins is the lowest for any regular 20th-century circulation-strike silver coin.

MARKET VALUES – CIRCULATION STRIKES

G-4	VG-8	F-12	VF-20	EF-40	AU-50	MS-60	MS-63	MS-65
$1,650	$2,200	$5,000	$7,500	$10,000	$12,750	$15,000	$20,000	$30,000

CERTIFIED POPULATIONS – CIRCULATION STRIKES

Fair	AG	G	VG	F	VF	EF	AU	MS-60
24	152	148	64	12	8	0	2	0

MS-61	MS-62	MS-63	MS-64	MS-65	MS-66	MS-67	MS-68	MS-69	MS-70
1	4	5	16	4	6	7	0	0	0

1914 Quarter

Circulation-strike mintage: 6,244,250
Proof mintage: 380

Availability in Mint State: One of the more available issues. ***Estimated number MS-65 or higher:*** 300 to 360.

Availability in circulated grades: 45,000 to 55,000. Most are G-4. Easy to find in any grade desired.

Characteristics of striking: Variable. Look for an exception.

Availability in Proof format: ***Proof-60 to 64:*** 275 to 325. ***Proof-65 or better:*** 50 to 60.

MARKET VALUES – CIRCULATION STRIKES

G-4	VG-8	F-12	VF-20	EF-40	AU-50	MS-60	MS-63	MS-65
$9	$10	$22	$40	$65	$115	$225	$400	$1,100

MARKET VALUES – PROOF STRIKES

PF-60	PF-63	PF-65	PF-65Cam
$450	$950	$2,100	$2,500

CERTIFIED POPULATIONS – CIRCULATION STRIKES

Fair	AG	G	VG	F	VF	EF	AU	MS-60
0	0	8	11	11	14	17	115	1

MS-61	MS-62	MS-63	MS-64	MS-65	MS-66	MS-67	MS-68	MS-69	MS-70
17	93	113	147	62	8	1	0	0	0

CERTIFIED POPULATIONS – PROOF STRIKES

PF-50	PF-60	PF-61	PF-62	PF-63	PF-64
1	1	6	8	20	55

PF-65	PF-66	PF-67	PF-68	PF-69	PF-70
39	40	21	12	0	0

1914-D Quarter

Circulation-strike mintage: 3,046,000

Availability in Mint State: Easy to find. ***Estimated number MS-65 or higher:*** 190 to 230.

Availability in circulated grades: 20,000 to 25,000. Most are G-4. Common in higher grades.

Characteristics of striking: Variable. Take time to find a sharp one.

MARKET VALUES – CIRCULATION STRIKES

G-4	VG-8	F-12	VF-20	EF-40	AU-50	MS-60	MS-63	MS-65
$9	$10	$22	$40	$65	$120	$240	$425	$1,100

CERTIFIED POPULATIONS – CIRCULATION STRIKES

Fair	AG	G	VG	F	VF	EF	AU	MS-60
0	0	4	6	6	7	16	49	0

12	38	69	82	31	6	1	0	0	0
74	191	260	342	139	68	23	0	0	0

1914-S Quarter

Circulation-strike mintage: 264,000

Availability in Mint State: MS–63 and 64 coins are somewhat scarce. ***Estimated number MS-65 or higher:*** 50 to 60. Low-mintage rarity.

Availability in circulated grades: 1,500 to 2,000. Most are G-4. Fine and VF coins are occasionally found, but higher-grade examples are elusive.

Characteristics of striking: Variable. Look for a sharp one.

Notes: The mintmark is often filled in and is a hallmark of certain authentic specimens according to David Lawrence's book. The same writer notes the existence of a slightly repunched date. This must mean a hub shift, as by this time date logotypes were not used.

MARKET VALUES – CIRCULATION STRIKES

G-4	VG-8	F-12	VF-20	EF-40	AU-50	MS-60	MS-63	MS-65
$125	$180	$375	$550	$825	$975	$1,400	$1,650	$3,500

CERTIFIED POPULATIONS – CIRCULATION STRIKES

Fair	AG	G	VG	F	VF	EF	AU	MS-60
1	56	93	75	25	22	5	10	0

MS-61	MS-62	MS-63	MS-64	MS-65	MS-66	MS-67	MS-68	MS-69	MS-70
6	5	10	8	11	3	3	0	0	0

1915 QUARTER

Circulation-strike mintage: 3,480,000
Proof mintage: 450

AVAILABILITY IN MINT STATE: One of the more plentiful issues. ***Estimated number MS-65 or higher:*** 300 to 360.

AVAILABILITY IN CIRCULATED GRADES: 20,000 to 25,000. Most are G-4. Easy to find in any grade desired.

CHARACTERISTICS OF STRIKING: Variable, but there are quite a few sharp strikes.

AVAILABILITY IN PROOF FORMAT: ***Proof-60 to 64:*** 275 to 325. ***Proof-65 or better:*** 40 to 50. The 1907 and 1915 are the rarest Barber quarters at the gem level.

MARKET VALUES – CIRCULATION STRIKES

G-4	VG-8	F-12	VF-20	EF-40	AU-50	MS-60	MS-63	MS-65
$9	$10	$22	$40	$65	$120	$240	$425	$1,200

MARKET VALUES – PROOF STRIKES

PF-60	PF-63	PF-65	PF-65Cam
$450	$1,000	$2,200	$2,600

CERTIFIED POPULATIONS – CIRCULATION STRIKES

Fair	AG	G	VG	F	VF	EF	AU	MS-60
0	1	3	7	10	6	10	67	0

MS-61	MS-62	MS-63	MS-64	MS-65	MS-66	MS-67	MS-68	MS-69	MS-70
15	57	88	117	60	9	1	0	0	0

CERTIFIED POPULATIONS – PROOF STRIKES

PF-50	PF-60	PF-61	PF-62	PF-63	PF-64
1	2	8	15	34	40

PF-65	PF-66	PF-67	PF-68	PF-69	PF-70
27	25	15	7	0	0

1915-D Quarter

Circulation-strike mintage: 3,694,000

Availability in Mint State: Plentiful. ***Estimated number MS-65 or higher:*** 500 to 600. At the gem level this is the second-most-common Barber quarter, but trailing the 1916-D by a long distance.

Availability in circulated grades: 25,000 to 30,000. Most are G-4. Easy to find in any grade desired.

Characteristics of striking: Another variety that is often weakly struck, but for which sharp coins can be found.

MARKET VALUES – CIRCULATION STRIKES

G-4	VG-8	F-12	VF-20	EF-40	AU-50	MS-60	MS-63	MS-65
$9	$10	$22	$40	$70	$120	$240	$425	$1,100

CERTIFIED POPULATIONS – CIRCULATION STRIKES

Fair	AG	G	VG	F	VF	EF	AU	MS-60
0	1	4	8	5	17	19	88	2

MS-61	MS-62	MS-63	MS-64	MS-65	MS-66	MS-67	MS-68	MS-69	MS-70
24	64	129	155	69	29	5	0	0	0

1915-S QUARTER

Circulation-strike mintage: 704,000

AVAILABILITY IN MINT STATE: Slightly scarce at the gem level, but easily available otherwise. ***Estimated number MS-65 or higher:*** 100 to 120.

AVAILABILITY IN CIRCULATED GRADES: 4,000 to 5,000. Most are G-4. Somewhat scarce in higher circulated grades.

CHARACTERISTICS OF STRIKING: Again, take time to find a sharp one.

NOTES: David Lawrence commented to me in 1997: "Most of the Mint State 1915-S quarters I have seen are rather 'ticky-tacky' in appearance and do not have smooth surfaces."

MARKET VALUES – CIRCULATION STRIKES

G-4	VG-8	F-12	VF-20	EF-40	AU-50	MS-60	MS-63	MS-65
$25	$40	$60	$85	$115	$200	$285	$475	$1,300

CERTIFIED POPULATIONS – CIRCULATION STRIKES

Fair	AG	G	VG	F	VF	EF	AU	MS-60
0	0	5	5	11	7	7	37	0

MS-61	MS-62	MS-63	MS-64	MS-65	MS-66	MS-67	MS-68	MS-69	MS-70
15	30	14	37	15	9	0	0	0	0

1916 Quarter

Circulation-strike mintage: 1,788,000

Availability in Mint State: Easy to find. ***Estimated number MS-65 or higher:*** 250 to 300.

Availability in circulated grades: 9,000 to 14,000. Most are G-4. Higher-grade circulated coins, while a tiny percentage of the overall population, are easily found.

Characteristics of striking: Variable, but examples usually occur with some lightness on the reverse. Sharp coins can be found, however.

MARKET VALUES – CIRCULATION STRIKES

G-4	VG-8	F-12	VF-20	EF-40	AU-50	MS-60	MS-63	MS-65
$9	$10	$22	$40	$70	$120	$240	$425	$1,000

CERTIFIED POPULATIONS – CIRCULATION STRIKES

Fair	AG	G	VG	F	VF	EF	AU	MS-60
0	0	3	7	5	4	8	75	1

MS-61	MS-62	MS-63	MS-64	MS-65	MS-66	MS-67	MS-68	MS-69	MS-70
7	50	79	106	55	13	2	0	0	0

1916-D QUARTER

Circulation-strike mintage: 6,540,800

AVAILABILITY IN MINT STATE: The most common Barber quarter. ***Estimated number MS-65 or higher:*** 1,500 to 2,000. At the gem level the 1916-D quarter is the only Barber silver coin with the estimated number of surviving gems crossing the 1,000 mark, and by a wide margin.[22]

AVAILABILITY IN CIRCULATED GRADES: 50,000 to 60,000. Most are G-4. The most common coin in the entire Barber quarter series.

CHARACTERISTICS OF STRIKING: Variable. Most have areas of lightness on the right side of the reverse.

NOTES: A large order for quarters was sent to the Denver Mint late in the year, causing the facility to produce these instead of additional 1916-D Mercury dimes, causing the latter to become a numismatic rarity.

MARKET VALUES – CIRCULATION STRIKES

G-4	VG-8	F-12	VF-20	EF-40	AU-50	MS-60	MS-63	MS-65
$9	$10	$22	$40	$70	$120	$240	$425	$1,000

CERTIFIED POPULATIONS – CIRCULATION STRIKES

Fair	AG	G	VG	F	VF	EF	AU	MS-60
0	0	12	9	11	29	35	227	5

MS-61	MS-62	MS-63	MS-64	MS-65	MS-66	MS-67	MS-68	MS-69	MS-70
56	177	239	413	182	64	12	2	0	0

VARIETIES: Some repunched mintmark varieties can be found with some searching and are collectible. These carry little or no price premium.

A Gallery of Barber Quarter Dollar Proof Coinage

Among Philadelphia issues in the Barber quarter series, Proofs were struck each year from 1892 through 1915. Most 1892 quarters had the Type II reverse. The last year, 1916, did not see a Proof coinage. See page 174 for a longer discussion.

1892, Type I Reverse, Proof, quarter.

1892, Type II Reverse, Proof, quarter.

1894, Proof, quarter.

1898, Proof, quarter.

1900, Proof, quarter.

1901, Proof, quarter.

1903, Proof, quarter.

1907, Proof, quarter.

1908, Proof, quarter.

1909, Proof, quarter.

1915, Proof, quarter.

Chapter Six

Barber Half Dollars 1892–1915

The Design of the New Half Dollar

The 1892 half dollar design by Charles E. Barber is a close copy of that used on the quarter. Liberty faces right, her hair is in a Phrygian cap, and a wreath of laurel encircles her head. The word LIBERTY appears on a small band or ribbon above her forehead. IN GOD WE TRUST is above, six stars are to the left, seven stars are to the right, and the date is below.

The reverse is an adaptation of the Great Seal of the United States and features a heraldic eagle grasping an olive branch and arrows, and holding in its beak a ribbon inscribed E PLURIBUS UNUM. A galaxy of stars is above. UNITED STATES OF AMERICA and HALF DOLLAR surround the design.

Pattern Coins

Five patterns are known for the Barber half dollar. Dated 1891, the obverses of four of the patterns very closely follow the adopted design of 1892, but with slight differences. These include adjustments of the border letters, the details of the ribbon and its relationship to the stars, and the position of the stars in relation to the portrait and lettering. The obverse of the fifth is divergent from the portrait that Mint Director Leech requested and shows Liberty standing near an eagle. With the exception of J-1763, the reverse dies differ from the adopted design and are described below. The only existing examples are in the National Numismatic Collection in the Smithsonian Institution.

The adopted design was used continuously from 1892 until the end of the series in 1915. Occasionally, suggestions were made to change it. For *The Numismatist*, in January 1908, Augustus G. Heaton submitted a sketch for a new half dollar design, featuring on the obverse "a group indicating labor, women's aid and the education of youth—the spirit of our progress," with the inscription surrounding: "LIBERTY AND EQUALITY UNDER LAW: PROSPERITY IN ENERGY AND INTEGRITY." The proposal was further described:

> On the reverse is the national shield and a spread eagle with a scroll in his beak on which is the number and name of the current president. This would be a historic record and give very interesting variety to our monotonous series. As a substitute for the contested "IN GOD WE TRUST" the Divine Eye (as used once by the Mormons) would be more impressive to old and young and not subjective trivial perversion . . .

Nothing came of the idea.

Pattern 1891 half dollar, Judd-1762. The obverse is a very close copy of that adopted in 1892, the only differences being minor positioning, most noticeable at the TR of TRUST in relation to the olive leaves. On the reverse, the clouds above the eagle are larger than on J-1764.

Pattern 1891 half dollar, Judd-1763. The obverse die is the same as the preceding. The reverse is very close to the adopted design, the differences being trivial, such as the position of some stars. For quick reference the star below the second S of STATES points directly to the S.

Pattern 1891 half dollar, Judd-1764. The obverse die is the same as the preceding. The clouds above the eagle are smaller than on J-1762, and the stars are positioned differently.

Pattern 1891 half dollar, Judd-1765. The obverse die is the same as the preceding. On the reverse, the eagle is smaller, and a heavy wreath of oak leaves surrounds it.

Pattern 1891 half dollar, Judd-1766. The obverse departs from the request of Director Leach and shows the standing figure of Liberty with a sword and cap on pole with a perched eagle behind. The reverse has an eagle smaller than the preceding and a heavier wreath of oak.

Mintages and Distribution

From 1892 onward, Barber half dollars were routinely released into circulation. Hardly any numismatic attention was paid to them. Pages of *The Numismatist* and the *American Journal of Numismatics* are devoid of information save for yearly mintage figures.

Within a few years, most Barber half dollars (and also dimes and quarters) were worn to the point at which the LIBERTY inscription on the portrait was mostly missing. Within 20 years it was gone completely. As the LIBERTY word is a key to assigning grades, Barber coins as a class are much rarer in Fine to AU grades than are, for example, Liberty Seated silver coins.

Mintages of Barber Half Dollars

Mintages of Barber quarters from highest to lowest, by issue, are as follows:

1892: 8,236,000	1897: 2,480,000	1912: 1,550,000	1909-O: 925,400
1899: 5,538,000	1906-O: 2,446,000	1902-S: 1,460,670	1896-O: 924,000
1908-O: 5,360,000	1909: 2,368,000	1911: 1,406,000	1898-O: 874,000
1902: 4,922,000	1898-S: 2,358,550	1893-O: 1,389,000	1901-S: 847,044
1900: 4,762,000	1912-D: 2,300,800	1912-S: 1,370,000	1893-S: 740,000
1901: 4,268,000	1903: 2,278,000	1908: 1,354,000	1911-D: 695,080
1894-S: 4,048,690	1894-O: 2,138,000	1911-S: 1,272,000	1897-O: 632,000
1907-O: 3,946,600	1903-O: 2,100,000	1907-S: 1,250,000	1905: 622,000
1907-D: 3,856,000	1910-S: 1,948,000	1915-D: 1,170,400	1913-S: 604,000
1908-D: 3,280,000	1903-S: 1,920,772	1894: 1,148,000	1904-S: 553,038
1906-D: 4,028,000	1895: 1,843,338	1896-S: 1,140,948	1913-D: 534,000
1904: 2,992,000	1893: 1,826,000	1901-O: 1,124,000	1905-O: 505,000
1898: 2,956,000	1895-O: 1,766,000	1904-O: 1,117,600	1910: 418,000
1900-O: 2,744,000	1909-S: 1,764,000	1895-S: 1,108,086	1892-O: 390,000
1906: 2,638,000	1906-S: 1,740,154	1892-S: 1,029,028	1913: 188,000
1907: 2,598,000	1899-O: 1,724,000	1914-S: 992,000	1915: 138,000
1900-S: 2,560,322	1899-S: 1,686,411	1896: 950,000	1914: 124,000
1902-O: 2,526,000	1908-S: 1,644,828	1892: 934,000	
1905-S: 2,494,000	1915-S: 1,604,000	1897-S: 933,900	

Comments and Reviews

Reviews and comments on all of the Barber coins were generally negative after their release in 1892. As noted in chapter 1, the quarters and half dollars would not stack properly, a complaint picked up by the press and printed in many newspapers. Beyond this aspect, the half dollar in particular elicited this criticism on January 20 in the *Tacoma Daily News:*

Just Our Luck:
The New Half Dollar is a Combination of Thirteens

The Washington National Bank has received 1,000 of the newly coined 50-cent pieces of the new design which are to be put into circulation. The new coin has a bird of undecipherable plumage, undistinguishable sex, unrecognizable genus, and might be a Chilean vulture or a spring capot ready for the fire as the glorious bird of freedom and independence. There are 13 stars above its head, 13 letters in E Pluribus Unum, 13 leaves on the olive branch in one claw and 13 arrows grasped in the other, 13 feathers are in its tail, 13 quills are in each wing, and no doubt all that restrained the engraver from putting 13 eyes in the bird was the limited space on the coin. It is an unlucky coin, and from the 13 combination it will doubtless very seldom be found in anyone's pocket.

Upon the other side of the coin is the head of Liberty looking west with her lips pursed up for a kiss and her nose slightly elevated. She's a pretty nice girl, but her complexion is a bit pale and her hair a trifle scant. She has a fine neck, just such a one as an erring son loves to throw his arms about. Liberty's cap is now away, but her eyes have a faraway dreamy look that makes the hope of winning many of her seem vain. She wears the crown of Liberty, is surrounded by 13 stars, and declares our trust in God. She is not as pretty as the girl on our dollars, has too high a cheek bone, and wears bangs. Her nose is straight, but she wears her head cut off too close to the shoulders to please everybody.

Half Dollar Hub Changes

In 1901 a new obverse hub die was introduced in the Barber half dollar series. The differences between the new and the old are very subtle and require magnification to detect. As a quick identifier the star next to TRUST points slightly to the right of the center of a denticle on Hub I and points slightly farther to the right on Obverse Hub II. Other differences are likewise microscopic.

For Philadelphia Mint coins of the transitional year 1900 circulation strikes are from Obverse Hub II while Proofs are from Obverse Hub I (Hub II was introduced on Proofs in 1902). Circulation strikes from all three mints can be found with both hubs.

Barber Half Dollars in Circulation

Half dollars were popular in commerce from the first year, 1892, onward, and mintage quantities were often substantial. After the silver dollar denomination was discontinued in 1904, the half dollar became the highest silver denomination of the realm. By that time silver dollars were not often seen in circulation, except in the Rocky Mountain states.

Half dollars were supplied in proportion to the call for them, as was done with the other two Barber denominations. Dimes and quarters were made in larger quantities. Both were used in vending machines and gambling devices, whereas very few were equipped with half-dollar slots. Production quantities for half dollars were smaller in most instances. Still, there was a steady demand for them through the years, and there were only a few years when a branch mint did not make them.

Barber half dollars were familiar sights in circulation into the early 1950s, by which time dimes and quarters were rarely seen.

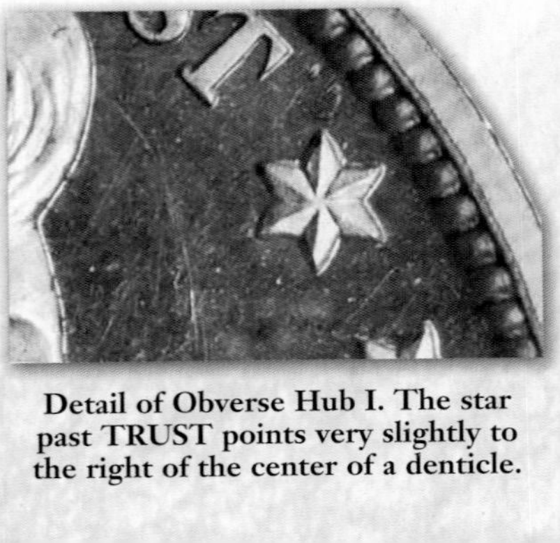

Detail of Obverse Hub I. The star past TRUST points very slightly to the right of the center of a denticle.

Detail of Obverse Hub II. The star past TRUST points slightly farther to the right.

Collecting Barber Half Dollars

Barber half dollars, generally ignored prior to the 1930s, attracted collectors with the popularization of coin albums and folders starting in that decade. Even so, the face value was a deterrent in the Depression years, and lower denominations, especially the Barber dime, were more widely sought. Raymond album pages were a popular way to store and display them.

By the 1940s, when these were still common in circulation, many enthusiasts built sets using Raymond pages and the more popular, inexpensive Whitman folders. Into the mid-1950s many collectors had sets of circulated Indian Head cents, Lincoln cents, Liberty nickels from the Liberty Head issues onward, and dimes, quarters, and half dollars from 1892 onward in Whitman folders. Most examples in numismatic channels were well worn, with AG-3 and G-4 being typical. Some dealers, Herbert Tobias being one, specialized in these. High-grade coins were hard to find—and still are—and certain issues are rare in Mint State, the 1904-S being the key in this regard.

The coin market changed direction beginning in 1960 when the launching of *Coin World* and the nationwide publicity given to the 1960, Small Date, cent (some $50 face-value bags sold for $12,000 or more), attracted hundreds of thousands of newcomers to become collectors and investors. Emphasis was placed on coins in higher grades. Barber coins were no longer in circulation, and the interest in filling Whitman albums faded. After the minting of 90-percent silver coins ceased in 1965, more emphasis was placed on high grades and investing. Interesting dates and mintmarks could no longer be found in pocket change. Barber coins were collected, but not many people concentrated on them.

Beginning in a large way in the late 1900s, Barber coins came to the fore with many specialists. *The Complete Guide to Barber Halves*, by David Lawrence, sold widely and provided information. Articles by David W. Lange and others added to the interest. Kevin Flynn's *Authoritative Reference on Barber Half Dollars*, published in 2005, featured many close-up illustrations of repunched dates and mintmarks and other information. The Barber Coin Collectors' Society today is a focal point for comments from members on various aspects. Despite these attractions, the number of collectors favoring Barber coins over other series was and is small. The membership of the BCCS is fewer than 300, although it has been growing in recent years. The number of collectors interested is much larger, however. Most have not joined the society. Acquisition alone rather than acquisition plus study and appreciation seems to be the rule.

Today in the marketplace many buyers, especially those building Registry Sets (a concept popularized by David Hall of PCGS), emphasize high grade rather than overall rarity. A number of Barber collections have been built this way. The process has resulted in coins that are common in such grades as MS–63, 64, or even 65 bringing very high prices if they are unique or very rare in population reports as MS-66. This was not a factor a generation ago.

Type-set collecting became especially popular following the market rise that began in early 1960. The introduction of the Library of Coins albums by the Coin and Currency Institute (founded as the publishing arm of Capital Coin Co. by Robert Friedberg) did much to further stimulate interest. Many buyers of Barber half dollars and other coins simply seek a single high-grade piece to illustrate the design.

PRICES IN 1946

The first edition of *A Guide Book of United States Coins* was issued in 1946 with a cover date of 1947. The most expensive Barber half dollar was the 1901-S, priced at $150.00 in Uncirculated grade. In fact, this was the only one with a three-figure valuation. The generic price for a common issue was $1.50 Fine, $2.50 Uncirculated. The cheapest Proofs were $8.50 each. Ranked in descending order, the top 20 1946 Uncirculated prices are given below against which you can compare current prices.

In 1946 the true rarity of certain issues was guesswork. Today there is more information from population reports and studies by specialists:

The Top 20 Barber Half Dollar Prices in 1946

1. 1901-S: $150.00	6. 1903-O: $30.00	11. 1902-O: $22.50	16. 1908-S: $20.00
2. 1901-O: $60.00	7. 1913-S: $30.00	12. 1894-O: $20.00	17. 1915-S: $20.00
3. 1904-S: $60.00	8. 1900-O: $25.00	13. 1895-O: $20.00	18. 1895-S: $18.50
4. 1902-S: $50.00	9. 1896-S: $22.50	14. 1896-O: $20.00	19. 1897-S: $18.50
5. 1903-S: $45.00	10. 1897-O: $22.50	15. 1906-S: $20.00	20. 1898-O: $18.50[1]

DIE VARIETIES

The most important die variety among Barber half dollars is the 1892-O, Micro o, which is a rarity in all grades. Beyond this there are many repunched-date varieties from 1892 through 1908, and across the entire series minor variations in mintmark placement and orientation are found. The Lawrence and Flynn books illustrate many of these. A number of misplaced dates (MPDs) are found in the form of traces of date numerals hidden in the denticles. These are believed to have been caused when the workman about to enter the date logotype touched it lightly on the edge of the die to evaluate the hardness of the metal.

ASPECTS OF STRIKING

Nearly all circulation-strike Barber half dollars show some weakness on the right side of the reverse. On the best strikes, the area where the eagle's wing meets the shield will be sharp, and the eagle's leg feathers and talons and the arrow feathers will be sharp. *However*, the details of the highest area of the eagle's talons will *not* be sharp in 99 percent of the coins seen (compared to the talons on the left which are usually sharp).

Of the four mints that struck Barber half dollars over the years, the New Orleans facility was the most casual and the most careless in its coinage. In order to enable workers to safely pay less attention to the coining presses, the dies were spaced slightly farther apart than they should have been,

The reverse of a 1903-O half dollar with areas of lightness as seen on nearly all New Orleans Mint half dollars and, to a lesser extent, on circulation strikes of other branch-mint issues. Among New Orleans coins this strike is better than usually seen.

The reverse of an 1893-O half dollar with extensive areas of light striking.

and the result was light striking on most coins made there. Similarly, collectors of Morgan silver dollars know well that O-Mint pieces usually come weakly defined.

As a general rule the San Francisco Mint Barber half dollars of this era are much better struck than are the New Orleans counterparts, but at the same time this striking was paid for with increased die cracks, which are much more numerous on extant San Francisco issues than issues from other mints. Among Philadelphia and San Francisco coins, those of the final 10 years of the series are usually not as well struck as the earlier dates. Such considerations combine to make the study of the series all the more interesting.

Proof Barber Half Dollars

Proofs of each year were made from 1892 to 1915, with the lowest mintages taking place in 1914 and 1915. These were sold in sets with other silver coins—dimes, quarters, and dollars through 1904, and dimes and quarters after that year.

Proofs of 1901 to 1904 typically have lightly polished portraits in the die and are not "cameo" or deeply frosted like the other years. Today, Proofs are readily collectible. Most of them survive in grades of Proof-63 or 64.

A gallery of Proof Barber half dollars can be found on page 343.

Grading Barber Half Dollars

1909. Graded MS-62.

MS–60 to 70 (Mint State). ***Obverse:*** At MS-60, some abrasion and contact marks are evident, most noticeably on the cheek and the obverse field to the right. Luster is present, but may be dull or lifeless. Many Barber coins have been cleaned, especially of the earlier dates. At MS-63, contact marks are very few; abrasion still is evident but less than at lower levels. Indeed, the cheek of Miss Liberty virtually showcases abrasion. This is even more evident on a half dollar than on lower denominations. An MS-65 coin may have minor abrasion, but contact marks are so minute as to require magnification. Luster should be full and rich. ***Reverse:*** Comments apply as for the obverse, except that in lower–Mint State grades abrasion and contact marks are most noticeable on the head and tail of the eagle and on the tips of the wings. At MS-65 or higher there are no marks visible to the unaided eye. The field is mainly protected by design elements, so the reverse often appears to grade a point or two higher than the obverse.

Illustrated coin: On this example, mottled light-brown toning appears over lustrous surfaces.

1915-D. Graded AU-53.

AU-50, 53, 55, 58 (About Uncirculated). ***Obverse:*** Light wear is seen on the head, especially on the forward hair under LIBERTY. At AU-58, the luster is extensive but incomplete, especially on the higher parts and in the right field. At AU-50 and 53, luster is less. ***Reverse:*** Wear is seen on the head and tail of the eagle and on the tips of the wings. At AU-50 and 53, there still is significant luster. An AU-58 coin (as determined by the obverse) can have the reverse appear to be full Mint State.

Illustrated coin: Areas of original Mint luster can be seen on this coin, more so on the reverse than on the obverse.

1908-S. Graded EF-45.

EF-40, 45 (Extremely Fine). ***Obverse:*** Further wear is seen on the head. The hair above the forehead lacks most detail. LIBERTY shows wear but still is strong. ***Reverse:*** Further wear is seen on the head and tail of the eagle and on the tips of the wings, most evident at the left and right extremes of the wings At this level and below, sharpness of strike on the reverse is not important.

1897-S. Graded VF-30.

VF-20, 30 (Very Fine). ***Obverse:*** The head shows more wear, now with nearly all detail gone in the hair above the forehead. LIBERTY shows wear, but is complete. The leaves on the head all show wear, as does the upper part of the cap. ***Reverse:*** Wear is more extensive, particularly noticeable on the outer parts of the wings, the head, the shield, and the tail.

Illustrated coin: This coin is seemingly lightly cleaned.

1909-O. Graded F-12.

F-12, 15 (Fine). ***Obverse:*** The head shows extensive wear. LIBERTY, the key place to check, is weak, especially at ER, but is fully readable. The ANA grading standards and *Photograde* adhere to this. PCGS suggests that lightly struck coins "may have letters partially missing." Traditionally, collectors insist on full LIBERTY. ***Reverse:*** More wear is seen on the reverse, in the places as above. E PLURIBUS UNUM is light, with one to several letters worn away.

1915-S. Graded VG-8.

VG-8, 10 (Very Good). ***Obverse:*** A net of three letters in LIBERTY must be readable. Traditionally LI is clear, and after that there is a partial letter or two. ***Reverse:*** Further wear has smoothed more than half of the feathers in the wing. The shield is indistinct except for a few traces of interior lines. The motto is partially worn away. The rim is full, and many if not most denticles can be seen.

1892-O. Graded G-4.

G-4, 6 (Good). ***Obverse:*** The head is in outline form, with the center flat. Most of the rim is there and all letters and the date are full. ***Reverse:*** The eagle shows only a few feathers, and only a few scattered letters remain in the motto. The rim may be worn flat in some or all of the area, but the peripheral lettering is clear.

Illustrated coin: On this coin the obverse is perhaps G-6 and the reverse AG-3. The grade might be averaged as G-4.

1892-O, Micro o, Half Dollar

Circulation-strike mintage: Smaller part of 390,000

Regular O mintmark.

Micro o mintmark.

Availability in Mint State: Probably 30 to 40 are known in lower levels of Mint State. ***Estimated number MS-65 or higher:*** 5 to 7. The finest by far is the Louis E. Eliasberg Collection MS-67 example auctioned in 1997, now in the Dale Friend Collection and graded MS-68 (by PCGS). A few other gem–Mint State coins are known and reside in several Registry Sets of Barber halves.

Availability in circulated grades: Most circulated examples are in grades AG to VG. Very few are known in F and VF, while more are known in EF and AU, following the grade distribution of the normal 1892-O coins. Basically, most examples are either in high grades or very low grades, with little in between.

There are likely a very small number of additional circulated examples out there to be found, and it is the collector's dream cherrypick. A new example in AU was reportedly discovered in early 2015.[2]

Characteristics of striking: The small o mintmark is asymmetrical and is much heavier on the right side than on the left, unlike the mintmarks on 1892-O quarters. After much research John Frost found several 1893-O quarters that had similarly asymmetrical mintmarks, but inverted with the heavier side to the left.

Notes: ***1892-O, Micro o (FS-501):*** This is the most important and most desired of the die varieties in the entire Barber series. The mintmark is significantly smaller than normal; the punch intended for a quarter dollar was inadvertently used on the half dollar die. It is a rarity in any grade.

In *Mint Marks*, in 1893, when this variety was scarcely a year old, Augustus G. Heaton commented:

After a long interval the half dollar was struck in 1892 with new bust and Heraldic Eagle dies. The date is small, and a small O [the regular 1892-O] is directly under the middle of the eagle's tail and over the D. There is one rare variety of this piece with an exceedingly small o, hardly larger than a period.

In Édouard Frossard's June 1894 sale of the William M. Friesner Collection a "Microscopic o, Sharp Uncirculated," sold for $2.10. An example of this variety was displayed by Howard R. Newcomb at the American Numismatic Society Exhibition of 1914. Subsequently, the variety was listed in the *Guide Book of United States Coins,* where it created widespread notice. Later, the listing was discontinued, and it became a footnote (*e.g.*, on page 163 of the 1996 edition). In recent years it has had a regular listing there.

MARKET VALUES – CIRCULATION STRIKES

G-4	VG-8	F-12	VF-20	EF-40	AU-50
$2,500	$4,250	$5,500	$7,500	$12,000	$18,500
AU-55	**MS-60**	**MS-62**	**MS-63**	**MS-64**	**MS-65**
$20,000	$28,000	$34,500	$40,000	$60,000	$80,000

CERTIFIED POPULATIONS – CIRCULATION STRIKES

Fair	AG	G	VG	F	VF	EF	AU	MS-60
2	0	2	1	1	0	0	1	0

MS-61	MS-62	MS-63	MS-64	MS-65	MS-66	MS-67	MS-68	MS-69	MS-70
0	1	0	1	1	0	0	1	0	0

1892-S HALF DOLLAR

Circulation-strike mintage: 1,029,028

AVAILABILITY IN MINT STATE: Scarce. Seemingly not many people in the West saved examples of this as the first year of issue. ***Estimated number MS-65 or higher:*** 45 to 55.

AVAILABILITY IN CIRCULATED GRADES: 2,250 to 2,750. Most are AG-3 or G-4. This is one of the more challenging issues to find in circulated grades, more so than for 1892-O.

CHARACTERISTICS OF STRIKING: Variable, but striking is usually quite good, this being generally true of early San Francisco issues.

Notes: Even though the mintage of 1892-S (1,029,028) is higher than the 1892-O (390,000), the 1892-S has emerged over the years as very important in its own right, for reasons that are not clear today. Even well-circulated specimens are rare. Mint State pieces are particularly desirable, although they do come on the market now and then, especially when fine cabinets are dispersed. More of these were saved, as the first year of issue, than were most later San Francisco issues through the very early 1900s.

MARKET VALUES – CIRCULATION STRIKES

G-4	VG-8	F-12	VF-20	EF-40	AU-50
$235	$340	$400	$500	$575	$700
AU-55	**MS-60**	**MS-62**	**MS-63**	**MS-64**	**MS-65**
$775	$950	$1,400	$2,250	$2,600	$4,350

CERTIFIED POPULATIONS – CIRCULATION STRIKES

Fair	AG	G	VG	F	VF	EF	AU	MS-60
9	41	43	32	8	11	9	46	0

MS-61	MS-62	MS-63	MS-64	MS-65	MS-66	MS-67	MS-68	MS-69	MS-70
11	21	17	8	10	0	2	0	0	0

1893 Half Dollar

Circulation-strike mintage: 1,826,000
Proof mintage: 792

Availability in Mint State: Easily obtained in lower–Mint State grades. ***Estimated number MS-65 or higher:*** 75 to 95.

Availability in circulated grades: 3,500 to 5,000. Mostly AG-3 or G-4. This is one of the more challenging issues to find in circulated grades above VG.

Characteristics of striking: Variable, but usually quite sharp.

Availability in Proof format: ***Proof-60 to 64:*** 500 to 600. ***Proof-65 or better:*** 50 to 60.

MARKET VALUES – CIRCULATION STRIKES

G-4	VG-8	F-12	VF-20	EF-40	AU-50
$20	$30	$80	$160	$210	$325
AU-55	**MS-60**	**MS-62**	**MS-63**	**MS-64**	**MS-65**
$350	$550	$850	$1,200	$2,000	$4,300

MARKET VALUES – PROOF STRIKES

PF-60	PF-63	PF-64	PF-65
$600	$1,200	$1,800	$3,250

CERTIFIED POPULATIONS – CIRCULATION STRIKES

Fair	AG	G	VG	F	VF	EF	AU	MS-60
1	1	4	0	6	19	12	78	3

MS-61	MS-62	MS-63	MS-64	MS-65	MS-66	MS-67	MS-68	MS-69	MS-70
24	39	39	25	12	5	1	0	0	0

CERTIFIED POPULATIONS – PROOF STRIKES

PF-50	PF-60	PF-61	PF-62	PF-63	PF-64
1	3	6	16	55	67
PF-65	**PF-66**	**PF-67**	**PF-68**	**PF-69**	**PF-70**
47	49	31	4	0	0

1893-O Half Dollar

Circulation-strike mintage: 1,389,000

Availability in Mint State: Somewhat scarce in lower–Mint State categories. ***Estimated number MS-65 or higher:*** 27 to 32. Examples are rare so fine. Lacking in most of the greatest collections to cross the auction block.

Availability in circulated grades: 4,000 to 5,000. This is one of the more challenging issues to find in circulated grades.

CHARACTERISTICS OF STRIKING: The 1893-O usually has areas of light striking, sometimes including stars on the lower right of the obverse, and typically at the inner wing and the talon and arrow feathers at the right of the reverse (as illustrated on page 262). Sharply struck coins exist and are hard to find. On some examples the obverse and reverse dies are very lightly clashed, notable on several areas of the coin, but in particular below Miss Liberty's chin on the obverse and at the left side of the reverse.

MARKET VALUES – CIRCULATION STRIKES

G-4	VG-8	F-12	VF-20	EF-40	AU-50
$35	$70	$130	$220	$350	$425
AU-55	**MS-60**	**MS-62**	**MS-63**	**MS-64**	**MS-65**
$525	$700	$1,000	$1,500	$2,250	$8,500

CERTIFIED POPULATIONS – CIRCULATION STRIKES

Fair	AG	G	VG	F	VF	EF	AU	MS-60
0	5	5	8	6	6	10	33	0

MS-61	MS-62	MS-63	MS-64	MS-65	MS-66	MS-67	MS-68	MS-69	MS-70
11	22	57	35	6	2	0	0	0	0

1893-S HALF DOLLAR

Circulation-strike mintage: 740,000

AVAILABILITY IN MINT STATE: MS–63 and 64 coins are scarce. ***Estimated number MS-65 or higher:*** 22 to 27. This is one of the rarer Barber half dollars at this level. With only a few exceptions, Barber half dollars of the 1890s are very difficult to find in gem preservation.

AVAILABILITY IN CIRCULATED GRADES: 2,000 to 2,500. Most are AG-3 or G-4. Any coin finer ranges from scarce to rare. This is one of the most challenging issues to find in circulated grades. David Lawrence considered this to be among the top-eight rarest half dollars in EF and AU.

CHARACTERISTICS OF STRIKING: The striking is usually quite good. When weakness is seen, it is usually on the eagle's talons and central tail feather. As many of these are in the marketplace, with careful hunting a sharp coin can be found (as illustrated above).

MARKET VALUES – CIRCULATION STRIKES

G-4	VG-8	F-12	VF-20	EF-40	AU-50
$140	$210	$500	$650	$850	$1,350
AU-55	**MS-60**	**MS-62**	**MS-63**	**MS-64**	**MS-65**
$850	$1,800	$2,450	$4,500	$7,750	$21,500

CERTIFIED POPULATIONS – CIRCULATION STRIKES

Fair	AG	G	VG	F	VF	EF	AU	MS-60
8	32	57	26	6	13	7	21	0

MS-61	MS-62	MS-63	MS-64	MS-65	MS-66	MS-67	MS-68	MS-69	MS-70
5	9	16	8	4	0	0	0	0	0

1894 Half Dollar

Circulation-strike mintage: 1,148,000
Proof mintage: 972

Availability in Mint State: Scarce, but one of the more available issues of the 1890s. Lower-level Mint State coins are easy to find. ***Estimated number MS-65 or higher:*** 90 to 110.

Availability in circulated grades: 3,000 to 4,000. Most are AG-3 or G-4. As is the case for many early Barber halves, this issue is challenging to find in grades VG and higher.

Characteristics of striking: The details are usually well defined.

Availability in Proof format: ***Proof-60 to 64:*** 600 to 700. ***Proof-65 or better:*** 75 to 90.

MARKET VALUES – CIRCULATION STRIKES

G-4	VG-8	F-12	VF-20	EF-40	AU-50
$30	$50	$110	$200	$300	$375
AU-55	**MS-60**	**MS-62**	**MS-63**	**MS-64**	**MS-65**
$425	$550	$750	$1,100	$1,600	$3,000

MARKET VALUES – PROOF STRIKES

PF-60	PF-63	PF-64	PF-65
$800	$1,200	$1,800	$3,250

CERTIFIED POPULATIONS – CIRCULATION STRIKES

Fair	AG	G	VG	F	VF	EF	AU	MS-60
2	0	10	7	9	14	9	31	3

MS-61	MS-62	MS-63	MS-64	MS-65	MS-66	MS-67	MS-68	MS-69	MS-70
8	22	27	38	16	9	0	0	0	0

CERTIFIED POPULATIONS – PROOF STRIKES

PF-50	PF-60	PF-61	PF-62	PF-63	PF-64
4	1	9	30	48	83

PF-65	PF-66	PF-67	PF-68	PF-69	PF-70
58	43	34	6	0	0

1894-O Half Dollar

Circulation-strike mintage: 2,138,000

Availability in Mint State: Lower-level Mint State coins are elusive and take some searching to find, especially if well struck (see characteristics of striking below). ***Estimated number MS-65 or higher:*** 25 to 33. Very rare.

Availability in circulated grades: 4,000 to 5,000. Most are AG-3 or G-4. This is one of the more challenging issues to find in Fine or higher grades.

Characteristics of striking: The 1894-O is usually seen with light striking. Check the inner wing and talons and the arrow feathers at the right of the reverse. The central tail feather is sometimes strong when the earlier-mentioned features are weak. Search for an above-average example, but do not expect full details everywhere. The best seen still has some weakness on the talons.

MARKET VALUES – CIRCULATION STRIKES

G-4	VG-8	F-12	VF-20	EF-40	AU-50
$25	$35	$90	$170	$300	$375
AU-55	**MS-60**	**MS-62**	**MS-63**	**MS-64**	**MS-65**
$425	$525	$750	$1,000	$1,750	$5,400

CERTIFIED POPULATIONS – CIRCULATION STRIKES

Fair	AG	G	VG	F	VF	EF	AU	MS-60
0	2	7	7	8	17	7	25	2

MS-61	MS-62	MS-63	MS-64	MS-65	MS-66	MS-67	MS-68	MS-69	MS-70
7	16	26	51	8	1	0	1	0	0

1894-S Half Dollar

Circulation-strike mintage: 4,048,690

Availability in Mint State: Another elusive issue from the 1890s. ***Estimated number MS-65 or higher:*** 40 to 50.

Availability in circulated grades: 8,000 to 10,000. Most are AG-3 or G-4. Due to the large mintage this is one of the most available Barber half dollars of the 1890s.

Characteristics of striking: Variable, but usually sharp.

MARKET VALUES – CIRCULATION STRIKES

G-4	VG-8	F-12	VF-20	EF-40	AU-50
$22	$25	$70	$140	$215	$365
AU-55	**MS-60**	**MS-62**	**MS-63**	**MS-64**	**MS-65**
$475	$600	$1,000	$1,500	$2,500	$8,500

CERTIFIED POPULATIONS – CIRCULATION STRIKES

Fair	AG	G	VG	F	VF	EF	AU	MS-60
1	1	11	13	10	15	15	39	2

MS-61	MS-62	MS-63	MS-64	MS-65	MS-66	MS-67	MS-68	MS-69	MS-70
16	25	33	29	7	0	1	0	0	0

1895 Half Dollar

Circulation-strike mintage: 1,843,338
Proof mintage: 880

Availability in Mint State: As is true of many if not most Philadelphia Mint Barber half dollars, dates that are rarities at the gem level exist by the hundreds in ranges such as MS–60 to 62. ***Estimated number MS-65 or higher:*** 75 to 95.

Availability in circulated grades: 3,500 to 5,000. Mostly AG-3 or G-4. This is among the scarcer issues to find in circulated grades. In F-12 and above they are especially elusive.

Characteristics of striking: Usually well struck.

Availability in Proof format: ***Proof-60 to 64:*** 550 to 650. ***Proof-65 or better:*** 75 to 90.

MARKET VALUES – CIRCULATION STRIKES

G-4	VG-8	F-12	VF-20	EF-40	AU-50
$18	$25	$70	$140	$210	$400

AU-55	MS-60	MS-62	MS-63	MS-64	MS-65
$475	$575	$800	$1,000	$1,600	$3,200

MARKET VALUES – PROOF STRIKES

PF-60	PF-63	PF-64	PF-65
$800	$1,200	$1,800	$3,250

CERTIFIED POPULATIONS – CIRCULATION STRIKES

Fair	AG	G	VG	F	VF	EF	AU	MS-60
0	0	12	7	2	12	8	38	0

MS-61	MS-62	MS-63	MS-64	MS-65	MS-66	MS-67	MS-68	MS-69	MS-70
14	30	28	25	10	4	0	0	0	0

CERTIFIED POPULATIONS – PROOF STRIKES

PF-50	PF-60	PF-61	PF-62	PF-63	PF-64
1	4	11	31	58	69
PF-65	**PF-66**	**PF-67**	**PF-68**	**PF-69**	**PF-70**
64	48	39	23	1	0

1895-O HALF DOLLAR

Circulation-strike mintage: 1,766,000

AVAILABILITY IN MINT STATE: As is true of many Barber half dollars, carefully purchased MS–63 and 64 coins are a practical alternative to MS-65 examples. ***Estimated number MS-65 or higher:*** 25 to 30. Rare at this level and seldom seen in auctions or otherwise.

AVAILABILITY IN CIRCULATED GRADES: 4,000 to 5,000. Most are AG-3 or G-4. Coins in higher grades are very hard to find. This is one of the more challenging issues to find in circulated grades.

CHARACTERISTICS OF STRIKING: The 1895-O is usually found with a fairly nice strike, an exception to the New Orleans Mint issues of the era. Seek one that has nearly full details, with only the eagle's talons weak.

MARKET VALUES – CIRCULATION STRIKES

G-4	VG-8	F-12	VF-20	EF-40	AU-50
$40	$60	$130	$180	$260	$385
AU-55	**MS-60**	**MS-62**	**MS-63**	**MS-64**	**MS-65**
$500	$625	$1,000	$1,300	$2,500	$6,000

CERTIFIED POPULATIONS – CIRCULATION STRIKES

Fair	AG	G	VG	F	VF	EF	AU	MS-60
0	5	13	4	8	10	7	25	2

MS-61	MS-62	MS-63	MS-64	MS-65	MS-66	MS-67	MS-68	MS-69	MS-70
8	12	9	18	11	0	1	0	0	0

1895-S Half Dollar

Circulation-strike mintage: 1,108,086

Availability in Mint State: Most of this issue must have been placed into circulation in quantity at or near the time of its mintage, for relatively few high-grade coins survived for later generations of numismatists. In fact, even in MS-60 the 1895-S is hard to find. ***Estimated number MS-65 or higher:*** 35 to 40. This is another key issue—a rarity at the gem level despite a mintage of over a million pieces.

Availability in circulated grades: 3,000 to 4,000. Most are AG-3 or G-4. This is one of the more challenging issues to find in circulated grades, especially in F-12 or higher.

Characteristics of striking: The details on a typical 1895-S half dollar are usually quite good, and on some even the eagle's talons are nearly full. Finding a nice coin will not be a challenge.

MARKET VALUES – CIRCULATION STRIKES

G-4	VG-8	F-12	VF-20	EF-40	AU-50
$30	$55	$140	$250	$300	$385
AU-55	**MS-60**	**MS-62**	**MS-63**	**MS-64**	**MS-65**
$500	$625	$1,000	$1,400	$2,750	$6,500

CERTIFIED POPULATIONS – CIRCULATION STRIKES

Fair	AG	G	VG	F	VF	EF	AU	MS-60
1	6	6	4	7	7	5	22	0

MS-61	MS-62	MS-63	MS-64	MS-65	MS-66	MS-67	MS-68	MS-69	MS-70
13	25	23	44	11	5	1	0	0	0

1896 Half Dollar

Circulation-strike mintage: 950,000
Proof mintage: 762

Availability in Mint State: Lower-level Mint State 1896 half dollars are relatively easy to find. ***Estimated number MS-65 or higher:*** 30 to 40.

Availability in circulated grades: 3,000 to 4,000. Most are AG-3 or G-4. This is one of the more challenging issues to find in circulated grades, especially F-12 or higher.

Characteristics of striking: Usually well struck.

Availability in Proof format: ***Proof-60 to 64:*** 400 to 500. ***Proof-65 or better:*** 55 to 65.

MARKET VALUES – CIRCULATION STRIKES

G-4	VG-8	F-12	VF-20	EF-40	AU-50
$20	$25	$90	$160	$240	$365
AU-55	**MS-60**	**MS-62**	**MS-63**	**MS-64**	**MS-65**
$450	$575	$750	$1,000	$2,200	$5,000

MARKET VALUES – PROOF STRIKES

PF-60	PF-63	PF-64	PF-65
$800	$1,200	$1,800	$3,250

CERTIFIED POPULATIONS – CIRCULATION STRIKES

Fair	AG	G	VG	F	VF	EF	AU	MS-60
0	1	4	3	7	10	4	20	3

MS-61	MS-62	MS-63	MS-64	MS-65	MS-66	MS-67	MS-68	MS-69	MS-70
5	16	18	15	8	3	2	0	0	0

CERTIFIED POPULATIONS – PROOF STRIKES

PF-50	PF-60	PF-61	PF-62	PF-63	PF-64
1	4	18	14	40	72
PF-65	**PF-66**	**PF-67**	**PF-68**	**PF-69**	**PF-70**
39	41	30	9	0	0

1896-O Half Dollar

Circulation-strike mintage: 924,000

Availability in Mint State: In Mint State the 1896-O is second only to the 1904-S in rarity. High-grade coins are a double whammy—rare and not sharply struck. When contemplating a coin such as this, reality is that a decade spent trying to build a full set of half dollars in MS-65 will come up short with some pieces lacking. This is sometimes difficult to understand, as other denominations of 1892 to 1916, *including gold*, are easier to complete! Regarding the 1896-O, there are a few dozen MS–63 and 64 coins, and these offer an alternative to the infrequently available MS-65 examples. ***Estimated number MS-65 or higher:*** 12 to 15. In the gem category the 1896-O half dollar is one of the rarest coins in the entire Barber silver series.

Availability in circulated grades: 2,000 to 2,500. This is one of the most challenging issues to find in circulated grades. David Lawrence considered this to be among the top-eight rarest half dollars in EF and AU, these being almost never seen.

Characteristics of striking: The 1896-O is usually (or perhaps always) seen with some lightness, typically most notable on the right side of the reverse, where the eagle's wing joins the shield and on the talons and lower arrows.

MARKET VALUES – CIRCULATION STRIKES

G-4	VG-8	F-12	VF-20	EF-40	AU-50
$50	$70	$210	$340	$550	$825
AU-55	**MS-60**	**MS-62**	**MS-63**	**MS-64**	**MS-65**
$975	$1,650	$2,900	$6,500	$13,000	$20,000

CERTIFIED POPULATIONS – CIRCULATION STRIKES

Fair	AG	G	VG	F	VF	EF	AU	MS-60
2	6	17	15	12	15	3	13	0

MS-61	MS-62	MS-63	MS-64	MS-65	MS-66	MS-67	MS-68	MS-69	MS-70
0	0	4	7	5	1	0	0	0	0

1896-S Half Dollar

Circulation-strike mintage: 1,140,948

Availability in Mint State: In all Mint State categories the 1896-S is eagerly sought. ***Estimated number MS-65 or higher:*** 40 to 50. This is another famous old-time rarity. Although a number of Barber half dollars are rarer at the gem level, a nice 1896-S always attracts attention when offered.

Availability in circulated grades: 2,500 to 3,000. Most are AG-3 or G-4. This is one of the most challenging issues to find in circulated grades, but it is slightly easier to find than 1896-O. Coins F-12 and above are in very high demand.

Characteristics of striking: Nearly all are well struck and have excellent details.

Notes: In the mid-1900s the 1896-S was considered one of the top several rarities in Mint State in the Barber half dollar series. Today it no longer has that ranking, but it certainly is a key issue.

MARKET VALUES – CIRCULATION STRIKES

G-4	VG-8	F-12	VF-20	EF-40	AU-50
$115	$165	$240	$385	$575	$825
AU-55	**MS-60**	**MS-62**	**MS-63**	**MS-64**	**MS-65**
$975	$1,550	$2,500	$3,700	$5,500	$9,500

CERTIFIED POPULATIONS – CIRCULATION STRIKES

Fair	AG	G	VG	F	VF	EF	AU	MS-60
8	21	33	15	13	9	5	12	0

MS-61	MS-62	MS-63	MS-64	MS-65	MS-66	MS-67	MS-68	MS-69	MS-70
1	6	12	15	5	6	0	0	0	0

1897 Half Dollar

Circulation-strike mintage: 2,480,000
Proof mintage: 731

Availability in Mint State: Lower-level Mint State coins are numerous. ***Estimated number MS-65 or higher:*** 90 to 110. Not hard to find.

Availability in circulated grades: 6,000 to 8,000. Most are AG-3 or G-4. One of the more available issues.

Characteristics of striking: The typical circulation strike has excellent details. Some have lightness at the inner feathers on the right reverse but are sharp otherwise.

Availability in Proof format: ***Proof-60 to 64:*** 375 to 475. ***Proof-65 or better:*** 50 to 60.

MARKET VALUES – CIRCULATION STRIKES

G-4	VG-8	F-12	VF-20	EF-40	AU-50
$20	$22	$45	$95	$200	$360
AU-55	**MS-60**	**MS-62**	**MS-63**	**MS-64**	**MS-65**
$400	$550	$700	$925	$1,200	$3,250

MARKET VALUES – PROOF STRIKES

PF-60	PF-63	PF-64	PF-65
$600	$1,200	$1,800	$3,250

CERTIFIED POPULATIONS – CIRCULATION STRIKES

Fair	AG	G	VG	F	VF	EF	AU	MS-60
0	2	3	3	7	14	14	49	0

MS-61	MS-62	MS-63	MS-64	MS-65	MS-66	MS-67	MS-68	MS-69	MS-70
12	18	29	43	22	6	2	0	0	0

CERTIFIED POPULATIONS – PROOF STRIKES

PF-50	PF-60	PF-61	PF-62	PF-63	PF-64
0	1	9	19	43	80
PF-65	**PF-66**	**PF-67**	**PF-68**	**PF-69**	**PF-70**
41	53	43	28	1	0

1897-O HALF DOLLAR

Circulation-strike mintage: 632,000

AVAILABILITY IN MINT STATE: Lower-level Mint State coins are scarce and enjoy a strong demand. ***Estimated number MS-65 or higher:*** 40 to 50. This has been a well-known rarity for many years. In the mid-1950s it was considered to be one of a handful at the very top. Since then data provided by population reports has given a better idea of relative availability, and some high-mintage Barber halves have emerged as being a bit rarer than some low-mintage issues, as is the case here. Still, a gem 1897-O is an object of great desire.

AVAILABILITY IN CIRCULATED GRADES: 2,000 to 2,500. Most are AG-3 or G-4. This is one of the more challenging issues to find in circulated grades. David Lawrence stated that the 1897-O and 1904-S coins were the most difficult to locate in EF and AU grades.

CHARACTERISTICS OF STRIKING: Most have light striking on the right side of the reverse, but not as soft as on other New Orleans half dollars of the era. With some searching, an above average coin can be found.

MARKET VALUES – CIRCULATION STRIKES

G-4	VG-8	F-12	VF-20	EF-40	AU-50
$160	$230	$500	$750	$1,050	$1,300
AU-55	**MS-60**	**MS-62**	**MS-63**	**MS-64**	**MS-65**
$1,450	$2,000	$3,100	$4,000	$5,750	$8,000

CERTIFIED POPULATIONS – CIRCULATION STRIKES

Fair	AG	G	VG	F	VF	EF	AU	MS-60
6	55	61	42	13	11	10	15	0

MS-61	MS-62	MS-63	MS-64	MS-65	MS-66	MS-67	MS-68	MS-69	MS-70
1	3	7	8	7	3	0	1	0	0

1897-S Half Dollar

Circulation-strike mintage: 933,900

Availability in Mint State: The 1897-S half dollar at this level has been recognized as a key issue for a long time. No surprise here. ***Estimated number MS-65 or higher:*** 35 to 45.

Availability in circulated grades: 2,000 to 2,500. Most are AG-3 or G-4. Examples are seldom seen F-12 or higher. Somewhat scarce and everlastingly popular, a key to the series, on par with the 1897-O. David Lawrence considered this among the top-eight rarest half dollars in EF and AU.

Characteristics of striking: High-grade examples from early strikes often show parallel raised die polish lines. Most Mint State coins have some light striking in the usual places, but some have nearly full sharpness.

MARKET VALUES – CIRCULATION STRIKES

G-4	VG-8	F-12	VF-20	EF-40	AU-50
$150	$220	$350	$550	$800	$1,000
AU-55	**MS-60**	**MS-62**	**MS-63**	**MS-64**	**MS-65**
$1,250	$1,550	$2,100	$3,650	$4,350	$6,600

CERTIFIED POPULATIONS – CIRCULATION STRIKES

Fair	AG	G	VG	F	VF	EF	AU	MS-60
6	39	30	36	21	23	6	9	0

MS-61	MS-62	MS-63	MS-64	MS-65	MS-66	MS-67	MS-68	MS-69	MS-70
0	5	3	37	7	3	2	1	0	0

1898 HALF DOLLAR

Circulation-strike mintage: 2,956,000
Proof mintage: 735

AVAILABILITY IN MINT STATE: MS–63 and 64 coins are readily located. ***Estimated number MS-65 or higher:*** 80 to 95. Not easy to find.

AVAILABILITY IN CIRCULATED GRADES: 7,000 to 9,000. Most are AG-3 or G-4. Easy to find in any circulated grade desired.

CHARACTERISTICS OF STRIKING: Circulation strikes are usually quite well detailed.

AVAILABILITY IN PROOF FORMAT: ***Proof-60 to 64:*** 400 to 550. ***Proof-65 or better:*** 50 to 60.

MARKET VALUES – CIRCULATION STRIKES

G-4	VG-8	F-12	VF-20	EF-40	AU-50
$18	$20	$45	$95	$200	$375
AU-55	**MS-60**	**MS-62**	**MS-63**	**MS-64**	**MS-65**
$475	$575	$650	$1,000	$1,400	$3,200

MARKET VALUES – PROOF STRIKES

PF-60	PF-63	PF-64	PF-65
$600	$1,200	$1,800	$3,250

CERTIFIED POPULATIONS – CIRCULATION STRIKES

Fair	AG	G	VG	F	VF	EF	AU	MS-60
0	0	4	3	7	23	13	47	0

MS-61	MS-62	MS-63	MS-64	MS-65	MS-66	MS-67	MS-68	MS-69	MS-70
12	17	36	33	15	2	0	0	0	0

CERTIFIED POPULATIONS – PROOF STRIKES

PF-50	PF-60	PF-61	PF-62	PF-63	PF-64
1	1	5	19	28	66
PF-65	**PF-66**	**PF-67**	**PF-68**	**PF-69**	**PF-70**
43	44	39	21	0	0

1898-O Half Dollar

Circulation-strike mintage: 874,000

Availability in Mint State: Scarce in MS–63 and 64 grades. ***Estimated number MS-65 or higher:*** 20 to 25.

Availability in circulated grades: 2,000 to 2,500 exist in grades AG-3 to VF-35. This is one of the most challenging issues to find in circulated grades, especially in higher levels. David Lawrence considered this to be among the top-eight rarest half dollars in EF and AU.

Characteristics of striking: The 1898-O is usually seen with light striking on the usual areas of the right side of the reverse. Some high-grade examples have proof-like surfaces, called "branch-mint Proofs" by some.

Notes: In the mid-1950s the 1898-O in Mint State was considered to be among the top rarities in the series. Today it is still a key issue, but not as much notice is given to it.

MARKET VALUES – CIRCULATION STRIKES

G-4	VG-8	F-12	VF-20	EF-40	AU-50
$38	$90	$240	$400	$540	$650
AU-55	**MS-60**	**MS-62**	**MS-63**	**MS-64**	**MS-65**
$850	$1,200	$2,300	$3,200	$4,200	$8,000

CERTIFIED POPULATIONS – CIRCULATION STRIKES

Fair	AG	G	VG	F	VF	EF	AU	MS-60	
1	4	18	10	10	11	9	15	0	
MS-61	**MS-62**	**MS-63**	**MS-64**	**MS-65**	**MS-66**	**MS-67**	**MS-68**	**MS-69**	**MS-70**
5	5	3	11	9	2	2	0	0	0

1898-S HALF DOLLAR

Circulation-strike mintage: 2,358,550

AVAILABILITY IN MINT STATE: Slightly scarce at lower–Mint State levels. ***Estimated number MS-65 or higher:*** 35 to 45. Rare as a gem, this being true of nearly all 19th-century Barber half dollars with mintmarks.

AVAILABILITY 3,000 to 3,500. Most are AG-3 or G-4. This is among the scarcer issues in circulated grades.

CHARACTERISTICS OF STRIKING: Most 1898-S half dollars have light striking on the wing at the upper right. Otherwise details are quite good.

NOTES: Some of this mintage was shipped to the Philippine Islands after the Spanish-American War ended in the summer of the year.

MARKET VALUES – CIRCULATION STRIKES

G-4	VG-8	F-12	VF-20	EF-40	AU-50
$30	$48	$90	$185	$340	$440
AU-55	**MS-60**	**MS-62**	**MS-63**	**MS-64**	**MS-65**
$625	$925	$2,200	$3,500	$6,000	$8,850

CERTIFIED POPULATIONS – CIRCULATION STRIKES

Fair	AG	G	VG	F	VF	EF	AU	MS-60
1	4	6	10	4	13	15	34	0

MS-61	MS-62	MS-63	MS-64	MS-65	MS-66	MS-67	MS-68	MS-69	MS-70
7	7	3	6	7	5	0	0	0	0

1899 Half Dollar

Circulation-strike mintage: 5,538,000
Proof mintage: 846

Availability in Mint State: Readily available. ***Estimated number MS-65 or higher:*** 90 to 110.

Availability in circulated grades: 20,000 to 25,000. Most are AG-3 or G-4. The most plentiful issue of the 1890s.

Characteristics of striking: Circulation strikes are usually well detailed.

Availability in Proof format: ***Proof-60 to 64:*** 300 to 400. ***Proof-65 or better:*** 35 to 45. Much rarer than the mintage would seem to indicate.

Notes: This is the largest circulation-strike mintage in the Barber half dollar series, edging out 1902 by a small margin. The same situation occurred for Barber quarters this year.

MARKET VALUES – CIRCULATION STRIKES

G-4	VG-8	F-12	VF-20	EF-40	AU-50
$18	$20	$45	$95	$200	$375
AU-55	**MS-60**	**MS-62**	**MS-63**	**MS-64**	**MS-65**
$475	$575	$700	$1,000	$1,300	$3,400

MARKET VALUES – PROOF STRIKES

PF-60	PF-63	PF-64	PF-65
$800	$1,200	$1,800	$3,250

CERTIFIED POPULATIONS – CIRCULATION STRIKES

Fair	AG	G	VG	F	VF	EF	AU	MS-60
0	3	8	10	18	31	22	90	2

MS-61	MS-62	MS-63	MS-64	MS-65	MS-66	MS-67	MS-68	MS-69	MS-70
24	37	33	41	18	7	0	0	0	0

CERTIFIED POPULATIONS – PROOF STRIKES

PF-50	PF-60	PF-61	PF-62	PF-63	PF-64
1	4	7	15	33	54
PF-65	**PF-66**	**PF-67**	**PF-68**	**PF-69**	**PF-70**
37	33	25	5	1	0

1899-O HALF DOLLAR

Circulation-strike mintage: 1,724,000

AVAILABILITY IN MINT STATE: MS–63 and 64 coins are not hard to find. ***Estimated number MS-65 or higher:*** 35 to 40. Repeating a familiar scene here is another high-mintage Barber half dollar for which gems are seldom seen.

AVAILABILITY IN CIRCULATED GRADES: 5,000 to 7,000. Most are AG-3 or G-4.

CHARACTERISTICS OF STRIKING: All 1899-O half dollars seen have had the usual light striking on the right side of the reverse. Some are sharper than others, however.

MARKET VALUES – CIRCULATION STRIKES

G-4	VG-8	F-12	VF-20	EF-40	AU-50
$25	$35	$80	$165	$275	$350
AU-55	**MS-60**	**MS-62**	**MS-63**	**MS-64**	**MS-65**
$450	$675	$975	$1,600	$3,150	$7,250

CERTIFIED POPULATIONS – CIRCULATION STRIKES

Fair	AG	G	VG	F	VF	EF	AU	MS-60
1	6	11	9	8	9	9	19	1

MS-61	MS-62	MS-63	MS-64	MS-65	MS-66	MS-67	MS-68	MS-69	MS-70
8	7	15	14	4	8	0	0	0	0

1899-S Half Dollar

Circulation-strike mintage: 1,686,411

Availability in Mint State: MS–60 to 64 coins are readily available, with those at the bottom of the scale being common in relation to the demand for them. ***Estimated number MS-65 or higher:*** 35 to 45. Very difficult to locate despite its high mintage.

Availability in circulated grades: 3,000 to 3,500. Most are AG-3 or G-4. This is one of the more challenging issues to find in circulated grades, especially in Fine or above.

Characteristics of striking: The 1899-S is usually found with excellent details.

Notes: Much of this coinage was shipped to the Philippine Islands for circulation there. In *The Numismatic Scrapbook Magazine*, in May 1938, Chuck Franzen, a Montana collector, reported owning an 1899-S half dollar with "mintmark upside down." Seemingly, this has not been listed in modern times.

MARKET VALUES – CIRCULATION STRIKES

G-4	VG-8	F-12	VF-20	EF-40	AU-50
$25	$40	$90	$175	$300	$400
AU-55	**MS-60**	**MS-62**	**MS-63**	**MS-64**	**MS-65**
$500	$685	$1,375	$2,150	$3,200	$5,900

CERTIFIED POPULATIONS – CIRCULATION STRIKES

Fair	AG	G	VG	F	VF	EF	AU	MS-60	
0	3	1	4	4	13	16	29	1	
MS-61	**MS-62**	**MS-63**	**MS-64**	**MS-65**	**MS-66**	**MS-67**	**MS-68**	**MS-69**	**MS-70**
3	6	10	10	6	8	3	0	0	0

1900 HALF DOLLAR

Circulation-strike mintage: 4,762,000
Proof mintage: 912

AVAILABILITY IN MINT STATE: Lower-level coins are common. ***Estimated number MS-65 or higher:*** 100 to 120. Readily available in the context of the number of buyers seeking gems.

AVAILABILITY IN CIRCULATED GRADES: 25,000 to 30,000. Most are G-4. Common.

CHARACTERISTICS OF STRIKING: The circulation strikes of this year are usually well struck, this being generally true of the Philadelphia Mint output during this time.

AVAILABILITY IN PROOF FORMAT: ***Proof-60 to 64:*** 450 to 600. ***Proof-65 or better:*** 65 to 80.

MARKET VALUES – CIRCULATION STRIKES

G-4	VG-8	F-12	VF-20	EF-40	AU-50
$17	$19	$45	$95	$200	$375
AU-55	**MS-60**	**MS-62**	**MS-63**	**MS-64**	**MS-65**
$475	$575	$700	$1,000	$1,300	$3,300

MARKET VALUES – PROOF STRIKES

PF-60	PF-63	PF-64	PF-65
$800	$1,200	$1,800	$3,250

CERTIFIED POPULATIONS – CIRCULATION STRIKES

Fair	AG	G	VG	F	VF	EF	AU	MS-60
0	0	7	9	7	28	22	74	4

MS-61	MS-62	MS-63	MS-64	MS-65	MS-66	MS-67	MS-68	MS-69	MS-70
24	43	48	57	16	6	1	0	0	0

CERTIFIED POPULATIONS – PROOF STRIKES

PF-50	PF-60	PF-61	PF-62	PF-63	PF-64
0	3	7	23	37	79
PF-65	**PF-66**	**PF-67**	**PF-68**	**PF-69**	**PF-70**
44	40	36	12	0	0

1900-O Half Dollar

Circulation-strike mintage: 2,744,000

Availability in Mint State: The 1900-O half dollar is rare in choice or gem Mint State although in worn grades (especially lower-level worn grades) it is not at all remarkable. ***Estimated number MS-65 or higher:*** 60 to 70.

Availability in circulated grades: 15,000 to 20,000. Most are AG-3 or G-4. Hard to find VF and higher.

Characteristics of striking: All examples seen have light striking on the right side of the reverse, but on most 1900-O half dollars this is more obvious where the wing joins the shield than on the leg and arrows.

MARKET VALUES – CIRCULATION STRIKES

G-4	VG-8	F-12	VF-20	EF-40	AU-50
$18	$25	$60	$170	$280	$435
AU-55	**MS-60**	**MS-62**	**MS-63**	**MS-64**	**MS-65**
$600	$875	$2,100	$3,400	$6,000	$13,000

CERTIFIED POPULATIONS – CIRCULATION STRIKES

Fair	AG	G	VG	F	VF	EF	AU	MS-60
0	0	8	7	7	13	14	15	0

MS-61	MS-62	MS-63	MS-64	MS-65	MS-66	MS-67	MS-68	MS-69	MS-70
0	10	6	10	3	1	1	0	0	0

1900-S HALF DOLLAR

Circulation-strike mintage: 2,560,322

AVAILABILITY IN MINT STATE: Lower-level Mint State coins are readily available. ***Estimated number MS-65 or higher:*** 30 to 35. By all logic this high-mintage issue should be readily available in gem Mint State. The opposite is true, as interest in mint-marked half dollars was minimal at the time. It is not known how many collectors ordered coins directly from the branch mints at the turn of the century, but I would estimate that for the half dollar denomination there were fewer than 10. The Louis E. Eliasberg Collection sales of Barber dimes (1996), quarters (1997), and half dollars (1997) offered coins bought directly from the mints by John M. Clapp. Nearly all were cataloged as gems. These coins had the advantage of never having been cleaned or brightened.

AVAILABILITY IN CIRCULATED GRADES: 12,000 to 15,000. Most are G-4.

CHARACTERISTICS OF STRIKING: The typical 1900-S half dollar is quite well struck, although there are scattered exceptions.

MARKET VALUES – CIRCULATION STRIKES

G-4	VG-8	F-12	VF-20	EF-40	AU-50
$17	$19	$45	$100	$210	$375
AU-55	**MS-60**	**MS-62**	**MS-63**	**MS-64**	**MS-65**
$500	$650	$1,500	$2,400	$4,000	$8,100

CERTIFIED POPULATIONS – CIRCULATION STRIKES

Fair	AG	G	VG	F	VF	EF	AU	MS-60
1	0	6	0	10	14	13	40	0

MS-61	MS-62	MS-63	MS-64	MS-65	MS-66	MS-67	MS-68	MS-69	MS-70
1	4	10	9	5	2	1	0	0	0

1901 Half Dollar

Circulation-strike mintage: 4,268,000
Proof mintage: 813

Availability in Mint State: Common in lower–Mint State grades. ***Estimated number MS-65 or higher:*** 50 to 60.

Availability in circulated grades: 14,000 to 18,000. Most are G-4. Easy to find in any circulated grade desired.

Characteristics of striking: The details are usually very good on circulation strikes.

Availability in Proof format: ***Proof-60 to 64:*** 400 to 500. ***Proof-65 or better:*** 70 to 85.

Proofs of this year of all denominations were made with the portrait features lightly polished in the die instead of frosted or cameo. This continued through 1904.

Notes: Obverse Hub II was introduced this year. Proofs are all from Obverse Hub I, while circulation strikes were made using both hubs. The differences are microscopic, resulting in no significant interest from collectors in acquiring one of each.

MARKET VALUES – CIRCULATION STRIKES

G-4	VG-8	F-12	VF-20	EF-40	AU-50
$17	$18	$45	$95	$200	$350
AU-55	**MS-60**	**MS-62**	**MS-63**	**MS-64**	**MS-65**
$450	$500	$700	$1,000	$1,300	$3,500

MARKET VALUES – PROOF STRIKES

PF-60	PF-63	PF-64	PF-65
$600	$1,200	$1,800	$3,250

CERTIFIED POPULATIONS – CIRCULATION STRIKES

Fair	AG	G	VG	F	VF	EF	AU	MS-60	
0	2	3	8	13	23	19	95	2	
MS-61	**MS-62**	**MS-63**	**MS-64**	**MS-65**	**MS-66**	**MS-67**	**MS-68**	**MS-69**	**MS-70**
15	37	38	36	11	3	0	0	0	0

CERTIFIED POPULATIONS – PROOF STRIKES

PF-50	PF-60	PF-61	PF-62	PF-63	PF-64
3	4	12	18	27	71
PF-65	**PF-66**	**PF-67**	**PF-68**	**PF-69**	**PF-70**
43	56	26	11	1	0

1901-O HALF DOLLAR

Circulation-strike mintage: 1,124,000

AVAILABILITY IN MINT STATE: MS–63 and 64 coins are rare. ***Estimated number MS-65 or higher:*** 12 to 13. This is among the top handful of Barber half dollar rarities at this level.

AVAILABILITY IN CIRCULATED GRADES: 5,000 to 6,000. Most are G-4. This is among the scarcer issues in circulated grades up to VF. EF and AU coins are elusive.

CHARACTERISTICS OF STRIKING: Most have some light striking on the reverse.

NOTES: Both obverse hub types were used for this issue. Obverse Hub II coins are seen more often. The differences are microscopic, resulting in no significant interest from collectors in acquiring one of each.

MARKET VALUES – CIRCULATION STRIKES

G-4	VG-8	F-12	VF-20	EF-40	AU-50
$17	$26	$80	$230	$350	$475
AU-55	**MS-60**	**MS-62**	**MS-63**	**MS-64**	**MS-65**
$625	$1,350	$3,000	$4,850	$9,000	$13,500

CERTIFIED POPULATIONS – CIRCULATION STRIKES

Fair	AG	G	VG	F	VF	EF	AU	MS-60
0	1	3	10	3	8	4	11	0

MS-61	MS-62	MS-63	MS-64	MS-65	MS-66	MS-67	MS-68	MS-69	MS-70
2	8	7	14	6	2	0	0	0	0

1901-S Half Dollar

Circulation-strike mintage: 847,044

Availability in Mint State: The 1901-S is rare in any Mint State level, and an MS–63 or 64 offered at auction will attract bids from far and wide. ***Estimated number MS-65 or higher:*** 22 to 26. This is one of the keys to the series.

Availability in circulated grades: 3,000 to 3,500. Most are G-4. This is one of the more challenging issues to find in circulated grades. David Lawrence considered this among the top-eight rarest half dollars in EF and AU. Such coins are in everlasting demand.

Characteristics of striking: Striking sharpness varies on this issue. Some have nearly full details, and others show lightness on the right side of the reverse. Careful searching for quality is advised.

Notes: Both hub types were used for this issue. Obverse Hub II coins are seen more often. The differences are microscopic, resulting in no significant interest from collectors in acquiring one of each.

This is one of the most famous of the Barber half dollars, probably not because of its absolute rarity, but because it has the same date and mintmark of the justifiably enshrined 1901-S quarter. When the first issue of *A Guide Book of United States Coins* was published in 1946 (with a cover date of 1947) the 1901-S, at $150 in Mint State, was far and away the most expensive coin in the series.

MARKET VALUES – CIRCULATION STRIKES

G-4	VG-8	F-12	VF-20	EF-40	AU-50
$32	$55	$165	$350	$700	$1,250
AU-55	**MS-60**	**MS-62**	**MS-63**	**MS-64**	**MS-65**
$1,700	$2,250	$5,000	$10,000	$12,500	$15,500

CERTIFIED POPULATIONS – CIRCULATION STRIKES

Fair	AG	G	VG	F	VF	EF	AU	MS-60
1	7	20	13	10	11	3	11	0

MS-61	MS-62	MS-63	MS-64	MS-65	MS-66	MS-67	MS-68	MS-69	MS-70
1	3	5	4	3	0	1	0	0	0

1902 HALF DOLLAR

Circulation-strike mintage: 4,922,000
Proof mintage: 777

AVAILABILITY IN MINT STATE: Mint State coins in lower grades are easy to find. ***Estimated number MS-65 or higher:*** 60 to 70. Slightly scarce.

AVAILABILITY IN CIRCULATED GRADES: 25,000 to 30,000. Most are G-4. Plentiful in all circulated grades.

CHARACTERISTICS OF STRIKING: Circulation strikes usually show some relatively minor weakness on the right side of the reverse.

AVAILABILITY IN PROOF FORMAT: ***Proof-60 to 64:*** 400 to 500. ***Proof-65 or better:*** 75 to 90.

MARKET VALUES – CIRCULATION STRIKES

G-4	VG-8	F-12	VF-20	EF-40	AU-50
$17	$18	$45	$95	$200	$350
AU-55	**MS-60**	**MS-62**	**MS-63**	**MS-64**	**MS-65**
$400	$500	$700	$950	$1,225	$3,400

MARKET VALUES – PROOF STRIKES

PF-60	PF-63	PF-64	PF-65
$600	$1,200	$1,900	$3,400

CERTIFIED POPULATIONS – CIRCULATION STRIKES

Fair	AG	G	VG	F	VF	EF	AU	MS-60
0	0	7	5	12	26	22	74	0

MS-61	MS-62	MS-63	MS-64	MS-65	MS-66	MS-67	MS-68	MS-69	MS-70
10	30	29	36	8	6	1	0	0	0

1903-S Half Dollar

Circulation-strike mintage: 1,920,772

Availability in Mint State: One of the scarcer issues among 20th-century dates and mintmarks. ***Estimated number MS-65 or higher:*** 30 to 35. Very difficult to locate in a combination of gem grade and good eye appeal, despite the fairly large mintage.

Availability in circulated grades: 7,000 to 9,000. Most are G-4. This is among the scarcer issues to find in circulated grades.

Characteristics of striking: Sharpness can vary and is usually quite strong. There are occasional exceptions such as the illustrated coin with weakness, highly usual for this extent to be seen on a San Francisco coin.

MARKET VALUES – CIRCULATION STRIKES

G-4	VG-8	F-12	VF-20	EF-40	AU-50
$17	$19	$60	$130	$230	$400
AU-55	**MS-60**	**MS-62**	**MS-63**	**MS-64**	**MS-65**
$500	$675	$1,300	$1,700	$3,000	$4,900

CERTIFIED POPULATIONS – CIRCULATION STRIKES

Fair	AG	G	VG	F	VF	EF	AU	MS-60
0	0	6	9	8	11	6	12	0

MS-61	MS-62	MS-63	MS-64	MS-65	MS-66	MS-67	MS-68	MS-69	MS-70
6	10	12	29	6	1	0	0	0	0

1904 HALF DOLLAR

Circulation-strike mintage: 2,992,000
Proof mintage: 670

AVAILABILITY IN MINT STATE: Mint State circulation strikes are very elusive despite the high mintage. Collectors seeking the date at the time of issue bought Proofs. MS–63 and 64 coins are not hard to find. ***Estimated number MS-65 or higher:*** 45 to 55.

AVAILABILITY IN CIRCULATED GRADES: 20,000 to 25,000. Most are G-4.

CHARACTERISTICS OF STRIKING: Usually well struck.

AVAILABILITY IN PROOF FORMAT: ***Proof-60 to 64:*** 350 to 450. ***Proof-65 or better:*** 50 to 60.

MARKET VALUES – CIRCULATION STRIKES

G-4	VG-8	F-12	VF-20	EF-40	AU-50
$17	$18	$35	$85	$200	$375
AU-55	**MS-60**	**MS-62**	**MS-63**	**MS-64**	**MS-65**
$450	$550	$900	$1,100	$1,400	$4,100

MARKET VALUES – PROOF STRIKES

PF-60	PF-63	PF-64	PF-65
$600	$1,200	$1,800	$3,250

CERTIFIED POPULATIONS – CIRCULATION STRIKES

Fair	AG	G	VG	F	VF	EF	AU	MS-60
0	2	2	5	6	21	11	47	0

MS-61	MS-62	MS-63	MS-64	MS-65	MS-66	MS-67	MS-68	MS-69	MS-70
13	19	15	34	7	3	0	0	0	0

CERTIFIED POPULATIONS – PROOF STRIKES

PF-50	PF-60	PF-61	PF-62	PF-63	PF-64
0	4	2	28	40	82
PF-65	**PF-66**	**PF-67**	**PF-68**	**PF-69**	**PF-70**
41	34	23	4	0	0

1904-O Half Dollar

Circulation-strike mintage: 1,117,600

Availability in Mint State: Again, MS–63 and 64 grades are a practical alternative to MS-65 coins. ***Estimated number MS-65 or higher:*** 30 to 35. Gems are seldom seen or offered.

Availability in circulated grades: 4,000 to 5,000. Most are G-4. This is one of the more challenging issues to find in circulated grades, especially VF or above. David Lawrence considered this to be among the top-eight rarest half dollars in EF and AU.

Characteristics of striking: While most 1904-O half dollars have areas of light striking on the reverse, there are exceptions worth tracking down.

MARKET VALUES – CIRCULATION STRIKES

G-4	VG-8	F-12	VF-20	EF-40	AU-50
$22	$35	$95	$235	$400	$600
AU-55	**MS-60**	**MS-62**	**MS-63**	**MS-64**	**MS-65**
$850	$1,250	$2,150	$3,750	$6,350	$10,750

CERTIFIED POPULATIONS – CIRCULATION STRIKES

Fair	AG	G	VG	F	VF	EF	AU	MS-60
1	1	5	5	8	10	8	22	0

MS-61	MS-62	MS-63	MS-64	MS-65	MS-66	MS-67	MS-68	MS-69	MS-70
4	5	1	10	4	0	0	0	0	0

1904-S Half Dollar

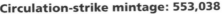

Circulation-strike mintage: 553,038

AVAILABILITY IN MINT STATE: Rare in any Mint State level, far more than population reports would indicate. Many certified coins have been resubmitted multiple times, and numerous original AU coins have been dipped and are now found in Mint State holders, often with light wear still apparent. Like the 1898-S quarter, a collector needs to buy the coin, and not the holder.[3] ***Estimated number MS-65 or higher:*** 10 to 12. This is the key to the Barber half dollar series. In the gem category, this joins the very slightly more available 1896-O half dollar as the rarest two coins in the entire Barber silver series except the 1894-S dime.

AVAILABILITY IN CIRCULATED GRADES: 1,500 to 2,000. Most are G-4. A challenge to find at any level, but especially VF or higher. David Lawrence stated that 1904-S was the most difficult to locate in EF and AU grades. Many coins are "generously" graded.

CHARACTERISTICS OF STRIKING: Striking varies, but all seen have some lightness of detail on the right reverse. Surfaces are often lackluster (literally). Patience is needed to find an above-average coin as opportunities to do so are usually spaced far apart.

MARKET VALUES – CIRCULATION STRIKES

G-4	VG-8	F-12	VF-20	EF-40	AU-50
$48	$115	$340	$775	$1,500	$2,300
AU-55	**MS-60**	**MS-62**	**MS-63**	**MS-64**	**MS-65**
$4,800	$9,500	$16,000	$19,500	$23,500	$39,000

CERTIFIED POPULATIONS – CIRCULATION STRIKES

Fair	AG	G	VG	F	VF	EF	AU	MS-60
0	7	45	31	21	15	9	18	0

MS-61	MS-62	MS-63	MS-64	MS-65	MS-66	MS-67	MS-68	MS-69	MS-70
4	3	4	5	2	1	1	0	0	0

1905 Half Dollar

Circulation-strike mintage: 622,000
Proof mintage: 727

Availability in Mint State: MS-63 and 64 coins are easy to find. ***Estimated number MS-65 or higher:*** 70 to 85. Somewhat scarce.

Availability in circulated grades: 2,500 to 4,000. Most are G-4. This is one of the most challenging issues to find in circulated grades.

Characteristics of striking: Luster can vary in its eye appeal. The low mintage of the year has made this a semi-key issue among Philadelphia Mint coins.

Availability in Proof format: ***Proof-60 to 64:*** 350 to 450. ***Proof-65 or better:*** 80 to 95.

MARKET VALUES – CIRCULATION STRIKES

G-4	VG-8	F-12	VF-20	EF-40	AU-50
$25	$29	$85	$185	$265	$365
AU-55	**MS-60**	**MS-62**	**MS-63**	**MS-64**	**MS-65**
$450	$550	$1,050	$1,500	$3,200	$5,350

MARKET VALUES – PROOF STRIKES

PF-60	PF-63	PF-64	PF-65
$800	$1,200	$1,800	$3,250

CERTIFIED POPULATIONS – CIRCULATION STRIKES

Fair	AG	G	VG	F	VF	EF	AU	MS-60	
0	2	6	8	6	7	5	25	1	
MS-61	**MS-62**	**MS-63**	**MS-64**	**MS-65**	**MS-66**	**MS-67**	**MS-68**	**MS-69**	**MS-70**
5	17	8	16	8	5	0	0	0	0

CERTIFIED POPULATIONS – PROOF STRIKES

PF-50	PF-60	PF-61	PF-62	PF-63	PF-64
4	3	9	21	32	53
PF-65	**PF-66**	**PF-67**	**PF-68**	**PF-69**	**PF-70**
36	29	21	4	0	0

1905-O Half Dollar

Circulation-strike mintage: 505,000

Availability in Mint State: In grades of MS–63 and 64 the 1905-O, while scarce, is offered for sale regularly. ***Estimated number MS-65 or higher:*** 50 to 60. Most of these survived as a matter of chance, not intent. At the time, probably no more than a dozen or so numismatists were assembling collections of Uncirculated coins.

Availability in circulated grades: 2,000 to 2,500. Most are G-4. This is among the scarcer issues to find in circulated grades.

Characteristics of striking: Most 1905-O half dollars have light striking on the reverse. Some are better than others, and with some searching a fairly sharp coin can be found. Check the obverse star centers too, especially at the lower right. High-grade coins usually have sub-par luster. Some have slightly raised areas on Liberty's neck, called "mumps" by David Lawrence.

MARKET VALUES – CIRCULATION STRIKES

G-4	VG-8	F-12	VF-20	EF-40	AU-50
$30	$45	$125	$225	$325	$450
AU-55	**MS-60**	**MS-62**	**MS-63**	**MS-64**	**MS-65**
$550	$750	$1,100	$1,650	$2,050	$3,900

CERTIFIED POPULATIONS – CIRCULATION STRIKES

Fair	AG	G	VG	F	VF	EF	AU	MS-60
0	0	9	5	6	5	3	10	2

MS-61	MS-62	MS-63	MS-64	MS-65	MS-66	MS-67	MS-68	MS-69	MS-70
2	20	21	26	7	3	2	1	0	0

1905-S Half Dollar

Circulation-strike mintage: 2,494,000

Availability in Mint State: Slightly scarce. ***Estimated number MS-65 or higher:*** 25 to 30. The rarity in gem Mint State of quite a few Barber half dollars is surprising in view of large mintages. Few numismatists were interested in them at the time, a comment that holds true for mintmarked issues in the entire Barber series.

Availability in circulated grades: 15,000 to 18,000. Most are G-4.

Characteristics of striking: Most 1905-S half dollars are quite well struck. Even among the better ones, the highest part of the eagle's talons on the right is weak, as nearly always in the series. Choice–Mint State coins are elusive.

MARKET VALUES – CIRCULATION STRIKES

G-4	VG-8	F-12	VF-20	EF-40	AU-50
$16	$19	$53	$140	$240	$400
AU-55	**MS-60**	**MS-62**	**MS-63**	**MS-64**	**MS-65**
$500	$650	$1,300	$1,950	$3,700	$8,500

CERTIFIED POPULATIONS – CIRCULATION STRIKES

Fair	AG	G	VG	F	VF	EF	AU	MS-60
0	2	10	8	11	13	9	22	0

MS-61	MS-62	MS-63	MS-64	MS-65	MS-66	MS-67	MS-68	MS-69	MS-70
6	4	15	15	6	0	1	0	0	0

1906 HALF DOLLAR

Circulation-strike mintage: 2,638,000
Proof mintage: 675

AVAILABILITY IN MINT STATE: The typical Mint State coin is well struck and lustrous. There are enough of these around that the date is inexpensive in the context of the series. ***Estimated number MS-65 or higher:*** 200 to 240.

AVAILABILITY IN CIRCULATED GRADES: 12,000 to 15,000. Most are G-4. Easy to find in any grade desired.

CHARACTERISTICS OF STRIKING: Usually very good.

AVAILABILITY IN PROOF FORMAT: ***Proof-60 to 64:*** 350 to 450. ***Proof-65 or better:*** 70 to 85.

MARKET VALUES – CIRCULATION STRIKES

G-4	VG-8	F-12	VF-20	EF-40	AU-50
$16	$17	$45	$95	$200	$375
AU-55	**MS-60**	**MS-62**	**MS-63**	**MS-64**	**MS-65**
$400	$550	$750	$1,000	$1,250	$3,200

MARKET VALUES – PROOF STRIKES

PF-60	PF-63	PF-64	PF-65
$600	$1,200	$1,800	$3,250

CERTIFIED POPULATIONS – CIRCULATION STRIKES

Fair	AG	G	VG	F	VF	EF	AU	MS-60
0	0	8	8	10	22	5	83	1

MS-61	MS-62	MS-63	MS-64	MS-65	MS-66	MS-67	MS-68	MS-69	MS-70
22	48	52	56	15	0	0	0	0	0

CERTIFIED POPULATIONS – PROOF STRIKES

PF-50	PF-60	PF-61	PF-62	PF-63	PF-64
0	2	6	13	40	79
PF-65	**PF-66**	**PF-67**	**PF-68**	**PF-69**	**PF-70**
50	38	23	5	0	0

1906-D Half Dollar

Circulation-strike mintage: 4,028,000

Availability in Mint State: Probably at least 500 lower-level Mint State coins survive. ***Estimated number MS-65 or higher:*** 70 to 90.

Availability in circulated grades: 15,000 to 18,000. Most are G-4. Easy to find in any grade.

Characteristics of striking: Most high-grade 1906-D half dollars show some lightness of strike at the usual spots on the right reverse. Sharp strikes can be found, with weakness only on the high part of the eagle's talons. Some have raised areas on the neck, popularly called "mumps" in various *Journal of the Barber Coin Collectors' Society* articles.

The luster is usually nice. Several examples with prooflike characteristics are noticed in the literature, including a piece which David Lawrence, in his book, calls a Proof or presentation example, also noting that in the Golden Jubilee Sale, 1950, B. Max Mehl offered a 1906-D having a brilliant Proof obverse and a brilliant Uncirculated reverse. Quite possibly during the initial coinage of the Denver Mint—this being the first year of extensive operations there—some 1906-D half dollars were struck for presentation. This is likely further still because half dollars were the largest silver denomination at the time.

MARKET VALUES – CIRCULATION STRIKES

G-4	VG-8	F-12	VF-20	EF-40	AU-50
$16	$17	$45	$95	$200	$375
AU-55	**MS-60**	**MS-62**	**MS-63**	**MS-64**	**MS-65**
$400	$550	$750	$1,000	$1,250	$3,200

CERTIFIED POPULATIONS – CIRCULATION STRIKES

Fair	AG	G	VG	F	VF	EF	AU	MS-60
0	1	13	13	10	20	20	59	0

MS-61	MS-62	MS-63	MS-64	MS-65	MS-66	MS-67	MS-68	MS-69	MS-70
15	27	36	38	8	4	0	0	0	0

1906-O HALF DOLLAR

Circulation-strike mintage: 2,446,000

AVAILABILITY IN MINT STATE: This date and mint is a major rarity in high–Mint State levels. One of the key issues among the later dates. The mint luster is usually very attractive. ***Estimated number MS-65 or higher:*** 40 to 50.

AVAILABILITY IN CIRCULATED GRADES: 9,000 to 14,000. Most are G-4. F-12 coins are hard to find, and EF and AU examples are even more so.

CHARACTERISTICS OF STRIKING: The 1906-O varies in sharpness, but there are quite a few examples that are above average for a New Orleans half dollar. These are worth tracking down.

MARKET VALUES – CIRCULATION STRIKES

G-4	VG-8	F-12	VF-20	EF-40	AU-50
$16	$19	$42	$95	$200	$350

AU-55	MS-60	MS-62	MS-63	MS-64	MS-65
$400	$600	$975	$1,400	$2,600	$5,150

CERTIFIED POPULATIONS – CIRCULATION STRIKES

Fair	AG	G	VG	F	VF	EF	AU	MS-60
0	2	6	9	10	15	8	21	1

MS-61	MS-62	MS-63	MS-64	MS-65	MS-66	MS-67	MS-68	MS-69	MS-70
3	6	12	11	6	5	0	0	0	0

1906-S Half Dollar

Circulation-strike mintage: 1,740,154

Availability in Mint State: Lower-grade examples are readily available. ***Estimated number MS-65 or higher:*** 45 to 55. Another 20th-century rarity in this grade.

Availability in circulated grades: 6,000 to 7,500. Most are G-4. This is among the scarcer issues to find in higher circulated grades.

Characteristics of striking: The 1906-S usually is well struck—amazingly sometimes even including details of the eagle's talon on the right.

MARKET VALUES – CIRCULATION STRIKES

G-4	VG-8	F-12	VF-20	EF-40	AU-50
$16	$19	$53	$115	$210	$350
AU-55	**MS-60**	**MS-62**	**MS-63**	**MS-64**	**MS-65**
$400	$600	$925	$1,350	$2,750	$4,750

CERTIFIED POPULATIONS – CIRCULATION STRIKES

Fair	AG	G	VG	F	VF	EF	AU	MS-60
0	0	1	8	9	6	5	28	1

MS-61	MS-62	MS-63	MS-64	MS-65	MS-66	MS-67	MS-68	MS-69	MS-70
4	10	11	25	9	3	1	1	1	0

1907 HALF DOLLAR

Circulation-strike mintage: 2,598,000
Proof mintage: 575

AVAILABILITY IN MINT STATE: Mint State examples are usually well struck and have excellent luster. ***Estimated number MS-65 or higher:*** 95 to 115.

AVAILABILITY IN CIRCULATED GRADES: 12,000 to 15,000. Most are G-4. Easy to find in any grade desired.

CHARACTERISTICS OF STRIKING: Usually well struck.

AVAILABILITY IN PROOF FORMAT: ***Proof-60 to 64:*** 290 to 340. ***Proof-65 or better:*** 45 to 55.

MARKET VALUES – CIRCULATION STRIKES

G-4	VG-8	F-12	VF-20	EF-40	AU-50
$16	$17	$45	$95	$200	$375
AU-55	**MS-60**	**MS-62**	**MS-63**	**MS-64**	**MS-65**
$450	$550	$800	$1,000	$1,300	$3,000

MARKET VALUES – PROOF STRIKES

PF-60	PF-63	PF-64	PF-65
$600	$1,200	$1,800	$3,250

CERTIFIED POPULATIONS – CIRCULATION STRIKES

Fair	AG	G	VG	F	VF	EF	AU	MS-60
0	0	3	5	12	19	6	56	2

MS-61	MS-62	MS-63	MS-64	MS-65	MS-66	MS-67	MS-68	MS-69	MS-70
19	37	42	74	19	3	0	0	0	0

CERTIFIED POPULATIONS – PROOF STRIKES

PF-50	PF-60	PF-61	PF-62	PF-63	PF-64
0	2	6	19	23	56
PF-65	**PF-66**	**PF-67**	**PF-68**	**PF-69**	**PF-70**
38	31	12	1	0	0

1907-D Half Dollar

Circulation-strike mintage: 3,856,000

Availability in Mint State: Attractive MS–63 and 64 coins can be found easily. ***Estimated number MS-65 or higher:*** 100 to 120. Somewhat scarcer than the large mintage might suggest.

Availability in circulated grades: 20,000 to 25,000. Most are G-4. Another issue that is easy to find in all circulated grades.

Characteristics of striking: Most have the usual weakness on the right side of the reverse, but there are some exceptions. Some have prooflike surfaces.

MARKET VALUES – CIRCULATION STRIKES

G-4	VG-8	F-12	VF-20	EF-40	AU-50
$16	$17	$45	$95	$200	$350
AU-55	**MS-60**	**MS-62**	**MS-63**	**MS-64**	**MS-65**
$375	$500	$625	$1,000	$1,175	$2,950

CERTIFIED POPULATIONS – CIRCULATION STRIKES

Fair	AG	G	VG	F	VF	EF	AU	MS-60	
0	2	10	10	15	19	21	69	0	
MS-61	**MS-62**	**MS-63**	**MS-64**	**MS-65**	**MS-66**	**MS-67**	**MS-68**	**MS-69**	**MS-70**
14	41	44	36	18	5	2	1	0	0

1907-O HALF DOLLAR

Circulation-strike mintage: 3,946,600

AVAILABILITY IN MINT STATE: In lower–Mint State grades probably 400 to 600 exist, making them quite collectible. ***Estimated number MS-65 or higher:*** 55 to 65.

AVAILABILITY IN CIRCULATED GRADES: 20,000 to 25,000. Most are G-4. Again, an issue easy to find in any grade desired.

CHARACTERISTICS OF STRIKING: The 1907-O is usually seen with weak striking in the usual areas on the right side of the reverse. David Lawrence considers the 1907-O to be the worst-struck issue in the entire Barber half dollar series. Well-struck pieces exist but are very rare.

MARKET VALUES – CIRCULATION STRIKES

G-4	VG-8	F-12	VF-20	EF-40	AU-50
$16	$17	$45	$95	$200	$375
AU-55	**MS-60**	**MS-62**	**MS-63**	**MS-64**	**MS-65**
$450	$550	$800	$1,000	$1,300	$3,000

CERTIFIED POPULATIONS – CIRCULATION STRIKES

Fair	AG	G	VG	F	VF	EF	AU	MS-60
1	5	9	6	8	19	16	46	0

MS-61	MS-62	MS-63	MS-64	MS-65	MS-66	MS-67	MS-68	MS-69	MS-70
7	38	45	42	18	6	3	0	0	0

1907-S Half Dollar

Circulation-strike mintage: 1,250,000

Availability in Mint State: Slightly scarce. ***Estimated number MS-65 or higher:*** 40 to 50. The 1907-S half dollar at the gem level is surprisingly rare for reasons unknown today. The same can be said of the 1907-S dime in particular and, to a lesser extent, the 1907-S quarter.

Availability in circulated grades: 5,000 to 6,000. Most are G-4. This is among the scarcer issues in circulated grades, and at F-12 or better it is a key. David Lawrence considered this to be among the top-eight rarest half dollars in EF and AU.

Characteristics of striking: Sharpness varies among 1907-S half dollars. The typical coin shows lightness on the right side of the reverse in the usual places, not what is expected for a San Francisco Mint coin. Sharply struck coins exist, but they still lack detail on the highest area of the eagle's talons on the right.

Notes: For half dollar specialists the 1907-S has long been known as a rarity. Although the mintage isn't high, it is not low either—1,250,000 pieces. Apparently the variety was virtually completely overlooked at the time it was released, and today the term *rarity* could be applied to a piece even at the AU level. David Lawrence says that the 1907-S "is the scarcest late date of the series in Mint State."[4]

MARKET VALUES – CIRCULATION STRIKES

G-4	VG-8	F-12	VF-20	EF-40	AU-50
$18	$30	$85	$185	$375	$650
AU-55	**MS-60**	**MS-62**	**MS-63**	**MS-64**	**MS-65**
$900	$1,275	$2,700	$5,700	$9,000	$11,000

CERTIFIED POPULATIONS – CIRCULATION STRIKES

Fair	AG	G	VG	F	VF	EF	AU	MS-60
0	1	18	5	10	7	10	12	0

MS-61	MS-62	MS-63	MS-64	MS-65	MS-66	MS-67	MS-68	MS-69	MS-70
3	6	5	7	7	2	1	0	0	0

1908 HALF DOLLAR

Circulation-strike mintage: 1,354,000
Proof mintage: 545

AVAILABILITY IN MINT STATE: Probably 500 or more exist in lower–Mint State grades. ***Estimated number MS-65 or higher:*** 60 to 70.

AVAILABILITY IN CIRCULATED GRADES: 6,000 to 7,500. Most are G-4. This is among the scarcer issues to find in circulated grades of F-12 and higher.

CHARACTERISTICS OF STRIKING: Half dollars of this date are usually quite well struck, the exception being details of the eagle's talons at the lower right of the reverse. The luster is usually quite nice.

AVAILABILITY IN PROOF FORMAT: ***Proof-60 to 64:*** 290 to 340. ***Proof-65 or better:*** 50 to 60.

NOTES: In the *Journal of the Barber Coin Collectors' Society*, Fall 1999, Michael S. Fey illustrated a well-worn 1908 with the reverse rotated 90 degrees clockwise.

MARKET VALUES – CIRCULATION STRIKES

G-4	VG-8	F-12	VF-20	EF-40	AU-50
$16	$17	$45	$95	$200	$375
AU-55	**MS-60**	**MS-62**	**MS-63**	**MS-64**	**MS-65**
$450	$550	$750	$1,000	$1,150	$3,000

MARKET VALUES – PROOF STRIKES

PF-60	PF-63	PF-64	PF-65
$600	$1,200	$1,800	$3,250

CERTIFIED POPULATIONS – CIRCULATION STRIKES

Fair	AG	G	VG	F	VF	EF	AU	MS-60
0	2	4	4	6	6	6	33	0

MS-61	MS-62	MS-63	MS-64	MS-65	MS-66	MS-67	MS-68	MS-69	MS-70
12	26	25	35	11	1	4	0	0	0

CERTIFIED POPULATIONS – PROOF STRIKES

PF-50	PF-60	PF-61	PF-62	PF-63	PF-64
0	2	13	18	24	38
PF-65	**PF-66**	**PF-67**	**PF-68**	**PF-69**	**PF-70**
31	31	20	4	0	0

1908-D Half Dollar

Circulation-strike mintage: 3,280,000

Availability in Mint State: Plentiful. Luster and eye appeal are usually very good on Mint State coins in all grades. ***Estimated number MS-65 or higher:*** 100 to 120.

Availability in circulated grades: 15,000 to 18,000. Most are G-4. Easy to find in any grade desired.

Characteristics of striking: The 1908-D half dollar is usually seen well struck except for details on the eagle's talon on the lower right of the reverse.

MARKET VALUES – CIRCULATION STRIKES

G-4	VG-8	F-12	VF-20	EF-40	AU-50
$16	$17	$45	$95	$200	$375
AU-55	**MS-60**	**MS-62**	**MS-63**	**MS-64**	**MS-65**
$450	$550	$750	$1,000	$1,150	$2,800

CERTIFIED POPULATIONS – CIRCULATION STRIKES

Fair	AG	G	VG	F	VF	EF	AU	MS-60
0	1	13	11	14	37	21	72	1

MS-61	MS-62	MS-63	MS-64	MS-65	MS-66	MS-67	MS-68	MS-69	MS-70
21	45	24	37	18	7	1	1	0	0

1908-O HALF DOLLAR

Circulation-strike mintage: 5,360,000

AVAILABILITY IN MINT STATE: Lower-level coins are available easily enough to supply the demand for them. ***Estimated number MS-65 or higher:*** 130 to 150.

AVAILABILITY IN CIRCULATED GRADES: 25,000 to 30,000. Most are G-4. Easy to find in any grade desired.

CHARACTERISTICS OF STRIKING: The typical 1908-O has light striking in the usual areas on the right side of the reverse, but not extensively so. The quality of the luster varies.

MARKET VALUES – CIRCULATION STRIKES

G-4	VG-8	F-12	VF-20	EF-40	AU-50
$16	$17	$45	$95	$200	$350
AU-55	**MS-60**	**MS-62**	**MS-63**	**MS-64**	**MS-65**
$400	$500	$675	$1,000	$1,150	$2,800

CERTIFIED POPULATIONS – CIRCULATION STRIKES

Fair	AG	G	VG	F	VF	EF	AU	MS-60
0	0	16	15	15	24	25	38	1

MS-61	MS-62	MS-63	MS-64	MS-65	MS-66	MS-67	MS-68	MS-69	MS-70
5	14	32	36	41	8	6	1	0	0

1908-S Half Dollar

Circulation-strike mintage: 1,644,828

Availability in Mint State: Many exist at lower–Mint State levels. ***Estimated number MS-65 or higher:*** 70 to 85.

Availability in circulated grades: 12,000 to 15,000. Scarce VF and higher.

Characteristics of striking: The usually-seen 1908-S is well struck except for minor details on the eagle's talon at the lower right. Luster and eye appeal are usually very good.

MARKET VALUES – CIRCULATION STRIKES

G-4	VG-8	F-12	VF-20	EF-40	AU-50
$16	$25	$75	$160	$275	$420
AU-55	**MS-60**	**MS-62**	**MS-63**	**MS-64**	**MS-65**
$650	$875	$1,400	$2,400	$3,650	$5,100

CERTIFIED POPULATIONS – CIRCULATION STRIKES

Fair	AG	G	VG	F	VF	EF	AU	MS-60
0	2	3	9	10	9	4	8	0

MS-61	MS-62	MS-63	MS-64	MS-65	MS-66	MS-67	MS-68	MS-69	MS-70
4	12	5	15	5	4	1	0	0	0

1909 HALF DOLLAR

Circulation-strike mintage: 2,368,000
Proof mintage: 650

AVAILABILITY IN MINT STATE: MS-63 and higher coins usually have nice luster and eye appeal. ***Estimated number MS-65 or higher:*** 210 to 240.

AVAILABILITY IN CIRCULATED GRADES: 9,000 to 14,000. Most are G-4. Easy to find in any grade desired.

CHARACTERISTICS OF STRIKING: Most 1909 half dollars are well struck.

AVAILABILITY IN PROOF FORMAT: ***Proof-60 to 64:*** 350 to 450. ***Proof-65 or better:*** 55 to 65.

MARKET VALUES – CIRCULATION STRIKES

G-4	VG-8	F-12	VF-20	EF-40	AU-50
$16	$17	$45	$95	$200	$375
AU-55	**MS-60**	**MS-62**	**MS-63**	**MS-64**	**MS-65**
$450	$550	$750	$1,000	$1,350	$3,250

MARKET VALUES – PROOF STRIKES

PF-60	PF-63	PF-64	PF-65
$600	$1,200	$1,800	$3,250

CERTIFIED POPULATIONS – CIRCULATION STRIKES

Fair	AG	G	VG	F	VF	EF	AU	MS-60
0	1	14	17	21	40	14	82	1

MS-61	MS-62	MS-63	MS-64	MS-65	MS-66	MS-67	MS-68	MS-69	MS-70
20	37	73	87	28	5	0	0	0	0

CERTIFIED POPULATIONS – PROOF STRIKES

PF-50	PF-60	PF-61	PF-62	PF-63	PF-64
3	1	7	23	38	70
PF-65	**PF-66**	**PF-67**	**PF-68**	**PF-69**	**PF-70**
50	52	29	10	0	0

1909-O Half Dollar

Circulation-strike mintage: 925,400

Availability in Mint State: Hundreds exist in lower–Mint State ranges. ***Estimated number MS-65 or higher:*** 55 to 65.

Availability in circulated grades: 4,000 to 5,000. Most are G-4. This is a challenging coin to find in higher circulated grades.

Characteristics of striking: The 1909-O half dollars usually have areas of light striking on the right side of the reverse, but rare exceptions are sharp, including talon details at the lower right.

MARKET VALUES – CIRCULATION STRIKES

G-4	VG-8	F-12	VF-20	EF-40	AU-50
$18	$22	$65	$175	$375	$650
AU-55	**MS-60**	**MS-62**	**MS-63**	**MS-64**	**MS-65**
$650	$1,400	$1,150	$1,600	$2,600	$4,200

CERTIFIED POPULATIONS – CIRCULATION STRIKES

Fair	AG	G	VG	F	VF	EF	AU	MS-60
0	1	11	23	18	13	9	11	0

MS-61	MS-62	MS-63	MS-64	MS-65	MS-66	MS-67	MS-68	MS-69	MS-70
3	1	9	17	21	4	0	0	0	0

1909-S Half Dollar

Circulation-strike mintage: 1,764,000

AVAILABILITY IN MINT STATE: Many can be found from MS–60 to 64. ***Estimated number MS-65 or higher:*** 5 to 55. Yet another 20th-century Barber half dollar that is seldom seen at the gem level.

AVAILABILITY IN CIRCULATED GRADES: 6,000 to 7,500. Most are G-4. This is among the scarcer issues in circulated grades.

CHARACTERISTICS OF STRIKING: Most 1909-S half dollars are very well struck. There are enough in the marketplace that finding a nice example will be no problem.

MARKET VALUES – CIRCULATION STRIKES

G-4	VG-8	F-12	VF-20	EF-40	AU-50
$16	$17	$45	$95	$200	$360
AU-55	**MS-60**	**MS-62**	**MS-63**	**MS-64**	**MS-65**
$410	$600	$900	$1,250	$2,600	$4,100

CERTIFIED POPULATIONS – CIRCULATION STRIKES

Fair	AG	G	VG	F	VF	EF	AU	MS-60
0	0	13	19	14	15	4	22	2

MS-61	MS-62	MS-63	MS-64	MS-65	MS-66	MS-67	MS-68	MS-69	MS-70
2	11	12	7	8	6	0	0	0	0

VARIETIES: ***1909-S, Inverted S Mintmark (FS-501):*** The mint worker mistakenly inverted the "S" mintmark punch on this die, creating an inverted S. The top-right serif is larger and heavier than the serif at the lower left. This variety is readily available and carries only a modest premium.

Detail of 1909-S, Inverted S, mintmark.

MARKET VALUES – CIRCULATION STRIKES

AU-50	AU-55	MS-60	MS-62	MS-63
$425	$500	$675	$1,150	$1,550

1910 Half Dollar

Circulation-strike mintage: 418,000
Proof mintage: 551

Availability in Mint State: Readily available in lower–Mint State grades. ***Estimated number MS-65 or higher:*** 80 to 95. Rare so fine. The demand for gems of any Philadelphia Mint year has been diminished by the availability of Proofs.

Availability in circulated grades: 3,500 to 4,500. Most are G-4. This low-mintage coin is available in G and VG, but is scarce in circulated grades of F-12 and above.

Characteristics of striking: Most 1910 half dollars have slight weakness at the usual places on the right side of the reverse. With searching, sharply struck coins can be found; these are distinguished by having details on the highest part of the eagle's talons on the right.

Availability in Proof format: ***Proof-60 to 64:*** 280 to 330. ***Proof-65 or better:*** 35 to 45. An unexpected rarity at the gem level.

MARKET VALUES – CIRCULATION STRIKES

G-4	VG-8	F-12	VF-20	EF-40	AU-50
$20	$30	$95	$175	$320	$410
AU-55	**MS-60**	**MS-62**	**MS-63**	**MS-64**	**MS-65**
$500	$600	$850	$1,100	$1,400	$3,400

MARKET VALUES – PROOF STRIKES

PF-60	PF-63	PF-64	PF-65
$800	$1,200	$1,800	$3,250

CERTIFIED POPULATIONS – CIRCULATION STRIKES

Fair	AG	G	VG	F	VF	EF	AU	MS-60
0	0	6	13	13	10	3	30	1

MS-61	MS-62	MS-63	MS-64	MS-65	MS-66	MS-67	MS-68	MS-69	MS-70
5	26	10	34	8	1	0	0	0	0

CERTIFIED POPULATIONS – PROOF STRIKES

PF-50	PF-60	PF-61	PF-62	PF-63	PF-64
2	0	4	11	46	73
PF-65	**PF-66**	**PF-67**	**PF-68**	**PF-69**	**PF-70**
43	31	33	9	0	0

1910-S HALF DOLLAR

Circulation-strike mintage: 1,948,000

AVAILABILITY IN MINT STATE: Readily available but hardly common in lower–Mint State categories. ***Estimated number MS-65 or higher:*** 65 to 75.

AVAILABILITY IN CIRCULATED GRADES: 6,000 to 7,500. Most are G-4. It is slightly scarce in EF and AU grades, but is readily available in lower categories.

CHARACTERISTICS OF STRIKING: Most 1910-S half dollars are similar to their Philadelphia Mint cousins and have slight weakness at the usual places on the right side of the reverse. Sharply struck coins exist but are in the minority.

MARKET VALUES – CIRCULATION STRIKES

G-4	VG-8	F-12	VF-20	EF-40	AU-50
$18	$20	$35	$95	$200	$375
AU-55	**MS-60**	**MS-62**	**MS-63**	**MS-64**	**MS-65**
$475	$650	$1,500	$2,000	$3,000	$5,750

CERTIFIED POPULATIONS – CIRCULATION STRIKES

Fair	AG	G	VG	F	VF	EF	AU	MS-60
0	1	8	11	10	16	8	16	0

MS-61	MS-62	MS-63	MS-64	MS-65	MS-66	MS-67	MS-68	MS-69	MS-70
5	10	11	10	3	6	1	1	0	0

1911 Half Dollar

Circulation-strike mintage: 1,406,000
Proof mintage: 543

Availability in Mint State: Readily available in lower–Mint State grades. ***Estimated number MS-65 or higher:*** 160 to 190.

Availability in circulated grades: 6,000 to 7,000. Most are G-4. Easy to find in any circulated grade desired.

Characteristics of striking: Most 1911 half dollars are quite well struck, which is above-average quality for the series. The high part of the eagle's talons is inevitably weak on all seen.

Availability in Proof format: ***Proof-60 to 64:*** 290 to 340. ***Proof-65 or better:*** 55 to 65.

MARKET VALUES – CIRCULATION STRIKES

G-4	VG-8	F-12	VF-20	EF-40	AU-50
$16	$17	$45	$95	$200	$375
AU-55	**MS-60**	**MS-62**	**MS-63**	**MS-64**	**MS-65**
$400	$550	$625	$1,000	$1,300	$2,900

MARKET VALUES – PROOF STRIKES

PF-60	PF-63	PF-64	PF-65
$800	$1,200	$1,800	$3,250

CERTIFIED POPULATIONS – CIRCULATION STRIKES

Fair	AG	G	VG	F	VF	EF	AU	MS-60
0	0	5	7	15	18	11	62	0

MS-61	MS-62	MS-63	MS-64	MS-65	MS-66	MS-67	MS-68	MS-69	MS-70
15	47	44	58	19	10	2	0	0	0

CERTIFIED POPULATIONS – PROOF STRIKES

PF-50	PF-60	PF-61	PF-62	PF-63	PF-64
0	2	7	12	31	73
PF-65	**PF-66**	**PF-67**	**PF-68**	**PF-69**	**PF-70**
43	38	18	9	1	0

1911-D HALF DOLLAR

Circulation-strike mintage: 695,080

AVAILABILITY IN MINT STATE: Scarce, especially in MS-63 and MS-64 grades. ***Estimated number MS-65 or higher:*** 30 to 35. At the gem level, this is one of the key Barber half dollars of the 20th century.

AVAILABILITY IN CIRCULATED GRADES: 2,500 to 3,000. Most are G-4. This is one of the more challenging issues to find in circulated grades, especially VF and above.

CHARACTERISTICS OF STRIKING: Most 1911-D half dollars are well struck except for the highest part of the eagle's talons on the right.

NOTES: The mintage was low, but enough were saved by chance that examples are easy enough to find.

MARKET VALUES – CIRCULATION STRIKES

G-4	VG-8	F-12	VF-20	EF-40	AU-50
$16	$17	$45	$95	$200	$350
AU-55	**MS-60**	**MS-62**	**MS-63**	**MS-64**	**MS-65**
$375	$500	$625	$1,000	$1,250	$3,100

CERTIFIED POPULATIONS – CIRCULATION STRIKES

Fair	AG	G	VG	F	VF	EF	AU	MS-60
0	0	3	4	9	11	3	26	0

MS-61	MS-62	MS-63	MS-64	MS-65	MS-66	MS-67	MS-68	MS-69	MS-70
5	13	16	36	15	5	1	0	0	0

1911-S Half Dollar

Circulation-strike mintage: 1,272,000

Availability in Mint State: Lower-grade Mint State coins are readily available. ***Estimated number MS-65 or higher:*** 45 to 55. One of the rarer 20th-century issues at the gem level.

Availability in circulated grades: 6,000 to 7,500. Most are G-4. Same comments as for 1911-D.

Characteristics of striking: Most 1911-S half dollars are quite well struck, this general comment being applicable to the majority of half dollars of this era from the three mints.

MARKET VALUES – CIRCULATION STRIKES

G-4	VG-8	F-12	VF-20	EF-40	AU-50
$18	$20	$40	$100	$210	$385
AU-55	**MS-60**	**MS-62**	**MS-63**	**MS-64**	**MS-65**
$450	$650	$1,050	$1,500	$2,650	$5,200

CERTIFIED POPULATIONS – CIRCULATION STRIKES

Fair	AG	G	VG	F	VF	EF	AU	MS-60
0	0	6	12	14	16	6	12	0

MS-61	MS-62	MS-63	MS-64	MS-65	MS-66	MS-67	MS-68	MS-69	MS-70
1	8	8	9	6	1	1	0	0	0

Varieties: ***1911-S, Repunched Mintmark (FS-501):*** On this variety the lower serif of the first mintmark is seen protruding from the serif of the second-punched, primary serif.

MARKET VALUES – CIRCULATION STRIKES

AU-50	AU-55	MS-60	MS-62	MS-63	MS-64	MS-65
$475	$550	$750	$1,200	$1,600	$3,150	$5,400

1912 Half Dollar

Circulation-strike mintage: 1,550,000
Proof mintage: 700

Availability in Mint State: Hundreds exist from MS–60 to 64. ***Estimated number MS-65 or higher:*** 60 to 70. This is another instance of gems being rare, but lower-level examples can be readily obtained.

Availability in circulated grades: 6,000 to 7,500. Most are G-4. Easy to find in any circulated grade desired.

Characteristics of striking: Most 1912 half dollars are well struck except for the high area on the eagle's talons at the lower right.

Availability in Proof format: ***Proof-60 to 64:*** 350 to 450. ***Proof-65 or better:*** 45 to 55. High-grade Proofs are much rarer than the generous mintage would suggest.

MARKET VALUES – CIRCULATION STRIKES

G-4	VG-8	F-12	VF-20	EF-40	AU-50
$16	$17	$45	$95	$200	$375
AU-55	**MS-60**	**MS-62**	**MS-63**	**MS-64**	**MS-65**
$400	$550	$625	$1,000	$1,300	$2,900

MARKET VALUES – PROOF STRIKES

PF-60	PF-63	PF-64	PF-65
$800	$1,200	$1,800	$3,250

CERTIFIED POPULATIONS – CIRCULATION STRIKES

Fair	AG	G	VG	F	VF	EF	AU	MS-60
0	0	11	9	11	24	17	73	1

MS-61	MS-62	MS-63	MS-64	MS-65	MS-66	MS-67	MS-68	MS-69	MS-70
16	46	70	81	13	0	0	0	0	0

CERTIFIED POPULATIONS – PROOF STRIKES

PF-50	PF-60	PF-61	PF-62	PF-63	PF-64
0	7	5	22	34	57
PF-65	**PF-66**	**PF-67**	**PF-68**	**PF-69**	**PF-70**
23	23	13	6	0	0

1912-D Half Dollar

Circulation-strike mintage: 2,300,800

Availability in Mint State: Readily available. ***Estimated number MS-65 or higher:*** 225 to 250. One of the more plentiful Barber half dollars in gem preservation. G-4. Easy to find in any circulated grade desired.

Characteristics of striking: Most are well struck except for the high area on the eagle's talons at the lower right.

MARKET VALUES – CIRCULATION STRIKES

G-4	VG-8	F-12	VF-20	EF-40	AU-50
$16	$17	$45	$95	$200	$375
AU-55	**MS-60**	**MS-62**	**MS-63**	**MS-64**	**MS-65**
$400	$550	$625	$1,000	$1,300	$2,900

CERTIFIED POPULATIONS – CIRCULATION STRIKES

Fair	AG	G	VG	F	VF	EF	AU	MS-60
0	0	12	26	20	32	25	108	2

MS-61	MS-62	MS-63	MS-64	MS-65	MS-66	MS-67	MS-68	MS-69	MS-70
19	56	78	114	30	8	0	0	0	0

1912-S Half Dollar

Circulation-strike mintage: 1,370,000

AVAILABILITY IN MINT STATE: Readily available in lower–Mint State grades. ***Estimated number MS-65 or higher:*** 80 to 95. Somewhat scarce in gem preservation.

AVAILABILITY IN CIRCULATED GRADES: 6,000 to 7,500. Most are G-4. This is among the scarcer issues to find in circulated grades EF and higher.

CHARACTERISTICS OF STRIKING: Most 1912-S half dollars are above average in sharpness. Some have the unusual characteristic of weakness at the upper right of the reverse in the shield and feather details, but at the lower right having part of the highest area of the talons sharp.

MARKET VALUES – CIRCULATION STRIKES

G-4	VG-8	F-12	VF-20	EF-40	AU-50
$16	$18	$45	$100	$200	$425
AU-55	**MS-60**	**MS-62**	**MS-63**	**MS-64**	**MS-65**
$475	$600	$850	$1,150	$2,200	$4,100

CERTIFIED POPULATIONS – CIRCULATION STRIKES

Fair	AG	G	VG	F	VF	EF	AU	MS-60
0	1	16	15	21	27	4	21	0

MS-61	MS-62	MS-63	MS-64	MS-65	MS-66	MS-67	MS-68	MS-69	MS-70
4	12	21	49	6	5	2	0	0	0

1913 Half Dollar

Circulation-strike mintage: 188,000
Proof mintage: 627

Availability in Mint State: Several hundred exist in lower–Mint State categories. ***Estimated number MS-65 or higher:*** 55 to 65.

Availability in circulated grades: 2,000 to 2,500. Most are G-4. Many well-worn coins were saved in the 1930s and 1940s when the low mintage figure was noted. David Lawrence considered this to be among the top-eight rarest half dollars in EF and AU.

Characteristics of striking: The strike is usually quite good.

Availability in Proof format: ***Proof-60 to 64:*** 350 to 450. ***Proof-65 or better:*** 50 to 60.

MARKET VALUES – CIRCULATION STRIKES

G-4	VG-8	F-12	VF-20	EF-40	AU-50
$75	$90	$210	$425	$650	$835
AU-55	**MS-60**	**MS-62**	**MS-63**	**MS-64**	**MS-65**
$950	$1,150	$1,375	$1,800	$2,775	$4,250

MARKET VALUES – PROOF STRIKES

PF-60	PF-63	PF-64	PF-65
$700	$1,300	$1,850	$3,500

CERTIFIED POPULATIONS – CIRCULATION STRIKES

Fair	AG	G	VG	F	VF	EF	AU	MS-60
0	9	158	86	12	27	8	25	2

MS-61	MS-62	MS-63	MS-64	MS-65	MS-66	MS-67	MS-68	MS-69	MS-70
5	11	7	16	8	2	0	0	0	0

CERTIFIED POPULATIONS – PROOF STRIKES

PF-50	PF-60	PF-61	PF-62	PF-63	PF-64
2	5	8	24	32	45
PF-65	**PF-66**	**PF-67**	**PF-68**	**PF-69**	**PF-70**
31	32	13	4	0	0

1913-D Half Dollar

Circulation-strike mintage: 534,000

Availability in Mint State: Lower-level Mint State coins appear with regularity. *Estimated number MS-65 or higher:* 50 to 60. Quite scarce.

Availability in circulated grades: 2,000 to 2,500. Most are G-4. This is a slightly scarce issue in F-12 and higher grades.

Characteristics of striking: The reverse of this issue typically shows light striking in the usual places. No example with full talon details has been seen.

MARKET VALUES – CIRCULATION STRIKES

G-4	VG-8	F-12	VF-20	EF-40	AU-50
$16	$17	$45	$95	$200	$375
AU-55	**MS-60**	**MS-62**	**MS-63**	**MS-64**	**MS-65**
$400	$550	$625	$1,000	$1,300	$4,350

CERTIFIED POPULATIONS – CIRCULATION STRIKES

Fair	AG	G	VG	F	VF	EF	AU	MS-60
0	1	7	4	8	11	10	71	1

MS-61	MS-62	MS-63	MS-64	MS-65	MS-66	MS-67	MS-68	MS-69	MS-70
9	22	38	61	17	5	0	0	0	0

1913-S Half Dollar

Circulation-strike mintage: 604,000

Availability in Mint State: Hundreds exist in lower–Mint State grades. ***Estimated number MS-65 or higher:*** 55 to 65.

Availability in circulated grades: 2,500 to 4,000. Most are AG-3 or G-4. This is one of the more challenging issues to find in F-12 and higher grades.

Characteristics of striking: Half dollars of this date and mint are above average in sharpness but have traces of the usual weakness at the right side of the reverse.

MARKET VALUES – CIRCULATION STRIKES

G-4	VG-8	F-12	VF-20	EF-40	AU-50
$16	$25	$55	$120	$275	$385
AU-55	**MS-60**	**MS-62**	**MS-63**	**MS-64**	**MS-65**
$450	$600	$975	$1,350	$2,450	$3,850

CERTIFIED POPULATIONS – CIRCULATION STRIKES

Fair	AG	G	VG	F	VF	EF	AU	MS-60
0	0	10	13	12	9	4	16	0

MS-61	MS-62	MS-63	MS-64	MS-65	MS-66	MS-67	MS-68	MS-69	MS-70
2	14	11	30	18	3	0	0	0	0

1914 Half Dollar

Circulation-strike mintage: 124,000
Proof mintage: 380

Availability in Mint State: The market demand for gem–Mint State coins is softened by the availability of Proofs. Many MS coins exist. In the mid-1970s Maurice Rosen handled a bank-wrapped roll of 40 pieces.[5] ***Estimated number MS-65 or higher:*** 30 to 35. Examples are rare so fine.

Availability in circulated grades: 2,000 to 2,500. Most are G-4 and were saved in the 1930s and 1940s. F-12 and higher coins are hard to find and are in strong demand.

Characteristics of striking: The 1914 Philadelphia Mint half dollars are usually seen with above average details, and a few have full talon details as well.

Availability in Proof format: ***Proof-60 to 64:*** 225 to 250. ***Proof-65 or better:*** 50 to 60.

R. Lawson Miles Jr., prominent in the oyster processing business in Norfolk, Virginia, formed a comprehensive collection of United States coins, which was eventually auctioned by Stack's in 1969. Apart from this endeavor, Miles liked and sought out Proof half dollars of 1914 and 1915, and for many years bought as many as he could, eventually acquiring more than 100 of each. Editions of *A Guide Book of United States Coins* in the 1950s show these two dates priced at multiples of any other years in the Barber series—reflecting Miles's hoarding of these issues (which was not disclosed until later years). Regrettably, his secretary, perhaps misunderstanding instructions, cleaned all of them with silver polish, destroying much of their numismatic value.

Notes: This is one of the most desired coins in the series. The fame of the 1914 is derived from the multiple consideration of the lowest Proof production in the Barber half dollar series (just 380 coins) with the lowest circulation-strike production as well (just 124,230).

There were no 1914-D coins minted, but some counterfeits were made and are occasionally seen in worn grades.

MARKET VALUES – CIRCULATION STRIKES

G-4	VG-8	F-12	VF-20	EF-40	AU-50
$150	$170	$315	$550	$775	$975
AU-55	**MS-60**	**MS-62**	**MS-63**	**MS-64**	**MS-65**
$1,125	$1,350	$1,500	$1,950	$3,150	$8,000

MARKET VALUES – PROOF STRIKES

PF-60	PF-63	PF-64	PF-65
$800	$1,450	$1,900	$3,600

CERTIFIED POPULATIONS – CIRCULATION STRIKES

Fair	AG	G	VG	F	VF	EF	AU	MS-60
0	10	151	112	27	19	9	23	1

MS-61	MS-62	MS-63	MS-64	MS-65	MS-66	MS-67	MS-68	MS-69	MS-70
1	15	23	34	10	1	0	0	0	0

CERTIFIED POPULATIONS – PROOF STRIKES

PF-50	PF-60	PF-61	PF-62	PF-63	PF-64
1	2	9	12	22	35
PF-65	**PF-66**	**PF-67**	**PF-68**	**PF-69**	**PF-70**
33	41	15	3	0	0

1914-S Half Dollar

Circulation-strike mintage: 992,000

Availability in Mint State: Several hundred exist in lower–Mint State grades. ***Estimated number MS-65 or higher:*** 60 to 70.

Availability in circulated grades: 4,000 to 5,000. Most are G-4. This is one of the more challenging issues to find in EF and AU grades, otherwise easily located.

Characteristics of striking: The 1914-S half dollars are usually of above-average sharpness.

MARKET VALUES – CIRCULATION STRIKES

G-4	VG-8	F-12	VF-20	EF-40	AU-50
$16	$20	$40	$100	$200	$400
AU-55	**MS-60**	**MS-62**	**MS-63**	**MS-64**	**MS-65**
$450	$600	$900	$1,150	$2,100	$4,350

CERTIFIED POPULATIONS – CIRCULATION STRIKES

Fair	AG	G	VG	F	VF	EF	AU	MS-60
0	2	19	15	13	20	7	22	0

MS-61	MS-62	MS-63	MS-64	MS-65	MS-66	MS-67	MS-68	MS-69	MS-70
4	8	9	39	16	4	0	0	0	0

1915 HALF DOLLAR

Circulation-strike mintage: 138,000
Proof mintage: 450

AVAILABILITY IN MINT STATE: Several-hundred lower-grade Mint State coins exist. ***Estimated number MS-65 or higher:*** 50 to 60.

AVAILABILITY IN CIRCULATED GRADES: 2,000 to 2,500. Most are G-4 and were plucked out of circulation in the 1930s and 1940s. David Lawrence considered this among the top-eight rarest half dollars in EF and AU.

CHARACTERISTICS OF STRIKING: Circulation-strike coins are above average in sharpness and are very attractive—when you can find them, that is.

AVAILABILITY IN PROOF FORMAT: ***Proof-60 to 64:*** 275 to 325. ***Proof-65 or better:*** 30 to 40. See comment under 1914, on page 338.

NOTES: The 1915 registered the second-lowest Proof mintage of the Barber series—only 450 coins. If this were not enough, it also checks in with the second-lowest circulation-strike mintage, 138,000. As such it is a cousin to the 1914 Philadelphia Mint half dollar.

MARKET VALUES – CIRCULATION STRIKES

G-4	VG-8	F-12	VF-20	EF-40	AU-50
$110	$140	$285	$375	$575	$850

AU-55	MS-60	MS-62	MS-63	MS-64	MS-65
$1,000	$1,350	$1,550	$2,250	$3,900	$5,600

MARKET VALUES – PROOF STRIKES

PF-60	PF-63	PF-64	PF-65
$800	$1,400	$1,900	$3,600

CERTIFIED POPULATIONS – CIRCULATION STRIKES

Fair	AG	G	VG	F	VF	EF	AU	MS-60
1	2	164	143	56	22	12	29	0

MS-61	MS-62	MS-63	MS-64	MS-65	MS-66	MS-67	MS-68	MS-69	MS-70
1	12	10	8	5	1	0	0	0	0

CERTIFIED POPULATIONS – PROOF STRIKES

PF-50	PF-60	PF-61	PF-62	PF-63	PF-64
0	1	7	6	23	69
PF-65	**PF-66**	**PF-67**	**PF-68**	**PF-69**	**PF-70**
25	19	16	8	0	0

1915-D Half Dollar

Circulation-strike mintage: 1,170,400

Availability in Mint State: One of the more available issues. ***Estimated number MS-65 or higher:*** 220 to 260.

Availability in circulated grades: 5,000 to 6,000. Most are G-4. Easy to find in any circulated grade desired.

Characteristics of striking: The 1915-D half dollars show the usual lightness on the right side of the reverse, more so than other half dollar issues of this late era. A needle-sharp example has not been seen.

MARKET VALUES – CIRCULATION STRIKES

G-4	VG-8	F-12	VF-20	EF-40	AU-50
$16	$17	$45	$95	$200	$375
AU-55	**MS-60**	**MS-62**	**MS-63**	**MS-64**	**MS-65**
$400	$550	$650	$1,000	$1,200	$3,200

CERTIFIED POPULATIONS – CIRCULATION STRIKES

Fair	AG	G	VG	F	VF	EF	AU	MS-60
0	1	4	17	26	25	29	129	0

MS-61	MS-62	MS-63	MS-64	MS-65	MS-66	MS-67	MS-68	MS-69	MS-70
26	61	89	137	51	9	1	0	0	0

1915-S HALF DOLLAR

Circulation-strike mintage: 1,604,000

AVAILABILITY IN MINT STATE: Readily available. *Walter Breen's Complete Encyclopedia of U.S. and Colonial Coins* mentioned five Mint State rolls (100 coins) that turned up decades ago. ***Estimated number MS-65 or higher:*** 150 to 180.

AVAILABILITY IN CIRCULATED GRADES: 6,000 to 7,000. Most are G-4. This is among the scarcer issues in circulated grades, but to a lesser extent than 1915-D.

CHARACTERISTICS OF STRIKING: There is the usual lightness on the right side of the reverse on all seen.

MARKET VALUES – CIRCULATION STRIKES

G-4	VG-8	F-12	VF-20	EF-40	AU-50
$16	$17	$45	$95	$200	$350
AU-55	**MS-60**	**MS-62**	**MS-63**	**MS-64**	**MS-65**
$375	$500	$625	$1,000	$1,150	$2,800

CERTIFIED POPULATIONS – CIRCULATION STRIKES

Fair	AG	G	VG	F	VF	EF	AU	MS-60
0	2	18	20	29	30	16	77	0

MS-61	MS-62	MS-63	MS-64	MS-65	MS-66	MS-67	MS-68	MS-69	MS-70
18	71	53	82	43	6	3	0	0	0

A Gallery of Barber Half Dollar Proof Coinage

Proofs half dollars of each year were made from 1892 to 1915, with the lowest mintages taking place in 1914 and 1915. None were made in 1916. See page 263 for a longer discussion.

1892, Proof, half dollar.

1894, Proof, half dollar.

1898, Proof, half dollar.

1900, Proof, half dollar.

1903, Proof, half dollar.

1904, Proof, half dollar.

1911, Proof, half dollar.

1915, Proof, half dollar.

APPENDIX I

Chief Engraver Charles E. Barber

Early Life

Charles Edward Barber, who served as chief engraver at the Philadelphia Mint from 1880 to 1917, was born in London on November 16, 1840, the son of William and Anna May (Coultart) Barber. Charles grew up in the engraving trade. His father, born in London on May 2, 1807, was the son of engraver John Barber. William Barber worked for several firms, including makers of silver plates, and for De La Rue & Co., for whom he made plates for embossing cards and labels. In September 1852, the family moved to the United States, which became their permanent home. William sought work in the line of designing coins and medals, but opportunities were slim and he mostly worked on political medalets, store cards, and related items.[1] Today, William is not remembered in this context, as his work was mostly or completely unsigned. In 1860 he was listed as a die sinker and letter cutter at 8 Congress Street, Boston. In 1865 James B. Longacre recommended that the elder Barber be hired to assist him at the Mint. This was done, and Barber remained in that position until after the death of Longacre on January 1, 1869. William Barber was named chief engraver in the same month.

Career Years

Beginning in January 1866, Charles E. Barber resided in Providence, Rhode Island, where he did engraving for Gorham, the eminent maker of silver tableware and other items. He is not known to have done any die engraving for tokens or medals. After his father was named chief engraver at the Mint, Charles was hired as an assistant and moved to Philadelphia. He worked in that capacity with another assistant, William H. Key, and he gained at least a modicum of proficiency. His salary was $4 per day.

In 1876 Mint Director Henry Linderman felt that the talent at the Mint, especially that of Chief Engraver William Barber, was less than he desired. Through contact with the Royal Mint, Linderman secured the service of George T. Morgan, whose work in England was highly acclaimed. Morgan signed on as an assistant engraver that year. Today he is best remembered for his silver dollar design of 1878, based on pattern half dollars he created in 1877.

In late August of 1879, Chief Engraver Barber experienced chills and a fever after bathing in the surf in Atlantic City. His condition worsened and he returned to Philadelphia, where he died in his home August 31. The chief engravership remained vacant. Charles was considered as a candidate, but it is said that he was not well liked by some of the Mint staff. Morgan was the favorite. Linderman, his mentor, was no longer living—otherwise Morgan's endorsement would have been certain.[2] Finally, in January 1880, Charles E. Barber was appointed to the post by President Rutherford B. Hayes.

Certain pattern coins produced prior to his chief engravership have been attributed to Charles E. Barber, although in many instances documentation of the pieces' authorship has not been located. It was not the standard practice of the Treasury Department when announcing new designs in that era to attribute them to specific engravers. Numismatic tradition has taken up the slack, with mentions of such information in auction catalogs of the time and the narrative by Edgar H. Adams and William H. Woodin in *United States Pattern, Trial and Experimental Pieces*, 1913.

In 1881 Barber set about making patterns for a proposed nickel design. The result, in 1883, was the Liberty Head nickel, a coin that has been a numismatic favorite for a long time. In the same year, he made dies for silver coins of Hawaii.

In the early 1890s he and Augustus Saint-Gaudens were commissioned to create the award medal for the World's Columbian Exposition. The two men became involved in a strong and ugly disagreement, and Saint-Gaudens, America's most honored sculptor, criticized Barber's ability, a sentiment echoed by Saint-Gaudens's friends in the artistic community in New York City. Matters between the two men did not get better when, in 1904, President Theodore Roosevelt spurned Barber's official inaugural medal and privately commissioned Saint-Gaudens to create another version.

In 1905 the Treasury Department sent Barber on a tour of European mints to study the equipment and procedures in use there. Upon his return he facilitated many improvements at the Philadelphia Mint, especially in the Medal Department.

His personal interests included nature study, reading, and taking extended walks. On March 4, 1875, Charles Barber married Martha E. Jones. The union produced one child, Edith (who married William T. Moseley of Wilmington, Delaware). Martha died in 1898, and on December 3, 1902, Barber married Caroline R. Gaston, a graduate of Swarthmore College and the University of Pennsylvania who was an instructor in Latin at the Philadelphia High School for Girls. The couple lived at 1625 North 17th Street in Philadelphia.

Charles E. Barber remained chief engraver until his death on February 18, 1917, after which he was followed in the office on April 10 by George T. Morgan. His obituary appeared in *The Numismatist* in April 1917:

> Mr. Charles E. Barber, chief engraver of the United States Mint at Philadelphia, died suddenly on Sunday, February 18, aged 77 years. Mr. Barber was born in London in 1840. He was appointed an assistant at the Philadelphia Mint in 1869, and became chief engraver in 1880 upon the death of his father, William Barber, who held the position from 1869 until his death in 1879.
>
> The latest coins designed by the younger Mr. Barber were the Panama-Pacific $2½ gold and the 50-cent silver pieces. Mr. Barber cut the dies for a number of the pattern series, and is said to have possessed a splendid collection of these pieces.

Barber's Other Work in Coinage

In addition to the Liberty Head coinage issues of 1892, which are studied in the present book, Barber created multiple patterns for contemplated United States coins, designs to alter existing coins, commemorative coins, along with coins designed for foreign governments, including the independent Kingdom of Hawaii. The following galleries highlight important examples from this body of work.

Today all of his coin issues are avidly collected.

UNITED STATES PATTERNS

Charles E. Barber designed many patterns from the time of his assistant engravership through his career as chief engraver. These are extensive and are delineated in *United States Pattern Coins,* by J. Hewitt Judd, M.D. Selected examples are shown here.

In 1879 Charles E. Barber created what collectors call the "Washlady" portrait of Liberty. This was used on pattern dimes, quarters (shown here on Judd-1590), half dollars, and dollars.

The pattern $4 gold Stella of 1879, J-1635, is a numismatic favorite. This design was also used in 1880.

In 1881 Barber designed a Liberty head that was used on pattern cents, three-cent pieces, and five-cent pieces. The portrait was adopted in 1883 for use on circulating nickels. The pattern cent, J-1667, is shown here.

A pattern 1883 five-cent piece, J-1712, one of many Liberty Head five-cent patterns of that year. The reverse inscription describes the coin's composition—an experimental alloy.

A pattern 1896 five-cent piece, J-1770.

CHANGES TO EXISTING COINS

Charles E. Barber's Liberty Head nickel, introduced in 1883, was first made with the denomination expressed only as V. After certain sharpers plated them with gold and passed them as $5 gold coins, the word CENTS was added. This design was produced in quantity for circulation through 1912. Today it is a numismatic favorite.

In 1907 Barber modified the MCMVII motif on the double eagle of the late Augustus Saint-Gaudens, lowering the relief to make the design possible to strike on high-speed presses. The MCMVII version took three blows of the press to bring the relief up fully and was impractical for that reason.

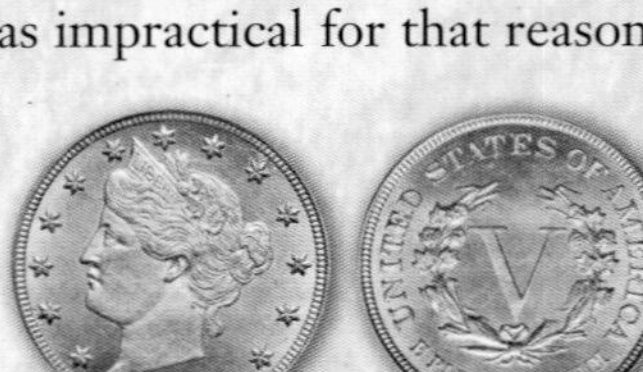

The first 1883, Liberty Head, nickel design with the denomination given as V.

The revised design, with CENTS added, became the standard.

MCMVII (1907), High Relief, double eagle by Augustus Saint-Gaudens.

The Saint-Gaudens design as modified by Charles E. Barber.

Commemorative Coinage

Charles E. Barber is credited with a number of commemorative coin designs from the 1892, World's Columbian Exposition, half dollar to the McKinley gold dollars of 1916–1917:[3]

Columbian half dollars of 1892 and 1893 (Barber did the obverse, Morgan the reverse; both designs were by Olin Levi Warner).

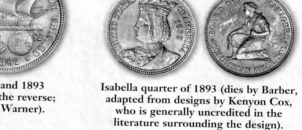

Isabella quarter of 1893 (dies by Barber, adapted from designs by Kenyon Cox, who is generally uncredited in the literature surrounding the design).

Lafayette silver dollar of 1900 (Barber did the obverse, copying the design from an 1881 medal by Peter L. Krider; the reverse, by Barber, shows an equestrian statue of Lafayette by Paul Wayland Bartlett and is signed with Bartlett's surname).

1903, Louisiana Purchase Exposition, gold dollar, obverse portraying Thomas Jefferson (copied from a medal by John Reich). The Exposition was held in 1904.

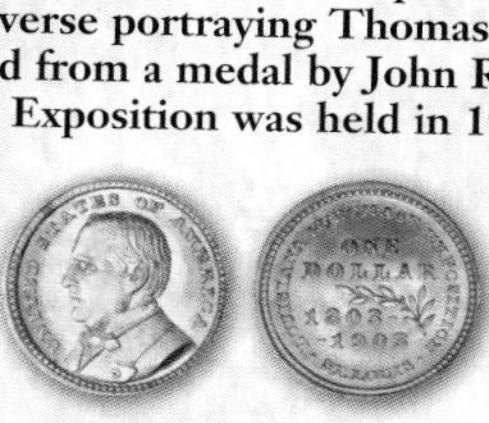

1903, Louisiana Purchase Exposition, gold dollar, obverse portraying William McKinley.

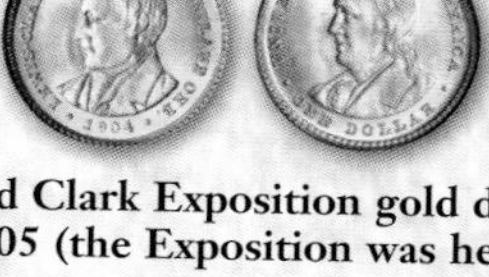

Lewis and Clark Exposition gold dollars of 1904 and 1905 (the Exposition was held in 1905).

Commemorative Coinage (continued)

1915-S, Panama-Pacific International Exposition, half dollar (obverse by Barber, reverse by Morgan).

Panama-Pacific International Exposition gold quarter eagle (obverse by Barber, reverse by Morgan, who adapted a motif he created in 1877 for a pattern half dollar).

McKinley Memorial gold dollars of 1916 and 1917 (obverse by Barber, reverse by Morgan).

Foreign Commissions

Barber is said to have designed coins for 14 Central and South American countries, as well as for China and Japan. Most of these are unsigned, some were by private (not Mint) commissions. No checklist of these has ever been prepared.

In 1883 he designed the silver dime, quarter, half dollar, and dollar for the Kingdom of Hawaii. These are well-known and are listed in *A Guide Book of United States Coins.*

1883 Hawaiian half dollar.

United States Medals and Related Work

Patterson DuBois, Mint historian in residence, discussed Charles E. Barber in the *American Journal of Numismatics*, July 1883:

> He was appointed as assistant in 1869 and became the official head by promotion in 1880, to fill the vacancy caused by his father's death. The appointment was not unmerited. Mr. Barber's latest card to the public is the new five-cent piece—a successful venture in very low relief.
>
> But his handiwork is more or less visible in all the principal medals executed since 1869. Since his appointment as chief engraver, the work of his department has been enormously increased by the number of medal dies demanded for the War Department and from other government sources. The medal dies made last year (1882) number twenty-eight.
>
> Mr. Barber's best work is seen in the medals of Snowden, Garfield, President Arthur, Indian Peace, Army-Marksmanship, and Great Seal. He is particularly happy in "catching a likeness." The head of Superintendent Snowden is a rare specimen of medallic portraiture. Messrs. Key and Morgan are the engraver's assistants.

The following listing of medals was compiled by Dick Johnson as part of a large data base, "Charles E. Barber," American Artists: Diesinkers, Medallists, Sculptors, accessible at Dick Johnson's Databank online. Many other references, exhibitions, and the like can be found in the Johnson data base. In the following list Julian numbers are listed, as given by R.W. Julian, in *Medals of the United States Mint. The First Century 1792–1892*. Dies attributed to William Barber are posthumous uses of this work; the senior Barber died on August 31, 1879.

Johnson points out the problem of attributing certain of the engraver's work:

> Barber frequently took credit for other artists' work. This includes Olin Levi Warner (Columbian half dollar), and earlier medals of Moritz Fürst and John Reich which he copied and signed his initials (Julian NA-8, NA-11, NA-15, List 513, and two Mint List medals are examples). He even signed a replacement reverse die originally engraved by his father, removing his father's initial and replaced his own C.E.B. initials (1881 Assay Medal, Julian AC- 24a).

Assay Commission Medals

1880 Assay Commission Medal (obverse by George T. Morgan, reverse by Charles E. Barber). [Julian AC-20]

1880 Assay Commission Medal (mule; both sides by Barber). [Julian AC-21]

1886 Assay Commission Medal (obverse by Barber, reverse by Morgan). [Julian AC-29]

1888 Assay Commission Medal (both sides by Barber). [Julian AC-31]

1889 Assay Commission Medal (both sides by Barber). [Julian AC-32]

1890 Assay Commission Medal (obverse by Barber, reverse by Morgan). [Julian AC-33]

1891 Assay Commission Medal (obverse by Barber, reverse by Morgan). [Julian AC-34]

1891 Assay Commission Medal (obverse by Barber, reverse by Morgan). [Julian AC-35]

1895 Assay Commission Medal. (shown reduced)

1894 Assay Commission Medal (obverse by Barber, reverse by Morgan). [Julian AC-38]

1895 Assay Commission Medal (obverse by Barber, reverse by Morgan). [Julian AC-39]

1896 Assay Commission Medal (obverse by Barber, reverse by Morgan). [Julian AC-40]

1897 Assay Commission Medal (obverse by Barber, reverse by Morgan). [Julian AC-41]

1898 Assay Commission Medal (obverse by Barber, reverse by Morgan). [Julian AC-42]

1899 Assay Commission Medal (obverse by Barber, reverse by Morgan). [Julian AC-43]

1900 Assay Commission Medal (obverse by Barber, reverse by Morgan). [Julian AC-44]

1901 Assay Commission Medal (obverse by Barber, reverse by Morgan). [Julian AC-45]

1906 Assay Commission Medal (obverse by Barber, reverse by Morgan). [Julian AC-50]

1907 Assay Commission Medal (obverse by Barber, reverse by Morgan). [Julian AC-51]

1908 Assay Commission Medal (obverse by Barber, reverse by Morgan). [Julian AC-52]

1910 Assay Commission Medal (obverse by Barber, reverse by Morgan). [Julian AC-54]

1911 Assay Commission Medal (obverse by Barber, reverse by Morgan). [Julian AC-55]

1912 Assay Commission Medal (obverse by Barber, reverse by Morgan). [Julian AC-56]

1913 Assay Commission Medal (obverse by Barber, reverse by Morgan). [Julian AC-57]

1914 Assay Commission Medal (obverse by Barber, reverse by Morgan). [Julian AC-58]

Indian Peace Medals

1881 James Garfield Indian Peace Medal (oval, obverse by Barber, reverse by Morgan). [Julian IP-44]

1883 Chester A. Arthur Indian Peace Medal (oval, obverse by Barber, reverse by Morgan). [Julian IP-45]

1885 Grover Cleveland Indian Peace Medal (oval, obverse by Barber, reverse by Morgan). [Julian IP-46]

1889 Benjamin Harrison Indian Peace Medal (oval, obverse by Barber, reverse by Morgan). [Julian IP-47]

1890 Benjamin Harrison Indian Peace Medal (round shape). [Julian IP-48]

Presidential Medals

1879 Ulysses S. Grant Presidential Medal (by Charles E. Barber and William Barber). [Julian PR-15]

Dated 1869 or 1873, the medal was first struck in 1879 from new dies commemorating Grant's first and second terms.

1881 James Garfield Presidential Medal. [Julian PR-20]

1881 James Garfield Presidential Medal. Muling (obverse of Julian PR-20, portrait by Barber; Lincoln reverse of Julian PR-12 by Morgan).

1881 James Garfield Presidential Memorial Medal (obverse by Barber, reverse by Morgan). The reverse gives dates of assassination and death; although dated 1881, it was first struck in 1886. [Julian PR-21]

1883 Chester A. Arthur Presidential Medal (obverse by Barber, reverse by Morgan). [Julian PR-22]

1885 Grover Cleveland Presidential First Term Medal. [Julian PR-23]

1889 Grover Cleveland Presidential Second Term Medal. [Julian PR-23A]

1889 Benjamin Harrison Presidential Medal (obverse by Barber, reverse probably by Morgan). [Julian PR-24]

1893 Grover Cleveland Second Inauguration Medal.

1897 William McKinley First Inauguration Medal (obverse by Barber, reverse by Morgan).

There is no mention of his assassination or death on the reverse.

1901 William McKinley Presidential Memorial Medal (obverse by Barber, reverse by Morgan).

This medal gives the dates of his assassination and death on the reverse.

1901 Theodore Roosevelt Presidential First Term Medal (obverse by Barber, reverse by Morgan).

1901 Theodore Roosevelt Presidential First Term Medal.

This medal has an experimental finish.

1905 Theodore Roosevelt Presidential Medal (obverse by Barber, reverse by Morgan).

This was struck by the Mint, and it is not the Inaugural Medal by the same artists struck by Davison's, see Miscellaneous Medals.

1909 William Howard Taft Presidential Medal (obverse by Barber, reverse by Morgan).

Secretaries of the Treasury Medals

1890 William Windom Medal. [Julian MT-25]

1891 William Windom Medal. [Julian MT-26]

1893 John Griffin Carlisle Medal.

1897 Lyman J. Gage Medal.

1902 Leslie M. Shaw Medal.

Mint Directors Medals

1885 Horatio Chapin Burchard Medal. [Julian MT-7]

1886 James Putnam Kimball Medal. [Julian MT-8]

1890 Edward Owen Leech Medal. [Julian MT-9]

1880 Archibald Loudon Snowden Medal (obverse designed by Joseph Alexis Bailly, engraved by Barber; reverse probably by Barber). [Julian MT-12]

1880 Archibald Loudon Snowden Medal (obverse by Barber, reverse by Anthony C. Paquet). [Julian MT-13]

1880 Archibald Loudon Snowden Medal. [Julian MT-14]

1880 Archibald Loudon Snowden Medal (obverse by Barber, reverse by Anthony C. Paquet). [Julian MT-15]

1886 Daniel Miller Fox Medal. [Julian MT-16]

1890 William Windom Medal. [Julian MT-25]

1891 William Windom Medal. [Julian MT-26]

1893 Robert E. Preston Medal.

1898 George Evan Roberts Medal.

United States Mint Superintendents Series

1894 Eugene Townsend Superintendent Philadelphia Mint Medal.

1895 Herman Kretz Superintendent Philadelphia Mint Medal.

United States Naval Victory Series, New Dies

1818 Stephen Cassin Medal (original dies by Moritz Fürst; reverse replacement die engraved by Charles E. Barber).

1817 Robert Henley Medal (original dies by Moritz Fürst; reverse replacement die engraved by Charles E. Barber, with the initials C.B.).

1818 Thomas Macdonough (original dies by Moritz Fürst, reverse replacement die engraved by Charles E. Barber in 1878).

Washington Alexandria Masonic National Monument Series

Common George Washington portrait after bust by Pierre Simon Benjamin Duvalier on obverse; reverse by topical device for each of four themes; all engraved by Barber. Struck at the Philadelphia Mint.

1902 George Washington. The Farmer Medal.

1902 George Washington. The Fireman Medal.

1902 George Washington. The Mason Medal.

1902 George Washington. The Surveyor Medal.

Miscellaneous Medals

1871 John Cleveland Robinson Medal. [Julian PE-28]

1873 Buffalo Schools Jesse Ketchum Medal (designed by Lars Gustaf Sellstedt, engraved by Charles E. Barber and William Barber). [Julian SC-15]

[Circa] 1874 Vessel Owners and Captains Association of Philadelphia medal.

1875 American Medical Association Nathan Smith Davis Medal (signed by both William and Charles E. Barber).

1875 Henry Draper Venus Transit Medal. [Julian PE-9]

1875 William Henry Furness Pastorate 50th Anniversary Medal.

1875 John Horn Congressional Lifesaving Medal. [Julian LS-14]

1875 Steamer Metis Congressional Lifesaving Medal (engraved by both Charles E. Barber and William Barber). [Julian LS-15]

1876 Knights of Pythias American Centennial Medal (unknown if Charles E. or William Barber engraved this medal; H. Joseph Levine attributes it to William).

1879 Army of the Cumberland Society Medalet (engraved by Barber, struck by Peter L. Krider). [Julian UN-2]

1879 Joseph Henry Medal (by both Charles and William Barber). [Julian PE-14]

This medal was reissued in 1967.

1879 Philadelphia Kennel Club Medal.

This medal was issued from 1879 to 1884.

1880 William Barber Chief Engraver Medal. [Julian MT-19]

1881 National Fair Association Medal.

This medal was struck by the Mint and issued during 1881 and 1882.

1881 National Fair Association Medal.

R.W. Julian states that this variety may not have been struck by the Mint. This medal was issued in 1881 and possibly later.

1882 Pennsylvania Bicentennial U.S. Mint Medal (Type II).

1882 Washington and Lee University Orators Medal (based on awards first made by the university in 1838; this medal issued from 1882 to 1921). Engraved by Barber; struck by the Mint. [Julian SC-66]

1883 Bethany Sabbath School Philadelphia 25th Anniversary Medal. Charles E. Barber sunk the dies using a Washington portrait engraved by his father, William, for the 1876 Assay Commission medal.

1883 Johns Hopkins University James Joseph Sylvester Medal.

1883 Augustus William Hoffman Medal.

1883 National Exposition of Railway Appliances Chicago Medal (by Barber and Morgan).

1884 Toronto Semi-Centennial Medal. [Julian CM-47]

1886 Statue of Liberty Medal (also called Liberty Enlightening the World Statue Medal).

1887 Henry Ward Beecher Medal.

1887 Washington Ninth International Medical Congress Medal.

1888 Spring Garden Institute Medal (portrait of John Baird).

1888 Spring Garden Institute Medal (allegorical female).

1889 Joseph Francis Congressional Lifesaving Medallion (designed by Zeleima Bruff Jackson, modeled by Louis Saint-Gaudens, reduced and retouched by Barber).

1891 Washington and Lee University Medal.

1892 Columbian Exposition Pattern Galvanos (obverse by Augustus Saint-Gaudens, reverse by Barber).

1892 Columbian Exposition Medal (obverse by Augustus Saint-Gaudens, reverse by Charles E. Barber).

The dies were made at Philadelphia Mint, and the medals were struck by the Scovill firm of Waterbury, Connecticut. The medal was made in 1894.

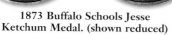

1873 Buffalo Schools Jesse Ketchum Medal. (shown reduced)

1892 Columbian Exposition Medal. (shown reduced)

1892 M. Richards Muckle 50th Anniversary with the Philadelphia Public Ledger Medal.

This medal was struck outside U.S. Mint.

1892 Washington & Lee University Cincinnati Orators Peace Medal.

1892 Wharton Street Methodist Episcopal Church Medal.

1894 Onondaga County New York Centennial Medal.

[Circa]1895 Philadelphia College of Pharmacy William Webb Medal.

1897 Tennessee Centennial Exposition Nashville Medal.

This medal was struck at the Mint exhibit on the exposition grounds.

1900 Cardenas Congressional Medal.

This is also called the Hudson Crew Lifesaving Medal.

1900 Russell H. Conwell Medal (attributed to Barber by J. Joseph Levine).

1900 National Capitol Centennial Relic Medal (designed by William Van Wickle, engraved by Barber).

Van Wckle served as the head of a 142-member design committee. Barber was a committee member. This medal was struck by Joseph K. Davison for R. Harris & Co, Washington, D.C., from metal from the Capitol.

1900 National Capitol Centennial Medal (same dies by Van Wickle and Barber).

These medals were made in gold and silver and were struck by the Philadelphia Mint.

1905 Denver Mint Opening Medal.

1905 Theodore Roosevelt Inaugural Medal (obverse by Barber, reverse by Morgan).

Roosevelt spurned this medal and privately commissioned Augustus Saint-Gaudens to make another version, a well-known imbroglio.

1906 Pike's Peak Discovery Centennial Medal.[4]

1907 Jamestown Tercentennial Exposition Medal (by Morgan with the assistance of Barber; struck on the exposition grounds).

1907 Atlantic Squadron World Cruise Plaquette (obverse by Barber, reverse by Morgan).

This is also called the Hampton Roads Plaquette or the Great White Fleet Medal.

1909 American Red Cross Medal.

1909 Commercial Commission of Japan United States Visit Medal (obverse portrait of William Howard Taft by Barber).

1913 Officers and Crew of S.S. Kroonland for Rescue of Survivors of the Volturno Medal.

1915 Panama-California Exposition Medal (designed by C.K. Berryman, engraved by Barber).

This was a relatively minor event held in San Diego the same year the Panama-Pacific International Exposition was held in San Francisco.

1915 Pan American Financial Conference Woodrow Wilson Medal.

Mint List Medals

Medals, many from new dies reproducing old motifs, on the Mint's list of medals for sale. These were available for sale to the general public. A number of them are also listed in the categories above.

1790 Washington Before Boston Medal (original by DuVivier; the fourth restrike [second U.S. restrike] is from new dies by Barber).

1818 Thomas Macdonough Naval Victory Medal (original dies by Moritz Fürst; reverse replacement die engraved by Charles E. Barber, with the initials C.B.).

Barber reproduced the reverse around 1878.

1818 Stephen Cassin Naval Victory Medal (original dies by Moritz Fürst; reverse replacement die engraved by Charles E. Barber, with the initials C.B.). [Julian NA-18]

Barber reproduced the reverse around 1878.

1818 Robert Henley Naval Victory Medal original dies by Moritz Fürst; reverse replacement die engraved by Charles E. Barber, with the initials C.B.).

Barber reproduced the reverse around 1878.

1875 John Horn Congressional Lifesaving Medal.

1875 Steamer Metis Congressional Lifesaving Medal (Charles E. Barber and William Barber). [Julian LS-15]

1905 Theodore Roosevelt Inaugural Medal. (shown reduced)

1906 Pike's Peak Discovery Centennial Medal. (shown reduced)

1879 Ulysses S. Grant Presidential Medal (by Charles E. Barber and William Barber). [Julian PR-15]

Dated 1869 or 1873, the medal was first struck in 1879 from new dies commemorating Grant's first and second terms.

1882 James Garfield Presidential Medal. [Julian PR-20]

1882 United States Great Seal Centennial Medal.

1889 Joseph Francis Congressional Lifesaving Medallion (by Zeleima Bruff Jackson, Louis Saint-Gaudens; reduced & retouched by Charles E. Barber). [Julian LS-13]

1889 Benjamin Harrison Medal (obverse by Barber, reverse by Morgan). [Julian IP-47]

This medal is an oval.

1891 William Windom Medal. [Julian MT-26]

1901 McKinley Memorial Medal.

1905 Theodore Roosevelt Second Term Presidential Medal (obverse by Barber, reverse by Morgan).

1909 William Howard Taft Presidential Medal (obverse by Barber, reverse by Morgan).

1909 Wright Brothers Plaquette (obverse by Barber, reverse by Morgan; the motif is a copy of an earlier medal by Victor Brenner, now with the positions of the Wright brothers changed).

1885 Horatio Chapin Burchard Medal. [Julian MT-7]

1886 James Putnam Kimball Medal. [Julian MT-8]

1890 Leech Edward Owen Medal. [Julian MT-9]

Replicas and Reissues

1876 United States Diplomatic Medal (original dies were by Augustin Dupré, and the medals were struck by Paris Mint; replicated by Barber in 1876, signed C. Barber).

1879 Joseph Henry Medal (by Charles E. Barber and William Barber).

This medal was reissued in 1967 by the Smithsonian Institution.

1884 Statue of Liberty Medal.

This medal was reissued by Medallic Art.

1893 Columbian Exposition Emmerich Prize Medal (obverse by Saint-Gaudens, reverse by Barber, advertising copy of prize medal won by Emmerich & Co.).

Decorations

1894 Sampson Medal (obverse by Barber, reverse by Morgan).

1898 West Indian Naval Campaign Medal (obverse by Barber, reverse by Morgan).

Relief

[Circa.] 1892 Grover Cleveland cast plaque (a different portrait from Charles E. Barber's presidential medal).

1818 Stephen Cassin Naval Victory Medal.
(shown actual size)

APPENDIX II

THE STORY OF THE 1894-S DIME

NOTES CONCERNING COINAGE

The 1894-S dime is the most famous and most rare coin in the entire Barber series. Although 10 pairs of dies were sent from Philadelphia to the San Francisco Mint for coining these, the only production was a short run of 24 coins on June 9, 1894, using just one die pair. Coins struck from this pair were prooflike in appearance, but they were not mirror Proofs in the style that would have been made for the numismatic trade. Nevertheless, in later years, collectors and dealers often described them as such.

Of the 24 1894-S dimes struck, five were submitted for assay. On June 9, the day of the coinage, two coins were sent to the director of the Mint in Washington to be assayed, which was done soon afterward. On June 25, two dimes are listed as part of the coins assayed by the San Francisco Mint during the month of June 1894. Another specimen was sent on June 28 to the superintendent of the Philadelphia Mint to be reserved for the annual Assay Commission to review coinage of 1894 early in the next year. No other orders for coinage were forthcoming, so the mintage for that year remained at just two dozen coins and the net distribution was just 19 coins.

The *Annual Report of the Director of the Mint,* dated November 24, 1894, covered the fiscal year that began on July 1, 1893, and ended on June 30, 1894. The production of dimes for that period was 1,491,425 pieces total. The *Annual Report of the Director of the Mint* for the next year, 1895, gave calendar year figures for 1894, including the production of just 24 dimes.[1]

AN EARLY ARTICLE

The *San Francisco Call* published this on August 25, 1895, by which time the dime had a recognized value:

> Whoever has a dime of 1894, coined by the San Francisco Mint, has a coin for which $5 has already been offered, and when all the facts are known regarding its scarcity it is not unlikely that it will command a much higher premium.
>
> Inquiry at the mint elicited the information that during the fiscal year of 1894 only twenty-four dimes were coined at the San Francisco Mint. How this came about was told by Chief Clerk Robert Barnett.
>
> "All undercurrent subsidiary coins, viz., those containing other than the design now being used when received at the sub-treasury, are not again allowed to go into circulation, but are sent to the mint to be recoined with the current design. In the course of the year 1894 we received a large sum in these coins, but having an ample stock of dimes on hand, it was not intended to coin any of that denomination in 1894.

However, when nearly all of this subsidiary coin bullion had been utilized, we found on our hands a quantity that would to advantage only into dimes and into dimes it was coined, making just twenty-four of them.

"My intention was first drawn to the matter particularly by the receipt of a letter from a collector somewhere East requesting a set of the coin 1894. In filling this order I found there were no dimes of that date on hand. Subsequently I received quite a number of similar letters, and in each case was, of course, unable to furnish the dimes.

"Plenty of dimes were coined that year at Philadelphia and New Orleans mints, but there are many collectors who accumulate the coinage of each mint, as each has its distinguishing mark. Those coined here bear a letter 'S' under the eagle. New Orleans used the letter 'O' and Carson City the letter 'C', while Philadelphia coins are identified by the absence of the letter.

"We receive each year about fifty requests from coin collectors for coins, mostly for those of silver."[2]

The Most Likely Explanation

Various accounts as to why only 24 were made have been printed over a long period of time, including the following. Farran Zerbe, who at the turn of the century was just beginning to travel around the United States to visit mints and collectors, claimed to have much information on the 1894-S dime and also the mysterious 1873-S, Liberty Seated, dollar (no example of which is known today). Years later, in "Two Extreme Rarities in Recent U.S. Coinage," in the April 1928 issue of *The Numismatist*, Zerbe discussed the 1913, Liberty Head, nickel and the 1894-S dime. Concerning the 1894-S dime:

> To close a bullion account at the end of the fiscal year, June 30, 1894, it was found necessary to show 40 cents, off in the year's coinage. The mint not having coined any dimes during the year, the dime dies were put to work, and to produce the needed 40 cents, 24 pieces were struck, any reasonable amount of even dollars over the 40 cents being readily absorbed in the account.
>
> It has been stated that at the time no thought was given by the mint people that a rarity had been produced, it being supposed that they would, as always in the past, be ordered to coin dimes before the close of the year. It so happened that no dime coinage was ordered, and the unintentional error was not realized until the year's coinage record was closed.
>
> It is said that two or three of the pieces were obtained by Mint people at the time of coinage, 'just to have a new dime,' and following the disclosure of rarity these were sold to collectors for $25 or more apiece. Except for these two or three pieces the coinage is said to have gone into a bag with other dimes and is supposed to have passed from the mint for circulation. . . . My information about the limited coinage was obtained at the San Francisco Mint in 1905.[3]

Frank C. Berdan's Account

Another explanation was given a good deal of attention because it was backed up by an employee from the San Francisco Mint, Frank C. Berdan. In the early 1900s Edgar H. Adams wrote a column on numismatics for the New York *Sun*. This was very popular, and excerpts from it were widely copied without credit by other newspapers. His column of March 29, 1908, was titled "Few Finds of Rare Coins" and included this:

There are right now in active circulation several issues of United States coins which if found by the average citizen would make the time he spends in glancing through his change profitable.

One of these is the United States dime dated 1894 that was struck at the branch mint in San Francisco. This coin bears on the reverse the little mint letter 'S' to distinguish it from all the other ten cent pieces of the year. Yet while the rest of the dimes exist in considerable numbers and are worth but their face value, the San Francisco dime would easily bring $50.

The available information regarding the coin shows that but twenty-four of the denomination were made in 1894. This figure is only an estimate, for the actual number does not appear in the records. That so few were coined was due to a peculiar circumstance.

Weigher [Frank C.] Berdan, now in the coiner's department of the San Francisco Mint, says that in July 1894 an order for $100,000 worth of silver coins had been completed and was ready for delivery. In order to provide specimens for assay purposes, the law requiring that a certain number of pieces from each melt, or order, be forward to the Mint headquarters for the purposes of annual assay, Mr. Berdan had the coining department strike a number of pieces from the dime dies.

He says there may have been twenty-four of these and there may have been less, probably not over twenty, as the matter of counting them was not deemed to be of importance. Two or three pieces in fact, he said, would have answered the requirements just as well.

He took a couple of ordinary dimes from his pocket and exchanged them for two of the new ten cent pieces merely from a desire to possess the first specimens that had come from the dies of this denomination for the year. He said that the idea of the dimes ever becoming scarce never entered his mind, for an order for 100,000 pieces might be expected any day, and no one would have imagined that the entire year would pass without the dies again being brought into requisition.

Yet 1894 did pass without any more coins of the denomination being struck there, and the only dimes dated 1894 and showing the 'S' mint mark were the two pieces referred to, which afterward fell into the hands of a well-known mint mark collector. The remainder of the pieces are right at the present moment passing from hand to hand, their temporary owners not being aware of their value to a coin collector.

The above would seem to indicate that no other San Francisco Mint officials obtained any at the time.

Explanations, Factual and Fictional

Various unsupported theories as to why only 24 examples were made have been printed over the years. It is said that Mint employees received some and that others were placed into circulation at face value. One possible reason for making just 24 1894-S dimes was for "testing the dies" (this supposition is another posed by from Farran Zerbe's article, "Two Extreme Rarities in Recent U.S. Coinage," referenced in part on page 355).

The Numismatic Scrapbook Magazine, February 1951, included this story:

Two 1894-S Dimes Sold

Wm. F. Bailey of San Francisco forwarded a newspaper clipping telling of the sale, by a non-collector, of two specimens of the 1894-S dime (24 were minted).

According to the story, back in 1894, a banker in Ukiah gave three dimes to his little daughter and told her to save them as they would someday be valuable. Recently

> the Ukiah woman sold two of them for $2,750.00 each. She looked high and low for the third specimen, but finally remembered that it was a hot day in 1894 when her father gave her those dimes and she visited an ice cream parlor on the way home.

Kevin Flynn told the latest theory in *The 1894-S Dime: A Mystery Unraveled*, 2005:

> In September 1972, James Johnson wrote an article in *Coin World* under Collectors' Clearinghouse attempting a complete accounting of the 1894-S story and including all known specimens.[4] In response to Mr. Johnson's article, Guy Chapman of California wrote a letter stating that Earl Parker brought the two 1894-S dimes to the Redwood Empire Coin Club in 1954 to sell.
>
> Mr. Parker told Mr. Chapman that the two dimes were purchased from Hallie Daggett, daughter of the Superintendent of the San Francisco Mint, in 1894. Chapman stated that Mr. Parker had told him that Hallie Daggett said the 24 dimes were struck in 1894 when a banker friend of her father's found there would be no dimes struck that year. So he asked Daggett to make some pieces especially for a small group of friends. There were 24 struck, and 8 people got 3, including Daggett. Daggett had given three to his daughter Hallie, one of which she spent on the way home on ice cream. John Daggett told his daughter to save the coins until she was his age and that someday the coins would be valuable. This theory has been widely accepted until now as to why the 24 1894-S dimes were struck.

The ever-inventive Walter Breen, in his *Complete Encyclopedia of U.S. and Colonial Coins*, swallowed the Earl Parker story. Breen went on to comment:

> Each of eight persons received three; Daggett gave his three to his daughter Hallie, telling her to put them away until she was as old as he was, at which time she would be able to sell them for a good price. On the way home the child supposedly spent one for a dish of ice cream, but kept the other two until 1954, when she sold them to coin dealer Earl Parker. . . .

It seems that closing a bullion account was the real reason. As noted earlier, the testing of the dies and the Daggett distribution have no backing.[5]

Early Numismatic Interest

In 1894 there were relatively few numismatists who collected coins from the branch mints. Although Augustus G. Heaton's *Mint Marks*, published the year before, enjoyed wide sales, the concept did not catch on widely until years later. Those who did collect mintmarked issues in 1894 did so from coins in circulation.

Among the exceptions was John M. Clapp, a Pennsylvania oil man, Washington, D.C., financier, and enthusiastic numismatist, who—in 1893—began ordering coins directly from each mint, including examples from the gold denominations. Although some collectors ordered silver coins from the branches, no record has been located of anyone other than Clapp seeking gold. On November 2, 1894, he wrote to San Francisco to order one example of each coin. Acting Superintendent Robert Barnett[6] replied on November 9, stating, "We have no coinage dimes 1894," and that the $10 eagles minted that year were in a sealed vault and would not be available until prior eagles on hand had been paid out.

During 1894 several others had written or sent orders for 1894-S dimes. George Evenson of Denver, Colorado, wrote on July 14 to order one each of the silver coins and was told by Barnett, "I have no dimes coined in 1894." This would seem to indicate that by autumn there were no 1894-S dimes on hand at the mint. If some employees had examples, this was not mentioned. It also gave no indication that coinage was expected.

Eugene B. Stevens, cashier of the First National Bank of Parsons, Kansas, charter no. 1951, sent a request which was answered by Barnett on October 29, 1894: "In reply to your favor 15th inst. I will respectfully say we have no dimes mintage 1894. In accordance with your suggestion I smiled." This would seem to imply that Barnett knew much and was aware of the numismatic significance of such dimes.[7]

On October 30, 1894, Augustus G. Heaton wrote from Washington and was told by Barnett, "We have no 10 cent pieces coinage 1894." Heaton communicated this to George F. Heath, editor of *The Numismatist*, who reported in the November issue that no 1894-S dimes had been coined. On November 28, H.M. Ensminger of Center Square, Pennsylvania, wrote to order silver coins of the year. Barnett furnished the others and stated, "We have no dimes coinage 1894." The most persistent applicant was Peter Mougey of Cincinnati, who first wrote on January 16 and was told, "I have no dimes of 94." Mougey sent other requests and on April 25, July 18, and November 8 was mailed similar replies from Barnett.[8] Other inquiries from various correspondents were answered in a similar manner in 1895.[9]

THE 1894-S DIME PUBLICIZED IN 1900

The earliest numismatic notice of the 1894-S dime seen by the author appeared in the March 1900 issue of *The Numismatist*, when Heaton updated his 1893 *Mint Marks* with an article, "Late Coinage of the United States Mint." He noted this:

> The San Francisco Mint takes proudly to itself the sensation of later U.S. coinage in striking but $2.40 worth of dimes, or *24 pieces* in all, in the year 1894. Of these, the writer possesses *the only one known* to the numismatic world.

At the very least, this suggests that by very early 1900 Heaton was not aware of any examples in private collections. It also suggest that the San Francisco Mint was proud of its accomplishment in creating such a rarity and gave details to Heaton, but they did not indicate that the locations of any other examples were known. Heaton told no more. As a follow-up to this article, George F. Heath, editor of *The Numismatist*, stated:

> J.C. Mitchelson of Kansas City, who has been spending much time in San Francisco, writes that he has uncovered an 1894-S dime. Mint authorities there informed him that while 24 were originally struck, only 14 went into circulation, the remaining 10 were restruck.[10] None remain in circulation.

John M. Clapp, who had unsuccessfully sought a dime from the San Francisco Mint in 1894, continued to build his collection until his passing in 1906, after which it was inherited and expanded by his son, John H. Clapp. The entries of the elder John in his notebook indicate that two specimens of the 1894-S dime, both Uncirculated, were in the cabinet by 1900. At least one had been obtained from a San Francisco source, but not from the San Francisco Mint during the year of issue (for such direct purchases were registered separately). When Heaton published notice of his coin in *The Numismatist* in 1900 he was not aware of Clapp's two coins.

He and Clapp knew each other and both resided in Washington, D.C., at the time. In 1901 Heaton sponsored Clapp for membership in the American Numismatic Association. Clapp is not known to have publicized the contents of his collection to anyone, and despite his friendship with Heaton he seems to have remained silent.

In his search for high-quality mintmarked coins from the West, John M. Clapp set up contact with several numismatists in San Francisco, including W.K. Cole, cashier of the San Francisco Mint; W.F. Greany; A. Reimers; Sutro & Co.; and John J. Valentine. This was a most impressive "network" for the time—and would be so even today—and probably resulted in the pair of 1894-S dimes being acquired promptly after local numismatists knew of them, whatever time that might have been.

Accordingly, in 1900 four 1894-S dimes were mentioned: one each in print by Heaton and Mitchelson and two in John M. Clapp's ledger. As weigher Frank C. Berdan later stated that the two he had obtained for face value in June 1894 went to a collector of mint-marked coins, he may have been the source of two of Clapp's coins.

Later Information

Over a number of decades the 1894-S dime was mentioned in print multiple times, and in time it became well known. Howard R. Newcomb, who in later years was to become very prominent on the numismatic scene, wrote an article entitled "Unappreciated Silver Mint Rarities—Dimes." It argued that everyone knew about the famous 1894-S dime as being the rarest in the series, but that other dimes were also deserving of attention, including the 1874-CC, of which Newcomb knew of fewer than a half dozen examples. Of the 1871-CC;1872-CC; and 1873-CC, With Arrows, only the 1871-CC was known to Newcomb in Uncirculated condition. Further, the 1885-S dime was identified as an undervalued issue.[11]

Examples were offered in a number of major auctions during the 20th century. Much was published about them, including estimates of rarity, which were typically given as close to a dozen, perhaps even 13 or 14. William A. Burd's "The Inscrutable 1894-S Dime," published in *The Numismatist*, February 1994, listed all of the examples known to him, two of which are well worn. This was a watershed study in the annals of this coin. In 2005 Kevin Flynn wrote and published *The 1894-S Dime: A Mystery Unraveled*, which contained much information from the San Francisco Mint archives. In 2006 Nancy Oliver and Richard Kelly, specialists in San Francisco Mint History, published new findings in *Coin World*.

The 1894-S dime has been a personal favorite of the present author ever since I acquired (via James F. Ruddy, who was commissioned to bid on it for me) the Charles A. Cass ("Empire") coin sold by Stack's in 1957, with Morton Stack at the auction podium. This piece later went into the collection of Emery May Holden Norweb, thus leading to a long-term friendship between myself and the Norweb family.

Registry of 1894-S Dimes

The following registry follows the sequence given by William A. Burd's aforementioned article (to which refer for details of the various coins), cross-referenced to David Lawrence's *Complete Guide to Barber Dimes*.[12] Burd's No. 5 and No. 7 are now known to be the same coin, and consequently I have delisted Burd-7.

No. 1: Newcomer Example • Burd-1; Lawrence-1. • Proof-60.

- Waldo C. Newcomer consigned this example, along with his entire collection, to B. Max Mehl in 1932. Mehl sold the coin for $1,000.
- Numismatic Gallery's sale of the F.C.C. Boyd "World's Greatest Collection," 1945, sold this coin as lot 756, for $2,350, to the Will W. Neil.

- B. Max Mehl's sale of the Will W. Neil Collection 1947, sold this coin as lot 1433, for $2,325, to Edwin Hydeman.
- Abe Kosoff's sale of the Edwin Hydeman Collection, 1961, sold this coin as lot 337, to Q. David Bowers for $13,000.
- The coin was next owned by Hazen B. and Buol Hinman, of Rome, New York.
- Paramount International Coin Co.'s sale of the Century (Hinman) Collection, 1965, sold this coin for $12,250.
- RARCOA's sale of the Leo A. Young Collection, 1980, sold this coin as lot 1578, for $145,000.
- Pacific Coast Auctions (Ron Gillio), 1986, sold this coin as lot 110, $91,300.

No. 2: First Clapp Example • B-2; L-2. • Gem Proof.

- This coin came into the J.M. Clapp Collection circa 1900, in 1906 it was inherited by John H, Clapp.
- John H. Clapp sold the coin as part of the Clapp estate through Stack's to Louis E. Eliasberg in 1942.
- In 1976 it was inherited by Richard A. Eliasberg.
- Richard A. Eliasberg consigned it to Bowers & Merena Galleries' sale of the Eliasberg Collection, 1996, where it sold as lot 1250, for $451,000.

No. 3: Second Clapp Example • B-3; L-3. • Gem Proof.

- This coin came into the J.M. Clapp Collection circa 1900, in 1906 it was inherited by John H, Clapp.
- John H. Clapp sold the coin as part of the Clapp estate through Stack's to Louis E. Eliasberg in 1942.
- It sold in the Stack's sale of the H.R. Lee Collection (which was composed of Eliasberg duplicates), 1947, as lot 348, for $2,150.
- It was next owned by James Aloysius Stack (no kin to the auctioneers), of Plandome, New York.
- In Stack's sale of the James A. Stack Collection, 1990, this coin sold as lot 206, for $275,000 to Armen Vartian, who was and agent for David "D."
- Jay Parrino, 1990,sold the coin for about $450,000, to DLRC.
- DLRC had purchased the coin to sell to Bradley Hirst of Indiana, as part of the "Richmond Collection," in 1998, for $825,000.
- The coin was sold along with the Richmond-Hirst Collection, to DLRC, in 2005.
- It was sold again in a private sale, in July 2007, for $1,900,000.
- It was next sold by John Albanese to a client.

No. 4: First Ukiah Example • B-4; L-5. • Gem Proof. Variously certified by PCGS as Proof–64 and 65 and by NGC as Proof–65 and 66.

- This example was sold by a lady from Ukiah, California, for $2,750 to San Francisco dealer Earl Parker, circa 1949, but the sale was not revealed until 1951.
- Earl Parker, who later claimed he bought this and another from Hallie Daggett, daughter of 1894 Mint Director John Daggett, Parker sold the two coins in 1954.
- The coin was then handled by unknown intermediaries, W.R. Johnson is the next recorded owner.
- Bowers and Ruddy Galleries, in 1974, *Rare Coin Review* No. 21, listed the sale of the coin at $97,500, to the Robert Delande, a Chicago dealer.
- Delande consigned it to Superior Galleries.
- Superior Galleries sale of August 1992, sold the coin as lot 104, $165,000, to Dwight N. Manley, president of Spectrum Numismatics.
- The next recored sale was by Kevin Lipton to John Feigenbaum and David Schweiz.
- Heritage Auction's January 2005 sale sold the coin for $1,035,000.

- The coin was next found in the Robert Simpson Collection.

No. 5: Second Ukiah Example • B-5 and B-7; L-6 and L-8. • Proof-60. There is a small rough area on the lower reverse.

- This example was sold by a lady from Ukiah, California, for $2,750 to San Francisco dealer Earl Parker, circa 1949, but the sale was not revealed until 1951.
- Earl Parker, who later claimed he bought this and another from Hallie Daggett, daughter of 1894 Mint Director John Daggett, Parker sold the two coins in 1954. This example was sold to James F. Kelly.
- The next recorded owner is Malcolm O.E. Chell-Frost.
- The coin was sold Stack's sale of the Fred S. Guggenheimer Collection, 1953, as lot 772, for $2,100.
- Abner Kreisberg next possessed the coin.
- Empire Coin Co. held the coin after that.
- The coin was a part of the Abraham J. Kaufman Collection.
- It passed from the Abraham J. Kaufman Collection to Joyce M. Kaufman.
- Kagin's 1973 Middle Atlantic Numismatic Association sale, sold the coin as lot 1114, for $52,000.
- Superior Galleries sale of the Jerry Buss Collection, 1985, sold the coin as lot 617, for $50,600, to Michelle Johnson acting on behalf of Robert Beaumont.
- It sold again in a Superior Galleries sale of 1988, for $70,400.

No. 6: Empire Example • B-6; L-7. • Choice Proof.

- Stack's sale of the Empire Collection (Charles A. Cass), 1957, sold this coin as lot 881, for $4,750, to James F. Ruddy, who acted as an agent for Q. David Bowers.
- Bowers sold it in 1958 for $6,000 to Ambassador R. Henry Norweb as a gift for his wife, Emery May Holden Norweb.
- Bowers & Merena Galleries Sale of the Norweb Collection, 1987, sold this coin as lot 584, for $77,000, to Allen Lovejoy.
- Stack's 55th Anniversary Sale, 1991, sold the coin as lot 504, for $93,000 to Jeffrey Bernberg.

No. 7: Friedberg Example • B-8; L-9. • G-4. This is popularly known as the "Ice cream specimen" that may have been spent on ice cream by the young girl who, as an adult in Ukiah, California, sold two Mint State coins to Earl Parker in the late 1940s.

- This coin was bought over the counter by Robert Friedberg in 1957.
- Arthur M. Kagin, consigned it to New Netherlands Coin Co.
- New Netherlands Coin Co. sold the coin in their sale of June 1958 as lot 581, for $3,200.
- In the Harmer-Rooke sale of November 1969, the coin sold as lot 1038, for $7,400, to James G. Johnson, a *Coin World* writer who had studied the history of the 1894-S dime.
- Steve Ivy sold it in the ANA Sale, 1980, as lot 1804, for $31,000, to the Numismatic Funding Corporation.
- It sold again in the Bowers and Ruddy Galleries ANA Sale, 1981, as lot 2921, for $25,500.
- Bowers and Ruddy Galleries sold it again in the Four Landmark Collections sale, 1989, as lot 191, for $33,000.

No. 8: Romito-Montesano Example • B-9; L-10. • AG-3, certified by NGC.

- Romito-Montesano example.[13]
- Laura Sperber to private client.

An Unclassified Example

The Charles M. Williams Collection 1894-S dime was sold by Numismatic Gallery in the "Adolphe Menjou Collection" sale in 1950. Menjou, a film actor, consigned some coins to the sale and allowed his name to be used. Numismatic Gallery had purchased the Williams Collection and was under a non-disclosure agreement at the time. It is not known if the Williams coin is a 9th example or if it is one of those listed above, perhaps No. 6.

APPENDIX III

Mints for the Barber Coinage

Overview of the United States Mints

Of the eight mints that have struck United States coins over the years, only four were used for Barber coinage. Extended descriptions of those follow; for the others, see below.

The Charlotte Mint opened in Charlotte, North Carolina, in 1838 and continued coinage until the Civil War in 1861, at which time the mint closed. Charlotte coins are identified by the mintmark C. All coins struck at Charlotte are either scarce or rare today.

The Dahlonega Mint was located in Dahlonega, Georgia, and operated during the same time span as the Charlotte Mint. Dahlonega coins have the mintmark D, not to be confused with the same mintmark later used for Denver coins—the Dahlonega Mint closed before the Denver Mint opened. All Dahlonega gold coins are either scarce or rare, and as a class they are more elusive than their Charlotte Mint counterparts.

The Carson City Mint opened in 1870 in Carson City, Nevada, to take advantage of silver and gold mined in the Comstock Lode. It produced coins which were used in the same region as the coins produced by the San Francisco Mint, and while the Bland-Allison Act increased the number of coins minted at the Carson City Mint, few were put into circulation. The mint ceased coining part way through 1885; then it opened again in 1889 and closed forever in 1893.

The West Point Mint was introduced in 1984 as a special minting facility located at West Point, New York (home of the Military Academy). It has produced certain gold commemorative coins, silver and gold bullion coins, and some other issues. The distinguishing mintmark W characterizes these pieces.

Denver Mint

The Denver Mint had its origin on April 21, 1862, when the Treasury Department bought the minting and assaying business of Clark, Gruber & Co. in Denver. They renamed the facility the Denver Mint, a title that afterward appeared in all *Annual Reports of the Director of the Mint.* However, that Denver Mint acted only as an assay office and depository. No coins were ever struck there.

On February 20, 1895, an act was passed to establish a new mint in Denver. The act was followed by legislation on March 2, 1895, authorizing the necessary expenses, including a site for $100,000 and a building not to exceed $500,000. A site was purchased for $60,261.61 on April 22, 1896. By the time it was completed, the cost of the building had mounted to $800,228.01.

The building was ready in 1904. Machinery costing $345,055 was subsequently installed. In 1905 three coinage presses were installed. A test run of $20-size copper tokens was made.

The *Denver Rocky Mountain News*, December 29, 1905, printed this:

> El Paso, Tex. Dec. 28. The police today found $500 in new dimes in a sack in a saloon in Mexico, where the bartender said that Louis Gonzales had left them. Gonzales was arrested yesterday on having robbed an express car in La Junta, Colo., when over $2,000 in dimes was stolen. He admits that he is from Colorado and says he worked on a sugar plantation at Lamar.

The same paper published this on January 4, 1906:

> Austin, Tex. Jan. 3. Sheriff John D. Brown of Bent County, Colo., was here today and obtained requisition papers from Governor Lanham for the return to Colorado of Louis Gonzales, a Mexican who is charged with stealing $1,000 in silver dimes of the first coinage of the Denver Mint, following the wrecking of a Santa Fe passenger train near Las Animas, Colo. recently. The money was being transported by Wells Fargo Express, and Gonzales was one of the section men sent to the scene of the accident to clear away the wreckage. He found the bags of silver dimes and disappeared. He was arrested at El Paso where he is now in jail.

As the Denver Mint had not started coining dimes by December 1905 it is assumed that the dimes, although they may have been shipped from Denver, were not from that mint. The amount of dimes stolen is inconsistent in the accounts.

The Denver Mint officially opened for business on New Year's Day 1906. At 10:59 A.M., Thursday, February 1, 1906, Superintendent F.M. Downer gave a signal, and as part of a public ceremony the first Denver Mint coins were struck. On hand was a crowd who heard commentaries and watched the machinery in motion.[1] Mintage at the event was limited to quarters and half dollars.

On March 16 the John Thompson Grocery Company in Denver ran this notice in *The Daily News* in that city:

> **New Coins from the Denver Mint:** Bright, new, glittering coins from our "home industry," the Denver Mint. Perhaps you would like to have some of them to keep as a memento of the opening of the Mint. To those who desire we will give in change new coins from the Denver Mint—new dimes, new quarters, new half dollars, and new ten-dollar gold pieces—and they are beauties. We will give you the new for the old.

By June 30 (the end of the fiscal year) 560,000 dimes, 195,000 quarters, and 128,000 half dollars had been struck.[2]

Coins produced in Denver bear a D mintmark on the reverse, not to be confused with the D for the Dahlonega Mint used from 1838 to 1861 in a different time period. An addition to the Denver Mint was built in 1936 and occupied in 1937.

The Denver Mint.

New Orleans Mint

The Coinage Act of 1835 provided for three branch mints to be constructed at Charlotte, North Carolina; Dahlonega, Georgia; and New Orleans, Louisiana. The extent of the United States had expanded greatly since the establishment of the Philadelphia Mint in 1792, and it was felt that additional mints would be beneficial. Charlotte and Dahlonega were in gold-mining districts and would be a convenience to that industry in those regions. New Orleans, on the lower Mississippi River, was the center of trade for the Midwest and was the busiest port on the Gulf of Mexico.

The New Orleans Mint was opened in 1838, and from that time until it closed early in the Civil War its mintage consisted of silver and gold coins of all denominations. After passage of the Bland-Allison Act on February 28, 1878, which provided that from two to four million ounces of silver must be purchased by the Treasury Department and coined into dollars, the New Orleans Mint was refurbished to help meet this challenge. It opened in 1879, in which year dollars and double eagles were minted. Silver dollars continued to be made there through 1904, when the denomination was suspended. The only later gold coins were eagles coined there through the early 1900s.

Barber dimes, quarters, and half dollars were made at the New Orleans Mint from 1892 until coinage ceased there forever in 1909, although not all denominations were made for every date. Each coin bore the mintmark O. As noted in the above text, many New Orleans Barber coins were carelessly struck, this being particularly true of the quarters and half dollars.

On April 1, 1909, coinage operations were suspended forever, as production could be accomplished more economically at the other mints.

Philadelphia Mint

In 1792 the government acquired a plot of land and several buildings in Philadelphia and set up the first federal facility for the production of coins. In the meantime, in July of that year, about 1,500 silver half dismes were struck in a private shop using equipment intended for the Mint. The foundation stones for the Mint were laid on July 31. Equipment was moved into the facility starting in September—two of the buildings remaining

The New Orleans Mint in 1906.

from earlier uses. In autumn and early winter of that year, limited numbers of pattern coins were struck there. Copper cents, the first coins made in quantity for general circulation, were issued in March 1793, followed by the first silver coins in 1794, and the first gold coins in 1795.

On July 4, 1829, the cornerstone for the second Philadelphia Mint was laid. A number of silver half dimes were struck for use at the ceremony. In 1832 the new facility opened for operations. In ensuing decades the facility struck coins of many denominations and also supplied dies for the various branches beginning with Charlotte, Dahlonega, and New Orleans in 1838. The Mint also performed assays, storage, and other functions. The Engraving Department created new designs and motifs. Proof coins for presentation and for collectors were struck there from about 1820 onward, with mintages for these specialized products expanding greatly after 1857, when numismatics became a widely popular hobby. The Mint Cabinet, a display initiated in 1838, was a focal point for numismatists. Barber silver patterns were made there in 1891 and coinage of circulation issues commenced in 1892. The last full year of operation was 1900.

On June 13, 1901, a ceremony was held to open the third Philadelphia Mint. By October machinery was in place, other facilities had been installed, and coinage commenced. Coinage of Barber denominations continued until 1916 for dimes and quarters, and until 1915 for half dollars.

The fourth and current Philadelphia Mint was opened in 1967 on Independence Square not far from the Liberty Bell and other historic attractions.

The second Philadelphia Mint in 1880.

The second Philadelphia Mint in 1900.

The third Philadelphia Mint as shown on a 1908 postcard.

The coining room in the third Philadelphia Mint.

San Francisco Mint

The first San Francisco Mint opened in March 1854, in a building that had been slightly expanded after the Treasury purchased it from Curtis, Perry, & Ward, private assayers and minters of gold coins. During the first year gold $1, $2.50, $5, $10, and $20 denominations were struck there. The first silver coins were minted in 1855. Cramped and poorly ventilated, it served its purpose but from the beginning was unsatisfactory in many ways. In time silver coins from the trime to half dollar and gold coins from the dollar to the double eagle were produced.

In 1870 the cornerstone for the second San Francisco Mint was laid. Opened in 1874, it produced exclusively silver and gold coins until the first bronze cents were struck there in 1908 and the first nickel five-cent pieces in 1912. Barber denominations were struck there from 1892 until 1916 for the dime and quarter, and 1915 for the half dollar.

After the earthquake and fire of April 1906, it was the only building left standing in its district. It became the headquarters for security and other government and banking activities while the rubble was cleared and other arrangements were made. In 1913 vaults believed to contain 61,395,000 silver dollars, which had been sealed for more than 30 years, were opened and the dollars counted. "Five bags were found to have been tampered with, 18 coins in all having been abstracted and iron washers substituted therefor."[3]

Gold coins were last struck there in 1930. In addition to federal coins, the Mint also struck coins for Hawaii, Japan, the Philippines, and certain Latin American countries. It also served as a storage depot for large quantities of silver dollars and gold coins. In 1937 the third and current San Francisco Mint was opened on Duboce Street and struck various bronze and silver denominations. After coining cents and dimes in 1955 the Treasury Department discontinued mintage operations. In 1962 it was renamed the San Francisco Assay Office. In the mid-1960s there was a nationwide coin shortage, and planchets were made there to be shipped to the Denver Mint. The Coinage Act of 1965 provided that the coining facilities be reactivated. In 1968 the Assay Office began striking Proof sets—an operation earlier conducted only in Philadelphia. On March 31, 1988, the San Francisco Mint name was officially restored. In recent decades the facility has made commemorative and Proof coins and other special issues as well as selected regular denominations, the last usually in lower quantities than have been made in Denver and Philadelphia.

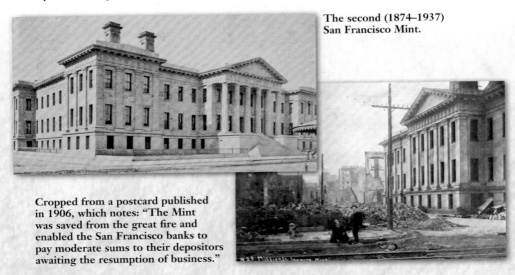

The second (1874–1937) San Francisco Mint.

Cropped from a postcard published in 1906, which notes: "The Mint was saved from the great fire and enabled the San Francisco banks to pay moderate sums to their depositors awaiting the resumption of business."

APPENDIX IV

Mint Directors and Superintendents 1892–1916

Mint Directors

The office of the director of the Mint was located in the Treasury Building in Washington, D.C. The appointment was made by the president of the United States, usually nodding to political considerations. The director was responsible for the Denver, Philadelphia, and San Francisco mints. The superintendents of those facilities reported to him or her. The director reported to the secretary of the Treasury. He or she was often called on by various congressional committees regarding coinage and monetary matters.

There was often a small gap between the term of one director and that of his or her successor. These gaps were filled by an appointed acting director. The Mint's fiscal year ran from July 1 of the first year into June 30 of the second. Most accounts and reports were on a fiscal year basis supplemented by some numbers calculated into calendar years (the last necessary for numismatists interested in mintage figures), such as the number of dies used in a calendar year, and related aspects. *The Annual Report of the Director of the Mint* was compiled by staff after the close of the fiscal year and published months later.

Mint Directors and Terms

Edward O. Leech: October 1889 to May 1893.

Robert E. Preston: November 1893 to February 1898.

George E. Roberts: February 1898 to July 1907.

Frank A. Leach: September 1907 to November 1909.

A. Piatt Andrew: November 1909 to June 1910.

George E. Roberts: July 1910 to November 1914.

Robert W. Wooley: March 1915 to July 1916.

F.H. von Engelken: September 1916 to March 1917.

Mint Superintendents and Terms

Each of the four mints active during the 1892 to 1916 era was under the direction of an appointed superintendent, again the position was usually a reward for good deeds performed for the party in control of Congress or for the president. Superintendents reported to the director of the Mint in Washington, D.C. The superintendent had charge of operations of the mint, including the processing of metal and planchets, coining to meet the requirements requested by the Treasury Department, and all other activities and departments.

The most important superintendency was at the Philadelphia Mint, where the Engraving Department was located and where dies for all three mints were made. The superintendent managed this and corresponded much more frequently with the director than did those of the other two mints. Each year he helped organize the Assay Commission to review the previous year's coinage of precious metals.

Col. Oliver C. Bosbyshell was particularly important in the development of designs for the 1891 patterns and 1892 coinage, working with Chief Engraver Charles E. Barber.

Denver Mint

Frank M. Downer: July 1902 to August 1913.[1]

Thomas Annear: August 1913 to July 1921.

New Orleans Mint

Gabriel Montegut: June 1885 to June 1893.

Overton Cade: July 1893 to 1898.

Charles W. Boothby: July 1898 to 1902.

Hugh S. Sithon: 1902 to 1911; the last coinage of this mint occurred in 1909.

Philadelphia Mint

Col. Oliver C. Bosbyshell: May 1889 to March 1894.

Dr. Eugene Townsend: March 1894 to May 1895.

Major Herman Kretz: May 1895 to January 1898.

Henry Boyer: January 1898 to April 1902.

John H. Landis: April 1902 to July 1914.

Adam M. Joyce: July 1914 to March 1921.

San Francisco Mint

W.H. Diamond: August 1889 to July 1893.

John Daggett: July 1893 to July 1897.

Frank A. Leach: August 1897 to November 1907.[2]

Edward Sweeney: November 1907 to August 1912.[3]

Frank A. Leach (2nd term): August 1912 to August 1913.

Thaddeus W.H. Shanahan: August 1913 to June 1921.

Notes

Chapter 1

1. Certain information is from R.W. Julian, "A Cut Above the Rest," *Coins* magazine, December 1998; other information is from Mint correspondence and contemporary published accounts.

2. *Annual Report of the Director of the Mint*, 1892.

3. It was déjà vu in 1907 when Saint-Gaudens submitted new designs for the double eagle, and Chief Engraver Barber protested that they were in high relief unsuitable for high-speed coinage.

4. R.W. Julian, "A Cut Above the Rest," *Coins* magazine, December 1998.

5. *Ibid.*

6. The clouds appeared on certain patterns but were dropped for the later circulating coins.

7. An allusion to *Aesop's Fables.*

8. Buckle is apparently taken from Petr Alekseevich Kropotkin, *Law and Authority: An Anarchist Essay*, London, 1886.

9. It was popular to liken George T. Morgan's eagle on the reverse of the dollar to a buzzard.

10. The *quadrature of the circle*, or the *squaring of the circle*, is a puzzle suggested by ancient mathematicians, who wished to find a simple rule that allowed them to construct a square with the exact same area of any given circle. Doing so was proved impossible in 1882, a mere decade before this review was written, yet more than three thousand years after the problem was first proposed. The author of this review may or may not have been aware that the ancient riddle had been proven unsolvable.

11. *Boston Herald*, Boston, Massachusetts, January 5, 1892, including a January 4 dispatch from Washington.

12. *Daily Illinois State Journal*, Springfield, Illinois, January 17, 1892.

13. This is taken from an unattributed clipping from "Numismatica Miscellanea," a scrapbook of the era owned by the author.

14. Exchange item in the Rockford, Illinois *Morning Star*, February 26, 1892. Citation furnished by David Sundman.

15. Additional press clippings can be found in Q. David Bowers, *Commemorative Coins of the United States a Complete Encyclopedia*, Bowers & Merena Galleries, 1992.

16. *Liberty Enlightening the World*, a.k.a. *The Statue of Liberty*, dedicated in 1886.

17. Although the World's Columbian Exposition was scheduled to open in 1892, construction delays occurred, and it did not open to the public until the spring of 1893.

18. Cornelius Vermeule, *Numismatic Art in America: Aesthetics of the United States Coinage,2nd edition*, Atlanta: Whitman Publishing, 2007.

19. Adapted from Russell Easterbrooks, "Statistical Die Data," *Journal of the BCCS*, Spring 1998.

20. From *The Annual Report of the Director of the Mint for Fiscal Year 1915* (which included certain 1914 calendar-year figures).

21. From *The Annual Report of the Director of the Mint for Fiscal Year 1915* (which included certain 1914 calendar-year figures).

Chapter 2

1. As cited by David W. Lange, *Journal of the BCCS*, Spring 1996.

2. Tim Glaue, "Barbers from a Fruit Cellar Find," *Journal of the BCCS*, 2014, No. 4.

3. Littleton marketed these as the Subway Hoard.

4. Working data supplied by Don Willis, PCGS president.

5. *The Numismatist*, August 1903.

Chapter 3

1. Later, in 1895, J.M. Walter of New Bethlehem, Pennsylvania, had a supply of these and advertised them for 25¢ each.

2. Various sources including the *Evening Star*, Washington, D.C., May 11, 1895.

3. "A Message from President Hooper," *The Numismatist*, March 1899.

4. Soon after, Elder was offered a position as a personal secretary to a gentleman in Alaska. He declined and returned to Pittsburgh, where he continued to grow his coin business.

5. *The Numismatist*, August 1903.

6. Today they are highly prized and expensive.

7. "The Stickney Sale," *The Numismatist*, July 1907.

8. Some 1909 coins show minute positional differences, as the catolger noted in an offering of the Eliasberg Collection of quarters in 1997.

9. *The Numismatist*, April 1909.

10. The information for 1916 is reprised from the author's book, *A Guide Book of Mercury Dimes, Standing Liberty Quarters, and Liberty Walking Half Dollars 1916–1947*, Atlanta: Whitman Publishing, 2015.

Chapter 4

1. Russell Easterbrooks, "Barber Coinage: Practicality Over Aesthetics," *Rare Coin Review* No. 105.

2. Correspondence with the author, November 26, 2014.

3. Michael S. Fey, "A New 1901-O / Horizontal O Barber Dime," *Journal of the BCCS*, Spring 1999, discusses this variety in detail.

4. Ed Rochette, "The Treasure of the Lost Dimes of Denver!" *Journal of the BCCS*, Summer 1990.

5. *The Numismatist*, December 1909, p. 338.

6. Letter to the author, January 27, 2015.

7. *The Numismatist*, March 1910, p. 93.

8. Russell Easterbrooks, "A Different Barber Dime," *Journal of the BCCS*, Fall 1994.

9. Letter to the author, January 27, 2015.

Chapter 5

1. R.W. Julian, "Barber Design Reigned on Quarters for 25 Years," *Journal of the BCCS*, 2010 No. 4, adapted from his article in *Numismatic News*, September 20, 2005.

2. For a detailed discussion see Steve Hustad, "Barber Quarter Design Varieties," *Journal of the BCCS*, 2011 No. 4.

3. William Cowburn, "Barber Quarter Dollars: Part 3, Mint Mark Positons & Reverse Varieties 1892–1900," *Journal of the BCCS*, 2007 No. 4.

4. These differences were first described in detail by George W. Rice in "United States Quarter Dollar of 1892," *The Numismatist*, May 1899.

5. For a detailed discussion see Steve Hustad, "Barber Quarter Design Varieties," *Journal of the BCCS*, 2011 No. 4.

6. John Frost, in a letter to the author, January 28, 2015.

7. Also, 1904-O and 1905-O are tied at $11.

8. John Frost, in a letter to the author, January 28, 2015.

9. Details on authenticating the 1896-S Barber quarter can be found on the BCCS website, www.barbercoins.org.

10. John Frost, in a letter to the author, January 28, 2015.

11. Letter to the author, January 28, 2015. His comment demonstrates the wisdom of not relying on the grades that are marked on holders.

12. Discovery reported by John A. Wexler, "Major Barber Quarter Doubled Die Discovered," *Journal of the BCCS*, Fall 1997.

13. From research by David W. Lange.

14. John Frost, letter to the author, January 28, 2015.

15. The BCCS website, barbercoins.org, has the diagnostics of the dies used to strike the 1901-S quarter.

16. R.W. Julian, "The Quarter that Might Not Have Been," *Journal of the BCCS*, Spring 1992, adapted from a *COINage* article of 1990.

17. Letter to the author, January 28, 2015.

18. John Frost, in a letter to the author, January 28, 2015.

19. *Ibid.*

20. *Ibid.*

21. Details on authenticating the 1913-S, Barber, quarter can be found on the BCCS website, www.barbercoins.org.

22. Mint State Barber coins by the roll are hardly ever seen. Stack's sale of August 10, 1990, had an original roll of 40 1916-D quarters.

Chapter 6

1. Also the 1914-S is tied at $18.50.

2. John Frost estimates, in a letter to the author, January 30, 2015.

3. *Ibid.*

4. Jack White, "1907-S Barber Coinage," *Journal of the BCCS*, Spring 1999, discusses this coinage in detail.

5. Communication with the author, February 18, 2015.

Appendix I

1. Patterson DuBois, "Our Mint and Engravers," *American Journal of Numismatics*, July 1883, p. 16.

2. R.W. Julian, in a letter to the author, April 24, 1996.

3. For press clippings and contemporary reviews of these commemoratives see Q. David Bowers, *Commemorative Coins of the United States a Complete Encyclopedia*, Bowers & Merena Galleries, 1992.

4. When the First National Bank of Colorado Springs, Colorado, building was razed in August 1955 to make way for another structure, some 4,000 of these medals were found. These were given to the Historical Society of the Pikes Peak Region to help finance the sesquicentennial of 1956. This group enlisted the aid of the Pikes Peak Coin Club to direct the sale.

Appendix II

1. The San Francisco information was supplied by chief coiner A.J. Spotts.

2. This is a reflection of the number of collectors interested in mintmarks by that time, a year after Heaton's *Mint Marks* was published.

3. His source was not identified. The account is similar in some respects to that of Frank C. Berdan below.

4. James Johnson, "Recounts History of Rare 1894-S Dime," *Coin World*, September 13, 1972.

5. Certain information is from Kevin Flynn, in a letter to the author, January 29, 2015, amplifying certain comments in his book on the 1894-S dime.

6. Barnett served as acting superintendent starting on July 18, 1893. Superintendent John Daggett was ill with sciatica.

7. Stevens, born in Michigan in 1857, became cashier of the First National Bank in July 1890. He served as mayor of Parsons from 1895 to 1897.

8. Mougey, ANA member no. 131 (listed in February 1893), lived at 42 York Street in Cincinnati. He died in 1898. His collection was bought intact by William H. Woodin, who extracted desired

gold coins and consigned the rest to Thomas L. Elder, who auctioned them on September 1 to 3, 1910, under the title of *Catalogue of the Forty-Third Public Sale. Magnificent rare Coin Collection of the Late Peter Mougey, Esqr. of Cincinnati, Ohio.*

9. Barnett correspondence excerpts can be found in Kevin Flynn's *The Authoritative Reference on Barber Dimes*, Brooklyn Gallery Coins and Stamps, 2004.

10. This may have meant "melted" or "reserved for assay." The location of the Mitchelson coin is not known today. His collection is preserved by the Connecticut State Library in Hartford.

11. The low-mintage 1885-S, while not a rarity, seems to have been viewed by Newcomb as underpriced.

12. The main sources for these provenances are the author's archives; William A. Burd, "The Inscrutable 1894-S Dime," The Numismatist 1994; Kevin Flynn, *The 1894-S Dime: A Mystery Unraveled*, 2005; Greg Reynolds, "Condition Ranking of 1894-S Dimes with Recent Histories," *Coin Week* 2013.

13. These surnames were published by Walter Breen. Nothing further has been learned about them.

Appendix III

1. Jacob G. Willson, "Denver Mints," *Numismatic Scrapbook*, June 1940.

2. *Annual Report of the Director of the Mint*, 1906; other sources.

3. *Annual Report of the Director of the Mint*, 1913.

Appendix IV

1. As superintendent before the mint opened, Downer helped supervise its construction and outfitting.

2. Resigned his superintendency to become director of the Mint in the same month.

3. Died in office.

Selected Bibliography

Adams, Edgar H., and William H. Woodin. *United States Pattern, Trial and Experimental Pieces.* New York City, NY: American Numismatic Society, 1913.

Ambio, Jeff. *Collecting & Investing Strategies for Barber Dimes.* Irvine, CA: Zyrus Press, 2009.

Bowers, Q. David. *United States Dimes, Quarters, and Half Dollars: An Action Guide for the Collector and Investor.* Wolfeboro, NH: Bowers and Merena Galleries, 1986.

——— "Barbers, a Unique Perspective to Their History, Beauty, and Rarity," *Journal of the Barber Coin Collectors' Society*, Summer 1989.

Many of his books were consulted as well, too numerous to list here.

——— *Liberty Head Double Eagles 1849–1907: The Gilded Age of Coinage.* Wolfeboro, NH: Stack's Bowers Galleries, 2014.

Breen, Walter H. *Walter Breen's Complete Encyclopedia of U.S. and Colonial Coins.* Garden City, NY: F.C.I. Press, Inc., 1988.

Bressett, Kenneth E. (senior editor). *A Guide Book of United States Coins.* Atlanta, GA: Whitman Publishing, various modern editions; earlier editions edited by Richard S. Yeoman.

Burd, William A., "The Inscrutable 1894-S Dime," *The Numismatist*, February 1994.

Coin World Almanac. Sidney, OH: Coin World, 2010.

Coin World. Sidney, OH: Amos Press, 1960 to date.

CoinWeek Internet site, various issues, 2012 to date.

Fivaz, Bill, and J.T. Stanton. *The Cherrypickers' Guide to Rare Die Varieties.* Fourth edition. Atlanta, GA: Whitman Publishing, 2006.

Flynn, Kevin. *The Authoritative Reference on Barber Dimes.* New York City, NY: Brooklyn Gallery, 2004.

——— *The Authoritative Reference on Barber Quarters.* New York City, NY: Brooklyn Gallery, 2005.

——— *The 1894-S Dime: A Mystery Unraveled.* Rancocas, NJ: Published by the author, 2005.

——— *The Authoritative Reference on Barber Half Dollars.* New York City, NY: Brooklyn Gallery, 2005.

Johnson, James G. "Recounts History of Rare 1894-S Dime," *Coin World*, September 13, 1972.

——— "Researching the 1894-S Dime," Wolfeboro, NH: Bowers and Merena Galleries, *Rare Coin Review*, Spring 1987.

Johnson, D. Wayne. "Charles E. Barber," American Artists: Diesinkers, Medallists, Sculptors. Data base in preparation, copy supplied.

Judd, J. Hewitt, *United States Pattern, Experimental and Trial Pieces*, Racine, WI, 1959; redone as *United States Pattern Coins*, Atlanta, GA: Whitman Publishing, various modern editions edited by Q. David Bowers.

Julian, R.W. *Medals of the United States Mint. The First Century 1792–1892.* Lake Mary, FL: The Token and Medal Society, 1989.

Julian, R.W., and Ernest E. Keusch. *Medals of the United States Assay Commission 1860–1977*. El Cajon, CA: Token and Medal Society, 1977.

Lawrence, David. *The Complete Guide to Barber Dimes*. Virginia Beach, VA: DLRC Press, 1991.

——— *The Complete Guide to Barber Quarters*. Second edition. Virginia Beach, VA: DLRC Press, 1994.

——— *The Complete Guide to Barber Halves*. Virginia Beach, VA: DLRC Press, 1991.

Numismatic Guaranty Corporation of America Census Report. Sarasota, FL: Numismatic Guaranty Corporation of America, various issues.

Numismatic Scrapbook Magazine. Chicago, IL, and Sidney, OH: 1935–1976.

Numismatic News. Iola, WI: Krause Publications, 1952 to date.

Numismatist, The. Colorado Springs, CO (and other addresses): The American Numismatic Association, various issues 1914 to date.

Oliver, Nancy, and Richard Kelly, "Newspaper Clipping May Clarify Pedigree of Dimes: Weigher Source of Clapp's 1894-S Dime?" *Coin World*, May 15, 2006.

PCGS Population Report. Newport Beach, CA: Professional Coin Grading Service, various issues.

Pessolano-Filos, Francis. *The Assay Medals, Assay Commission, 1841–1977*. New York City, NY: Eros Publishing Company, 1983.

Pollock, Andrew W. III. *United States Patterns and Related Issues*. Wolfeboro, NH: Bowers and Merena Galleries, 1994.

Raymond, Wayte. *Standard Catalogue of United States Coins and Paper Money* (titles vary). New York City, NY:, Scott Stamp & Coin Co. (and others), 1934 to 1957 editions.

Records of the Bureau of the Mint, National Archives.

Reynolds, Greg. "Condition Ranking of 1894-S Dimes with Recent Histories," *CoinWeek*, July 23, 2013.

Schwarz, Ted, *A History of United States Coinage*, San Diego, CA, and New York City, NY: A.S. Barnes and Co., 1980.

Taxay, Don. *U.S. Mint and Coinage*. New York City, NY: Arco Publishing, 1966.

Treasury Department, United States Mint, *et al. Annual Report of the Director of the Mint*. 1892 to 1916.

Vermeule, Cornelius. *Numismatic Art in America: Aesthetics of the United States Coinage*. Atlanta, GA: Whitman Publishing, 2007.

Wikipedia. (www.wikipedia.org) General information on American history.

CREDITS AND ACKNOWLEDGEMENTS

Mark Borckardt, Heritage Auctions, helped in several ways. **Karen Bridges** provided many images. **Wynn Bowers** helped with proofreading. **Phil Carrigan**, long-time president of BCCS, reviewed the manuscript and made suggestions. **John Dannreuther** helped with research on certain varieties. In 1996 **Beth Deisher** assisted with research on the 1894-S dimes. **Kevin Flynn** made suggestions concerning 1894-S dimes and other issues. **John Frost**, president and webmaster of BCCS, reviewed the manuscript with regard to every date and mintmark issue and made suggestions concerning strike, rarity and other aspects; he was one of the major contributors. The postal collection of the late **Bernard Heller** provided images from exposition postcards. **Heritage Auctions (HA.com)** provided access to images from their Permanent Auction Archives. **D. Wayne Johnson** shared his archives on Charles E. Barber and provided nearly all of the information on Barber medals featured in appendix I. **R.W. Julian** furnished information about the design competition of 1891 and answered research inquiries. **David W. Lange** reviewed the manuscript, made suggestions, and helped with pictures. **Nancy Oliver** and **Rich Kelly** shared correspondence regarding 1894-S dimes (February 17, 2006), and in 2015 reviewed part of the manuscript. **Evelyn Mishkin** helped with copy editing and made suggestions. **Numismatic Guaranty Corporation (NGC)** supplied certain images. **Gary Parietti** was the source for the 1947 savings bank dime folder. **Maurice Rosen** sent information about a hoard of 1914 half dollars. **Peter K. Shireman** provided images of coins in his collection of Barber half dollars. **David Sundman**, Littleton Coin Co., provided historical information and images. **Stephanie Westover**, Littleton Coin Co., provided images.

To the late **David Lawrence (David Lawrence Feigenbaum)** I owe a debt of gratitude for his sharing information on the three denominations via his essential reference books and also for letters and conversations about Barber coin technicalities in the 1990s, including reviews and comments on coins in collections we were offering at auction, including those of Ambassador and Mr. R. Henry Norweb and Louis E. Eliasberg.

To the **Barber Coin Collectors' Society** and its ***Journal*** a special nod for the wealth of information shared by members since its founding in 1989. For more information, see the BCCS website at **www.barbercoins.org**.

About the Author

Q. David Bowers became a professional numismatist as a teenager in 1953. He is chairman emeritus of Stack's Bowers Galleries and is numismatic director of Whitman Publishing. He is a recipient of the Pennsylvania State University College of Business Administration's Alumni Achievement Award (1976); has served as president of the American Numismatic Association (1983–1985) and of the Professional Numismatists Guild (1977–1979); is a recipient of the highest honor bestowed by the ANA (the Farran Zerbe Award); was the first ANA member to be named Numismatist of the Year (1995); and has been inducted into the ANA Numismatic Hall of Fame, one of only 12 living members and the only professional numismatist among these. He has also won the highest honors given by the Professional Numismatists Guild. In July 1999, in a poll published in *COINage*, "Numismatists of the Century," Dave was recognized in this list of just 18 names. He is the author of over 50 books; hundreds of auction and other catalogs; and several thousand articles, including columns in *Coin World* (now the longest-running by any author in numismatic history), *The Numismatist*, and other publications. His books have earned more "Book of the Year Award" honors bestowed by the Numismatic Literary Guild than have those of any other author. He was involved in the sale of five of the six most valuable collections ever sold at auction—the Ambassador and Mrs. R. Henry Norweb Collection ($24 million), the Garrett Collection for The Johns Hopkins University ($25 million), the Harry W. Bass, Jr. Collection ($45 million), the Eliasberg Collection ($55+ million), and the John J. Ford, Jr. Collection (nearly $60 million). When the all-time record for any rare coin ever sold at auction was achieved, a gem 1794 dollar in 2013, he cataloged it and his firm sold it. Dave is a trustee of the New Hampshire Historical Society and a fellow of the American Antiquarian Society, American Numismatic Society, and Massachusetts Historical Society. He has been a consultant for the Smithsonian Institution, Treasury Department, and U.S. Mint, and is research editor of *A Guide Book of United States Coins* (the annual best-selling book in numismatics, the standard guide to prices). In Wolfeboro, New Hampshire, he is on the Board of Selectmen and is the town historian. This is a short list of his honors and accomplishments.

About the Foreword Author

Kenneth E. Bressett has been involved in numismatics since the 1940s. He has written many numismatic articles and is author or editor of more than a dozen related books; a past governor, vice president, and president of the American Numismatic Association; and a highly accomplished teacher, researcher, and student. He has served for many years as the editor of *A Guide Book of United States Coins*, popularly known as the "Red Book"—at more than 23 million copies, one of the best-selling nonfiction titles of all time. As a former consultant to the United States Mint, he was instrumental in originating the 50 State Quarters® Program, and in selecting many of the coins' reverse designs. Ken is a recipient of the Numismatic Literary Guild's Clemy Award and is an inductee in the Numismatic Hall of Fame (at ANA Headquarters in Colorado Springs).

INDEX